## DATE DUE

| | |
|---|---|
| APR 1 9 1995 | Richmond Public |
| JUN 1 4 1995 | due Dec 20/03 |
| JUN 2 7 1995 | DEC 6 2004 |
| JUL 1 1 1995 | |
| JUL 25 1995 | |
| DEC 18 1995 | |
| FEB 21 1996 | |
| MAR 0 6 1996 | |
| NOV 2 9 1996 | |
| FEB 0 5 1997 | |
| OCT 2 9 1997 | |
| NOV 26 1997 | |
| MAR 2 3 1998 | |
| OCT 2 0 1998 | |
| NOV 3 0 1998 | |
| FEB - 9 2000 | |
| MAR 0 3 2003 | |

Cat. No. 23-221

# Ego Defenses

# An Einstein Psychiatry Publication

*Einstein Psychiatry Publication No. 10*

# Ego Defenses

## Theory and Measurement

*Edited by*

## HOPE R. CONTE
## ROBERT PLUTCHIK

A Wiley-Interscience Publication

John Wiley & Sons, Inc.

New York • Chichester • Brisbane • Toronto • Singapore

*Library of Congress Cataloging in Publication Data:*

Ego defenses : theory and measurement / edited by Hope R. Conte and
  Robert Plutchik.
     p.  cm.—(Einstein psychiatry publication ; no. 10)
    "A Wiley Interscience publication."
    Includes index.
    ISBN 0-471-05233-7 (alk. paper : cloth)
    1. Defense mechanisms (Psychology)  2. Defense mechanisms
(Psychology)—Testing.  I. Conte, Hope R., 1929–  .  II. Plutchik,
Robert.  III. Series: Publication series of the Department of
Psychiatry Albert Einstein College of Medicine of Yeshiva University
; 10.
    [DNLM: 1. Defense Mechanisms.  2. Ego.  3. Psychoanalytic Therapy—
methods.    WM 193 1994]
RC455.4.D43E36  1994
150.19'52—dc20
DNLM/DLC
for Library of Congress                      94-7484

Printed in the United States of America

10 9 8 7 6 5 4 3 2 1

# Contributors

**Alan Apter, M.D.** Associate Professor of Psychology, Chairman, Child and Adolescent Section, Sackler School of Medicine, University of Tel Aviv, Israel

**Stephen F. Bauer, M.D.** Associate Professor of Clinical Psychiatry, Associate Chairman, Educational Training, North Shore University Hospital-Cornell University Medical College, Manhasset, New York

**Lorna Smith Benjamin, Ph.D.** Professor of Psychology, University of Utah, Salt Lake City, Utah

**Michael P. Bond, M.D.** Associate Professor of Psychiatry, McGill University, Montreal, Canada

**Peter Buckley, M.B., Ch.B.** Professor of Psychiatry, Director, Residency Training, Albert Einstein College of Medicine, Bronx, New York, Faculty, New York Psychoanalytic Institute, New York, New York

**Hope R. Conte, Ph.D.** Professor of Psychiatry, Director, Psychodynamic Psychotherapy Research Program, Albert Einstein College of Medicine, Bronx, New York

**Hartvig Dahl, M.D.** Professor of Psychiatry, SUNY Health Science Center, Brooklyn, New York, Director of Research, New York Psychoanalytic Institute, New York, New York

**Goldine C. Gleser, Ph.D.** Professor Emeritus of Psychology, Department of Psychiatry, University of Cincinnati College of Medicine, Cincinnati, Ohio

**Steven N. Gold, Ph.D.** Associate Professor of Psychology, Nova University School of Psychology, Director, Sexual Abuse Survivors Program, Nova University Community Mental Health Center, Fort Lauderdale, Florida

**Don Greif, Ph.D.** Clinical Fellow in Psychiatry, Massachusetts General Hospital/Harvard Medical School, Director, New England Conservatory of Music Counseling Center, Boston, Massachusetts

**Stuart T. Hauser, M.D., Ph.D.** Professor of Psychiatry, Harvard Medical School, Laboratory for Social Psychiatry, Boston, Massachusetts

**Mardi J. Horowitz, M.D.** Professor of Psychiatry, Director, Center for the Study of Neuroses, Langley Porter Psychiatric Institute, University of California, San Francisco, California

**David Ihilevich, Ph.D.** Adjunct Professor of Psychology, Michigan State University, East Lansing, Michigan

**Nancy L. Johnson, Ph.D.** Private Practice, formerly Associate Professor of Psychology, Nova University School of Psychology, Fort Lauderdale, Florida

**Marianne E. Kardos, M.D.** Instructor of Psychiatry, Harvard Medical School, Boston, Massachusetts, Associate Director of Psychopharmacology, Cambridge Hospital, Cambridge, Massachusetts

**J. Christopher Perry, M.P.H., M.D.** Associate Professor of Psychiatry, Director of Research, Department of Psychiatry, Sir Mortimer B. Davis-Jewish General Hospital, Montreal, Quebec, Canada

**Robert Plutchik, Ph.D.** Professor of Psychiatry, Albert Einstein College of Medicine, Bronx, New York

**Barry Ritzler, Ph.D.** Professor of Psychology, Long Island University, Brooklyn, New York, Member, Adjunct Faculty Rorschach Workshops, Inc., Asheville, North Carolina

**Lawrence H. Rockland, M.D.** Associate Professor of Clinical Psychiatry, Director, Adult Outpatient Services, The New York Hospital-Cornell Medical Center, Westchester Division, White Plains, New York

**Andrew W. Safyer, Ph.D.** Assistant Professor of Social Work, School of Social Work, Boston University, Research Associate, Harvard Medical School, Boston, Massachusetts

**Malcolm Owen Slavin, Ph.D.** Director of Training, Tufts University Counseling Center, Medford, Massachusetts, Faculty and Board of Directors, Massachusetts Institute for Psychoanalysis, Boston, Massachusetts

**Charles H. Stinson, M.D.** Associate Adjunct Professor of Psychiatry, Codirector of Program on Conscious and Unconscious Mental Processes, Center for the Study of Neuroses, Langley Porter Psychiatric Institute, University of California, San Francisco, California

# A Note on the Series

Psychiatry is in a state of flux. The excitement springs in part from internal changes, such as the development and official acceptance (at least in the U.S.A.) of an operationalized, multiaxial classification system of behavioral disorders (the DSM-IV), the increasing sophistication of methods to measure abnormal human behavior, and the impressive expansion of biological and psychological treatment modalities. Exciting developments are also taking place in fields relating to psychiatry, in molecular (brain) biology, genetics, brain imaging, drug development, epidemiology, experimental psychology, to mention only a few striking examples.

More generally speaking, psychiatry is moving, still relatively slowly, but irresistibly, from a more philosophical, contemplative orientation, to that of an empirical science. From the fifties on, biological psychiatry has been a major catalyst of that process. It provided the mother discipline with a third cornerstone, that is, neurobiology, the other two being psychology and medical sociology. In addition, it forced the profession into the direction of standardization of diagnoses and of assessment of abnormal behavior. Biological psychiatry provided psychiatry not only with a new basic science and with new treatment modalities, but also with the tools, the methodology and the mentality to operate within the confines of an empirical science, the only framework in which a medical discipline can survive.

In other fields of psychiatry, too, one discerns a gradual trend towards scientification. Psychological treatment techniques are standardized and manuals developed to make these skills more easily transferable. Methods registering treatment outcome—traditionally used in the behavioral/cognitive field—are now more and more requested and, hence, developed for dynamic forms of psychotherapy as well. Social and community psychiatry, until the sixties more firmly rooted in humanitarian ideals and social awareness than in empirical studies, profited greatly from their liaison with the social sciences and the expansion of psychiatric epidemiology.

Let there be no misunderstanding. Empiricism does *not imply* that it is only the measurable that counts. Psychiatry would be mutilated if it would neglect that which cannot be captured by numbers. It *does imply* that what is measurable should be measured. Progress in psychiatry is dependent on ideas and on experiment. Their linkage is inseparable.

This Series, published under the auspices of the Department of Psychiatry of the Albert Einstein College of Medicine, Montefiore Medical Center, is meant to keep track of important developments in our profession, to summarize what has been achieved in particular fields, and to bring together the viewpoints obtained from disparate vantage points—in short, to capture some of the ongoing excitement in modern psychiatry, both in its clinical and experimental dimensions. The Department of Psychiatry at Albert Einstein College of Medicine hosts the Series, but naturally welcomes contributions from others.

Bernie Mazel originally generated the idea—an ambitious plan that we all felt was worthy of pursuit. The edifice of psychiatry is impressive, but still somewhat flawed in its foundations. May this Series contribute to consolidation of its infrastructure.

HERMAN M. VAN PRAAG, M.D., PH.D.
*Professor and Chairman*
*Academic Psychiatric Center*
*University of Limburg*
*Maastricht*
*The Netherlands*

# Preface

Among the important contributions psychoanalysis has made to personality theory and to the theory of psychological adaptation is the concept of defense mechanisms. Just one indication of its importance is that whereas some aspects of psychoanalytic theory have not generally been accepted by psychiatrists, psychologists, social workers, and clinicians, the concept of defenses has been embraced by all disciplines. It has, in fact, become part of everday language.

Despite the wide acceptance of the general concept, there has been increasing divergence of opinion among clinicians and theoreticians about the precise meaning and function of defenses. There is disagreement on the issue of whether ego defenses are adaptive or maladaptive, flexible or rigid, problem-solving oriented, or forms of self-deception. These issues have led to debate over their role in the clinical situation. A question that has been raised is to what extent an individual's use of defense mechanisms is associated with psychopathology. Another question concerns whether only some defenses, used to excess, can be considered psychopathological. There is also disagreement on how many defenses there are, how they should be labeled and defined, and whether or not they can form an hierarchical order of degree of primitiveness, maturity, or maladjustment. There is also the question of the extent to which ego defenses may be measured in psychometrically valid ways.

In recent years, a number of researchers and theoreticians have proposed answers to these questions and, at the same time, have developed methods for the measurement of defense mechanisms. These techniques vary widely, ranging from ratings made from video- or audiotaped interviews or transcripts, to projective tests, and to self-report ratings made by patients or subjects themselves. To a great extent, the technique chosen for measurement is related to the author's theoretical conceptualization of the defenses.

We have had a continuing interest in these issues, and since 1979—when we presented a new conceptualization of defenses based on their relation to emotion and to one another, and an instrument for their measurement—we have closely followed the defense mechanism literature.

We therefore invited some of the most prominent people in the field to contribute their ideas and insights into both theoretical and measurement issues. The result is the present volume, which brings together in one place diverse theoretical views about the nature of defenses as well as current information on the different methods that have been developed for measuring them.

The book is divided into two parts. Part I contains theoretical papers dealing with the conceptual issues previously described. Part II presents descriptions of the many methods that have been developed for measuring defenses. The contributors, all of whom have written their chapters specifically for this volume, provide the rationale for their measurement technique, describe it in detail, present reliability and validity data, and include illustrations of the usefulness of their methodology. Thus, the present book provides both a modern explication of the concept of defenses and a source of practical methods for their measurement. It should therefore be of value to theoreticians and clinicians, as well as researchers interested in finding appropriate tools of measurement.

HOPE R. CONTE
ROBERT PLUTCHIK

*Albert Einstein College of Medicine*
*Bronx, New York*
*September 1994*

# Contents

# Introduction

This introduction provides a summary of the key ideas considered by each of the contributors to the volume. In Part I, which deals with theoretical issues, Plutchik (Chapter 1) examines the relations between his psychoevolutionary theory of emotion and ego defenses. His theory includes the premise that a number of conceptual domains such as personality, diagnoses, and ego defenses are derivatives of emotions. Another aspect of the theory is that a circle or circumplex is the most adequate description of the similarity relations among emotions as well as among ego defenses. Empirical data are presented that support this idea.

In addition, an explicit model is presented of the relations between a set of eight ego defenses and the eight emotions that Plutchik considers to be primary or basic. An analysis is given of the underlying structure of ego defenses. This structure includes the *traits* associated with each major defense, the *social need* the defense acts to express, the *method* each defense uses to deal with the need, and the *function* of each defense. For example, the traits associated with repression are timidity, passivity, and obedience; the social need is to avoid or withdraw from social relationships; the method used is to forget painful events; and the function of the defense is to avoid decisions and subjective anxiety.

Another important idea of the theory concerns the question of the adaptiveness of defenses. The view presented is that a distinction should and can be made between defenses, conceived as relatively rigid, stereotyped, and primitive, in contrast to coping styles, which are seen as flexible, open to choice, and problem oriented. The theory has provided the conceptual basis for the development of new self-report measures of both ego defenses and coping styles.

In Chapter 2, Buckley provides a historical review of the development of the concept of ego defenses from Freud's initial conceptualization of the idea to the recent work of object relations and other psychoanalytically oriented theorists. He points out that the idea of ego defenses is among the most robust and least controversial aspects of psychoanalytic theory. Although Freud initially used the terms "defense" and "repression" synonymously, by the mid-1920s repression was recognized as only one method of defense among others. The study of defenses has led to the study of resistances to therapy and to the analysis of resistances as a basic technique of psychoanalysis. This is because of the belief that defenses against former dangers recur in treatment as resistance against recovery, since recovery itself is perceived as a new danger.

The history and psychoanalytic conceptualizations of a number of defenses are described. These include sublimation, reaction formation, undoing, isolation, introjection, identification, projection, regression, reversal, and denial. Anna Freud's elaboration of these concepts is also presented, with particular emphasis on a developmental hierarchy. Also of interest is her idea that several defenses may be combined in relation to a particular stressor. Buckley concludes by describing ideas of object relations theorists such as Melanie Klein, who postulates that defense mechanisms such as projection and introjection occur so early in life that they contribute to the development of the ego. These theorists have added other ego defense concepts such as splitting, omnipotence, devaluation, and primitive idealization to earlier formulations. Some of them claim that certain defenses are more likely to occur in certain personality disorders; for example, primitive idealization and denial are considered characteristic of borderline personality disorder. Among the most recent psychoanalytic ideas about defenses is that defenses are available simultaneously and/or sequentially for whatever stress is most important at any given moment in the life of a particular individual.

Benjamin, in Chapter 3, challenges the psychoanalytic view that defenses keep people from becoming aware of their own thoughts and behaviors resulting from severe conflicts and anxiety. She proposes that normal defenses are consistent with wishes and fears that enhance the likelihood of behaviors associated with "attachment affects," namely affirmation, love, and protection. In contrast, abnormal defenses are associated with wishes and fears that usually result in disruptive behaviors such as blaming, attack, and ignoring. Although she believes that, in the long run, it is better not to involve defenses because they distort perception, mental processing, or responses, sometimes defenses are necessary to preserve attachments to others.

The idea of normal and abnormal defenses is related to Benjamin's circumplex model of intrapsychic and interpersonal relations, her Structural Analysis of Social Behavior (SASB) model. She also makes some points about the concepts of adaptive and maladaptive behaviors in relation to normal and abnormal behavior. Depending on the context, she claims that certain adaptive behaviors may be abnormal, while certain maladaptive behaviors may be normal.

Several vignettes illustrate the defenses of pathological repression, denial, and lying. Benjamin concludes by stating that defenses may or may not be unconscious or maladaptive. Their main purposes is to satisfy wishes and fears that arise in relation to the defender's relationship to important people in his or her life, or their internalized representations. Some implications for psychotherapeutic treatment are also given.

A new approach to understanding defenses called "control process theory" is presented by Horowitz and Stinson (Chapter 4). Control process theory attempts to identify the verbal and nonverbal processes that individuals use to modify, ward off, or modulate states of mind generated by strong affects, conflicts, or stress. Some examples of control processes are focus of attention, thresholds for decision or interruption, action planning, and thresholds for arousal. The function of all control processes is to reduce emotions to tolerable limits.

Control process theory is related to another set of theoretical ideas that these authors call "Personal Schemas Theory," which is defined as the ways that individuals integrate knowledge about self and environment into internal meanings. Examples of such schemas are self schemas, value schemas, and role-relationship models. These schemas increase the person's sense of temporal continuity and identity. They help the individual interpret his or her relations to others. Schemas act as motivators and may organize desirable or undesirable states of mind or adaptive compromises.

Horowitz and Stinson then present general clinical vignettes that attempt to relate patients' use of defense mechanisms to various control categories. For example, the passive-aggressive defense was related to a change in the role-relationship between patient and therapist. Thus, control process theory provides a microanalytic statement of how defensive episodes are formed. By focusing on this microanalysis of defense formation, the clinician may gain more insight into how to help a patient make small, but incremental, changes in attention and interpersonal roles.

An "information feedback" theory of emotions and its relation to defenses is presented in Chapter 5, by Dahl. He begins by describing his theory, which classifies all emotions in terms of orientation (it or me), valence (attraction or repulsion), and activity (active or passive). For animals (or humans) without symbolic language, emotions are the primary system for surviving in a world of dangers and for communicating and recognizing the intentions of members of one's own species.

From the point of view of this theory, defenses serve two main functions: (a) to restrict awareness of emotional experiences and wishes and (b) to inhibit acts related to wishes. Dahl also states that one emotion may be substituted for another and thus function as a defense. He also proposes that differences in the intensity of emotional experience may reflect the operation of defenses. For example, it is possible that people who almost never express strong emotions have strong defenses. Defenses against the expression of emotions may result in personality traits. For example, strong defenses against the expression of any emotion may lead to the so-called stoic personality. In contrast, the lack of defenses against the expression of emotions may lead to the traits of a histrionic personality. Dahl also believes that persisting defenses may account for the variations in the language of emotions that expresses intensity of feeling.

In Chapter 6, Safyer and Hauser explore the idea that defenses may be conceptualized along a developmental continuum based on level of maturity or degree of pathology. One such approach groups defenses into three levels: (a) narcissistic defenses, (b) affective defenses, and (c) neurotic defenses. Patients are said to shift from primitive narcissistic defenses to neurotic defenses during clinical improvement. A second approach describes immature, neurotic, and mature defenses. Longitudinal studies of normal individuals have found that mature defenses are used more frequently as people age, while the use of immature defenses declines.

Still another approach reviewed in this chapter attempts to relate defenses to ego development. For example, individuals at the lowest levels of ego development are more likely to use primitive defenses such as regression or projection, whereas individuals with high levels of ego development would be expected to show more mature defenses such as empathy and intellectualization.

The research of Hauser has indicated that individuals can use defenses in adaptive as well as maladaptive ways. It has been found that individuals at higher levels of ego development use more differentiated and "engaging" defenses, whereas individuals at lower ego development levels are more likely to use "constricting/detaching" defenses. There is continued debate about the relative validity of the various proposed hierarchies and the methods used to measure them. Research is hampered by the lack of an agreed-on common list of defenses based on conceptual and empirical consensus.

In the last chapter of Part I, Slavin and Grief state that the concept of repression is at the heart of psychoanalytic theory, but that considerable controversy exists over *what* is repressed and *why* it is repressed. The classical psychoanalytic view is said to assume that repression regulates conflicts between self-centered motives and the demands of the parental environment. The more contemporary interpersonal view sees repression as the individual's method of protecting parts of the self to enable future growth.

These conflicting positions on the nature of repression are related by Slavin and Grief to issues of parent-child conflict as understood by modern evolutionary biology. This theory recognizes that conflict is an expected feature of parent-offspring relations because the self-interests (inclusive fitness) of parents are not identical to the self-interests of their children. Repression is interpreted as a diversion of subjective experience to preserve access to temporarily unacceptable but potentially important needs. Repression allows the child to identify with the parents' identities without sacrificing his or her own long-term interests. Repression is a form of strategic self-deception designed to deceive others into greater investment and reciprocity than would obtain if the person's true intentions were known.

These ideas lead to the notion that development in the child is the negotiation of a series of provisional identities. Maturation involves a shift from an environment of interactions between kin to an environment of mostly unrelated individuals bound together primarily by ties of reciprocity and exchange. In general, Slavin and Grief argue that the basic patterns of our mental systems are evolved adaptations designed to regulate the inherently conflicting pressures of the interpersonal world. The human social self must be equally rooted in culture and biological nature.

Part II of this volume is devoted to measurement issues and covers a number of methodologies that different investigators have used for the assessment of defense mechanisms. Chapter 8, by Conte and Apter, describes the background, construction, and use of the Life Style Index (LSI), both in English and in translations. As developed by Plutchik, Kellerman, and Conte, the LSI consists of 97 items in a Yes-No, self-report format, designed to assess an individual's use of behavioral derivatives of eight defense mechanisms.

In choosing these eight defenses—repression, regression, projection, intellectualization, compensation, denial, displacement, and reaction formation—the authors remained close to the Freudian notion of defenses as unconscious mechanisms, preferring to label the more conscious adaptive processes as "coping styles." The choice of items for the LSI was guided by both an extensive review of the psychodynamic literature and by Plutchik's theoretical model, which considers ego defenses to have an implicit circular similarity and polarity structure.

The reliability of the scales of the LSI, on which normative data are available, is presented in terms of test-retest and alpha coefficients. A number of studies are described that provide evidence for its discriminant, predictive, and construct validity. It has been shown, for example, to discriminate between psychiatric patients and normals and between patients high on potential risk for suicide as compared with those at high risk for other-directed violence. The Hebrew version demonstrated the ability of LSI scales and total score to discriminate among Israeli adolescents who were suicidal, destructive, and neither suicidal nor destructive. Another study suggested its value in predicting rehospitalization of a group of schizophrenics.

Construct validity of the LSI is supported by significant positive correlations between LSI scale scores and anxiety, significant positive correlations with life problems or stresses, and significant negative correlations with measures of self-esteem and with ego strength. Further evidence for construct validity is provided by relations between its scale scores and measures of personality disorders and clinical syndrome categories. Translated into Norwegian, both the subscales and total score of the LSI have shown interesting relations with other variables such as psychological stress factors and levels of immunoglobulins.

Chapter 9 presents Bond's description of the development and properties of the Defense Style Questionnaire (DSQ). This self-report 87-item instrument is designed to measure conscious manifestations of defense mechanisms. It does not assess any of the 24 identified defenses or coping mechanisms separately but, rather, seeks to measure four clusters of defenses that Bond and his colleagues have called defense styles.

Statistical analyses confirmed the hypothesis that these four clusters could be empirically derived and could also be ranked according to developmental level, ranging from immature to mature. In developmental terms, there is a progression from the maladaptive action patterns (e.g., regression and acting out) through the image-distorting defenses (e.g., splitting and primitive idealization) and the self-sacrificing defenses (e.g., pseudoaltruism), to the adaptive defenses (e.g., suppression and sublimation) along the line of increasingly constructive dealing with the vicissitudes of life.

Evidence for the reliability and validity of the four defense styles is presented. Some specific defenses may be associated with some specific psychiatric disorders; however, in most cases the correlations are not high enough or exclusive enough to use defenses, as measured by the DSQ, as an indicator of diagnosis. The DSQ seems to be most accurate when discriminating between adaptive and maladaptive defense styles, which in turn allows predictions about level of development and measures of health and outcome, at least in psychodynamically oriented therapy.

After a review of theorists' thinking about the nature and function of defense mechanisms since Freud's original conceptualization, Ihilevich and Gleser (Chapter 10) describe the development of their classification system for the Defense Mechanism Inventory (DMI). This is also in a self-report format, but of a different type. They found that defensive responses to three conflictual story vignettes could be classified into five styles: (1) Turning against Object, which includes the defenses of identification with the aggressor and displacement; (2) Projection; (3) Principalization, which subsumes such defenses as intellectualization and rationalization; (4) Turning against Self, subsuming pessimistic and masochistic responses; and (5) Reversal, which includes such defenses as denial and reaction formation. For each vignette, respondents are asked four questions to which they must choose the response alternative representing one of the five defense styles that best typifies their reaction to the question.

Psychometric data are presented that support the face validity of the defensive responses, justify the use of a forced choice format, and show that intercorrelations among the defense styles are in the expected direction. The DMI scores are correlated with gender, age, education, and intelligence, making it important that scores be interpreted with respect to the appropriate normative group. Average internal consistency estimates for the five defense styles range from .61 to .80, while average stability estimates range from .62 to .81. Construct validity data showing convergence with other measures of defense as well as with theoretically relevant variables are presented. Significant correlations with other constructs in the behavioral, cognitive, affective, and personality domains are also given.

In the last two sections of their chapter, Ihilevich and Gleser illustrate possible clinical applications of the DMI in terms of defenses and anxiety, aggression, and self-esteem. They conclude with a brief review of the implications of empirical findings gathered with the DMI for several theoretical issues pertaining to defenses.

In Chapter 11, Johnson and Gold describe the development and use of their Defense Mechanism Profile (DMP), a self-administered, projective sentence completion instrument. It is their belief that the open-ended aspect of this measure has the advantage of permitting the respondent a complete range of expression without forcing a response that may be neither representative nor accurate. Respondents are instructed to state what they would do behaviorally in relation to each of 40 sentence stems that present a psychologically uncomfortable situation or distressing affect. Each response is assigned to one of 14 scoring categories, which include both precursors of defenses, or tension reducers, and early, middle range, and advanced defenses selected from the literature. A scoring manual defines each category and gives specific criteria and behavioral examples for scoring.

After approximately 6 weeks of training, a satisfactory level of interrater agreement on the categorization of the open-ended responses can be achieved. Test-retest reliability has been shown to be satisfactory for all but four scales. A normative profile, based on a nonpsychiatric sample is available, and the influences of gender, age, educational, and social desirability factors are discussed. Evidence for the convergent validity of the DMP is presented in terms of the consistency between DMP ratings and observer ratings and the consistency between DMP scores and daily behavioral diary entries. Support for the DMP's discriminant validity is provided by results comparing normal with psychiatric inpatient populations and substance abusers with medical outpatients.

As the authors point out, further examination of normative performance by age and gender groupings is needed as is work on increasing the test-retest stability of some of the scales. Nevertheless, this chapter reflects encouraging preliminary work with a projective measure.

Ritzler (Chapter 12) investigates whether the Rorschach can adequately operationalize defense mechanisms as distinct psychological structures or whether work on Rorschach assessment of defenses has merely identified differences in levels of adaptation. He presents a review and critique of the interpretive systems of Schafer; Holt; Lerner; and Cooper, Perry, and Arnow.

Schafer's system, which covers repression, projection, regression, isolation, intellectualization, reaction formation, and undoing is the most comprehensive in terms of using the total Rorschach protocol for interpretation. However, with the exception of some suggestive work by Haan, little research validation for this system has appeared in the literature. Holt, unlike Schafer, did not focus on specific defenses, but rather, used the Rorschach to assess four defensive operations and three overall estimates of their effectiveness. There is research support for the reliability of the overall scores, but reliability estimates for the specific defensive operation scores has been poor. The Lerner Defense Scales, derived from Kernberg's theory of borderline personality, provide the first Rorschach method that promotes validation research on specific defense mechanisms. There are five, including splitting and devaluation, that are designed to measure defenses at a lower, more pathological level of functioning. Most of the definitions for the scoring system are clear, and reliability estimates have been adequate. However, with the exception of the definitions used to score splitting, the amount of inference required to make the connections greatly reduces face validity. Cooper, Perry, and Arnow's Rorschach Defense Scale is similar in format to Lerner's but longer, measuring 15 defenses, is applicable to a wider range of psychopathology, and is based on somewhat different theoretical concepts (e.g., Kohut's narcissism and object relations theory). While it has reliability problems, it has shown some modest discriminatory power.

To date, none of these systems has given much reason to believe that what is assessed as defenses on the Rorschach is what Freud, or the ego psychologists, or the object relation theorists meant by defenses. Until studies are conducted that provide convincing evidence of significant relations between Rorschach measures and clinical or behavioral assessments of defenses, Ritzler believes that the status of the Rorschach as a technique for assessing defense mechanisms must be considered "uncertain."

The last two chapters deal with the assessment of defenses through the use of rating scales. Chapter 13 (Perry and Kardos) reviews research on defense mechanisms using the Defense Mechanisms Rating Scale (DMRS), developed by the first author and incorporating Vaillant's and Kernberg's conceptualizations about levels of defense. This method for rating defenses from interview or other clinical data has a manual-based scoring system for guiding and justifying inferences regarding the use of 28 different defense mechanisms. Now in its fifth edition, directions are given for making both qualitative and quantitative ratings. In either case, an individual's Overall Defense Maturity score may be calculated. The advantage of the quantitative method is that it permits quantitative comparisons of defensive functioning within individuals over time, thus allowing assessment of change, as well as comparisons between groups of individuals.

The DMRS is organized around the concept of a hierarchy of the adaptiveness of defenses and divides them among seven levels, within each of which the defenses share some functional properties. These levels range from the low adaptation *action defenses* (e.g., acting out and passive-aggression) to high adaptation *mature defenses* (e.g., sublimation, suppression, and humor).

Empirical data on the reliability and validity of the DMRS are presented. Higher reliabilities are obtainable with the quantitative than with the qualitative method, and summary scores calculated by combining the ratings for each level of defense prove to be more reliable than ratings of individual defenses. Studies are cited that support both the concurrent validity of the DMRS and the construct validity of the hierarchical adaptive value of defenses.

Studies cited also suggest that the DMRS adds predictive information over and beyond data on Axis I and Axis II disorders, implying that it may be useful for dynamically oriented clinicians in planning treatment. It may also play a useful scientific role in addressing clinically meaningful questions in the area of psychotherapy process and outcome studies and in research dealing with stress and conflict.

In Chapter 14, Bauer and Rockland present a concise review of the psychoanalytic theory of defense mechanisms before describing their new rating scale measures of defenses. This review includes the views of Freud and elaborations by Anna Freud, Klein's concept of primitive defenses, and Kernberg's integration of these primitive defenses into an object relations/ego psychological model.

They also describe trends that have emerged in psychoanalytic understanding of the concept of defenses. These include debate over whether mechanisms of defense are ego functions used solely for defense or whether all mental products may be used defensively; the controversies surrounding the developmental level of defenses; and the relation between defense and coping.

Bauer and Rockland discuss four major approaches to the empirical study of defenses, as typified by Gleser and Ihilovich (ratings of standard conflicts), Bond (self-report questionnaire), Vaillant (coding of case histories), and Hauser and Perry (ratings of interview material). They then describe their new measure, the Inventory of Defense-Related Behaviors (IDRB), which asks raters to identify the presence or absence of behaviors that are considered to be manifestations of defense rather than the defenses themselves.

The IDRB is a 60-item inventory of the type of behaviors exhibited by patients in clinical interviews. A clinician agreement study confirmed that each of 20 defenses, selected to be representative of the domain of defenses in the literature, was reliably related to its postulated clinical behaviors. A preliminary interreliability study, using ten 45-minute videotaped sessions, produced encouraging, if mixed, results depending on the technique used for measurement of agreement.

It is suggested that the IDRB can be useful for studies of shifts in defensive functioning during single therapy session as well as throughout the course of an entire psychotherapy. It also may be useful in studies to determine whether specific diagnostic entities are characterized by specific constellations of defenses.

# PART I
# Theory

# 1

# A Theory of Ego Defenses

## ROBERT PLUTCHIK

The concept of ego defenses has been acknowledged as one of the most important contributions of psychoanalysis. Ego defenses are recognized as relevant to drives, affects, development, personality, adaptation, and psychotherapy. Although other aspects of psychoanalytic theory have been challenged, and sometimes greatly modified, the theory of ego defenses has been widely accepted and is presented in many textbooks in quite similar ways.

Despite the importance and usefulness of the concept, a number of issues have not been resolved. The present chapter will therefore examine the classical psychoanalytic view of defenses and the modifications that have been suggested, and will then present a theory of defenses that will be shown to have systematic relevance to a theory of emotions, as well as to social relations, personality disorders, psychotherapy, and test construction.

## THE CLASSICAL PSYCHOANALYTIC VIEW OF EGO DEFENSES

Freud assumed that anxiety occupies a unique position in the economy of the mind; it is, he believed, the cause of both repression and symptom formation. Anxiety is also believed to be the trigger that initiates defensive functioning in a weak or immature ego, (Freud, 1926/1957). "Defense mechanisms are fixations on a small and rigid repertoire of attempts, primitive and inadequate, to solve the ego's task of adapting the claims of the instinctual drives to reality's conditions for their gratification" (Sjoback, 1973).

The first situation of danger faced by an infant is helplessness. Freud assumed that defensive processes emerge during this very early stage of mental development (Freud, 1915/1957) and that they have one or more of three functions: (1) blocking or inhibition of mental contents; (2) distortion of mental content; or (3) screening and covering of mental contents by use of opposite contents.

This concept of defense is at the core of Freud's theory of neurosis. Defenses invariably lead to self-deception. Freud puts this idea in the following way: "Repression is fundamentally an attempt to flight. . . . But we cannot flee from oneself; flight is no help against internal dangers. And for that reason the defensive mechanisms of the ego are condemned to falsify one's internal perception and to give only an imperfect and distorted picture of one's id" (Freud, 1937/1957, p. 237). By implication, Freud's theory of neurosis is in essence a theory of the effects of self-deception and self-concealment resulting from the operation of defensive processes.

How do psychoanalysts recognize a defensive process? Since defenses by definition are theoretical constructs that can only be inferred from indirect evidence, what is the nature of the evidence used to infer them? Defenses are inferred from overt behavior and from the contents of communications. Such behavior and communications have certain characteristics:

1. The behaviors are rigid.
2. There is the sense of little control over them.
3. Anxiety occurs when defense-related behavior is blocked.
4. Incongruities exist between verbal communications and facial expressions or posture.

These are complex criteria and a great deal of observation is needed to make such inferences, and they are, at best, uncertain.

## Questions Related to Ego Defenses

Three other questions frequently arise in psychoanalytic discussions of ego defenses:

1. How many defenses are there?
2. Can we order defenses in terms of levels of primitiveness?
3. Can defenses be adaptive?

### How Many Ego Defenses Are There?

In 1936, Anna Freud listed nine defenses: regression, repression, reaction formation, isolation, undoing, projection, introjection, turning against the self, and reversal. Ten years later (A. Freud, 1936/1946), she added intellectualization and identification. In S. Freud's writings, along with the defenses already cited, he included denial, displacement, rationalization, and derealization. At various times, psychoanalysts have proposed a number of other concepts as defenses: compensation, fantasy, idealization, substitution, somatization, acting out, sublimation, magical thinking, asceticism, avoidance, negation, and splitting (Bibring, Dwyer, Huntington, & Valenstein, 1961; Kaplan & Sadock, 1989; Moore & Fine, 1990; Sjoback, 1973). Bond, Gardner, Christian, and Sigal (1983) describe 24 defenses including inhibition, pseudoaltruism, as-if behavior, and clinging. And Perry (1990) lists and defines 28 defenses including affiliation, anticipation, self-observation, and hypochondriasis. The Diagnostic and Statistical Manual of Mental Disorders (DSM III-R; American Psychiatric Association, 1987) adds the following defenses: autistic fantasy, devaluation, dissociation, passive-aggression, and suppression. Given this diversity, it is not surprising that Schafer (1954), presciently, has written: "There cannot be any "correct" or "complete" list of defenses, but only lists of varying exhaustiveness, internal theoretical consistency, and helpfulness in ordering clinical observation and research findings" (p. 161). In this connection, it is also worth quoting another analyst who wrote:

Many psychoanalysts use the term "mechanism of defense" . . . in so many and ill-defined senses, and often in a sense which seem in various ways to deviate from Freud's conceptions of defense mechanisms, that to list everything that has been labeled a "defense" would entail a grave dilution . . . of the essence of the theory of defensive processes as constructed by Freud and the more prominent theorists among his followers. (Sperling, 1958, p. 25)

This issue will be examined in a different context shortly.

*Levels of Primitiveness*

Although the question of the degree of primitiveness of ego defenses has occupied many psychoanalysts over the years, Freud did not much discuss the question of when mechanisms of defense other than repression have their onset. And Anna Freud wrote: "The chronology of psychic processes is still one of the most obscure fields of analytic theory" (A. Freud, 1936/1946, p. 56). Similarly, the British psychoanalyst Edward Glover wrote: "Practically all reconstructions of early phases of development are in the nature of guesses and are strongly influenced by the prejudices and preconceptions of the observer" (Glover, 1949, p. 27).

Despite these cautions, various proposals have been made concerning the chronology of the appearance of ego defenses. Fenichel (1946) suggests the following order from more to less primitive: denial, projection, introjection, repression, reaction formation, undoing, isolation, and regression. Consistent with this proposal is the statement by English and Finch (1964) that projection is primitive, and by Arieti (1974) that denial is primitive. Inconsistent with the chronology is the statement by Ewalt and Farnsworth (1963) that regression is a primitive defense.

The most detailed attempt to order ego defenses in terms of levels of maturity has been made by Vaillant (1971; 1976). According to him, the most primitive ("narcissistic") defenses are denial, projection, and distortion. The "immature" defenses typical of character disorders include fantasy, hypochondriasis, acting out, and passive-aggressive behavior. "Neurotic" defenses include intellectualization, repression, displacement, reaction formation, and dissociation. At the top of this theoretical hierarchy are the "mature defenses of sublimation, suppression, altruism, anticipation, and humor. It is worth noting that Vaillant considers certain concepts to be defenses (particularly the so-called mature defenses) that are not on the lists of other psychoanalysts and at the same time ignores the defenses of regression and rationalization.

Perry (1990) has suggested another classification system for defenses. He proposes seven classes of defenses that he labels in the following ways: (a) action defenses (e.g., passive-aggression); (b) borderline defenses (e.g., splitting); (c) disavowal defenses (e.g., denial); (d) narcissistic defenses (e.g., omnipotence); (e) other neurotic defenses (e.g., repression); (f) obsessional defenses (e.g., undoing); (g) and mature defenses (e.g., sublimation). It is worth noting that the language of personality disorders is used to describe some of these types of defenses, an important point to which I will return later.

In addition to Vaillant's attempt to group defenses in terms of levels of maturity, several other groupings not involving the concept of maturity have been proposed. For example, Verwoerdt (1972) has suggested that three classes of defense mechanisms deal with threats and influence the development of pathophysiological reactions. The first type of defense is a form of retreat from the threat. It implies regression revealed by hypochondriasis, dependency, and self-centeredness. The second class of defense is an attempt to exclude the threat from awareness. This includes denial, suppression, rationalization, projection, and introjection. The third way to deal with threat is to overcome it. According to Verwoerdt, this is done by intellectualization, isolation, counterphobic reactions, obsessive-compulsive styles, and sublimation. This model also provides for various combinations of these defensive maneuvers.

Ihilevich and Gleser (1991) have proposed yet another classification system. They suggest that all defenses can be classified in terms of five general defensive styles. The first class is called "Turning against an object," and it is one that manages internal conflicts or threats by attacks on the presumed source of danger. "Projection" is a style that handles threat by attributing negative intent to others on the basis of distorted evidence. "Principalization" is a defense style that involves platitudes and rationalizations to deal with threat. "Turning against self" manages threat by disapproval of self. And "Reversal" handles threat by minimizing the threat or blocking it from awareness. Each of these styles presumably reduces anxiety in a different way.

## Are Defenses Adaptive?

Psychoanalysts assume that "normality" is an ideal fiction and that the difference between neurosis and normalcy is only a matter of degree. This implies that defensive processes occur to some degree in everyone. However, the fact that defenses can be recognized at some levels in all individuals does not mean that they are desirable or particularly useful. Freud concluded that repression is always a pathogenic process and cannot be considered "the watchman of our mental health" (Freud, 1916/1963, p. 294). He added, "The work of analysis aims at inducing the patient to give up the repressions (using the word in the widest sense) belonging to his early development and to replace them by reactions of a sort that would correspond to a psychically mature condition" (Freud, 1937/1964, p. 257).

Similarly, Fenichel (1946) says that defenses have unfavorable effects on mental functioning and do not promote mental health. Loewenstein (1967) describes defenses as rigid, inappropriate, stereotyped, and oriented toward substitute gratifications inconsistent with the reality principle. Freud concludes:

> The mechanisms of defense serve the purpose of keeping off dangers . . . and it is doubtful whether the ego could do without them during its development. But it is also certain that they may become dangers themselves. . . . These mechanisms are not relinquished after they have assisted the ego during the difficult years of its development. . . . This turns them into infantilisms. . . . Thus . . . the defense mechanisms, by bringing about an ever more extensive alienation from the external world and a permanent weakening of the ego, pave the way for, and encourage, the outbreaks of neurosis. (Freud, 1937/1964, p. 237)

Thus it is evident that the classical psychoanalysts interpreted ego defenses as unfavorable and undesirable modes of mental functioning. They believed that defenses should be abandoned when they have fulfilled their task of protecting the young and immature ego from disruptions due to anxiety and possibly other painful affects. They should then be replaced by nondefensive means of controlling and modulating emotions.

In more recent years, several psychoanalysts have attempted to expand the classical notion of defenses as infantile, rigid, and stereotyped, and have suggested that some ego defenses are "good," flexible, and adaptive. These ideas stem from the work of Hartmann (1958) who emphasized that not all developments arise from instinctual conflict. The growth of locomotion, the capacity to postpone or control impulses, the ability to make realistic anticipations are all part of a conflict-free innate ego structure that is a product of evolution.

Based partly on these ideas, Vaillant (1971, 1975, 1976) has proposed a fourfold classification of ego defenses ranging from the most "primitive," to those that are "immature," to those that are "neurotic," and finally to those that represent good adaptation or "maturity." Mature defenses include sublimation, altruism, and humor. The concept of mature defenses is inconsistent with the thinking of most classical analysts, and it is questionable whether humor, for example, should be thought of as a defense or as an independent coping style.

White (1963) points out that although defense mechanisms, as seen in neurotic patients, are primitive and inappropriate and are based on a sense of helplessness in the face of painful reality, there are in each person's life, adaptations that make primitive defense mechanisms unnecessary. Adaptive or coping behavior does not literally repeat earlier behaviors, but accommodates to present circumstances. Adaptive processes include locomotion, language, motor skills, play, investigation, postponement, anticipation as well as logical reasoning. These characteristics typically develop independently of psychosocial conflicts.

The distinction between defenses and coping styles has been elaborated most thoroughly by Haan (1977). Based partly on the work of Piaget, she proposes that ego processes may be divided into at least two broad categories—defense processes and coping processes. Defenses are characterized by rigidity, distortion of present reality, pressure from the past, undifferentiated thinking, magical thinking, and gratification of subterfuge. In contrast, coping processes are flexible, open to choice, oriented to present reality as well as the future, and focused on realistic compromises between wishes and affects. Defenses are forms of negation (of logic, of causality, of self-evaluation, of present reality, etc.), whereas coping styles are modes of problem solving of general problems of living.

To illustrate some differences between ego defenses and copying styles, Haan (1977) briefly describes the results of various studies. For example, defenses have been found to be negatively related to IQ and socioeconomic status, and positively related to psychopathological functioning, low ego strength, extremist political attitudes, adverse drug reactions, and problem drinking. In contrast, coping styles have been reported to be positively correlated with IQ, socioeconomic status, measures of nonpathological functioning, and moral development. Negative correlations have been found between coping styles and adverse drug reactions, obesity, and problem drinking. These findings suggest that coping styles have a different relation to reality issues than do defenses, and support the value of such a dichotomy. Other studies have shown that measures of defensiveness correlate positively with anxiety and with jealousy (Lougeay, 1986; Plutchik, Kellerman, & Conte, 1979).

Given these observations what can be concluded about the question of whether defenses are adaptive? The view suggested here is that defenses are of limited adaptive value. They are relatively primitive, unconscious methods used initially by children to deal with threats, anxiety, and conflict. When they are used by adults they represent unconscious, often inflexible, methods for dealing with anxieties. Ego defenses should be contrasted with coping styles, which are methods adults consciously use to solve problems. What Vaillant calls mature defenses are from this point of view adaptive adult coping styles. They are conscious, flexible, and often creative means for handling conflicts, anxiety, anger, and other emotions as well.

In examining these and related ideas concerning the meaning of defenses, it becomes evident that they relate to many important clinical issues. The following section describes some of the properties of defenses in more detail, from which the outlines of a general theory will emerge.

## General Characteristics of Ego Defenses

A careful reading of the literature on ego defenses leads to the conclusion that there is a considerable overlap of meaning of many of the defenses. For example, English and Finch (1964) point out that it is not always easy to distinguish between the various mechanisms of defense and that there are no distinct boundaries limiting one from the other. They note that some defenses are related quite closely to each other, such as reaction formation and undoing, or denial and projection. Noyes and Kolb (1963) point out that projection is, in many respects, a form of identification. Freedman, Kaplan, and Sadock (1975) argue that although the term introjection has been applied to the symbolic taking into oneself of other individuals, it has been discarded as unsatisfactory by many analysts. In a similar vein, Arieti (1974) notes that isolation and splitting are two names for the same concept. Bellak, Hurvich, and Gediman (1973) point out that the psychoanalytic literature uses the terms internalization, identification, introjection, and incorporation interchangeably and inconsistently. And Vaillant (1971) states that the term intellectualization includes the concepts of isolation, rationalization, ritual, undoing, and magical thinking.

Freud did not distinguish between identification and introjection and used them occasionally as synonyms (White, 1963). Repression and isolation have sometimes been used to refer to the same ideas, and repression has not always been clearly separated from denial (Fenichel, 1946). Both isolation and denial produce partial expulsion of ideas from consciousness. In the sense that isolation tends to separate ideas from affects, it is like splitting. Undoing has been described as being related to reaction formation (Fenichel, 1946). Humor and wit have been described as forms of denial (Sjoback, 1973).

In addition to the similarity of meaning of many defenses, the literature also hints at the idea of polarity in relation to ego defenses. For example, Arieti (1974) considers reaction formation as the replacement of an unacceptable drive derivative by its opposite. Both Chapman (1967) and English and Finch (1964) point out that introjection and incorporation are the opposite of projection. Acting out may be seen as the opposite of repression, just as identification may be considered the opposite of projection.

The literature thus implies at least two concepts in relation to defenses. One is that defenses overlap and vary in their degree of similarity to one another. The second is that some defenses are interpreted as polar opposites. From an analogue point of view, the concepts of similarity and polarity can be represented schematically by means of a circle. These observations have important implications for theory.

## TOWARD A THEORY OF EGO DEFENSES

The definitions of the different ego defenses each seem to have a theme. For example, *displacement* is generally defined as the discharge of *anger* toward individuals who are less dangerous than the "real" object of the anger. *Projection* is associated with the *hostile rejection* of other individuals because they are believed to possess the person's own unacceptable or dangerous traits or feelings. *Compensation* refers to the attempt to find substitutes for real or imagined *losses* or inadequacies.

What is implied by each of these examples is that the defense is a reaction to a complex, mixed emotional state that involves a particular emotion plus anxiety. Thus, for example, *displacement* involves anger mixed with anxiety over the expression of the anger. *Projection* involves disgust with (or rejection of) self mixed with anxiety over the self-hatred. *Compensation* involves sadness about a loss and anxiety over whether the lost object can be regained. *Denial* involves a person's uncritical acceptance or falsification of his or her perception of a potentially dangerous or unpleasant object mixed with anxiety over the possible consequences. *Reaction formation* involves the desire for lustful experiences mixed with anxiety over the expression of such feelings. And *regression* involves the desire for help with dangerous events mixed with anxiety over the need for help. All these events are unconscious. These observations suggest that emotions are intimately involved in the conceptual system of ego defenses. To elaborate this idea more fully, the following section will provide a brief overview of the author's "psychoevolutionary theory of emotion" and will then show how it throws light on the question of the relations between defenses and emotions.

## Overview of the Psychoevolutionary Theory of Emotion

There are three major aspects or models within this general theory. The first is called the "sequential model" and is concerned with describing the complex sequence of events that define an emotion, from the initial triggering event to the final action. The second aspect is called the "structural model" and is concerned with the concept of a limited number of basic or primary emotions and the relations among them. The third is called the "derivatives model" and is concerned with specifying the relations between emotions and other conceptual domains such as personality, diagnoses, and ego defenses. The following remarks will primarily address the derivatives model.

From a psychoevolutionary point of view, emotions are complex psychobiological processes that have evolved to deal with emergency or unusual situations in an individual's life. Emotions have two purposes. One is to communicate intentions from one individual to another. Another is to support behavior that increases long-term chances of survival. Fundamentally, emotions are basic adaptive processes, identifiable in all organisms.

The concept of basic emotions is fairly widely accepted although there is disagreement on the exact number and terminology used to describe them. The psychoevolutionary theory assumes that there are four pairs of basic bipolar emotions varying in degree of similarity to one another as well as in levels of intensity. The three concepts of similarity, polarity, and intensity define a three-dimensional structure shaped like a cone. Any cross section of this cone is a circle or circumplex.

Most people tend to think of emotions in terms of feeling states, but feelings are too idiosyncratic, ambiguous, and unreliable to serve as the basis for a general theory of emotion. We know, for example, that verbal reports of emotions may be deliberate attempts to deceive another person or may simply be conventional responses. We believe that in some cases, because of repression or denial, no reports of emotion are available even though other types of evidence suggest that emotions are present. Emotions are also believed to occur in animals from whom verbal reports are not available. These observations do not mean that a person's report of an emotional feeling is necessarily incorrect or meaningless. It only implies that subjective reports are not "gold standards," or the ultimate definers of emotion, but are subject to error, as are all forms of measurement.

The concept of derivatives implies that many conceptual domains are derived from the general conception of emotions. Table 1–1 illustrates this idea by showing the subjective language, the behavioral language, and the trait language of emotions. In each case, two examples are given to emphasize the idea that emotions refer to complex dimensions, for which there are multiple descriptive terms.

Emotions are typically transient events described by such subjective terms as fearful, sad, angry, or surprised. Such subjective feelings have a high probability of being associated with various classes of behavior; for example, avoidance behavior when fearful, attacking behavior when angry, and distress signals such as crying when sad. If for some reason, an emotional reaction occurs with high frequency or occurs consistently to a certain stimulus, we use the language of personality traits to describe the individual. For example, someone who is frequently fearful is described as timid or shy; someone who is frequently sad is described as gloomy or passive; and someone who is frequently disgusted is described as hostile or distrustful. In this context, the same words are often used to describe emotions and personality traits.

**TABLE 1–1**
**Three Languages That Describe Emotional States**

| *Subjective Language* | *Behavioral Language* | *Trait Language* |
|---|---|---|
| Fearful, terrified | Escaping, avoiding | Timid, shy |
| Angry, furious | Attacking, biting | Quarrelsome, irritable |
| Joyful, ecstatic | Cooperating, mating | Sociable, friendly |
| Sad, griefstricken | Crying for help, distress signals | Gloomy, pensive |
| Accepting, open | Affiliating, grooming | Trusting, gullible |
| Disgusted, loathful | Rejecting, vomiting | Distrustful, hostile |
| Anticipating, expectant | Exploring, mapping | Controlling, manipulative |
| Surprised, astonished | Losing control, disorienting | Dyscontrolled, impulsive |

The results of a study by Sanderson, Wetzler, Beck, and Betz (1992) are consistent with these ideas. They systematically evaluated a large number of patients who showed high levels of depression and/or dysthymia. They found that most of these patients received a diagnosis of personality disorder. The most common personality disorders associated with depression were avoidant personality, dependent personality, and obsessive-compulsive personality. This illustrates how an emotion (depression) may be intimately related to certain personality traits.

Important implications of the psychoevolutionary theory are that the relations between emotions can be described by means of a circle or circumplex and that the same idea applies to the other derivative languages. This is represented in Figure 1–1 where subjective language, behavioral

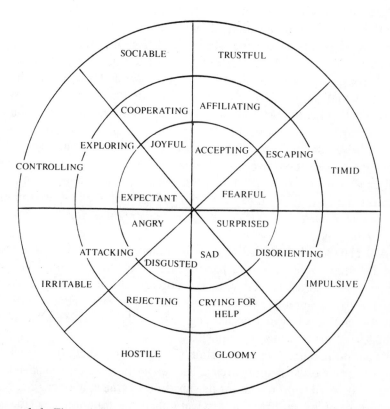

**Figure 1–1.** Three derivative languages for emotions. The inner circle refers to the subjective language, the middle circle to the behavioral language, and the outer circle to the trait language.

language, and trait language are shown on the same diagram. Various studies have shown empirically that the subjective language can be represented by means of a circumplex (Fisher, Heise, Bohrnstedt, & Lucke, 1985; Plutchik, 1980; Russell, 1989). Other studies have revealed that the language of personality traits can also be represented by means of a circumplex (Conte & Plutchik, 1981; Kiesler, 1983; Wiggins, 1982).

The psychoevolutionary theory also assumes that personality disorders, ego defenses, and coping styles are all derivatives of the basic emotions, and that all these different languages are systematically related. This concept of emotion derivatives is illustrated in Table 1–2.

Table 1–2 describes nine different conceptual domains related directly or indirectly to emotions. The first domain or conceptual language refers to the stimulus events that tend to initiate the complex chains of events that we call emotions. These stimuli refer to biologically important, survival-related events that have significance to all living organisms, which is one of the reasons for calling the theory a psychoevolutionary theory of emotions. However, events alone do not automatically produce emotional states; these events need to be interpreted before the subsequent links in the chain can occur. Thus, certain stimuli are cognitively evaluated as "dangerous," others as "enemies," and still others as "friends." Such cognitions, which are not always conscious, may be inferred on the basis of antecedent and consequent events. Based on such cognitions, the subjective feelings of emotion occur. These feelings (e.g., anger, joy, sadness, and surprise), are what are often defined as an emotion. In actuality, they are only one aspect of the complex state here called an emotion, and clinical experience confirms that such feelings are often vague, confusing, inconsistent, and difficult to report or specify. Such feelings are too limited and unstable to use as the only or even central basis for the definition of an emotion.

Associated with each feeling state is an impulse to act in a certain way and a certain probability of a particular type of overt action. Thus, for example, fear is associated with the impulse and the act of escaping, anger with the impulse and act of attacking a barrier, sadness with the impulse and act of crying or uttering distress signals. These acts are referred to as the behavioral language.

In addition, these acts have certain functions: to protect the individual in the case of escape; to destroy a barrier in the case of attack; and to reintegrate with a lost object (or its substitute) in the case of crying. Each basic emotion has a different survival-enhancing function described by such terms as rejection of a noxious stimulus, exploration of new territory, and orientation to an unexpected stimulus.

**TABLE 1–2**
**Emotions and Their Derivatives**

| Stimulus Event | Inferred Cognition | Subjective Language | Behavioral Language | Functional Language | Trait Language | Diagnostic Language | Ego-Defense Language | Coping-Style Language |
|---|---|---|---|---|---|---|---|---|
| Threat | "Danger" | Fear | Escape | Protection | Timid | Passive | Repression | Avoidance |
| Obstacle | "Enemy" | Anger | Attack | Destruction | Quarrelsome | Antisocial | Displacement | Substitution |
| Potential mate | "Possess" | Joy | Mate | Reproduction | Sociable | Manic | Reaction formation | Reversal |
| Loss of valued individual | "Abandonment" | Sadness | Cry | Reintegration | Gloomy | Depressed | Compensation | Replacement |
| Member of one's group | "Friend" | Acceptance | Groom | Incorporation | Trusting | Histrionic | Denial | Minimization |
| Unpalatable object | "Poison" | Disgust | Vomit | Rejection | Hostile | Paranoid | Projection | Fault finding |
| New territory | "What's out there?" | Expectation | Map | Exploration | Curious | Obsessive-Compulsive | Intellectualization | Mapping |
| Unexpected object | "What is it?" | Surprise | Stop | Orientation | Indecisive | Borderline | Regression | Help seeking |

When an individual shows an emotion frequently or in a wide variety of situations, the language of personality traits is used to describe the resulting patterns. A person who frequently shows fear is usually described as timid or shy; someone who is frequently angry may be described as quarrelsome or irritable; someone who is frequently open, friendly, and unaggressive may be called trusting. These are personality traits, although it should be evident that a number of different trait terms could be used to describe the personality derivatives of each basic emotion dimension, depending on the intensity and frequency of the emotional expressions. Thus, for example, someone who is frequently joyful could be described in the personality trait language as sociable, friendly, hypomanic, or enthusiastic.

Of great clinical interest is that extreme forms of certain personality traits are generally considered to create problems for the individual and those others with whom he or she is in contact. When timidity, for example, becomes extreme in an individual, we tend to use the language of personality disorders, describing such a person as passive or submissive. When anger and irritability in an individual becomes extreme, we tend to describe such a person as aggressive or antisocial. The extremely sad person is diagnosed as depressed or dysthymic, and the extremely hostile person may be seen as paranoid. It is possible to identify a personality disorder diagnoses for extreme forms of each of the basic emotion dimensions and personality derivatives, although we recognize that several additional elements often enter into a specific diagnosis. In addition, even if clinicians disagree with the specific terminology proposed in Table 1–2, the general idea is certainly a reasonable one.

We come now to the heart of the present theory of ego defenses. The theory postulates that the many terms that have been described as ego defenses are in fact synonyms or closely related concepts reflecting a small number of "basic" defenses. The eight basic defenses have been called repression, displacement, reaction formation, compensation, denial, projection, intellectualization, and regression. These terms were selected because of the overlap of meanings in published papers plus factor-analytic work described in Plutchik et al. (1979). One of the reasons for the complexity associated with ego defense concepts is that emotions frequently are mixed and that the basic defenses are also combined in subtle ways, perhaps sufficiently so to sometimes justify the use of special terms. It is assumed that each ego defense developed in infancy or childhood to help the individual deal with a particular emotional state in conflict with anxiety, as described earlier.

Finally, we may consider the domain or language of coping styles. The theory assumes that for each primitive, unconscious ego defense, there is a corresponding realistic, conscious coping style. Thus, for the defense of repression there is the conscious coping style of "avoidance"; for denial there is "minimization"; and for regression there is "help seeking." The definitions of each defense and each corresponding coping style are presented later.

A final point should be made about Table 1–2 and the concept that emotions have derivatives. The concept of derivatives is one of the most important ideas of the psychoevolutionary theory. This term may be used in three different senses. It can mean that certain human behaviors are seen in lower animals; for example, the sneer of the human may be said to be derived from the snarl of the wolf. It can also mean that certain behaviors seen in adults are derivatives of certain behaviors seen in infants. An example might be the feeding and babyish behaviors sometimes seen between adult lovers. A third meaning of the concept is the that certain conceptual domains are derivative of other more primitive events or concepts. This is the sense in which the term is used here. It means that a number of conceptual domains are systematically related to one another.

The concept of derivatives does not mean that the different related domains are identical to, or even highly correlated with, each other. In chemistry, all organic compounds are derived from carbon, yet their properties may differ considerably depending on the other elements or components involved. Similarly, if an individual frequently uses repression as a defense, it does not necessarily mean that he or she also uses "avoidance" as a conscious coping style. If an individual uses regression as a defense, this does not necessarily imply that he or she uses "help seeking" as a conscious coping style. The defenses reflect early stages of mental development, whereas coping styles reflect mature methods of problem solving resulting from life experiences. Perhaps another way of saying this is that whereas all defenses tend to be immature, all coping styles tend to be reasonably mature attempts to solve a variety of problems.

## THE STRUCTURE OF EGO DEFENSES

From the point of view of the present theory, all ego defenses have a basic underlying structure. For each defense, there is a set of *associated personality traits*, a *social need*, a characteristic *method*, and a purpose or *function*. This idea is shown in detail in Table 1–3, and is elaborated in part from the description provided by Kellerman (1979).

Let us consider several examples of these hypotheses. People who use displacement a lot tend to be aggressive, provocative, or cynical. Their

**TABLE 1-3**
**The Underlying Structure of Ego Defenses**

| Ego Defense | Associated Traits | Social Needs | Method | Function |
|---|---|---|---|---|
| Repression | Timid<br>Passive<br>Lethargic<br>Obedient | Need to avoid or withdraw from social relationships | Forget painful events | To maintain passivity and avoid decisions and anxiety |
| Displacement | Aggressive<br>Provocative<br>Cynical | Need to find scapegoats who will absorb hostility | Attack a symbol or substitute for source of frustration | To express anger without fear of retaliation |
| Reaction Formation | Altruistic<br>Puritanical<br>Conscientious<br>Moralistic | Need to show good (or correct) behavior | Reverse feelings of interest to their opposite | To hide interest in bad and especially sexual behavior |
| Compensation | Boastful<br>Daydreamer<br>Worried about inadequacies | Need to be recognized, admired, and applauded | Exaggerate positive aspects of self | To improve a perceived weakness or replace a loss |
| Denial | Uncritical<br>Trusting<br>Suggestable<br>Gullible<br>Romantic | Need to avoid conflict in social relationships | Interpret threats and problems as benign | To maintain feeling of being liked or loved |
| Projection | Critical<br>Fault finding<br>Blaming | Need to identify imperfections in others | Blame or be hypercritical | To decrease feelings of inferiority, shame, or personal imperfections |
| Intellectualization | Obsessional<br>Domineering<br>Possessive | Need to control all social relationships | Find a rational justification for all acts | To prevent the expression of sudden or unacceptable impulses |
| Regression | Impulsive<br>Restless<br>Undercontrolled | Need to act out all impulses | Express impulsive and immature behaviors | To achieve acceptance of impulsive acts |

From R. Plutchik, 1991.

*need* is to find scapegoats to whom hostility can be safely directed. The *method* used is to attack a substitute for the source of the frustration, and the *function* of displacement is to express anger without fear of retaliation.

To take another example, people who use denial a lot are likely to be suggestible, trustful, and gullible. Their *need* is to avoid conflict with others in social relationships. The *method* they use, in contrast to the individual who uses repression, is to interpret social problems as benign, trivial, or even desirable. The function of this unconscious strategy is to maintain the feeling of being liked or loved. From this description, it is evident that denial and repression have certain similarities. Both imply a need to avoid pain or conflict in social relationships. The differences between them are in the methods used, and in the ultimate purpose of the behavior. The fact that there are various degrees of overlap between the different ego defenses helps explain why so many overlapping names have been proposed over the years, and why an implicit similarity structure exists among all the defenses. The present theory assumes that this implicit structure is, in fact, a circumplex.

## The Circumplex Structure of Ego Defenses

If the theory of defenses as derivatives of emotions is correct, then we would expect that the circumplex structure of emotions would be reflected to some degree in the relations among ego defenses. A study dealing with the relative similarity of a set of 16 ego defenses was carried out several years ago, the results of which helped determine the eventual set of 8 defenses described in this chapter.

Figure 1–2 shows the results of using similarity scaling on a set of 16 ego defense concepts. Experienced psychiatrists were asked to make paired comparisons of these concepts in terms of degree of similarity. The details of the method have been described by Plutchik et al. (1979). The results of the analysis reveal an approximate circumplex showing the degree of nearness of all defenses, and polarities as well. Thus, for example, denial, repression, and undoing are considered to be relatively similar in meaning, just as intellectualization, rationalization and isolation are relatively similar in meaning. The cluster of projection, displacement, and acting out are also found near one another and thus represent similar methods by which the ego defends itself.

Polarities may also be seen in Figure 1–2: The displacement ego defense is opposite the defenses of fantasy and introjection; sublimation is opposite regression and reaction formation, acting out is opposite repression. These are all relations that make clinical sense.

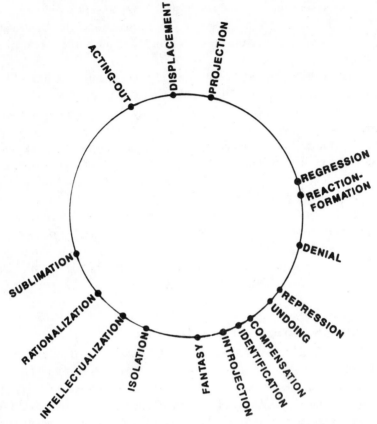

**Figure 1–2.** Similarity scaling of 16 ego defenses by direct comparison method.

## The Concept of Coping Styles

The theory makes a distinction between ego defenses and coping styles. As described earlier, ego defenses are unconscious, rigid, and of limited adaptive value to an immature ego. In contrast, coping styles are conscious methods of solving problems, are flexible, and generally are adaptive. For each defense, a corresponding conscious coping style is postulated. Thus, for repression, there is conscious *avoidance,* for displacement, there is conscious *substitution,* and for denial there is conscious *minimization.* These are all shown in Table 1–2. Table 1–4 provides brief definitions of the eight basic defenses and the eight corresponding coping styles.

The defenses cover all the classical ones. The terms used to describe the coping styles were created to emphasize the key aspect of each coping

## TABLE 1-4
### The Eight Basic Defenses and Coping Styles

1. Defense: *Repression, Isolation, Introjection.* Exclusion from consciousness of an idea and/or its associated emotions to avoid painful conflicts or threats.

   Coping: *Avoidance.* An attempt to solve a problem by avoiding the person or situation believed to have created the problem, or by "thought-stopping" or turning attention away from the problem.

2. Defense: *Denial.* Lack of awareness of certain events, experiences, or feelings that would be painful to acknowledge.

   Coping: *Minimization.* An attempt to solve a problem by assuming that the problem is not as important as other people think it is.

3. Defense: *Displacement.* Discharge of pent-up emotions, usually of anger, on objects, animals, or people perceived as less dangerous to the individual than those that originally aroused the emotions.

   Coping: *Substitution.* An attempt to solve a problem by doing unrelated pleasurable activities; for example, reducing tension-related problems by using meditation, exercise, or alcohol.

4. Defense: *Regression, Acting-Out.* Retreat under stress to earlier or more immature patterns of behavior and gratification.

   Coping: *Help Seeking.* Asking assistance from others to help solve a problem.

5. Defense: *Compensation, Identification, Fantasy.* The development of strength in one area to offset real or imagined deficiency in another.

   Coping: *Replacement.* Solving a problem by improving weaknesses or limitations that exist either in yourself or in the situation you are in.

6. Defense: *Intellectualization, Sublimation, Undoing, Rationalization.* Unconscious control of emotions and impulses by excessive dependence on rational interpretations of situations.

   Coping: *Mapping.* Getting as much information about a problem as possible before acting or making a decision.

7. Defense: *Projection.* Unconscious rejection of emotionally unacceptable thoughts, traits, or wishes, and the attribution of them to other people.

   Coping: *Blaming.* Blaming other people for the existence of a problem, or blaming the "system."

8. Defense: *Reaction Formation.* Prevention of the expression of unacceptable desires, particularly sexual or aggressive, by developing or exaggerating opposite attitudes and behaviors.

   Coping: *Reversal.* Solving a problem by doing the opposite of what you feel; for example, smiling even when you feel angry.

---

method. In each case, the defense refers to an unconscious process designed to hide, avoid, or modify some threat, conflict, or danger. The coping styles refer to methods of problem solving. These methods of problem solving, although conceptually related to the defenses are not equivalent to them; they are conscious strategies each of which can be applied to a wide variety of problems.

## IMPLICATIONS

The conception of ego defenses presented here has been described as one aspect of a more general theory of emotions. All organisms are born with certain genetically determined biobehavioral mechanisms that deal with environmental emergencies. There are a limited number of such mechanisms, and they are concerned with such survival-related activities as avoiding predators, finding prey, incorporating food, expelling waste products or toxins, and sexual behavior to ensure genetic survival.

In humans, particularly during early stages of growth and development, the infant and young child are relatively helpless and have few methods for dealing with dangers. These reactions include calling for help (distress signals), ignoring the danger, and making believe that the danger is not serious, as well as a few others. They are the prototypes of the ego defenses that we recognize in adults. As mentioned earlier, the defenses are relatively limited, rigid, unconscious and primitive methods that both children and adults use to deal with anxiety-provoking situations. They are related not only to the eight basic emotions postulated by the psychoevolutionary theory of emotions but to clusters of personality traits, and to diagnoses of personality disorders. As the ego strengthens and matures, dangers and difficulties are seen as problems to be dealt with in relatively more conscious ways. These conscious and therefore flexible problem-solving methods are what we call coping styles; and although they bear some resemblances to defenses, they have emergent properties that make them different.

Given these general ideas, what are some implications? Three implications will be briefly explored: (1) for test construction, (2) for assessment, and (3) for psychotherapy.

### Implications for Test Construction

The ideas described in this chapter have been the basis for the development of a number of psychological tests. They have provided the conceptual basis for scales designed to measure personality dimensions, ego defenses, and coping styles. These are described in other sources and will not be elaborated here (Plutchik, 1989; Plutchik & Conte, 1989). However, Chapter 8 of this volume provides extensive data on the construction and use of the ego defense scales in the United States and in several other countries.

### Implications for Assessment

The use of these scales for individual assessment may be illustrated through an unusual symposium sponsored by a private foundation concerned with supporting research in cardiology. A number of professionals representing different disciplines (e.g., cardiology, psychotherapy, psychology, nutrition, homeopathy, etc.) were asked to discuss two cardiac cases from their perspectives. The two patients gave permission to allow their medical records to be reviewed and were willing to be interviewed as well (Plutchik, 1992).

The following case history describes the use of the ego defense scales with one of the patients, Mr. Joseph (a pseudonym).

Mr. Joseph is a 55-year-old white male who is overweight, has mild diastolic hypertension, and has had an occlusion of a coronary artery that has been treated successfully with angioplasty. His father died at age 80, cause unknown, while his mother died at age 55 after a series of strokes. He has had several major stresses in his life including the death of his wife in 1992 of cancer. He does not smoke or drink but has a heavy coffee intake. During his adult life, he has been a very successful businessperson.

Mr. Joseph took several tests designed to measure personality, ego defenses, and coping styles. His personality profile on the Emotions Profile Index (EPI) (Plutchik & Kellerman, 1974) suggests a person who is quite sociable, yet not fully trusting of other people. He sees himself as moderately self-controlled and yet at the same time describes himself as impulsive, eager to try new experiences, and adventurous. There thus seems to be some conflict between his interest in new experiences and his need to keep things under control and predictable.

Figure 1–3 shows Mr. Joseph's ego defense profile based on the ego defense scales of the Life Style Index (Plutchik et al., 1979; Plutchik & Conte, 1989). It attempts to measure unconscious defenses. Mr. Joseph has very high scores on *denial* suggesting that he sees himself as easy to get along with, free of prejudice, and always optimistic. Such attitudes, when extreme as they are here, imply that the individual has unrealistic and somewhat grandiose beliefs about him- or herself, associated with an urge to show off. Often adjustment is good in such persons. High scores on *repression* tend to be associated with high anxiety (which Mr. Joseph denies) and with great difficulty in directly expressing emotions in a warm and open way. This point is consistent with the case history description of his unsatisfactory relation to his children.

The high score on *intellectualization* reveals Mr. Joseph as a person who sees himself as highly rational, objective, hard working, and self-controlled. On the other hand, such persons are often seen by other people as cold and somewhat critical. High scores on *intellectualization, denial,* and *repression* reveal a person under high *stress* who is largely unaware of it. The high *compensation* score suggests an underlying feeling of inadequacy and a need to engage in activities to compensate for these

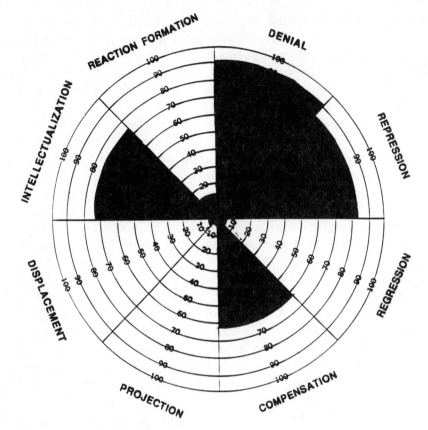

**Figure 1–3.** Ego defense profile for Mr. Joseph.

supposed shortcomings. Such individuals often become preoccupied with accumulating possessions, and they have a strong urge to prove themselves when faced with direct or indirect challenges.

In summary, Mr. Joseph is unusually high on minimizing problems and hiding or reversing his feelings. He is very high on intellectualizing. This implies that he is not in touch with his inner feelings of love, fear, anger, or joy. Whether this inhibition of feelings has anything to do with his heart condition is unknown, but it is likely that he would feel closer to other people and perhaps happier if he were more open, less intellectual, and more willing to accept help from others.

## Implications for Psychotherapy

One value of the proposed model of ego defenses is that it focuses attention on a small number of "basic" defenses. Rather than having to remember and search for as many as 28 overlapping and obscurely defined defenses, the therapist can attempt to thoroughly understand the key ones. Once defenses are identified, it is then possible to infer the existence of certain personality traits that tend to be associated with each defense. Also of great interest is the likelihood of being able to infer the existence of certain personality disorders as well. The chain of relations works both ways and a knowledge of traits and diagnoses implies the likely existence of certain defenses. Finally, recognition of defenses may provide insight into the kinds of affects an individual finds conflictful or dangerous.

These implications do not exhaust the range of possibilities. Research based on this model of defenses should clarify and enlarge both the postulates and the deductions.

## REFERENCES

American Psychiatric Association. (1987). *Diagnostic and statistical manual of mental disorders* (3rd ed.-rev; DSM-III-R). Washington, DC: Author.

Arieti, S. (Ed.). (1974). *American handbook of psychiatry.* New York: Basic Books.

Bellak, L., Hurvich, M., & Gediman, H. K. (1973). *Ego functions in schizophrenics, neurotics, and normals.* New York: Wiley.

Bibring, G. L., Dwyer, T. F., Huntington, D. S., & Valenstein, A. F. (1961). A study of the psychological processes in pregnancy and of the earliest mother-child relationship. Appendix B. Glossary of defenses. *Psychoanalytic Study of the Child, 16,* 62–72.

Bond, M., Gardner, S. T., Christian, J., & Sigal, J. J. (1983). Empirical study of self-rated defense styles. *Archives of General Psychiatry, 40,* 333–338.

Chapman, A. H. (1967). *Textbook of clinical psychiatry: An interpersonal approach.* Philadelphia, PA: Lippincott.

Conte, H. R., & Plutchik, R. (1981). A circumplex model for interpersonal traits. *Journal of Personality and Social Psychology, 2,* 823–830.

English, O. S., & Finch, S. M. (1964). *Introduction to psychiatry.* New York: Norton.

Ewalt, J. R., & Farnsworth, D. L. (1963). *Textbook of psychiatry.* New York: McGraw-Hill.

Fenichel, O. (1946). *The psychoanalytic theory of neurosis.* London: Routledge & Kegan Paul.

Fisher, G. A., Heise, D. R., Bohrnstedt, G. W., & Lucke, J. F. (1985). Evidence for extending the circumplex model of personality trait language to self-reported moods. *Journal of Personality and Social Psychology, 49,* 233–242.

Freedman, A. M., Kaplan, H. I., & Sadock, B. J. (Eds.). (1975). *Comprehensive textbook of psychiatry* (Vol. 2). Baltimore, MD: Williams & Wilkins.

Freud, A. (1946). *The ego and the mechanisms of defense.* New York: International Universities Press. (Original work published 1936)

Freud, S. (1957). Repression. In J. Strachey (Ed. and Trans.), *The standard edition of the complete words of Sigmund Freud* (Vol. 14, pp. 146–158). London: Hogarth Press. (Original work published 1915)

Freud, S. (1957). Inhibitions, symptoms and anxiety. In J. Strachey (Ed. and Trans.), *The standard edition of the complete words of Sigmund Freud* (Vol. 20, pp. 87–174). London: Hogarth Press. (Original work published 1926)

Freud, S. (1957). Analysis terminable and interminable. In J. Strachey (Ed. and Trans.), *The standard edition of the complete words of Sigmund Freud* (Vol. 23, pp. 216–253). London: Hogarth Press. (Original work published 1937)

Freud, S. (1963). Introductory lectures on psycho-analysis. In J. Strachey (Ed. and Trans.), *The standard edition of the complete words of Sigmund Freud* (Vol. 16, pp. 243–483). London: Hogarth Press. (Original work published 1916)

Freud, S. (1964). Constructions in analysis. In J. Strachey (Ed. and Trans.), *The standard edition of the complete words of Sigmund Freud* (Vol. 23, pp. 257–269). London: Hogarth Press. (Original work published 1937)

Glover, E. (1949). *Psycho-analysis: A handbook for medical practitioners and students of comparative psychology.* New York: Norton.

Haan, N. (1977). *Coping and defending: Processes of self-environment organization.* New York: Academic Press.

Hartmann, H. (1958). *Ego psychology and the problem of adaptation.* New York: International Universities Press.

Ihilevich, D., & Gleser, G. C. (1991). *Defenses in psychotherapy: The clinical application of the Defense Mechanisms Inventory.* Odessa, FL: Psychological Assessment Resources.

Kaplan, H. I., & Sadock, B. J. (Eds.). (1989). *Comprehensive textbook of psychiatry.* New Haven, CT: Yale University Press.

Kellerman, H. (1979). *Group therapy and personality: Intersecting structures.* New York: Grune & Stratton.

Kiesler, D. J. (1983). The 1982 Interpersonal Circle: A taxonomy for complementarity in human transactions. *Psychological Review, 90,* 185–214.

Loewenstein, R. M. (1967). Defensive organization and autonomous ego functions. *Journal of the American Psychoanalytic Association, 15,* 795–809.

Lougeay, D. C. (1986). *Relationship of jealousy to defensiveness and anxiety: A correlation-descriptive study.* Ph.D. Dissertation. San Diego, CA: United States International University.

Moore, B. E., & Fine, B. D. (Eds.). (1990). *Psychoanalytic terms and concepts.* New Haven, CT: Yale University Press.

Noyes, A. P., & Kolb, L. C. (1963). *Modern clinical psychiatry.* Philadelphia, PA: Saunders.

Perry, J. C. (1990). *Defense mechanism rating scales.* (5th ed.). Boston, MA: Harvard Medical School.

Plutchik, R. (1980). *Emotion: A psychoevolutionary synthesis.* New York: Harper & Row.

Plutchik, R. (1989). Measuring emotions and their derivatives. In R. Plutchik & H. Kellerman (Eds.), *Emotion: Theory, research, and experience: Vol. 4. The measurement of emotions.* San Diego, CA: Academic Press.

Plutchik, R. (1992). *Personality, ego defenses and coping styles in relation to health and disease.* Paper presented at a symposium on New Perspectives in Cardiology, The Russek Foundation. Boca Raton, Florida.

Plutchik, R., & Conte, H. R. (1989). Measuring emotions and their derivatives: Personality traits, ego defenses, and coping styles. In S. Wetzler & M. Katz (Eds.), *Contemporary approaches to psychological assessment.* New York: Brunner/Mazel.

Plutchik, R., & Kellerman, H. (1974). *Manual of The Emotions Profile Index.* Los Angeles, CA: Western Psychological Services.

Plutchik, R., Kellerman, H., & Conte, H. R. (1979). A structural theory of ego defenses and emotions. In C. E. Izard (Ed.), *Emotions in personality and psychopathology.* New York: Plenum Press.

Russell, J. A. (1989). Measures of emotion. In R. Plutchik & H. Kellerman (Eds.), *The measurement of emotions.* New York: Academic Press.

Sanderson, W. C., Wetzler, S., Beck, A. T., & Betz, F. (1992). Prevalence of personality disorders in patients with major depression and dysthymia. *Psychiatry Research, 42,* 93–99.

Schafer, R. (1954). *Psychoanalytic interpretation in Rorschach testing.* New York: Grune & Stratton.

Sjoback, H. (1973). *The psychoanalytic theory of defensive processes.* New York: Wiley.

Sperling, S. J. (1958). On denial and the essential nature of defense. *International Journal of Psychoanalysis, 39,* 25–38.

Vaillant, G. E. (1971). Theoretical hierarchy of adaptive ego mechanisms. *Archives of General Psychiatry, 24,* 107–118.

Vaillant, G. E. (1975). Natural history of male psychological health: III. Empirical dimensions of mental health. *Archives of General Psychiatry, 32,* 420–426.

Vaillant, G. E. (1976). Natural history of male psychological health: The relation of choice of ego mechanism of defense to adult adjustment. *Archives of General Psychiatry, 33,* 535–545.

Verwoerdt, A. (1972). Psychopathological responses to the stress of physical illness. In Z. J. Lipowski (Ed.), *Psychosocial aspects of physical illness.* Advances in psychosomatic medicine, 8. Basil, Switzerland: Karger.

White, R. W. (1963). *Ego and reality in psychoanalytic theory.* New York: International Universities Press.

Wiggins, J. S. (1982). Circumplex models of interpersonal behavior in clinical psychology. In P. C. Kendall & J. N. Butcher (Eds.), *Handbook of research methods in clinical psychology.* New York: Wiley.

# 2

# Ego Defenses
## A Psychoanalytic Perspective

### PETER BUCKLEY

Of all psychoanalytic concepts, that of ego defenses has proven to be among the most robust, enduring, and least controversial, accepted widely as a crucial aspect of clinical assessment. The reasons for this ready acceptance, even in circles outside of psychoanalysis, are not difficult to discern. Ego defenses—or at least their manifestation as defensive behaviors, ideas or affects—can be directly observed as part of the phenomenology of the clinical situation as well as at work in everyday life. Thus the recognition of ego defenses as psychological phenomena does not require the use of levels of theoretical inference far removed from the data at hand.

This chapter will trace the historical and theoretical evolution of the concept of ego defenses from the viewpoint of psychoanalytic theory. It was within psychoanalysis that the idea of ego defenses first originated and the gradual expansion of the concept in the writings of Freud will be reviewed here and later developments and controversies within psychoanalysis concerning ego defenses will be outlined.

## EGO PSYCHOLOGY AND DEFENSE MECHANISMS

### Sigmund Freud's Views

Anna Freud (1966) observed that the term *defense* was the earliest representative of the dynamic viewpoint in psychoanalytic theory, appearing for the first time in 1894 in Freud's *The Neuro-Psychoses of Defense.*

Freud (1894/1962) stated "I shall call this form *defense* hysteria—the designation of the ego's response to "incompatible ideas"—pushing the thing away, of not thinking of it, of suppressing it" (p. 47). Defense was thus a description of the ego's battle against painful or intolerable ideas or affects.

Freud initially used the terms *defense* and *repression* synonymously. The concept of repression had made its original appearance in Breuer and Freud's *Preliminary Communication* of 1893 where it was defined as the mechanism that governed "things which the patient wished to forget and therefore intentionally repressed from his conscious thought" (1893/ 1955, p. 10). It was not until after the development of the structural model of id, ego, and superego, and the publication of *Inhibitions, Symptoms and Anxiety* (1926/1959) that repression was defined as a special method of defense, and defense became "a general designation for all the techniques which the ego makes use of in conflicts which may lead to a neurosis" (p. 163). Subsequently, Freud proceeded to describe a number of defense mechanisms separate from repression, but as Wallerstein has pointed out, since repression "is characteristically operative alongside almost every other defense mechanism it has also always been considered primus inter pares" (1983, p. 202).

Symptom formation was seen by Freud to be intimately related to the action of repression:

A symptom arises from an instinctual impulse which has been detrimentally affected by repression. If the ego, by making use of the signal of unpleasure, attains its object of completely suppressing the instinctual impulse, we learn nothing of how this has happened. We can only find out about it from those cases in which repression must be described as having to a greater or less extent failed. In this event the position, generally speaking, is that the instinctual impulse has found a substitute in spite of repression, but a substitute which is very much reduced, displaced and inhibited and which is no longer recognizable as a satisfaction. (1926/1959, pp. 95–96)

This thesis is delineated in the first of Freud's major case studies, *Fragment of an Analysis of a Case of Hysteria* (1905/1953a). Two dreams and their painstaking analysis form the centerpiece of the report, and Freud uses them to explicate the repressed unconscious meaning of Dora's hysterical symptoms. The case goes awry (Dora abruptly terminated treatment after 3 months) because Freud fails to recognize and address the transference and instead pursues a single-minded scientific quest with regard to the analysis of Dora's two dreams and the unconscious repressed meaning of her symptoms.

Freud came to divide repression into two forms, *primal* repression and repression proper. Primal repression was seen as occurring in childhood and being responsible for the universally observed amnesia of childhood.

The motivation for primal repression was postulated to be the avoidance of the specific stimulus that would produce unpleasure. Because of the immaturity of the psychic apparatus, the threatening or forbidden instinctual wishes that underwent primal repression in early childhood did not have a preconscious representation, hence Freud postulated that they were inaccessible to consciousness. This was in contrast to the repression of conflictual events or forbidden wishes that took place in late childhood, adolescence, or adulthood. Potentially, these repressed ideas or feelings could be brought into consciousness through the analytic method since, in Freud's view, such repression did possess preconscious representation.

## Repression and Therapy

Freud's model of the nature of therapeutic action was intimately connected to the concept of repression. His early "cathartic" view postulated that therapy worked through the release of dammed-up affects that had been warded off from consciousness because of the pain they would cause. As Cooper (1986) has commented, Freud thought that these warded-off noxious feelings and thoughts acted as a kind of mental abscess emitting toxins that poisoned the mental system, thus causing conversion symptoms and hysteria. The curative catharsis was achieved by bringing into consciousness the painful or unendurable ideas or affects; that is, by undoing the repression.

As Freud developed his theories, however, concepts of defense and resistance become more prominent. Resistance was now related to the whole range of the patient's defense mechanisms: "The defense mechanisms directed against former danger recur in the treatment as resistances against recovery. It follows from this that the ego treats recovery itself as a new danger" (1937/1964, p. 238).

As Sandler, Dare, and Holder (1973) have commented, because resistances reflect the type of conflict and the defenses used, they have become an object of analytic study in themselves. The analysis of resistances can be viewed as the analysis of those aspects of the patient's defenses that enter into and contribute to the pathological outcome of conflicts. Thus "defense-analysis"—the analysis of resistances—has come to play a central role in the therapeutic technique of the ego psychological school of psychoanalysis.

## Sublimation and Reaction Formation

In *Three Essays on the Theory of Sexuality* (1905/1953b), Freud described the defense mechanisms of *sublimation* and *reaction formation:*

What is it that goes to the making of these constructions which are so important for the growth of a civilized and normal individual? They probably emerge at the cost of the infantile sexual impulses themselves. Thus the activity of those impulses does not cease even during this period of latency, though their energy is diverted, wholly or in great part, from their sexual use and directed to other ends. Historians of civilization appear to be at one in assuming that powerful components are acquired for every kind of cultural achievement by this diversion of sexual instinctual forces from sexual aims and their direction to new ones—a process which deserves the name of "sublimation" . . . these impulses . . . arise from erotogenic forces and derive their activity from instincts which, in view of the direction of the subject's development, can only arouse unpleasurable feelings. They consequently evoke opposing mental forces (reacting impulses), which, in order to suppress this unpleasure effectively, build up the mental dams that I have already mentioned—disgust, shame and morality. (p. 178)

## Undoing and Isolation

In *Inhibitions, Symptoms and Anxiety* (1926/1959), Freud defined the defense mechanisms of *undoing* and *isolation,* both commonly seen in obsessional neuroses. He defined undoing as follows:

It is, as it were, negative magic, and endeavors, by means of motor symbolism, to "blow away" not merely the *consequences* of some event (or experience or impression) but the event itself—in which one action is cancelled out by a second, so that it is as though neither action has taken place, whereas, in reality, both have. (p. 119)

Isolation, as a defense, was felt by Freud to be

peculiar to obsessional neurosis. It, too, takes place in the motor sphere. When something unpleasant has happened to the subject or when he himself has done something which has a significance for his neurosis, he interpolates an interval during which nothing further must happen—during which he must perceive nothing and do nothing. This behaviour, which seems strange at first sight, is soon seen to have a relation to repression. We know that in hysteria it is possible to cause a traumatic experience to be overtaken by amnesia. In obsessional neurosis this can often not be achieved: the experience is not forgotten, but, instead, it is deprived of its affect, and its associative connections are suppressed or interrupted so that it remains as though isolated and is not reproduced in the ordinary processes of thought. The effect of this isolation is the same as the effect of repression with amnesia. (1926/1959, p. 120)

In his case study *Notes upon a Case of Obsessional Neurosis* (1909/1955) Freud provided graphic clinical examples of the operation of these defense mechanisms. Meticulously, Freud interpreted to the Rat Man (as the patient in this case report was to become known) the unconscious meaning of the various elements of his obsessional symptoms. At this stage of his thinking, Freud believed this meticulous "uncovering" of repressed memories was the primary therapeutic component of analysis.

Freud had thus suggested that a connection existed between special forms of defense and particular illnesses (e.g., between repression and hysteria), and between undoing and isolation and obsessional neurosis. This idea was further developed in *Certain Neurotic Mechanisms in Jealousy, Paranoia and Homosexuality* (Freud, 1922/1955), where *introjection* or *identification* and *projection* were mentioned as important defense mechanisms. Projection was identified as the primary defense mechanism of paranoid illnesses.

## Projection

The mechanism of *projection* had been adumbrated by Freud in the Schreber case study (1911/1958) to explain how internal perceptions were replaced by external perceptions. Projection was seen to be at the heart of the paranoic's symptom formation. For Freud, all the common forms of paranoia could be represented as contradictions of the single proposition: "I (a man) love him (a man)," which is contradicted by "I do not love him—I hate him." This belief was transformed by projection into "He hates (persecutes) me, which will justify me in hating him." As Freud stated, "And thus the impelling unconscious feeling makes its appearance as though it were the consequence of an external perception 'I do not love him—I hate him, because he persecutes me.' Observation leaves room for no doubt that the persecutor is some one who was once loved" (1911/1958, p. 63).

Fenichel further developed Freud's ideas on projection:

Like elements of the body, one's mental characteristics, too, may be projected onto the persecutor. This occurs not only in the projection of the hatred which is basic for the delusion; certain definite attitudes and expressions, which are ascribed to the persecutor, also correspond to traits of the patient and especially often to demands of the patient's superego. The persecutor, then, observes and criticizes the patient; the persecutors themselves represent projections of the patient's bad conscience—the projection of the superego is most clearly seen in ideas of reference and of being influenced. The patient feels that he is being controlled, observed, influenced, criticized, called upon to account for himself, and punished. The voices he hears utter criticisms of him, usually referring to his sexual activities which are depicted as dirty or homosexual. The patient hears himself reproached for his homosexuality and pregenital tendencies, just as severe parents might have talked to their naughty child. (1945, p. 430)

## Identification

*Identification* was felt by Freud to be an important mechanism in the genesis of depressive illness. In *Mourning and Melancholia* (1917/1957), he felt that melancholia, like mourning, was a reaction to the loss of a loved object, with the distinction that "in mourning it is the world which has become poor and empty; in melancholia it is the ego itself" (p. 246). The self-reproaches of the depressive were seen by him to be reproaches against a loved object; an identification of the ego had occurred with the lost object. Identification for Freud was an early stage of object choice: "The ego wants to incorporate this object into itself and, in accordance with the oral or cannibalism phase of libidinal development—it wants to do so by devouring it" (1917/1957, pp. 249–250).

Although identification is often used for the purpose of defense, as Brenner (1973) has pointed out, no general agreement exists as to whether it should be classified as a defense mechanism as such or whether it is a general tendency of the ego that is frequently used in a defensive manner. As he observed, "The ego can and does use as a defense anything available to it that will help to lessen or avoid the danger arising from the demands of an unwanted instinctual drive" (1973, p. 102). Brenner, in accordance with Freud, further suggests that when identification is used by the ego in a defensive way, it is unconsciously modeled on the physical action of eating or swallowing. Unconsciously, the individual using the mechanism of identification fantasizes that he is eating or being eaten by the person with whom he becomes identified. Such a fantasy is postulated by Brenner to be the reverse of that associated with projection where the unconscious model is that of defecation.

## Regression

Another defense mechanism described by Freud, *regression,* like identification, has to be viewed as a general tendency of the ego, but one that can be employed for defensive purposes. Regression can be defined as a return to a less developmentally mature level of psychological functioning. Implicit in this is the proposition that during development each individual passes through a specific series of psychological phases with particular characteristics. Arlow (1963) has noted that regression is an essential feature of almost all symptom formation in adults, and it involves not only the functions of the id but also the functioning of the ego and superego. Arlow comments that most regressions are transient and reversible, but that "the regressions which concern symptom formation are persistent and involve derivatives of the instinctual drives. Symptoms are formed on the basis of a conflict over some regressive reactivated instinctual wish from childhood" (1963, p. 16).

Freud (1916/1963) felt that *fixation* (of the instinct) and regression were not independent of each other:

> The second danger in the development by stages of this sort lies in the fact that the portions which have proceeded further may also easily return retrogressively to one of these earlier stages—what we describe as a regression. The trend will find itself led into a regression of this kind if the exercise of its function—that is, the attainment of its aim of satisfaction—is met, in its later or more highly developed form, by powerful external obstacles. It is plausible to suppose that fixation and regression are not independent of each other. The stronger the fixations on its path of development, the more readily will the function evade external difficulties by regressing to the fixations—the more incapable, therefore, does the developed function turn out to be of resisting external obstacles in its course. Consider that, if a people which is in movement has left strong detachments behind at the stopping-places on its migration, it is likely that the more advanced parties will be inclined to retreat to these stopping-places if they have been defeated or have come up against a superior enemy. But they will also be in the greater danger of being defeated the more of their number they have left behind on their migration. (Freud, 1916/1963, pp. 340–341)

## Reversal

Finally, in *Instincts and their Vicissitudes* (1915/1957), Freud described the processes of *turning against the self* and *reversal.* Reversal of an instinct into its opposite was seen by Freud as involving two different processes: a change from activity into passivity, and a reversal of its content. Examples of the former were seen in the two pairs of opposites: sadism-masochism and scopophilia—exhibitionism whereby "the active aim (to torture, to look at) is replaced by the passive aim (to be tortured, to be looked at)" (p. 127). An example of reversal of content was the transformation of love into hate. Reversal of an instinct was intimately connected with turning against the self: "Masochism is actually sadism turned around upon the subject's own ego, and exhibitionism includes looking at his own body—the essence of the process is thus the change of the object, while the aim remains unchanged" (1915, p. 128). Anna Freud suggested that these two processes

> also must come under the heading of methods of defense, for every vicissitude to which the instincts are liable has its origins in some ego-activity. Were it not for the intervention of the ego or of those external forces which the ego represents, every instinct would know only one fate—that of gratification. (1966, p. 47)

Thus, scattered throughout his clinical and theoretical writings, Freud had described 10 mechanisms of defense—repression, sublimation, reaction formation, isolation, undoing, projection, introjection or identification, regression, turning against the self, and reversal.

### Anna Freud's Views

In her classic monograph *The Ego and the Mechanisms of Defense* (1966), Anna Freud built on her father's concepts. In the second part of this work, she delineated further defensive methods of the ego. She first examined *denial,* which is directed against some painful or potentially overwhelming aspect of external reality, unlike the other defense mechanisms, which are brought into play to ward off painful or dangerous instinctual forces emanating from within. Denial plays a normal role in childhood and is often seen in the psychoses (e.g., the delusional belief that someone who died is actually alive, thus denying the painful reality). Denial, however, is also seen in everyday life (e.g., the cigarette smoker who denies the possibility of developing a fatal illness as a consequence).

Because of its prominence in childhood and frequent appearance in psychotic states, denial, like projection, has frequently been viewed as a "primitive" defense mechanism. Implicit in this view is the idea that there is a developmental hierarchy of defenses—certain primitive defense mechanisms are used by the ego very early in life, whereas others are seen as "higher level" defenses coming into play after object constancy has been established and hence are associated with a later stage of development. This thesis has been criticized by Willick (1983), who has contended:

> Defenses should not be designated as primitive or mature without an evaluation of the total ego organization. What appears to be the operation of a primitive defense in an adult depends not merely on the type of defense employed, but on the nature of the ego involved. The sicker a patient is, the more we see poor ego integration, poor ego organization, and breakdown of ego functions. The defensive processes called into service in such patients appear primitive primarily because of the low level of ego functioning. (1983, pp. 176–177)

In contrast to this view, Vaillant (1976), in his quantitative studies of adult male development, demonstrated the use of "immature" defenses negatively correlated with the presence of good adult adjustment and positively correlated with psychopathology. Vaillant's findings are consistent with the generally accepted clinical view that the predominant use of immature defenses compromises an individual's psychological and social functioning and may be as much trait as state determined.

Anna Freud demonstrated that defense mechanisms could be combined, sometimes against an internal and sometimes against an external force. She illustrated this in her description of two defense operations—*identification with the aggressor* and what she called *a form of altruism.* In the case of the former, identification is combined with the turning of passivity into activity, thus providing "one of the ego's most potent weapons in its dealings with external objects which arouse its anxiety" (1966, p. 117). Simultaneously, Anna Freud felt that the mechanism of identification with the aggressor was supplemented by another defensive mechanism, the *projection of guilt.* She saw both as processes of a preliminary phase of normal superego development in childhood when the ego was employed in conflicts against external authority. It became pathological, and an intermediate stage in the development of paranoia, when it was carried on into adult love life; for example, "When a husband displaces onto his wife his own impulses to be unfaithful and then reproaches her passionately with unfaithfulness, he is really introjecting her reproaches and projecting part of his own id" (1966, p. 130). She postulated that underlying a *form of altruism* was a type of projection combined with identification whereby instinctual impulses were surrendered in favor of other people so that they could be fulfilled vicariously.

## OBJECT RELATIONS THEORY AND
## DEFENSE MECHANISMS

In her "suggestions for a chronological classification," Anna Freud (1966) speculated that possibly each defense mechanism first evolved to master some specific instinctual urge and thus was associated with a particular phase of infantile development. Nonetheless, she finally acknowledged that this was an unresolved and obscure issue. However, the "British" school of object relations, exemplified by the work of Melanie Klein, specifically designated the defense mechanisms of projection and introjection in the infant as the very processes by which the structure of the ego differentiated and developed, a far cry from the ego psychological view promulgated by Anna Freud, in which such mechanisms could only take place after the ego had differentiated.

### Melanie Klein

Melanie Klein, through her clinical experience with children and patients suffering from severe psychiatric illness, developed an influential "internal objects" theory. She postulated a developmental theory in which the psychological growth of the infant is governed by defense mechanisms of introjection and projection:

> From the beginning the ego introjects objects "good" and "bad" for both of which its mother's breast is the prototype—for good objects when the child obtains it and for bad when it fails him. But it is because the baby projects its own aggression onto these objects that it feels them to be "bad" and not only in that they frustrate its desires: The child conceives them as actually dangerous—persecutors who it fears will devour it, scoop out the inside of its body, cut it to pieces, poison it—in short encompassing its destruction by all the means which sadism can devise. These images, which are a fantastically distorted picture of the real objects upon which they are based, are installed by it not only in the outside world but, by the process of incorporation, also within the ego. Hence quite little children pass through anxiety-situations (and react to them with defense-mechanisms), the content of which is comparable to that of the psychoses of adults. (1935, p. 145)

Of major importance in Klein's theory is the defense mechanism of *splitting,* whereby the primary object, the breast, is split into the ideal breast and the persecutory breast, both of which are introjected into the internal object world. With later development, the inner world of the individual is organized around complementary fantasies of internal good and bad objects. The sense of self as good or bad is related to the relative predominance of good or bad objects in the internal object world.

## W. Ronald D. Fairbairn

Fairbairn, taking as his starting point Melanie Klein's conception of internalized objects, rejected Freud's instinct theory and put in its place object relationships: "The object, and not gratification, is the ultimate aim of libidinal striving" (1952, p. 60). For Fairbairn, "The pristine personality of the child consists of a unitary dynamic ego," and "the first defense adopted by the original ego to deal with an unsatisfying personal relationship is mental internalization, or introjection of the unsatisfying object" (1952, p. 134). Hence the child begins with a structured ego complete with defenses that are object related.

Fairbairn applied his psychology of object relationships to a revision of the classical theory of repression. For him, the nature of the repressed lay in the relationship of the ego to bad internalized objects. Unlike Freud, who viewed the repressed as consisting of intolerably guilty impulses or intolerably unpleasant memories, Fairbairn saw the repressed as consisting of intolerably bad internalized objects. In his theory of therapy, Fairbairn conceived the psychotherapist as an exorcist who casts out the devils (the bad objects) from the patient's unconscious, by providing the therapist's self as a powerful good object who gives the patient sufficient sense of security to allow the terrifying bad objects to slowly emerge into the light of day.

In later developments within object relations theory on the nature of therapeutic change, internalization of aspects of the interaction between patient and analyst was felt to be crucial. Hence in this view, greater emphasis is placed on the importance of the therapeutic relationship in effecting change than is the case with the *ego psychological school.*

## Otto Kernberg

Kernberg (1975) in his descriptions of the borderline syndrome, relies heavily on the work of Melanie Klein to explain the particular defensive mechanisms seen in patients suffering from this disorder. Kernberg postulated that a central difficulty of borderline patients lies in their inability to integrate positive and negative fantasies of both their self and object representations, which are "split" to prevent the anxiety that would occur if they were experienced simultaneously. "Splitting" is thus seen as a specific defense of infancy retained by the borderline individual and as Shapiro (1978) has commented:

> These positive or negative stereotyped fantasies are activated in a relationship depending on the degree of gratification or frustration perceived by the patient. In a gratifying relationship, the patient develops positive fantasies, with the negative ones dissociated or "split off" and therefore unavailable. When frustrated, the patient elaborates negative fantasies and loses all memory of the positive relationship. (p. 1307)

Kernberg viewed borderline pathology, and the use of splitting in particular, as a result of a developmental failure occurring after self-object differentiation but before the development of object constancy.

Kernberg further enumerated other defense mechanisms occurring in the borderline disorders, including *primitive idealization, primitive denial, omnipotence, devaluation,* and *projective identification.* Projective identification was first described by Melanie Klein and has been defined by Segal as follows: "Parts of the self and internal objects are split off and projected into the external object, which then becomes possessed by, controlled and identified with the projected parts" (1964, p. 27). In a recent review of this term, Goldstein (1991) pointed out that there has not been a consensus as to its meaning. Ogden (1979) defined projective identification as referring "to a group of fantasies and accompanying object relations having to do with the ridding of the self of unwanted aspects of the self; the depositing of those unwanted 'parts' into another person; and finally the 'recovering' of a modified version of what was extruded" (p. 357). Ogden postulates that the individual using such a defensive process is functioning, in part, at a developmental level where there is a blurring of the boundaries between self and object representations. He notes, "The projector feels that the recipient experiences his feeling, not merely a feeling like his own, but his own feeling that has been transplanted into the recipient" (1979, p. 358). This is in contrast to projection where the individual involved in projection feels little, if any, identification with the projection.

Although considerable controversy surrounds both the definition and validity of the defense mechanisms described by Kernberg as central to borderline disorders, they have proven to be useful conceptualizations that provide an explanation for the nature of the often tempestuous, confusing, and unpredictable clinical phenomenology and treatment course of these patients.

## CONCLUSION

In an effort to oppose overly simplistic views of the concept of ego defenses, Wallerstein (1983) has made an important distinction between defense *mechanisms* as constructs or conceptual abstractions and defensive *behaviors* as an observable phenomena. He provided a specific example: "An exaggerated sympathy can be a *defense* against an impulse to cruelty. The postulated operative mental *mechanism* by which this is explained is called reaction formation" (1983, p. 205). He noted that since defense mechanisms are theoretical abstractions describing a way of working of the mind, they cannot be conscious, but the contents of the defenses—the simple or complex behaviors, affects, and ideas that serve defensive purposes—can be either unconscious or conscious. He further contended that the concept of defense mechanisms could be usefully broadened from the view of simple ego defense against instinctual impulse to a wider view of ego mechanisms "available simultaneously and/ or sequentially for whatever organismic need or pressure—defensive, adaptive, impulsive etc.—perceived (at some level) as most salient at any given moment and in whatever complexly configured expression" (1983, p. 223). He thus postulates a more complex and less specific model of the mind than that expressed in Anna Freud's *The Ego and the Mechanisms of Defense* (1966), but one far less prone to the danger of reification.

Finally, notwithstanding the major debates coursing through modern psychoanalysis concerning the structure and nature of the psychic apparatus and the causes of therapeutic change, the overall concept of ego defenses has proven to be comparatively free of controversy and an integral part of disparate theoretical persuasions. In the final analysis, this attests to the central role an understanding and recognition of ego defenses has in helping to make sense out of the often bewildering complexity of the individual clinical situation.

## REFERENCES

Arlow, J. A. (1963). Conflict, regression, and symptom formation. *International Journal of Psychoanalysis, 44,* 12–22.

Brenner, C. (1973). *An elementary textbook of psychoanalysis.* New York: International Universities Press.

Breuer, J., & Freud, S. (1955). On the physical mechanism of hysterical phenomena. In J. Strachey (Ed. and Trans.), *The standard edition of the complete psychological works of Sigmund Freud* (Vol. 2, pp. 3–17). London: Hogarth Press. (Original work published 1893)

Cooper, A. (1986). Concepts of therapeutic effectiveness in psychoanalysis: A historical review. *Psychoanalytic Inquiry, 9,* 4–25.

Fairbairn, W. R. D. (1952). *Psychoanalytic studies of the personality.* London: Tavistock Publications.

Fenichel, O. (1945). *The psychoanalytic theory of neurosis.* New York: Norton.

Freud, A. (1966). *The ego and the mechanisms of defense.* London: Hogarth Press.

Freud, S. (1953a). Fragment of an analysis of a case of hysteria. In J. Strachey (Ed. and Trans.), *The standard edition of the complete psychological works of Sigmund Freud* (Vol. 7, pp. 7–122). London: Hogarth Press. (Original work published 1905)

Freud, S. (1953b). Three essays on the theory of sexuality. In J. Strachey (Ed. and Trans.), *The standard edition of the complete psychological works of Sigmund Freud* (Vol. 7, pp. 125–245). London: Hogarth Press. (Original work published 1905)

Freud, S. (1955). Notes upon a case of obsessional neurosis. In J. Strachey (Ed. and Trans.), *The standard edition of the complete psychological works of Sigmund Freud* (Vol. 10, pp. 153–318). London: Hogarth Press. (Original work published 1909)

Freud, S. (1955). Certain neurotic mechanisms in jealousy, paranoia and homosexuality. In J. Strachey (Ed. and Trans.), *The standard edition of the complete psychological works of Sigmund Freud* (Vol. 18, pp. 223–232). London: Hogarth Press. (Original work published 1922)

Freud, S. (1957). Instincts and their vicissitudes. In J. Strachey (Ed. and Trans.), *The standard edition of the complete psychological works of Sigmund Freud* (Vol. 14, pp. 111–140). London: Hogarth Press. (Original work published 1915)

Freud, S. (1957). Mourning and melancholia. In J. Strachey (Ed. and Trans.), *The standard edition of the complete psychological works of Sigmund Freud* (Vol. 14, pp. 239–258). London: Hogarth Press. (Original work published 1917)

Freud, S. (1958). Psychoanalytic notes on an autobiographical account of a case of paranoia. In J. Strachey (Ed. and Trans.), *The standard edition of the complete psychological works of Sigmund Freud* (Vol. 12, pp. 3–82). London: Hogarth Press. (Original work published 1911)

Freud, S. (1959). Inhibitions, symptoms and anxiety. In J. Strachey (Ed. and Trans.), *The standard edition of the complete psychological works of Sigmund Freud* (Vol. 20, pp. 77–174). London: Hogarth Press. (Original work published 1926)

Freud, S. (1962). The neuro-psychoses of defence. In J. Strachey (Ed. and Trans.), *The standard edition of the complete psychological works of Sigmund Freud* (Vol. 3, pp. 43–68). London: Hogarth Press. (Original work published 1894)

Freud, S. (1963). Introductory lectures on psychoanalysis. In J. Strachey (Ed. and Trans.), *The standard edition of the complete psychological works of Sigmund Freud* (Vol. 16, pp. 243–463). London: Hogarth Press. (Original work published 1916)

Freud, S. (1964). Analysis terminable and interminable. In J. Strachey (Ed. and Trans.), *The standard edition of the complete psychological works of*

*Sigmund Freud* (Vol. 23, pp. 211–253). London: Hogarth Press. (Original work published 1937)

Goldstein, W. N. (1991). Clarification of projective identification. *American Journal of Psychiatry, 148,* 153–161.

Kernberg, O. F. (1975). *Borderline conditions and pathological narcissism.* New York: Jason Aronson.

Klein, M. (1935). A contribution to the psychogenesis of manic depressive states. *International Journal of Psychoanalysis, 16,* 145–174.

Ogden, T. H. (1979). On projective identification. *International Journal of Psychoanalysis, 60,* 357–373.

Sandler, J., Dare, C., & Holder, A. (1973). *The patient and the analyst.* New York: International Universities Press.

Segal, H. (1964). *Introduction to the work of Melanie Klein.* New York: Basic Books.

Shapiro, E. R. (1978). The psychodynamics and developmental psychology of the borderline patient. *American Journal of Psychiatry, 135,* 1305–1315.

Vaillant, G. E. (1976). Natural history of male psychological health: The relation of choice of ego mechanisms of defense to adult adjustment. *Archives of General Psychiatry, 33,* 535–545.

Wallerstein, R. S. (1983). Defence mechanisms and the structure of the mind. *Journal of the American Psychoanalytic Association, 31,* 201–225.

Willick, M. S. (1983). On the concept of primitive defences. *Journal of the American Psychoanalytic Association, 31* (Suppl.), 175–200.

# 3

# Good Defenses Make Good Neighbors

## LORNA SMITH BENJAMIN

In his 1914 poem, "Mending Wall," Robert Frost (1949) described an encounter with a New England neighbor who was repairing his fence. The neighbor explained, "Good fences make good neighbors." Frost objected: "Something there is that doesn't love a wall, that wants it down." The neighbor continued to shore up his fence, maintaining that good boundaries preserve good relations with others. In an interpersonal sense, Frost might have been arguing for more intimacy, while the neighbor favored better differentiation. The debate is neither trivial, nor easy to resolve.

Psychoanalysts have implicitly sided with Frost, at least in the special context of describing the war within the self. Pathology arises from internal conflict, they assume. It is manifest by defenses that keep forbidden wishes from emerging to awareness. A key feature of the psychoanalytic definition of a defense is that it keeps the person from becoming aware of his or her own mental operations. An intervention that breaks down defenses and releases the unconscious energies should diminish pathology. "Material" (e.g., wishes and fears) against which defenses have been erected must be brought to awareness. A healthy person is not defensive. The walls within the self must come down.

This perspective has been the basis of widespread devotion to an array of therapeutic techniques that facilitate the discovery and expression of unacknowledged feelings. Unfortunately, awareness and insight alone rarely effect a cure in practice. Psychoanalysts recognize the need to then go on to help the ego "work through" the new "material" so that the emergent conflict can be resolved in a nondefensive way. The algorithm

The author would like to thank the editors and friends and colleagues who made helpful comments on earlier versions of this chapter. They include Hope Conte, Rob Plutchik, Marjorie Klein, Norman Greenfield, Bill Henry, and Jules Strand.

for what to do once the "unconscious" has been exposed has not yet been written and widely disseminated. The presumption is that therapist facilitation of "working through" is a complex skill that comes from years of supervised training in an analytic institute. Perhaps the key to improving efficacy of psychotherapy does lie in learning how to better train therapists to help the patient uncover unconscious conflicts and work them through. On the other hand, perhaps the underlying drive model is inadequate. Maybe its treatment implications are not optimal. Perhaps psychotherapies that seek to "break down defenses," to bring conflicts to awareness, or encourage the expression of feeling are misguided. The idea that there are deficiencies in drive theory has been recognized within psychoanalysis itself.

In this chapter, I will side with Frost's neighbor to assert that (de)fences can support normal function and improve social relations. It is not always good to break them down. The arguments invoke interpersonal modifications of psychoanalytic drive theory. The British school of object relations (Greenberg & Mitchell, 1983) has deepened understanding of the human psyche by transforming the language of psychoanalysis into more human terms. A parallel shift in the interpersonal direction was offered by Sullivan (1953), who translated psychoanalytic concepts into interpersonal terms. He argued that basic anxiety is generated in defective mother-infant interactions. Defenses evolve primarily to defend the ego against dreaded anxiety experienced in relation to the primary caregiver. Sullivan emphasized actual social learning more than abstract concepts such as id, ego, and superego.

Resolution of questions about the nature and function of defenses will follow the development of formulations that can be empirically confirmed or disproved. Classical psychoanalysis has not yet become amenable to tests by scientific methods. However, there have been many attempts to use the rules of scientific method to capture the grains of truth in psychoanalysis. The interpersonal translations of analytic theory, like those suggested by Sullivan, seem most promising to me. The language I prefer to use to describe mental operations in interpersonal terms is set forth by a substantial variation of an interpersonal circle as described by other investigators (Conte & Plutchik, 1981; Kiesler, 1983; Leary, 1957; Lorr, Bishop, & McNair, 1965; Wiggins, 1982). That approach is called Structural Analysis of Social Behavior (SASB, Benjamin, 1974; 1984; 1993b). A simplified version appears in Figure 3–1. (For a complete explanation of the SASB model, see Chapter 3 of Benjamin, 1993b.)

The terms shown in bold print in Figure 3–1 describe behaviors that are prototypically parentlike and involve focus on another person. The terms

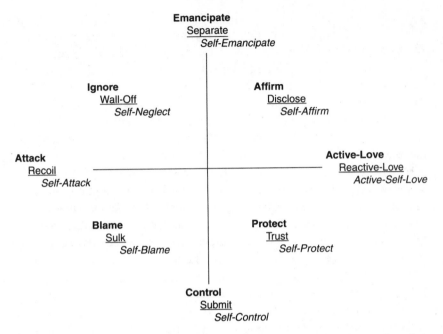

**Figure 3–1.** The simplified SASB Cluster model. The horizontal axis runs from hate to love, and the vertical axis represents a continuum from enmeshment to differentiation. The three types of focus are represented on three surfaces by different styles of print. Complementarity is shown by adjacent **bold** and underlined points. Inrojection is shown by adjacent **bold** and *italicized* points. From *Interpersonal Diagnosis and Treatment of Personality Disorders* (p. 54) by L. S. Benjamin, 1993, New York: Guilford Press. Copyright 1993 by Guilford Press. Reprinted by permission.

shown in underlined print are prototypically childlike and involve reactive interpersonal focus on the self. The terms shown in *italics,* indicate introjections that are associated with the adjacent behaviors. For example, the parentlike behavior, **Affirm** is likely to be complemented by the childlike behavior, Disclose. This context is likely to strengthen a self-concept best described as *Self-Affirm.*

SASB differs from the conventional interpersonal circles in many ways. The most obvious is that there are three surfaces rather than one. One advantage of using three circumplexes is that links between social input and self-concept can be detailed (e.g., the principle of introjection, just illustrated). Another important difference is that the SASB model opposes **Control** with **Emancipate** rather than with Submit. The premise that **Emancipate** rather than Submit is the opposite of **Control** has many clinically useful implications. The addition of a region to mark separate psychological space permits articulation of the clinically vital concept of differentiation (**Emancipate** or Separate).

On the assumption that behavior, affect, and cognition evolved in parallel, models for affect and cognitive style have been proposed to parallel the SASB model for social behavior (Benjamin, 1986). For example, the behavior **Blame** is presumed to be associated with the affects of arrogance and vengefulness, and with a narrowly focused cognitive style. The opposite behavior, **Affirm** may be associated with the affects of tolerance and permissiveness, and a broad and open cognitive style. Most of the unpleasant affects characteristic of patients are associated with behaviors shown on the hostile side of the childlike surface of the SASB model. Submit is associated with helplessness and depression; Sulk is associated with humiliation and defeat; Recoil is accompanied by fear and hatefulness; Wall-Off is marked by loneliness, bitterness and pessimism. Cognitive styles associated with these particular affects include suggestibility, constriction, rumination, looseness, incoherence, and tuning out.

These parallel cognitive and affect models have not been validated. They are mentioned here primarily to mark the idea that everything said about behaviors probably has theoretically parallel affects, and cognitions. This understanding of parallels can be very useful clinically. For example, at the moment that a problematic social situation is being discussed, the therapist can ask, "How do you feel about that?" to elicit affect. He or she also could say, "What do you think about that?" to elicit cognition. The therapist might ask, "Then what did you do?" to elicit more detail about behavior. And so on. Belief in parallelism among behavior, affect, and cognition allows the clinician to move easily among the three domains, each enriching the understanding of the other. The parallelism hypothesis allows one to analyze a given pathological or normal event by starting in any domain: cognition, affect, or behavior. An effective clinician consistently attends to all three.

The SASB dimensional model has been applied (Benjamin, 1993b) to the *Diagnostic and Statistical Manual of Mental Disorders* (DSM-III-R); (American Psychiatric Association, 1987; 1993) Axis II descriptions of personality disorder. The resulting "categories" are exclusively interpersonal. The "traits" of personality disorder are interpreted in interpersonal contexts. The predictive properties of the SASB model generate developmental hypotheses that have specific psychosocial treatment implications for the various DSM personality disorders. For example, Obsessive Compulsive Personality Disorder (OCD) is described interpersonally:

There is a fear of making a mistake or being accused of being imperfect. The quest for order yields a baseline interpersonal position of blaming and inconsiderate control of others. The OCD's control alternates with blind obedience to authority or principle. There is excessive self-discipline, as well as restraint of feelings, harsh self-criticism, and neglect of the self.

The hypothetical interpersonal history includes a history of coercion to be perfect regardless of the personal consequences. There were harsh consequences for mistakes and no rewards for success. These experiences lead to a need to control in the quest to be perfect and the lack of enjoyment of anything but the quest for excellence. (Benjamin, 1993b, pp. 406–407)

The treatment implications are that the OCD must learn to distance from or transform internalized figures that demand perfection; he or she must learn to enjoy warm interactions with loved ones in the present. The approach represents a testable interpersonal version of the psychoanalytic hypothesis that adult character is shaped by developmental (learning) experiences and is organized by (sometimes unconscious) wishes and fears that arise naturally from that learning.

## THE APPLICATION OF THE SASB MODEL TO DEFENSES

This chapter explores the application of the SASB model to the psychoanalytic idea of defenses. Psychoanalytic definitions are translated to interpersonal terms and greatly simplified. Different assumptions are made about the nature and function of defenses. There are different views of what must be defended against.

The application begins with a definition of defenses. The ordinary meaning of the word "defense" is "protection." If the psychoanalytic view of fixed energies bouncing within the walls of the individual is rejected, then defenses need not offer protection from forbidden impulses. Still, if defenses are to be defined from an interpersonal perspective, the question must be answered: protection from *what?* The alternative proposal begins with a list of assumptions about mental function. These assumptions are discussed in the following sections.

### Mental Operations

A key idea is that the substance of mental operations is primarily interpersonal in nature. Mental operations are built on inherited temperaments and are specifically shaped by past and current family and other important social relationships. Mental operations are internalized *interpersonal events*. They are associated with specific cognitions and affects.

Interpersonal mental operations can be SASB coded. So long as referents are properly defined, the "interpersonal" approach can include any interactive events, including pain from bodily harm and loss of loved ones, even if the injury or loss is not due to social causes. For example, it is normal to show fear of bodily harm, or **Attack.** Even if the source of bodily harm is not social, it often is SASB codable. Consider the event: being hit by lightning. Lightning is named as one referent, and the victim is the other. Since SASB coding attends strictly to verbal or nonverbal behavior, one need not attribute intention to the lightning to code **Attack.** The hostile impact of being struck by lightning can be recorded without attributing love or hate to the lightning. Other nonsocial interactive events can likewise be coded by any of the points on the SASB model. The only requirement for SASB coding is that there be at least two interactants, and that available information is specific enough to support judgments about the components of interactant's focus, friendliness-hostility, and enmeshment-differentiation.

### *I*mportant *P*eople and Their *I*nternalized *R*epresentations (IPIRs)

Three developmental concepts are vital to the discussion of defenses: identification, internalization, and introjection. These three forms of "copying" are assumed to be basic and universal mechanisms of socialization. They are not unique to psychopathology.

The principle of *identification* means simply that the young child is very likely to act like important others. It is a long-term form of imitation, and is described by the SASB principle of similarity. For example, if a child is raised in a home saturated with **Blame,** he or she is very likely to become a **Blame**r.

The SASB version of *introjection* specifies that the person treats him- or herself as important others have treated him or her (Sullivan, 1953). For example, a girl who is raised in a setting of gross neglect (parental **Ignore**) is very likely to *Self-Neglect.* If nobody cared about and for her, she will not care about and for herself.

The principle of *internalization* encompasses the idea that mental representatives of important other people become a part of mental operations. Within his or her mind, the individual relates to the mental representatives as if the transactions were in fact interpersonal. For example, a toddler who contemplates touching the stereo is likely to "hear" his father saying "No," and Submit to that memory. The child reaches toward but does not touch the stereo as he reacts to the internalization of his father. Again, the only requirement for SASB coding is that interactive referents be identified, and that the concepts be concrete enough to yield judgments about focus, love-hate, and enmeshment-differentiation. Speaking more informally, social operations unfold within the person's mind just as they did or do in the interpersonal world. Mental operations replay family scenarios again and again.

Individuals often strive to realize wishes or avoid fears in relation to important others or their internalizations. The acronym IPIR (Benjamin, in press) stands for Important People or their Internalized Representations. IPIRs are generated by any or all of the copying processes: imitation, introjection, or internalization. IPIRs and the wishes and fears and the associated behavioral patterns can be SASB coded if the interviewer elicits descriptions that are specific enough to yield judgments of love-hate and enmeshment-differentiation.

In young children, current social relationships (IP) have priority over internalizations (IRs). The reason is that attachment is vital to the survival of the young child. The child's need to maintain proximity to and good will from the caregiver is overwhelming in early childhood. As the child grows older, current figures have progressively less relevance to wishes and fears that organize behavioral patterns. In adulthood, internalizations retain their power and often have marked priority over current relationships and current reality. It appears that the desire for attachment is most powerful in relation to earlier important others.

Long term, much loved sexual partners in adulthood may provide an exception to the principle that the earliest internalized figures prevail. Beloved children, psychotherapists, or other viable parental substitutes also can become effective internalizations, but not as easily as can earlier caregivers or sexual partners. If psychotherapy is to be successful, destructive internalizations must be transformed or replaced.

## Attachment and Disrupted Attachment

Normal wishes are to be a participant in interactive events that correspond to *attachment* as it is marked by the SASB model (Figure 3–1). The social behaviors characteristic of normal attachment include **Affirm**/Disclose/*Self-Affirm;* **Active-Love**/Reactive-Love/*Active-Self-Love;* **Protect**/Trust/*Self-Protect.* Call this the Attachment Group (AG). The AG of social behaviors is associated with specific affects (e.g., exuberance, love) and cognitive styles (e.g., encouragement, rationality).

It is normal to fear being subjected to events that are described by the respective opposing regions on the SASB model. These include **Blame**/Sulk/*Self-Blame;* **Attack**/Recoil/*Self-Attack;* **Ignore**/Wall-Off/*Self-Neglect.* Call this the Disaffiliative or Disrupted Attachment Group (DAG). Behaviors in the DAG group are associated with specific affects (e.g., fear, anger, helplessness) and cognitive styles (e.g., appeal to authority, narrow focus). The individual fears behaviors that are described by points located within the DAG group. Fears also can be defined in terms of threatened loss of AG.

Because SASB codes can be assigned to social or asocial interactive events, even fears and wishes that are not social can be SASB coded and assigned to the AG or DAG groups for the analysis of defenses. Fear of bodily harm (Recoil), for example, belongs to the Disrupted Attachment Group. Wishes for happiness (Reactive-Love in relation to the desired person, thing, event, circumstance) belong to the Attachment Group of social behaviors.

Normal wishes for attachment can be transformed by abnormal interpersonal experiences. The most common way to interfere with the development of attachment is to have primary caregivers fail to deliver appropriate behaviors from the Attachment Group. The developing child who receives hostile messages from the primary caregivers still attempts to comply with their wishes. The child wishes that the hostile caregiver will become friendly. For example, the little girl who is incestually abused and told she is a whore will take in that message and believe it is true. She may neglect and punish herself and recklessly exploit her body. She may insist she hates her abuser. However, if she treats herself in ways that he modeled, it is likely that she remains attached and that he is an IPIR. In other words, her self-defeating "maladaptive" patterns are driven by a wish to be loved by, to receive attachment behaviors from the (internalizations of) her abuser: "You hurt me so I hurt me. Obviously, this is what you want. Since I am what you say, and do what you want, please love me now." Every psychopathology is a gift of love* (Benjamin, 1993a). She will not stop self-destructive behavior until she transforms the wishes and fears and the associated disaffiliative behaviors that arise in relation to this IPIR.

This principle, "Every psychopathology is a gift of love," does not apply in cases where attachment has been essentially disrupted, as in Antisocial Personality Disorder (ASP). If infants and toddlers are consistently subjected to abandonment alternating with cruel, arbitrary control, they will form weak attachments at best. Such deprived children are likely to behave in ways that are designed to keep them either in **Control**

---

*The theoretically minded reader may by now have realized that the IPIR is on a continuum with a hallucination. Indeed, the present perspective would normalize certain forms of psychosis. There is a continuum that ranges from self-talk at the normal end, through the IPIR (which often is an unconscious entity), to the auditory hallucination. I have developed this idea more fully elsewhere (Benjamin, 1989; Benjamin, in press).

(and **Blame**) or out of reach of others' control (Wall-Off, Separate). The domain of attachment behaviors is not of interest to the individual with ASP. When viewed from the perspective of the person, the ASP "disorder" represents an attempt to adjust to social learning experiences. However, because there is no interest in attachment, the principle, "Every psychopathology is a gift of love" does not apply. For the person with ASP, defenses are not organized by a wish for some form of attachment. The ASP wants only to meet basic asocial needs such as food, sex, power, and so on. He or she will be organized primarily by the wish to have **Control** or to be Separate, rather than to receive behaviors from the Attachment Group, or avoid behaviors from the Disrupted Attachment Group.

Behaviors that reflect extreme differentiation or extreme enmeshment are not necessarily pathological. However, the extremes shown by the individual with ASP are pathological because the ASP also is typically detached (Wall-Off), and has easy access to **Attack** and **Blame**. On the other hand, a parent who shows extreme enmeshment (**Control**) in a developmentally appropriate way does not exhibit pathology. If the parent does not enmesh by showing **Control** and insist that the child Submit in certain contexts, the toddler will not be properly socialized. In fact, the parent who fails to set limits can be classified as hostile due to dereliction of duty (**Ignore**). Similarly, an adolescent who goes through a characteristic phase of extreme differentiation (Separate) is normal, not antisocial. The adolescent needs to shape the parameters of his or her own self separately from the parents. Once the adolescent develops a more secure sense of a separate self, he or she is likely to resume friendly relations with the parent. The test of whether habitual positions of extreme enmeshment or differentiation are normal or not, is in their contextually interpreted result.

## The Function of Defenses

Defenses enhance wishes or reduce fears. Normative wishes are defined by the AG sector of the SASB model, while normative fears are characterized by loss of AG, or by the introduction of DAG. Normal defenses are consistent with wishes and fears that enhance the likelihood of behaviors associated with AG and minimize the likelihood of behaviors characterized by DAG. Abnormal or psychopathological defenses are aligned with wishes and fears that usually result in DAG behaviors.

A summary of the proposed relations between defenses and normal and pathological behavior is shown in Figure 3–2. It is normal to function in ways (behavioral, affective, cognitive) that enhance friendliness and diminish hostile behavior in the present. Individuals who seek attachment

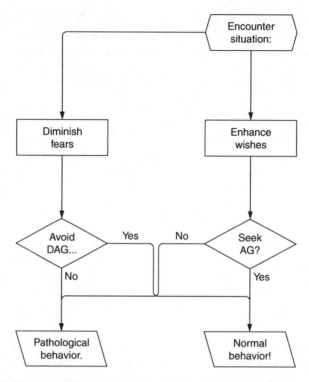

**Figure 3–2.** Functions of normal and pathological defenses. All defenses enhance wishes and diminish fears. These wishes and fears often exist in relation to important other people or their internalization (IPIRs). If the wishes and fears result in behaviors described by the Attachment Group on the SASB model, the defenses are normal. If the wishes and fears result in hostile behaviors described by the Disrupted Attachment Group on the SASB model, they are pathological. Pathological defenses are often the result of attachment to destructive IPIRs.

behaviors from normal friendly IPIRs characteristically exhibit friendly behaviors. Those individuals who seek attachment behaviors from hostile IPIRs fail to be habitually friendly. So do those who do not seek attachment from anyone (e.g., ASP). Without attachment that results in habitual friendliness, there is pathology.

It should be noted that in certain contexts, a normal person can exhibit hostile behavior. For example, a normal mother can become murderous if the life of her child is threatened. It also should be noted that the superficial friendliness of a person with ASP, or with Histrionic Personality Disorder (HPD) does not qualify as normal. Friendliness in normals is "clean," while pathological friendliness is "contaminated." SASB codes of behaviors typical of the ASP yield a complex combination of friendliness, coercion, and detachment. Codes of a person with HPD yield a complex picture of a demanding dependency that may also involve detachment. These complex combinations of friendliness and hostility are not normal (see Benjamin, 1993b for further detail).

### The Role of Awareness

Wishes and fears that organize interpersonal defenses may be conscious or unconscious. Awareness is not critical to the definition of interpersonal defenses. For example, consider the normal child who is jealous of a new baby sibling. The child fears loss of parental attachment because parents seem so busy with the new family member. It is natural for the child to reason that he or she must get rid of the challenger to preserve parental behaviors from the AG, namely **Active-Love**, **Affirm**, and **Protect**. However, the normal child learns that the parents are angry about attacks on the baby, and they are pleased with demonstrations of generosity to the baby. So the child learns to be generous in order to preserve attachment behaviors from the parents and their internalizations (IPIR).

The adult may or may not remember this context in which generosity was first learned. Memory of the learning experience is not so important to the understanding of interpersonal defenses. What is vital to the understanding of defenses is that generosity was learned for the purpose of maintaining parental attachment. In the sense that generosity is cultivated to enhance attachment, it is a "defense." The defensive status of the interpersonal trait (generosity) is not altered by whether or not the person knows he or she has it. A trait also is not more or less defensive if the person can remember when and why he or she learned it (e.g., to be generous in order to receive parental love).

Lack of awareness may be passive or active. Passive lack of awareness means the attentional spotlight is directed elsewhere for the moment. With little effort, the individual can bring the event to awareness. The deflected attentional spotlight is what Freud called the preconscious. Active lack of awareness is apparent when the person is unable even with effort to bring the thought or idea to consciousness. Freud called this the unconscious.

If defenses do not succeed, the person experiences pain. It is assumed that *it is natural to defend against experiences of too much loss or too much pain by banishing them from awareness.* Freud named the process of forgetting an event that is too painful, repression. A very common example of normative repression is the extreme pain of childbirth. It is hardly noted either in the literature or the folklore. Many women forget the pain from the birth of one child to the next, and from one generation to the next. It is simply too intense to remember and talk about.* And no useful function can be served by making note of it. It could even be argued that it would be maladaptive for the species to enhance awareness of the pain of childbirth.

The phenomenon of normative repression is most likely to occur in relation to catastrophic events, like the pain of childbirth. A child is calmed when important people show attachment and becomes anxious when important people threaten behaviors described by the DAG. But a normal child will not repress mild versions of these fearful or painful events. For example, if a child breaks his father's favorite tool, he may or may not "forget" his mistake. A working hypothesis is that the child will not repress if the fear is mild, but he will if it becomes too intense. The strength of the child's fear probably will relate sensibly to the strength of his attachment to and fear of his father. It will be important to conduct research studies of the conditions under which repression occurs.

In addition to the normal process of forgetting if the event involves threat of too much pain, forgetting also is enhanced if the child is specifically threatened with punishment for remembering. For example, suppose a young girl is incestually attacked by her father and informed that if she tells anyone, he will kill her, or he will be sent to jail, or that the family will be broken up. These messages help her to banish the incestual attacks from awareness. She can preserve attachment to her father and to her family if she "forgets." And so she will.

### The Role of Adaptation

When seen from the perspective of the individual, mental operations are adaptive. Both mental "health" and mental "disorder" reflect attempts at adjustment. Mental disorder is not a breakdown, but rather, an attempt to cope. Mental operations are organized by attempts to implement or create wished-for interpersonal conditions and to avoid feared interpersonal conditions. These conditions often are determined by a relationship with an IPIR. For example, consider the toddler who inhibits his reach for the stereo to avoid the disapproval of his father (IPIR). This evidence of a developing normal conscience reflects an adaptation.

Defenses driven by the desire to receive AG behaviors from earliest internalizations often "account for" grossly maladaptive behavior. For

---

*One colleague who read an earlier version of this chapter commented that women's views of childbirth are comparable to men's "war stories." Another confirmed that there are subgroups of women who do compare notes and dwell at length on the nature of the experience. This "war stories group" would not fit the present analysis. There remain, however, a large number of women who say: "It hurt a lot, but shortly afterward, I just forgot all about it."

example, consider the exemplary normal child mentioned earlier who learned that his or her mother disapproved of attacking and exploiting the younger sibling. He became generous. Suppose his parents died, and when he was older, the young man was thrust into an urban street culture wherein he was mocked and beaten for failing to attack and exploit weaker victims. In this new setting, the moral position that he learned in his family of origin would be maladaptive. Nonetheless, out of internalized loyalty to his mother and her values, he might stick to his principle of generosity, and refuse to become a predator. In so doing, this young man would seek AG behaviors from the internalized representations of very important others, his deceased parents. His behavior would be a defense against loss of the approval of his *internalization* of loved ones. This process takes place despite external events that strongly discourage such loyalty. It serves to maintain "maladaptive" behavior. The example reverses the usual diagnostic implication that maladaptive is abnormal, whereas adaptive is normal.

Defenses serve to avoid loss of friendly behaviors defined in the AG, or the initiation of hostile behaviors from the DAG. The source is the IPIRs. In other words, the individual defends against loss of love or attack from Important People and their Internal Representations. Defenses are associated with disorder or psychopathology only if they result in cognitions, behaviors, affects, and self-concepts that are not aligned with normal behaviors described by the Attachment Group. The exemplary generous child already mentioned remained generous even when the trait became maladaptive. His principled behavior as a young man was not disordered because it was consistent with the idealized norm in relation to others that is defined by the SASB model. His behavior was consistent with the AG positions: **Affirm**/Disclose/*Self-Affirm;* **Active-Love**/Reactive-Love/*Active-Self-Love;* **Protect**/Trust/*Self-Protect.* His behavior was saturated with attachment, while that of his peers and his social context was not.

On the other hand, the defenses used by the young man's peers were disordered even though they were adaptive in their setting. The mechanism sustaining the defense of exploitativeness in the peer group was the same as the mechanism sustaining the defense of generosity in the exemplary young man. The difference was that the exemplary young man had internalized parents who provided AG behaviors for generosity. The gang members had no experience with "attachment objects." Their natural primate tendencies for affiliation had to unfold mostly within the peer group. This means that the gang members were driven by the standards of the group in order to receive AG behaviors from its leaders, if from anyone. Consider a particular younger group member who had very little Attachment Group behaviors at home, and frequent exposure to Disrupted Attachment Group behaviors. His wish for the leader's **Affirm**, **Active-Love** and **Protect** could drive him to performs acts of special violence "for" the gang. His reckless lack of regard for others (nongang members) might be a defense in service of attachment to an important other person, the group leader. Devoted members to destructive cults might be described in similar terms.

As previously indicated, asocial as well as social interactive events can be assigned to the AG and DAG groups. Defenses also exist against asocial events described by the DAG. For example, it is natural to fear asocial **Attack** (e.g., bodily harm from a nonsocial source like disease); **Blame** (e.g., existential responsibility); and **Ignore** (e.g., deprivation of basic needs like food, water).

Researchers hope that studies from the cognitive sciences will enhance understanding of how and why such early learning prevails over current events and determines the patterns of mental processing in adulthood (e.g., see Benjamin & Friedrich, 1991). This phenomenon of loyalty to internalizations has a great deal to do with why adults persist in patterns that are grossly maladaptive despite their stated wish to change. It is one way of explaining Freud's idea of "repetition compulsion" and Allport's "functional autonomy."

## Mechanisms of Defense

Defenses are implemented in one or more of three ways. These are (a) distorted perceptions; (b) blocks in awareness or blocks in linkages among the domains of affect, cognition, and behavior; (c) distorted responses. These three categories of defensive processes emerged from an interpersonal analysis of defenses described in the psychoanalytic literature. A summary appears in Figure 3–3. Brief sketches of the three groups follow.

### Transformation (Distortion) of Input

For example, projection, splitting, idealization and devaluation all involve distortion of perceived social input. Affect, cognition and behavior are properly linked, but the input, the initial perception, is not reality based.

A classical example of pathological projection is the paranoid's misperception of pervasive hostility. He or she is ever ready to lash out, and sees others in the same terms. On the other hand, his or her affects and behaviors are quite appropriate, once the distorted perception is accepted. The paranoid has learned to see the world as hostile, and so he or

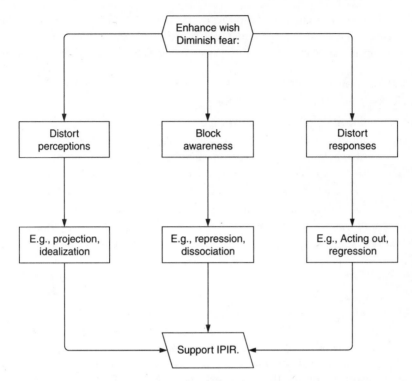

**Figure 3–3.** Mechanisms of normal and pathological defenses. Defenses described by psychoanalysts are implemented in the three different ways shown in the figure. These distortions and blockages support the individual's relationship with IPIRs. As Figure 3–2 suggested, defenses are normal if they result in better attachment. A normal person can selectively choose defensive mechanisms to maintain a friendly orientation. In the long run, it is better if there are no distortions or blockages because attachment is better supported by the real-life data stream if no distortion is required.

she feels hostile and "detects" hostility even if it is not present.* Because the paranoid person's typical orientation is hostile, his or her defensive system is pathological.

An example of normative projection is the optimist's cheerful persistence in face of daunting odds. The psychometric literature of the 1960s was dominated by concerns about "social desirability," the normative tendency of people to see and describe themselves in an inappropriately positive light. Those concerns persist in the current literature

---

*It should be noted that the paranoid person does not always distort. Because of his or her sensitivity, the paranoid individual sometimes is extraordinarily accurate in perceptions. He or she can, for example, detect hidden hostility in co-workers who are colluding to contain his or her perceived "dangerousness" to the organization (see Lemert, 1962).

on "depressive realism" (Taylor & Brown, 1988). It holds that depressed people perceive themselves more accurately than normals because depression strips away the normal person's rose-colored glasses.

### Blocked Awareness of a Social Pattern, or of Links among the Domains of Cognition, Affect, and Behavior

In the section "The Role of Awareness," it was noted that defenses need not preclude awareness. An important group of defenses, however, does compromise awareness. Repression, denial, somatization, intellectualization, lying, dissociation, and isolation all involve blockage. The defense of isolation provides one of many possible examples of blocked awareness (cognition). In special situations, the isolator is aware of relevant events, and his or her affect and behavior are appropriately linked to that cognition. When not in that special situation, the isolator is not aware.

For an example of pathological isolation, consider a patient who successfully uncovered and experienced affect about childhood trauma in his therapy sessions. The defense of isolation would be apparent if the insights and experiences from therapy failed to have a discernible impact on his personal life. He continued in a neurotic (hostile to others or self) pattern despite the achievement of insight in therapy.

A normative example of isolation is offered by the surgeon who had just learned of the death of a loved one, but nonetheless went ahead to successfully perform the life-saving surgery that a patient needed immediately. The surgeon, who had isolated awareness of the terrible personal event and all the associated affect, then went home and collapsed with grief. The defense permitted the surgeon to **Protect** the patient, despite his or her own pain. Because the result was fundamentally friendly, the defense was normal.

### Transformation (Distortion) of Responses

Displacement, acting out, and sublimation are defenses that *change the situation in which the response is given.* Compensation, regression, and undoing are implemented in the original situation, but involve *changing the response itself.*

A common example of pathological acting out is offered by the patient who does not acknowledge his anger at his parent or his transference reaction to the therapist, and who instead rages at his wife. The hostile result classifies the defense as pathological. A normative example of acting out is the therapist who had a traumatic childhood filled with suffering, but who devotes his or her life to relieving suffering in others. The therapist cannot redo his or her own childhood in a better way. But he or she can help others repair themselves, and help prevent a replication of problems with their own children. The friendly result suggests the defense is normative.

The boundaries among these three categories of defensive process are fuzzy. Some defenses involve more than one category. For example, the defense of acting out involves blockage in awareness as well as an inappropriate change of situation. Displacement is identical to acting out, except that displacement does not involve a block in awareness. The husband who acted out would have shown displacement if he knew he was angry at his boss, and deliberately "took it out" on his wife. Similarly the helpful therapist was acting out if he or she was not aware of the reasons for the devotion to helping others. On the other hand, if he or she was aware of the connection to an abusive childhood, then the defense would represent displacement.

While acknowledging that defensive distortion or blockage can be normal, I am not advocating a deconstructivist's view that all perception is defensive and relative to the eyes and needs of the beholder. It is argued that defenses support relationships with IPIRs. Wishes and fears in relation to IPIRs organize behavior as well as the associated cognitions and affects. Defenses that support relationships with destructive IPIRs result in hostile behavior and they are therefore pathological. They also can support friendly IPIRs and therefore result in friendly, normal behavior. A normal person can selectively choose defensive mechanisms in order to serve attachment behaviors. In the long run, however, attachment is better served if there are no distortions or blockages in awareness or linkages. Ultimately, attachment is better served by clarity and integrity in perception, processing, and responding. The reason is simple. Realistic, undistorted interactions are better supported in the long run by the continuing data stream. Attachments that do not involve distortions can be sustained under a variety of conditions. If little distortion or blockage is involved, the attachments become enriched over time.

## CLINICAL EXAMPLES

### Repression

*Pathological repression* is active forgetting of events, thoughts, or feelings associated with wishes and fears that results in increases in hostile behaviors described by the DAG. Normative repression is the same except that it enhances affiliative behaviors described by the AG. Pathological repression is illustrated by the forgetting of incestual attacks that forms the basis of self-mutilation (see Benjamin, 1993b, Chapter 5). The repressed events, thoughts, and feelings, and the associated wishes and fears, embroil the patient in hostile behaviors toward self and others. Normative repression would be illustrated by forgetting the pain of childbirth. The repression of the event facilities wishes and fears that optimize attachment to the baby, its father, and babies yet to come.

The following example of pathological repression illustrates the interpersonal definition of repression in a clinical context:

A mother was chronically embattled with her adolescent daughter and had become suicidal. The daughter had become increasingly involved with dangerous sexuality and use of drugs. She was very critical of her mother and the patient seemed unable to assume a parental role by setting even the most reasonable of limits on the girl. The therapist asked the patient why she had such difficulty saying, for example, that the daughter would need to be home by midnight, or face consequences. The patient explained that she was terrified that she would be a "bad guy" in her daughter's eyes. She felt that if she tried to exert control, she would be rejected by her daughter. Her ex-husband would come and take her daughter to live with him.

The therapist, wondering why the patient was so sure she was going to lose her daughter, asked, "Can you recall an earlier time when something you loved was taken away?" The patient said: "If I verbalize it, I have to feel it. I don't want to feel it. I know where it came from. It came from home. From Dad and Mother. . . . My mind goes blank sometimes. I know it is because I don't want to deal with things."

With a little encouragement from the therapist, the patient remembered a cat that she had as a child. She loved the cat. It slept with her every night, and she was greatly comforted by petting it. The cat clearly liked to be with her and that was the only relationship she had where she felt valued. One day, her mother and father told her the cat had to go because its fur was too difficult to clean up. She had to put it in the cage that was used to take the cat to the animal shelter, where it was destroyed. The patient also was offered a bicycle she had long wished for to help her get over her grief. She said, "Nobody would listen to how much I loved her. I had no say in anything that happened to me. I still feel guilty. I didn't realize how much hurt I suffered because of that."

The therapist encouraged the patient to look at the incident from the perspective of an adult to try to help her see that she indeed had little choice and need not take responsibility for the cat's death. She then said: "I didn't realized how I hated myself. I thought I was just mad at my mother. I see it wasn't my fault."

The therapist asked the patient how she felt now and she said: "Relieved. I can put down a load. Something I have been carrying. A heavy rock. I had no idea it was that devastating. I never dealt with it."

The story reveals the uncovering of a forgotten memory during psychotherapy. It appears that the woman's relationship with her daughter was crippled by her wish to avoid taking control because that would replicate her own earlier experience with arbitrary and devastating parental control. She did not want to be a "bad guy" like her parents. Her own actions as a mother were deeply affected by an incident that she could not remember. She had experienced a major attachment loss and was convinced she was responsible. She accepted the idea that she had destroyed the cat by putting it in the carrying cage and criticized herself for being "bought off" because she accepted the offer of a bicycle. The loss combined with guilt formed an unbearable combination. A vital part of the story had to be repressed. It was more painful to think about her own perceived responsibility for the cat's death than to think about the loss itself. The patient repressed her belief that she had been as destructive as her mother.

That guilt crippled her ability to set appropriate limits with her own daughter. "I don't want to be a bad guy." The result was that her attachment with her own daughter was compromised severely. The woman was unable to set appropriate limits (**Control, Protect**) and the daughter's defiance led to a relationship characterized by hostility and ambivalence. The repression was pathological because it was associated with the fear (she was like her mother) that resulted in behaviors described by the DAG.

The patient's statement: "I thought I was mad at my mother, but I realize I hated myself" suggests the defensive process involved more than repression. She punished herself out of loyalty to the cat (introjection of generic maternal attack), but says she directed her anger instead toward her mother (displacement). The defense ended up directing the anger appropriately. The pathology remained in her relationship with her own daughter.

It is vitally important to discover how and why the patient was able to recall this episode in therapy. What enabled her to remember? It was a brief therapy with an inexperienced but gifted student therapist. The patient had very strong and positive feelings about her therapist, and he reciprocated. He was able quickly to see interpersonal patterns and to draw connections among them. He offered compassionate and well-focused advocacy for her battles with herself and others.

A working hypothesis for why she was able to remember the details of the forgotten episode is that she had a good attachment to this therapist, who offered behaviors from the AG sector: **Affirm** and **Protect**, if not also **Active-Love**. He disclosed to the supervisory group that he liked the patient very much. His audiotapes showed that he was warm, and appropriately differentiated and professional. His communications were clear and relevant. This relationship gave her the security to tolerate the pain of recalling the loss of a very important early attachment object, the cat. Perhaps the therapist's affection for her was internalized, and her self-esteem boosted enough that she could face her guilt.

This patient was aware of the wish to do better than her mother, fearing that she would recapitulate in her children her own early trauma. She was not aware that the rigid and overdetermined quality of her refusal to take control was from her belief that she herself had been a fatal bad guy in relation to the cat. In alliance with her therapist, she was able to look back at the episode and blame herself less. This had the effect of enabling her to feel she had more choice in how to relate to her own daughter.

**Denial**

Pathological *denial* is unwillingness to acknowledge certain events or thoughts or feelings because of their association with wishes or fears that enhance hostile behaviors described by the DAG. Normative denial is the same except that it enhances attachment behaviors described by the AG.

It is appropriate to distinguish among the closely related defenses of repression—denial and lying. To explore the differences, consider the patient who recalled in therapy that she had put her pet cat in the cage and that she felt responsible for its subsequent death. Until she remembered the episode in therapy, the event had a deep impact on her own parenting behavior. The example illustrated repression.

That patient might have exhibited the defense of denial if she had remembered putting the cat in the cage and felt guilty about it, but said that the episode had nothing to do with her own hostile behavior as a mother. It should be noted that unless there was convincing other evidence that the episode was affecting her parenting, the therapist should not assume the patient was denying. The patient's perceptions are the primary data source that informs understanding of the patient's mental operations. The therapist should not take the liberty to declare a patient is engaging in defensiveness unless the patient has provided data that directly support the interpretation.

A common form of denial is shown by the cheerful masochist who hardly acknowledges the presence or significance of her frequent batterings. She is aware of the attacks, but maintains a friendly presentation to her spouse, children, and the world. The SASB analysis of her pattern in relation to her battering spouse is summarized by a complex code: **Active-Love** plus Sulk plus *Self-Neglect*. Although she seems friendly, she shows hostile compliance to his bullying behavior and neglects herself. The hostile consequences described by the DAG behaviors Sulk and *Self-Neglect* mark her denial as pathological.

A specific clinical example of denial is offered by the passive-aggressive personality discussed in Benjamin, 1993b, pp. 282–284. During a dynamic interview in front of the hospital staff who had cared for her during many hospitalizations for suicidal depression, the patient discovered that her suicidal episodes were motived by a desire to show her father that he had harmed her. As soon as she herself affirmed that interpretation on the basis of her own words, she retracted it. She said: "I'm not doing it to hurt him." Immediately after she had uncovered a wish for her father to feel sorry for harm done and to make it up to her, she denied it was true. She had said the purpose of her suicidal activity (*Self-Attack*) was to **Blame** her father. She hoped he would Submit to her wish and do a better job at **Active-Love**ing and **Protect**ing her. Presumably the denial that followed was inspired by recognition that the staff might dismiss her depression as invalid and thereby block the potential for the wish to be realized.

It will be important to discover why some wishes and fears and associated episodes are denied and others are repressed. In both cases, the pain or fear associated with full awareness is probably too great. The line between denial and repression probably is thin. Perhaps repression kicks in when the pain of acknowledgment becomes great enough. It is likely that the woman just described quickly forgot about (repressed) the interview during which the connection between her wish for restitution and her suicidal depressions was uncovered.

## Lying

The pathological defense of lying is defined as active efforts to disguise or conceal events or thoughts or feelings because they are associated with wishes or fears that enhance behaviors described by the DAG. The normative defense of lying is the same except it enhances behaviors described by the AG.

An example of normative lying would be the efforts of the French, Dutch, and Danish families who protected Jewish families by hiding them during the Nazi occupation. They conspired to support elaborate lies, all in service of preservation of life. Their behaviors would be coded as **Affirm**ing, **Active-Love**ing and **Protect**ion of the victims of the Nazi ideology.

Pathological lying often characterizes interactions in psychotherapy, but it is rarely discussed in the literature or in practice. Some common lies from patients have to do with their distrust of the therapist, their sexual love for the therapist, their unwillingness to discuss certain embarrassing but vital topics, deceptions concerning their ability to pay the therapist's bill, their distortions of stories to manage the therapist's impression of them. These lies stem from wishes and fears about the relationship with the therapist and/or the IPIRs, and they enhance DAG behaviors. The wishes and fears interfere with the patients' ability to engage in the main task of therapy, which is to learn about patterns, where they came from and what they are for, and decide to change. The patient who lies to the therapist might believe he or she is engaged in AG behaviors such as *Self-Protect,* but actually is implementing *Self-Neglect.*

Consider a woman who tells her therapist a distorted story about an exchange with a supervisor that suggests the patient was victimized when in fact she was simply confronted with inadequate performance. Her lie interferes with her opportunity to learn about her patterns and develop better alternatives. She compromises her opportunity to develop a typical position of friendliness described by the Attachment Group.

The therapist needs to be aware of the possibility of lying and help the patient approach the painful subject of the lies as he or she is ready. In the example of the encounter with the supervisor, for example, the therapist might ask for more specific data, with questions such as "What did she [the supervisor] say to you? What did you say then? How did you feel? What did you think?" "What did you do?" This level of specificity is likely to make the truth apparent to the patient as well as the therapist. Collaboratively, patient and therapist can discuss how threatened the patient felt, and trace her inappropriate pain back to its earlier roots of confrontations in childhood. Eventually, she might also discuss the defense of lying and its relation to those early roots. No doubt lying and exaggerating the story had earlier served the patient well and/or was modeled by important early figures. Therapists should avoid endorsing a moral hierarchy that is most respectful of repression and least respectful of lying. They all have their defensive reasons, and should be treated comparably.

**Other Defenses**

The same approach could be applied to other defenses discussed by psychoanalysis. Examples were mentioned in the section "Mechanisms of Defense." They include projection, splitting, idealization, devaluation, repression, denial, somatization, intellectualization, lying, dissociation, isolation, displacement, acting out, sublimation, compensation, regression, and undoing. Each defense represents different cognitive processes involving an interaction between the defender and wishes and fears connected with important external or internalized others (IPIRs). The patterns can be identified by SASB codes. Pathological versions disrupt attachment and enable DAG behaviors. Normative versions support transactions characterized by the Attachment Group.

## SUMMARY

Defenses invoke distortions in perception, awareness, or response. Defenses may or may not be unconscious, or maladaptive in the current social context. The main purpose of defensive distortions or blockages is to satisfy wishes and fears that arise in relation to the defender's relationships with IPIRs. If the IPIR is destructive, then the defenses that support the relationship result in behavior that is typically hostile. These defenses are pathological. If the IPIR supports a friendly orientation toward self and others, the associated defenses are normal. Factors that create and maintain IPIRs and their associated wishes and fears have yet to be well articulated. It is clear that early caregivers have high priority. In addition to age of exposure, the dimensions of power and sexuality probably also enhance the development of IPIRs.

In the long run, it is better not to invoke defenses (i.e., to distort perception or processing or responses) because attachment is better supported over time and context if no distortion is required. However, sometimes defenses are necessary to preserve attachment to self and others. It must be noted that SASB codes of pseudo, forced, or false friendliness include a hostile component, and therefore classify them as pathological.

## COMPARISON OF THE PRESENT APPROACH WITH THE PSYCHOANALYTICAL APPROACH

This approach deviates from the psychoanalytic in important ways. An important difference is the demotion of the role of making the unconscious conscious. Lack of awareness is a major feature for some defenses (e.g., repression), but not for others (e.g., lying). The present perspective acknowledges that banishing thoughts, affects, memories of incidents from awareness is an important defense. But lack of awareness is by no means the only mental tactic that can be used to serve the wishes and fears associated with IPIRs.

Another important difference is that defenses are not automatically seen as pathological or maladaptive. Normal behavior, including repression, can be defensive too. The distinction between normal and pathological defenses hinges on the results of the defense. Pathological defenses result in hostile behaviors, and their associated cognitions and affects. Normative defenses result in friendly behaviors and their associated cognitions and affects.

There are many other differences, but these do not relate directly to the topic of defenses, and psychoanalysis itself is divided on many topics. One example is the present assumption that attachment is primary. According to classical drive theory, hostility and self-centered sexuality are primary. Defenses must be erected against these natural forces of destruction if civilization is to survive. Friendliness is the result of a fragile truce between the id and the superego, and it is manifest only if the ego is very clever. The present proposal that attachment is primary, while destructiveness is deviant essentially reverses the perspective on what is primary and what is derivative.

The present analysis can explain some unusual problems that are not addressed by traditional views of defenses. These include maladaptive behavior that is normal (the generous child in the street culture); adaptive behavior that is pathological (the devoted Satanic cult member); abnormal behavior that does not involve distorted perceptions (the sensitive paranoid); normal behavior that involves distorted perceptions (the loving child who ignores or immediately forgets his mother's outrageous behavior, thereby preserving attachment; the terminally ill cancer patient who maintains a cheerful attitude and therefore survives longer).

## TREATMENT IMPLICATIONS

In both the British and the Sullivanian psychoanalytic approaches, conflicts are defined in terms of "object relations" rather than abstract energies. Nonetheless, psychotherapy based on object relations theory continues to assume that the treatment challenge is to help the patient break defenses, uncover unconscious conflicts, express and work through thoughts and feelings that have been banished from awareness.

The treatment implications of the present approach are different. Treatment is not focused on breaking down defenses and uncovering unconscious material. Instead, it is assumed that no matter what the school or approach, psychotherapy is a social learning experience. Under this social developmental learning model of therapy, insight is not the end point. When the patient learns about his or her defenses, the therapy is progressing but is by no means finished. To expect that insight effects a "cure" would be the same as to expect to be able to serve a tennis ball well after learning that one is not holding the racket properly. From the perspective of a learning model, the "insight" is little more than a "diagnosis" of the problem.

Under the developmental social learning model, the therapy task is to help the patient learn to recognize his or her interpersonal and intrapsychic patterns, where they came from, and what they are for. In other words, the patient learns to recognize destructive patterns and their connection to wishes and fears that arise in relation to IPIRs. In the process, he or she learns about the defensive distortions and blockages that support the relationships with the IPIRs. To the extent therapists can be aware of the connections between patterns and wishes and fears about IPIRs, and of the role defenses play in supporting these relationships, they will be able to help patients learn to recognize and deal with them.

Insight may combine with the relationship with the therapist, plus current life experiences, to help the patient mobilize the will to "betray" the IPIRs, and move on to a happier and more constructive way of being. A simple model is offered by the dieter who makes little progress until he or she decides the excess weight truly is worse than the loss of the pleasure of indulgent eating. Similarly, the psychotherapy patient will make little significant progress until he or she decides that the rewards of engaging in healthy patterns outweigh the fears associated with better function and which often include the threat of loss of the IPIRs' love. With respect to defenses, therapy learning must focus on the distorting and blocking mechanisms that support the relationship with the IPIRs. As the patient changes the relationship with the IPIRs, the need for the defensive distortions and blockages should diminish. The normal individual would be aware of defenses and be able to choose to use them or not. Once the decision to give up or significantly transform the attachment to the old IPIRs has been made (usually gradually and unconsciously), new learning can take place. Behaviors described by the Disrupted Attachment Group, and the associated cognitions and affects will shift more reliably in the direction of the Attachment Group of behaviors, cognitions, and affects. Ideally, few defenses will be needed, except under extraordinarily stressful conditions.

## REFERENCES

American Psychiatric Association (1987). *Diagnostic and statistical manual of mental disorders* (3rd ed., rev.; DSM-III-R) Washington, DC: Author.

Benjamin, L. S. (1974). Structural Analysis of Social Behavior. *Psychological Review, 81,* 392–425.

Benjamin, L. S. (1984). Principles of prediction using Structural Analysis of Social Behavior. In R. A. Zucker, J. Aronoff, & A. J. Rabin (Eds.), *Personality and the prediction of behavior* (pp. 121–173). New York: Academic Press.

Benjamin, L. S. (1986). Adding social and intrapsychic descriptors to Axis I of DSM-III. In T. Million & G. Klerman (Eds.), *Contemporary directions in psychopathology* (pp. 599–638). New York: Guilford Press.

Benjamin, L. S. (1989). Is chronicity related to the quality of the relationship with the hallucination? *Schizophrenia Bulletin, 15,* 291–310.

Benjamin, L. S. (1993a). Every psychopathology is a gift of love. *Psychotherapy Research, 3,* 1–24.

Benjamin, L. S. (1993b). *Interpersonal diagnosis and treatment of personality disorders.* New York: Guilford Press.

Benjamin, L. S. (in press). An interpersonal theory of the personality disorders. In J. F. Clarkin (Ed.), *Major theories of personality disorder.* New York: Guilford Press.

Benjamin, L. S., & Friedrich, F. J. (1991). Contributions of Structural Analysis of Social Behavior (SASB) to the bridge between cognitive science and a science of object relations. In M. J. Horowitz (Ed.), *Person schemas and maladaptive behavior* (pp. 379–412). Chicago, IL: University of Chicago Press.

Conte, H. R., & Plutchik, H. R. (1981). A circumplex model for interpersonal personality traits. *Journal of Personality and Social Psychology, 40,* 701–711.

Frost, R. (1949). *The complete poems of Robert Frost.* New York: Holt.

Greenberg, J. R., & Mitchell, S. A. (1983). *Object relations in psychoanalytic theory.* Cambridge, MA: Harvard University Press.

Kiesler, D. J. (1983). The 1982 interpersonal circle: A taxonomy for complementarity in human transactions. *Psychological Review, 90,* 185–214.

Leary, T. (1957). *Interpersonal diagnosis of personality: A functional theory and methodology for personality evaluation.* New York: Ronald Press.

Lemert, E. M. (1962). Paranoia and the dynamics of exclusion. *Sociometry, 25,* 2–20.

Lorr, M., Bishop, P. F., & McNair, D. M. (1965). Interpersonal types among psychiatric patients. *Journal of Abnormal Psychology, 70,* 468–472.

Sullivan, H. S. (1953). *The interpersonal theory of psychiatry.* New York: Norton.

Taylor, S. E., & Brown, J. D. (1988). Illusion and well-being: A social psychological perspective on mental health. *Psychological Bulletin, 103,* 193–210.

Wiggins, J. S. (1982). Circumplex models of interpersonal behavior in clinical psychology. In P. C. Kendall & J. N. Butcher (Eds.), *Handbook of research methods in clinical psychology* (pp. 183–221). New York: Wiley.

# 4

# Defenses as Aspects of Person Schemas and Control Processes

## MARDI J. HOROWITZ AND CHARLES H. STINSON

Control process theory aims to describe how defensive operations are formed. This permits a microanalysis of warding-off behaviors and points to selective interventions to alter attention deployment. The theory stems from observation of patterns of resistances to disclosure in exploratory psychotherapies. Some of these control processes involve shifts in schemas of self and relationships; other control processes involve shifts in topics and representations that are organized by particular schemas of self and others. This chapter focuses on control processes that affect these person schemas and briefly reviews other aspects of control process theory.

## BACKGROUND

Psychoanalytic theory of defense mechanisms began with studies of repression (Breuer & Freud, 1895/1958; Freud, 1900/1953). The terms *defense mechanisms* and *repression* were used interchangeably until a variety of defense mechanisms were described (A. Freud, 1936; Vaillant, 1992). Table 4–1 presents six examples of our most recent list of 30 defenses, with definitions that use the same theoretical language about person schemas as does control process theory (Horowitz, 1988a).

We and our colleagues have examined defensive states in intensive single-case studies (Horowitz, 1987; Horowitz, Milbrath, Jordan et al., 1994; Horowitz, Stinson, Curtis et al., 1993). We found that many defenses were combined, even in a short episode of warding-off behavior. It

This chapter is based on a presentation at the American Association for the Advancement of Science, Washington, DC, 1991, and research supported by the John D. and Catherine T. MacArthur Foundation's Program on Conscious and Unconscious Mental Processes.

**TABLE 4–1**
**Some Defense Mechanisms Related to Person Schemas**
**and Control Process Definitions**

| Defense Mechanism | Description |
|---|---|
| Conversion of Passive to Active. | To defend against the threat of a weak, passive, and vulnerable position, the person may conceptually place self in the active role of a model of relationship with another person. Identification with an aggressor for whom the self is a victim is one form of this defensive role reversal. |
| Displacement. | The avoided ideas and feelings are transferred from a targeted other in a role-relationship model to some other person, situation, or object. A targeted aspect of self may also be shifted to some other aspect. For example, in hypochondriacal displacement, a person may displace worry and ward off a concern that his or her mind is failing, and focus concern instead on the possibility of a body part failing. |
| Dissociation. | The individual deals with emotional conflicts or sharp increases in stress by a temporary alteration in the integrative functions of consciousness, and in more enduring ways by segregating memories by changing self schemas and/or role-relationship models. |
| Omnipotent Control. | To defend against the stress produced by others abandoning or failing to attend properly to the self, the person shifts to a role-relationship model in which self has total control of the object, who may be viewed as an extension of self. Sometimes, omnipotent control also includes attitudes of an irrational but grandiose nature, in which the person believes that wishes or rituals involving the self will bend environmental forces to his or her will. |
| Projection. | A warded-off impulse, emotion, or trait is attributed to others instead of the self. For example, people who struggle with their own hatred may develop a delusion that others are out to get them. This provides an acceptable rationale to switch into a role-relationship model in which self hates the other as a response and allows the individual to avoid recognition of his or her own destructive impulses. |
| Splitting. | The person deals with emotional conflicts by segregated views of self, others, or relationships between self and other(s) as all good or all bad. Integration of positive and negative qualities of self and others into cohesive images and supraordinate relationship schemas does not occur. Instead, "either/or" states occur in which the self and/or other is either idealized or devalued rather than seen as having both good and bad characteristics. |

*Note:* Adapted from *Introduction to Psychodynamics: A New Synthesis* (p. 191–196) by M. J. Horowitz, 1988a, New York: Basic Books. Copyright 1988 by Basic Books. Reprinted by permission.

seemed best to describe how multiple processes of control act together in forming any communication or conscious representation of an idea or feeling.

In such research, it is important to develop reliable methods of locating increases in defense activity. By defining a variety of control processes, and how they might manifest themselves, we were able to arrive at reliable measures of verbal efforts at dyselaboration (obscuring, obstructing, or misleading the flow of information) nonverbal measures of warding-off behavior (signs of stifling emotion in the face or body), and global efforts at stifling emotionality (as in overmodulated or shimmering states of mind) (Horowitz, Ewert, & Milbrath, 1992; Horowitz, Milbrath, Jordan et al., 1994; Horowitz, Stinson, Curtis et al., 1993).

To examine the overlaps in control processes and classically defined defenses, we subjected the same clinical material to analysis by categories of defense mechanisms and also by categories of control processes (Horowitz, Cooper, Fridhandler et al., 1992). The latter seemed better able to specify what was happening on a moment-to-moment basis. The control process categories used in such work include those that affect selection of a topic, those that affect the form of expression of that topic, and those that affect schemas that organize thought or communication. These control processes are summarized in Table 4–2 (from Horowitz, Cooper, Fridhandler et al., 1992).

Control processes that affect person schemas relate to defense mechanisms described after Freud's initial discoveries. These defense mechanisms have been called the "image-distorting defenses" (Bond, Gardner, Christian, & Sigal, 1983). The term *image distortion* refers to modifications of internalized knowledge structures about self and others; that is, defenses that affect internalized object relations. These defenses are formed by control processes that shift which schemas actively organize a state of mind. Microanalytic studies of such image-distorting defense mechanisms such as splitting (Horowitz, 1977), undoing (Horowitz, 1988b), devaluation (Horowitz, 1975), displacement (Horowitz, Stinson, & Fridhandler, 1991), and role reversal (Horowitz, Merluzzi et al., 1991) led us to the categories of control processes we now use.

## PERSON SCHEMAS THEORY

Person schemas theory evolved from a synthesis of cognitive science concepts and psychoanalytic concepts of internalized object relation theory (Greenberg & Mitchell, 1983; Horowitz, 1991a; Kernberg, 1969; Rowan,

**TABLE 4–2**
**Cognitive Operations in the Control Process**

**Control of Content**

1. *Focus of attention:* The setpoint for attentional focus determines in part the probabilities for the next topics for conscious representation.
2. *Concepts:* Shifts in settings at this level may facilitate or inhibit different types of concepts relative to one another. The settings will affect how a chain of concepts on the topic of attention is formed and represented.
3. *Appraisal of importance of a chain of concepts:* Chains of concepts are weighed for their relative importance in terms of their implications for the motives or intentions of self and others. By shifting the appraisal and valuation of a chain of concepts, a person can alter the emotional consequences of ideas, memories, fantasies, or plans that are involved.
4. *Threshold for decision or interruption:* One may change the setting of the threshold for shifting attention to a new topic, allowing a point of decision or interruption.

**Control of Form**

1. *Modes of representation:* These settings determine the ratio of words, quasi-sensory images, and enactions in the sphere of conscious representation.
2. *Time span:* The setting of time span establishes a focus for considering a topic in terms of past, present, or future as well as a temporal range from very short to very long periods.
3. *Quality of logical contemplation:* The setting for type of logic and organization determines in part the forms that will be used for the simultaneous and sequential organization of concepts. The forms used may vary from the logic of rational problem solving to reverielike rules.
4. *Action planning:* Settings for level of action planning may vary from using thought as nonaction, to thought as trial action, to rehearsals of action, to reflexive actions.
5. *Arousal or vigilance level:* The setting of arousal level involves thresholds for excitation or dampening of how various systems react to input from other systems.

**Control of Repertoires of Schematization**

1. *Self schemas:* In any state of mind, one of several potential self schemas tends to be dominant. Shifting which schema is primed may change the state of mind.
2. *Other person schemas:* Shifting which schema is primed will affect how the behaviors, intentions, and motives of the other person are interpreted.
3. *Role-relationship models:* By shifting which role-relationship model is used for interpreting an interpersonal situation, a person may change mood, states, plans, and actions, and may alter how a topic is contemplated.
4. *Value schemas (critic roles):* The appraisal of a topic, chain of concepts, or remembered action sequence includes judgments in relation to values. The judgments can range from harsh to accepting views. Judgments can be experienced in thought as if they were made by critics. By shifting schemas and values, a person may vary the degree of praise and blame.
5. *Executive-agency schemas:* A person may view the body and mind as that of an individual (I, me) or as that belonging to another person or larger group (we). Shifts in how topics are viewed may occur with changes in which executive schemas are currently primed.

*Note:* From "Control Processes and Defense Mechanisms" by M. J. Horowitz, Cooper et al., 1992, *Journal of Psychotherapy Practice and Research, 1*, pp. 324–336. Copyright 1992 by University of Chicago Press. Reprinted by permission.

1990). Person schemas are internal structures of meaning that integrate knowledge about physical, psychological, and social characteristics.

As stated elsewhere (Horowitz, 1988b), the properties of person schemas have been defined:

> . . . by such authors as Bartlett (1932); Asch (1946); Piaget (1979); Neisser (1976); Markus (1977); Horowitz (1979, 1987, 1991b); Hastie (1981); Bandura (1982); Marcel (1983a, 1983b); Taylor and Crocker (1981); Ostrom, Pryor, and Simpson (1981); Krumhansl and Castellano (1983); Horowitz and Zilberg (1983); Luborsky (1984); and Rummelhart (1986). These properties include the following:

1. Schemas generalize past experiences into holistic, composite forms, thus allowing incoming information to be measured against the existing composite for "goodness of fit." In forming a conscious experience of thought, information from the internal composite may be used to fill out forms missing from the external stimulus information. Although this may enable rapid perception in some ways, it may also lead to patterned and recurrent errors in interpreting and responding to stimuli that are actually different from the schematic forms.

2. Schemas that accord well with real stimuli permit a more rapid organization of incoming information than those that match poorly with the actual situation. Therefore, schemas enhance stimuli that fit the schematic view and impede recognition of stimuli that do not.

3. Schemas of self and others enhance a sense of temporal continuity and coherence of identity. Conversely, aschematic conditions seem to lead to a loss of coherence of identity, experienced subjectively and symbolically as fragmentation of self and a loss of location of self in time.

4. As an encapsulation or a composite view of a role, a person schema can be named. Hence, it may be possible to represent consciously by symbols a meaning form that usually operates unconsciously. Naming and conscious reflection may facilitate changes in how schemas are used in appraisals, decisions, and plans and may lead to rehearsals that can build new schemas or that integrate schemas into supraordinate forms. Such deliberate trials and rehearsals may lead to changes in automatic behavioral sequences. This is believed to be a change

process in dynamic, cognitive, and behavioral psychotherapies. Unless they are modified, defensive control processes
may ward off conscious reflection and impede change.

5. Multiple schemas may be applied simultaneously and unconsciously to the interpretation of a given stimulus such as a
changing social situation. Multiple parallel channels operate
in unconscious information processing, but conscious
thought tends to proceed in one or only a few channels. As a
result, there may be competition for priority and goodness
of fit among these multiple schemas as information processing results approach channels for conscious representation. The outcome of the competition determines which
derivatives of schemas and information processing gain conscious recognition.

6. Schematic transorderings of information may effect the
"mysterious leaps" between body and mind, mind and body,
as well as the mysterious transmissions of mood between persons in families, group processes and crowds. (pp. 13–14)

Taking self schemas as the most central example of person schemas,
many theorists now see each person as having a repertoire of systematic
(but not necessarily compatible) views of self. This multiplicity can lead
to different qualities of conscious identity, the sense of being an "I" or
"me," in different states of mind. Some identities are desired, others
dreaded. A clinical example may clarify the relationship between
dreaded self schemas and the schemas defensively used to avoid them.

## Clinical Example of Defensive Layering of Multiple Self Schemas

A man entered treatment for an array of social inhibitions that prevented
him from having either deep friendships or loving attachments. During
the initial months of his treatment, he complained of feeling lonely even
during therapy hours. He felt reasonably strong, but walled off from others, including the therapist.

During a transference regression, he experienced earnest and intense
desires to be intimately joined with the therapist in an empathic, exhila-
rating, and insightful exploration of his life story. As the regression deepened, his desires gained sensuous tinges. Concerns about a dreaded
consequence began to emerge: he feared inappropriate and dangerous
sexual closeness because he would be used, abused, and then abandoned.
The desired state of closeness and the dreaded state of abandonment were
linked together in an obligatory script sequence: one state, it seemed to

him, necessarily led to the other. His strong aloof stance (that is, his distant state of relating), though lonely, was a defense to ward off the onset of the use, abuse, abandonment cycle or script. Within this distant and walled-off state, he projected his desire for closeness and so experienced a state of mind in which he worried that his therapist was yearning to be "too close" to him. He was alert and ready to fend off such closeness.

The multiple self schemas were of self as a strong, self-protective, and aloof man; self as an attractive but manipulable child; and self as a deserted, degraded waif. The first schema could be activated to ward off weak self-states and anxious feelings.

## PERSON SCHEMAS AND CONTROL PROCESSES

### Patterns in Interpersonal Transactions

An advantage of person schemas theory is that it helps us explain repetitions of inappropriate beliefs, feelings, and actions in persons with exceptionally rigid patterns. These people do not change according to a real situation but react to all contexts too excessively according to inner enduring attitudes about self and other in interpersonal transactions. They repeat maladaptive patterns in an obligatory scriptlike manner. Typological patterns have been identified. Clinicians have noted sudden shifts between all-good and all-bad views of self and others in borderline personality (e.g., Kernberg, 1969); shifts among the inferior-self-in-desperate-need-of-a-self-object, the entitled and grandiose self, and the quasi-realistic self schemas of the narcissistic personality (e.g., Kohut, 1972); shifts among the incompatible and unstable too-strong and too-weak self-concepts of the compulsive personality disorder (e.g., Salzman, 1968); shifts between the confusing levels of self-as-active and self-as-passive of the attention-seeking histrionic disorder (e.g., Horowitz, 1991a); and shifts from a socially shy self to a fantasied star-like self in some avoidant personalities (e.g., Eells, Horowitz, Stinson, & Fridhandler, 1993).

Person schemas theory describes the self as having component or modular parts such as a repertoire of body images and roles; as mentioned, within an overall self-organization each person may have multiple self schemas. These self schemas, in turn, may be contained within and contribute structure to schematized views of relationships with others. A repertoire of self schemas may or may not be integrated into supraordinate self schemas.

Larger supraordinate structures foster integration and control. Hatred toward a frustrating person would be mitigated by a schematic knowledge that in other states the other person was not frustrating but giving. Such gestalts can be symbolized, permitting conscious representation, self-reflection, and volitional choice among otherwise contradictory attitudes. With development of higher levels of integration and control, self-regulatory capacities are heightened and refined.

A person schema contains traits, characteristics, attributes, and roles of people (self, others) and also a sequence of wishes, fears, aims, responses, and reactions. These sequences constitute a scriptlike set of actions. Together, a schema of self, a schema of other, and a script for interaction between the two can be called a *role-relationship model* (Horowitz, Merluzzi et al., 1991).

## Role-Relationship Models

For a specific real-life relationship, such as with a sibling, spouse, child, parent, friend, or employer, there may be a repertoire of role-relationship models. Emotionality and style of relating to the other will vary not only according to the real-life situation and activities of mutual engagement but according to which relationship schema is actively organizing a state of mind.

Schemas develop from life experiences. Some have their genesis in repeated social experiences, which are then generalized into the form of the schema. Temperament may dispose a person to develop certain schemas. Sometimes, however, with traumatic events, the schema is born from a single episode, although the schema takes shape in part through the repetition of that episode in the form of recurrent memories.

As the individual learns from social experiences, he or she learns to take either role in a role-relationship model. Both roles in a repeated relationship transactional pattern become familiar. By identification, a weak self learns the aggressor role of a stronger other who has victimized the self. By reversing roles, the negative emotions of fear and pain are not felt by self so this may be learned as a preferable organization. In such ways, defensive uses of schemas such as role reversal are learned.

Existing schemas are probably not erased but may gradually be modified, and newer schemas may become more active. Integrative schemas may be formed from views of prior experience. Supraordinate schemas may schematize subordinate ones and contain them in ways that reconcile previous incompatibilities. Mourning provides an example: A person may mourn a loss that occurred many years or even decades before. Shortly after the loss, the person may have believed that the negative feelings activated could not be tolerated. Review of role-relationship models around a relationship with the person lost might have been inhibited. Later, as in the safe context of psychotherapy, the person may allow memories and schemas to be consciously symbolized once again. As that happens, the person can undertake the reschematization that is an important part of completing a mourning process, including schematization of a view of self as capable of withstanding the loss and continuing with life.

The processing of any theme can occur in parallel according to different self schemas and role-relationship models, leading to different ideas and feelings en route. *Control processes can determine which of several parallel channels of unconscious information processing gain access to conscious representation.*

## PROPERTIES OF SCHEMAS

Schemas have motivational properties and can be activated by biological, social, or psychological needs. Some schemas organize desirable states of mind, others undesirable or dreaded states of mind. Still other schemas, considered adaptive compromises, might organize states of mind that avoid risks. Any given topic may tend to activate schemas of desire, fear, or more defensive states.

A specific topic may contain so many contradictions between wishes and fears, as well as so many dilemmas of choice and discrepancies in beliefs, that contemplation of the topic becomes alarmingly emotional. To reduce emotional responses, processes of control may inhibit expression of or attention to the topic or elements within the topic. Processes of control may also facilitate some self schemas and inhibit others, affecting all aspects of information processing and behavior in relation to that conflictual topic. The outcome of all control processes may be regarded as adaptive or maladaptive if the processes succeed in reducing emotion to tolerable limits, or as dysregulation if emotional flooding still occurs.

*Adaptive regulation* would be an outcome of multiple processes of control appraised as useful in solving problems or dealing with life. Conversely, *maladaptive regulation* would be an outcome of multiple processes of control appraised as costly to the organism (not coping well with stress or conflict). In outcomes called states of *dysregulation,* control processes did not operate in a satisfactory way to protect the subject from vulnerabilities that could have been warded off had there been adequate regulation of ideas, feelings, or interpersonal acts.

## CATEGORIES OF CONTROL OF PERSON SCHEMAS

Each category of processes of control of person schemas can have outcomes that represent adaptive regulation, maladaptive regulation, or dysregulation, as shown in Table 4–3. The first category, *shifting self*

**TABLE 4–3**
**Control of Person Schemas and Role-Relationship Models**

| Level | Description of the Level |
|---|---|
| A. Shifting self schemas | Assume that each person has a repertoire of self schemas and that in any state one of these tends to be a dominant referent for appraisal of experiences and actions. Altering which schema is dominant as an organizer affects the estimation of the significance of acts, memories, or plans as well as how themes are thought about or actions carried out. |
| B. Shifting schemas of other persons | Assume that each person can view another person not only by the actions and expressions of that person but by a variety of prototypes. Which prototype is selected from a repertoire of person schemas will affect how the behaviors, intentions, and motives of the other person are interpreted. By altering the schemas selected for interpreting the other person, a subject may alter emotional responses to interpersonal situations. |
| C. Shifting role-relationship models | Schemas of self and other may be combined in role-relationship models. These include scripts for sequences of action and reaction. By altering which role-relationship model is used for interpreting an interpersonal situation (current, remembered, or fantasied), a person may change mood, states, plans, and actions. |
| D. Shifting person appraisal schemas (critic roles) | After a sequence of actions, or in taking mental perspective on potential actions, a person may appraise the social, moral, or value significance of the happenings. This appraisal can be from various perspectives within the overall self-organization of a person. There may be sets of values organized by various critic roles. These can be based on personifications or introjects of real or fictitious people, spirits, or ideological groups. By altering which of these critical vantage-points is the current appraisal schema, a person may vary between degrees of praise and blame for the self or other. |
| E. Shifting executive "we" schemas | A person may view self as an individual (I, me) or as a large group (we). A person may set the executive agency schema as the separate "I" or as a "we" (marital unit, family, group, ideology, tribe, nation), which transcends the "my body" framework. |

*Note:* From "Role Relationship Models Configuration (RRMC)" by M. J. Horowitz et al., in M. J. Horowitz (Ed.), *Person Schemas and Maladaptive Interpersonal Patterns*, 1991, Chicago: University of Chicago Press. Copyright 1991 by University of Chicago Press. All rights reserved. Reprinted by permission.

*schemas,* can alter a sense of identity and perhaps a style of interpersonal expression. The second category, *shifting schemas of significant others,* can alter views about the intentions of others, the interpretation of their behavior, and plans for how to act accordingly.

The third category, *shifting role-relationship models* can more globally change a state of mind. Suppose the topic is mourning the loss of a deceased person. If the self and the deceased are viewed in terms of a relationship of mutuality and caretaking, then the state will be one of sad pining. If, however, the relationship is viewed as one in which there was constant frustration and annoyance because of the bad acts of the other, the loss of the other might be seen as an occasion for relief. It is not uncommon in the course of mourning to alternate states of such negative and positive valences. The presence of ambivalence prior to the loss, for example, can lead to such alternating states following the loss. The confusing oscillation between states, as well as the fact that ambivalence during mourning is felt at all, can lead to yet other states such as shame and guilt.

This leads us to the fourth level listed in Table 4–3, which is *shifting value schemas* or critic roles. All mental intentions and memories of behaviors are at some time usually appraised in relation to schematized values. Values may be arranged according to the standpoint of various possible internalized critics or introjects (Horowitz, 1991b; Loevinger, 1976). Which schema of values and which critic role are most active in a given state of mind will affect the experience of esteem (or its deflation) in that state of mind, whether the person feels pride or shame, guilt or self-reward. These include the imagined perspectives of gods and ideological groups as well as parental introjects and other sources of value.

The final level described in Table 4–3 has to do with *shifting executive "we" schemas.* The emotion and attitude, as well as styles of action, may vary, whether the person centers on the self as an individual "I" or views the self as part of a larger grouping or a "we." Patriotic martyrdom may occur in the latter organization, selfish flight in the former.

As mentioned earlier, the outcome of regulation can be examined and defined in terms of intrapsychic or interpersonal levels. It is much more difficult to be reliable about the intrapsychic level, because the inferences must rest entirely on self-report and observations of expressive behavior in very intimate situations such as psychotherapy. The interpersonal outcomes are usually easier to recognize but may have their own complexity. It is helpful to separate the intrapsychic effects from the interpersonal outcomes of altering person schemas. Table 4–4 shows the former, and Table 4–5 the latter.

TABLE 4-4

**Control of Person Schemas and Role-Relationship Models: Intrapsychic Outcome**

| Level | Outcome of Regulation | | Outcome of Dysregulation |
|---|---|---|---|
| | Adaptive | Maladaptive | |
| A. Altering self schemas | Improved understanding of situation; enriched sense of identity | Excessively grand or inferior beliefs about self; taking on a bad self schema to avoid identity diffusion; alternating "personalities" | Identity diffusion, states of depersonalization |
| B. Altering schemas of other person | Enriched understanding of the intentions, motives, and predictable patterns of other | Disregard of nature of other to preserve fantasy or personal stereotypes; changing the object of a feeling, wish, source of threat from a more or less pertinent one (displacement) | Impoverished understanding of other as a center of feelings and initiative |
| C. Altering role-relationship models | Resilient change in internal working model of a current situation; useful learning by identification of self to role of other | Role reversals in a way inappropriate to the situation; switching working models into all-good or all-bad views of the relationship; changing the agent or source of an activity, wish, or feeling from self to other or other to self (role-reversal, projecting) | Annihilation anxiety or panic on separations, states of derealization |
| D. Altering person appraisal schemas (critic roles) | Sagacious monitoring and judging of self and others, and of future critique of present choices; maintaining useful vows and commitments | Unrealistic devaluation or idealization of self and/or others; switching values so rapidly that doubt paralyzes thought or action so that good intentions are not maintained | Inability to evaluate moral consequences |
| E. Altering executive "we" schemas | Restorative sense of being a part of something beyond self; generating responsibility for others | Excessive surrender of best interests of self; excessive self-centeredness | States of alienation |

Note: From "Role Relationship Models Configuration (RRMC)" by M. J. Horowitz et al., in M. J. Horowitz (Ed.), *Person Schemas and Maladaptive Interpersonal Patterns*, 1991, Chicago: University of Chicago Press. Copyright 1991 by University of Chicago Press. All rights reserved. Reprinted by permission.

**TABLE 4–5**

**Control of Person Schemas and Role-Relationship Models: Interpersonal Outcomes**

| Level | Adaptive | Outcome of Regulation — Maladaptive | Outcome of Dysregulation |
|---|---|---|---|
| A. Altering self schemas | Increases in competence and resilience within a situation; improved fit of behavior to the situation | Jarring shift in "personality"; acting in a too-superior or too-inferior way; using others as if they were part of or extensions of the self | Inability to use relationships with others to stabilize a sense of identity |
| B. Altering schemas of other person | Increases in understanding, empathy, and "reading" of another during an interaction | Reacting by an internal misperception of the other; provoking the other to conform to an internal misperception (projective identification); short circuiting to an inappropriate all-good or all-bad view of other. Changing the object of a feeling, wish, source of threat from the most pertinent one to a less pertinent one (displacement) | Chaotic views about another in a situation |
| C. Altering role-relationship models | Useful trials of a new pattern for a situation | Disguising or undoing an intended script sequence by running an alternative, compromise, or opposite one (undoing, passive-aggression). Shimmering alterations of contradictory patterns; pretense of roles that are not felt authentically; acting out an "obligatory script" rather than acting flexibly as an actual situation unfolds; changing the agent or source of an idea, emotion, or act from self to other or other to self | Inflexible preservation of an inappropriate interaction pattern |
| D. Altering person appraisal schemas (critic roles) | Pointing out following of or deflections from values, rules, commitments in self and others in a useful way to give rewards, pride, or to improve situation in future | Irrational assumption of other's values to avoid a social tension; inhibition of spontaneity by excessive monitoring; attributing blame outward irrationally to protect self-esteem | Impulsive punitive or revenge behaviors against self or others |
| E. Altering executive "we" schemas | Acting responsibly to care for others and to care for self as situations demand | Unrealistic abnegations of self; suddenly selfish or autistic acts that disrupt relationship | Inability to take care of others |

*Note:* From "Role Relationship Models Configuration (RRMC)" by M. J. Horowitz et al., in M. J. Horowitz (Ed.), *Person Schemas and Maladaptive Interpersonal Patterns,* 1991, Chicago: University of Chicago Press. Copyright 1991 by University of Chicago Press. All rights reserved. Reprinted by permission.

91

A person can ward off certain views of self, others, role-relationship models and cycles of role-relationship models by the use of defenses. In addition, dreaded states of mind can also be defensively avoided by shifting values, activating or inhibiting different personifications of critic roles, and by changing executive agency schemas (e.g., shifting from a "we" to an "I" or vice versa).

## Control Processes and Psychotherapy Technique

If we want to help a person gain conscious awareness and so conscious control we can do so best by interpretation of how and why that which is warded off is warded off. Using the special property of consciousness that allows a deliberate focusing of attention, the person may be able to alter control processes. Telling someone, "You are repressing your anger at your mother because you are afraid of hurting her and feeling guilty," may work because the person then can stop inhibiting ideas and feelings by attending to the target object (mother) and the target topic (self feeling anger, self feeling afraid, and self imagining feeling guilty). We know this can and does happen in therapy and analysis; however, it may *not* work because the interpretation does not tell the patient how he avoids or distorts conscious thought and how he may consciously refocus attention.

By getting to the level of control processes, interventions can be made that say how the patient may use increased mindfulness to change. This would lead to therapist statements such as, "You are avoiding the topic of your mother," "You are avoiding remembering how you felt last month when . . . ," and "You are organizing your experiences by a view of yourself as the strong protector of your weak mother to numb your feeling of resentment that your mother was not a strong protector of you when you felt weak."

## Microanalysis of Psychotherapy Discourse

How defensive control processes occur during the actual statements in psychotherapy is shown in the following example (Horowitz, Cooper et al., 1992, pp. 331–333).

The subject was a young married woman who suffered from a social phobia. She was seen in exploratory psychotherapy in a research context that involved recording of all sessions. By a variety of maneuvers, she warded off entry into states of intense shame characterized by ideas that she had performed badly before others. In the state of *shame,* there was a dreaded self schema of being worthless, degraded, and weak. She protected herself from feeling ashamed with states of *surly sarcasm,* organized by a stronger self schema as a critical observer of others; by a state of *irritable whining,* organized by a self schema as a disappointed but needy person; or by a state of *withdrawal,* organized by a self schema as an eccentric loner. Each of these states and self schemas was experienced as less dangerous than a desired state of *excitement,* and its obligatory linkage in a script that led toward humiliation because, in this script, as in the earlier example, she might become enthralled with another person and the other then might abuse and abandon her.

In an hour rated by both a team using defense mechanisms categories and a team using control process categories, the patient was referring ambiguously toward some before-the-hour experiences that had positive transference elements, including ones in which she felt at risk of becoming too excited about the relationship with the therapist.

She began this hour with an episode that was judged as passive-aggression by defense mechanism categories and that, in control process categories, involved a change in role-relationship models from being an interesting, trusting, and vulnerable patient wanting attention from a trustworthy therapist to being an inferior, vulnerable patient wanting attention from an indifferent, self-centered therapist to whom she responded with passive-aggressive hostility by provocatively neglecting to follow his leads for discussion in the therapy hour.

She then shifted the topic under discussion away from the relationship with the therapist and told a story about how her husband had neglected one of her creative products. This was a relatively minor incident that was less threatening than the feeling she was experiencing, or vulnerable to experiencing, within the transference and toward the therapist. This story about how the husband had neglected her creative product was judged as displacement. Here we can analyze that episode of displacement in control process terms.

The patient said she was still mad that her husband, by neglect, had harmed one of her creative products. The therapist repeated a phrase the patient had just uttered with a questioning tone. She responded, "Yes, and it turned into more of a symbol of something else." She did not clarify what that "something else" was, but it seemed to be her anger at her husband for using and then neglecting her (just as she anticipated the therapist would use and then neglect her). Instead of dealing with the central relationship concepts, she stayed on the topic of the husband's neglect of and harm to the creative product. She said, "I accused him of not thinking of [the product] as very significant; it was so trivial to him and I had worked really hard on it." She continued by telling the therapist some details about the product. She then shifted to describing her resentment targeted at a friend of her husband who she felt had neglected her.

This episode was judged as a displacement because the patient shifted annoyance about her husband not caring for her to her husband not caring for a product of her creation. Because the particular item could be taken as trivial, she could dismiss the episode—and so her anger—as unimportant, thus reducing the danger of excessive rage, humiliation for being enraged, and the threat of rejection and abandonment because she got angry. She also displaced anger from her husband to his friend.

In terms of processes of control, this episode involved shifting concepts, shifting the appraisal of importance of a chain of concepts, and shifting schemas of the other person. The topic was now her husband's attitude toward her and her things. Of the array of concepts on this topic, she facilitated expression of a relatively minor concept (his neglect of a thing) and inhibited a major concept (his neglect of her). She even underplayed the importance to herself of her creative product. The evidence was in the videotape of this episode that showed a discord between the higher intensity of anger in her voice prosodics and the lower intensity of the mild language she used verbally.

She shifted from a self schema to an object-symbol-of-self schema. As already mentioned, her husband neglecting "it" is less anxiety-provoking than her husband neglecting her (see Figure 4–1). In a later moment, she

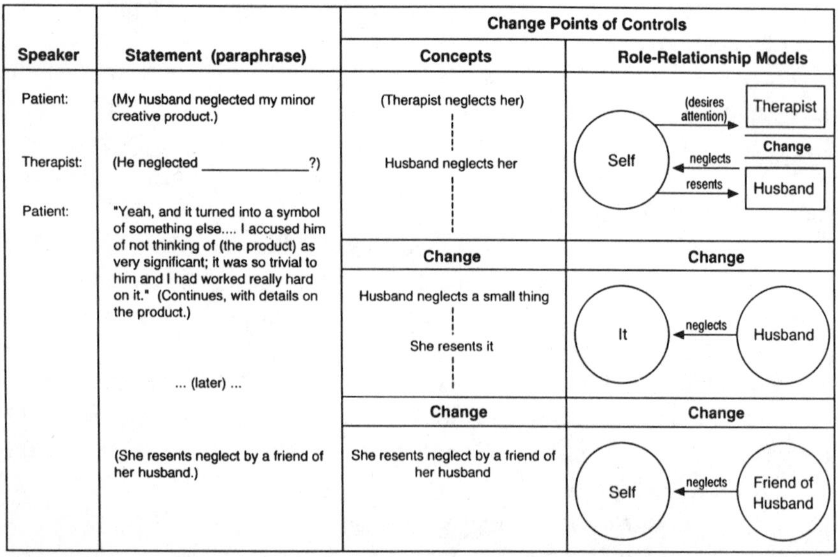

**Figure 4–1.** Modeling the episode of displacement. From "Control Process and Defenses Mechanisms" by M. J. Horowitz et al., 1992, *Journal of Psychotherapy Practice and Research,* 1, pp. 324–336. Copyright 1992 by University of Chicago Press. Reprinted by permission.

focused on a friend of her husband rather than on the husband or the therapist as the target object. This change is shifting the schemas of other persons in the role-relationship model of being neglected by the other and then reacting resentfully. The other is shifted from "husband" to "his friend."

## CONCLUSION

Control process theory is derived from studies of how people under conflict modify their thought and communication to avoid states of unwanted emotion. Control process theory is integrated with defense mechanisms theory from psychoanalysis and information processing theory from cognitive science; it can provide a microanalytic statement of how defensive episodes are formed. By focusing on this microanalysis of formation, the clinician may gain more insight into how to help a patient make small but incremental changes in attention deployment. Gradually, this can alter habitual styles of avoidance or distortion. Focused as it is on small-order changes in ideas, forms, and schemas of organization, control process theory may also help researchers develop new measures of warding-off behaviors.

## REFERENCES

Asch, S. (1946). Forming impressions of personality. *Journal of Abnormal and Social Psychology 41,* 258–90.

Bandura, A. (1982). The self and mechanisms of agency. In J. Suls (Ed.), *Psychological perspectives on the self* (vol. 1). Hillsdale, NJ: Erlbaum.

Bartlett, R. C. (1932). *Remembering: A study in experimental and social psychology.* Cambridge: Cambridge University Press.

Bond, M., Gardner, S., Christian, J., & Sigal, J. S. (1983). Empirical study of self-rated defense styles. *Archives of General Psychiatry, 40,* 333–338.

Breuer, J., & Freud, S. (1958). Studies on hysteria. *The standard edition of the complete psychological works of Sigmund Freud* (Vol. 2). London: Hogarth Press. (Original work published 1895)

Eells, T., Horowitz, M. J., Stinson, C., & Fridhandler, B. (1993). Self-representation in anxious states of mind: A comparison of psychodynamic models. In Z. V. Segal & S. J. Blatt (Eds.), *Self-representation and emotional disorder: cognitive and psychodynamic perspectives.* New York: Guilford Press.

Freud, A. (1936). *The ego and mechanisms of defense.* New York: International Universities Press.

Freud, S. (1953). The interpretation of dreams. In J. Strachey (Ed.), *The standard edition of the complete psychological works of Sigmund Freud.* London: Hogarth Press. (Original work published 1900)

Greenberg, J. R., & Mitchell, S. A. (1983). *Object relations in psychoanalytic theory.* Cambridge, MA: Harvard University Press.

Hastie, R. (1981). Schematic principles in human memory. In E. T. Higgins, C. P. Herman, & M. Zanna (Eds.), *Social cognition: The Ontario symposium.* Hillsdale, NJ: Erlbaum.

Horowitz, M. J. (1975). Sliding meanings: A defense against threat in narcissistic personalities. *International Journal of Psychoanalytic Psychotherapy, 4,* 167–180.

Horowitz, M. J. (1977). Cognitive and interactive aspects of splitting. *American Journal of Psychiatry, 134,* 549–553.

Horowitz, M. J. (1979). *States of mind* (1st ed.). New York: Plenum Press.

Horowitz, M. J. (1987). *States of mind: Configurational analysis of individual psychology* (2nd ed.). New York: Plenum Press.

Horowitz, M. J. (1988a). *Introduction to psychodynamics.* New York: Basic Books.

Horowitz, M. J. (Ed.). (1988b). *Psychodynamics and cognition.* Chicago: University of Chicago Press.

Horowitz, M. J. (1991a). Introduction to the hysterical (histrionic) personality disorder: Core traits. In M. J. Horowitz (Ed.), *Hysterical personality style and histrionic personality disorder* (2nd ed.). Northvale, NJ: Aronson.

Horowitz, M. J. (1991b). *Person schemas and maladaptive interpersonal patterns.* Chicago: University of Chicago Press.

Horowitz, M. J., Cooper, S., Fridhandler, B., Perry, J. C., Bond, M., & Vaillant, G. (1992). Control processes and defense mechanisms. *Journal of Psychotherapy Practice and Research, 1,* 324–336.

Horowitz, M. J., Ewert, M., & Milbrath, C. (1992). *States of mind: Rating to assess control of emotion during discourse.* Manuscript submitted for publication.

Horowitz, M. J., Merluzzi, T. V., Ewert, M., Ghannam, J. H., Hartley, D., & Stinson, C. H. (1991). Role-relationship models configuration (RRMC). In M. J. Horowitz (Ed.), *Person schemas and maladaptive interpersonal patterns.* Chicago: University of Chicago Press.

Horowitz, M. J., Milbrath, C., Jordan, D., Stinson, C. H., Ewert, M., Redington, D., Fridhandler, B., Reidbord, S., & Hartley, D. (1994). Expressive and defensive behavior during discourse on unresolved topics: A single case study. *Journal of Personality.*

Horowitz, M. J., Stinson, C. H., Curtis, D., Ewert, M., Redington, D., Singer, J. L., Bucci, W., Mergenthaler, E., Milbrath, C., & Hartley, D. (1993). Topics and signs: Defensive control of emotional expression. *Journal of Clinical and Consulting Psychology, 61,* 421–430.

Horowitz, M. J., Stinson, C. H., & Fridhandler, B. (1991). Person schemas and emotion. *Journal of the American Psychoanalytic Association, 39* (Suppl.), 173–208.

Horowitz, M. J., & Zilberg, N. (1983). Regressive alterations in the self-concept. *American Journal of Psychiatry, 140*(3), 284–89.

Kernberg, O. (1969). *Borderline conditions and pathological narcissism.* Northvale, NJ: Aronson.

Kohut, H. (1972). Thoughts on narcissism and narcissistic rage. *Psychoanalytic Study of the Child, 27,* 360–400.

Krumhansl, C., & Castellano, M. (1983). Dynamic processes in music perception. *Memory and Cognition, 11,* 325–34.

Loevinger, J. (1976). *Ego development.* San Francisco: Jossey-Bass.

Luborsky, L. (1984). *Principles of psychoanalytic psychotherapy.* New York: Basic Books.

Marcel, A. J. (1983a). Conscious and unconscious perception: An approach to the relations between phenomenal experience and perceptual processes. *Cognitive Psychology, 15,* 238–300.

Marcel, A. J. (1983b). Conscious and unconscious perception: Experiments on visual masking and word recognition. *Cognitive Psychology, 15,* 197–237.

Markus, H. (1977). Self-schemas and processing information about the self. *Journal of Personality and Social Psychology, 35,* 63–78.

Neisser, U. (1976). *Cognition and reality.* San Francisco: Freedman.

Ostrom, T. M., Pryor, J. B., & Simpson, D. D. (1981). The organization of social information. In E. T. Higgins, C. P. Herman, & M. Zanna (Eds.), *Social cognition: The Ontario symposium.* Hillsdale, NJ: Erlbaum.

Piaget, J. (1979). *Structuralism.* New York: Basic Books.

Rowen, J. (1990). *Subpersonalities: The people inside us.* London; New York: Routledge Press.

Rummelhart, D. E., Smolensky, P., McClelland, J. L., & Hinton, G. E. (1986). Schemata and sequential thought processes in PDP models. In D. E. Rummelhart & J. L. McClelland, (Eds.), *Parallel distributed processors: Studies in the microstructure of cognition.* Cambridge, MA: MIT Press.

Salzman, L. (1968). *The obsessive personality.* New York: Science House.

Taylor, S. E., & Crocker, J. (1981). Schematic bases of social information processing. In E. T. Higgins, C. P. Herman, & M. Zanna (Eds.), *Social cognition: The Ontario symposium.* Hillsdale, NJ: Erlbaum.

Vaillant, G. E. (1992). *The ego and mechanisms of defense.* Washington, DC: APA Press.

# 5

# An Information Feedback Theory of Emotions and Defenses

## HARTVIG DAHL

If we are ever to have a general theory of how the psychotherapeutic process works, then it is essential to base it on a clear and widely accepted theory of emotions. But it is equally apparent that at the present time there is no general acceptance of even a few competing theories. Since this is not to be a review of such theories, and since a theory is particularly essential to understand the relationship between emotions and defenses, I have little recourse but to first offer the one I know best, my own. My claim is simple: a vast amount of our knowledge of ourselves, of our goals, of the behavior of other human beings, and of that all-pervasive but elusive thing called our common sense, is based on the *implicit information content* of emotions. To the degree that this knowledge is implicit, we need a coherent, testable theory of emotions, such as the one I shall outline. This theory was originally part of a general "model of motivation," called "the appetite hypothesis of emotions" (Dahl, 1978, 1979), which I referred to as a "bio-psycho-social" model.

But first, to anchor the theory to some data, let's look at a real-life illustrative example of the expression of a powerful emotion and a significant defense. When I was a resident in training at the Menninger School of Psychiatry in Topeka in 1951, Dr. Karl, as he was familiarly known, taught a seminar in which the residents helped him write whatever book he was working on. On this occasion, our 11 A.M. class began with his asking for volunteers to read their assignments for the day, to wit, a description of a recent new patient. I raised my hand and he called on me. I began, "The patient was a warm and friendly 28-year-old single male . . . " He looked at me quizzically and asked, "What do you mean warm?" I replied, "I think you know what I mean, Dr. Karl." He leaned forward and looked down at his huge desk with his hands folded in front of him. After fully a minute of total silence in the room, he resumed by calling on another resident and there was no mention of the incident. After class, as we were on our way to lunch, one of my fellow residents asked me where I would be going next. How would I like leaving Topeka? When I got back to my ward after lunch, there was a sealed envelope, addressed to me. It had obviously been hand-delivered. I'm not sure what I felt as I opened it and read the following on his private note stationery:

Dear Dr. Dahl–

I sincerely apologize for losing my temper and speaking so sharply to you today. There is no way for you to know how much I *want* to get certain ideas across in a too short period. As one of the more alert and responsive students, you surprised me so with your reaction that I was thrown off balance. I don't mean to justify myself or neutralize this apology with this explanation.

I know you are working hard and trying to cooperate and improve. You've been a distinct help to me in the course. I'd be very sorry to think I did anything to discourage or hurt you permanently.

KAM

Common sense permits us to identify the central emotion and defense in this anecdote but it does not offer a coherent theory about the function of either the emotion or the defense. Nor does it help us with the disparate state of our theories of emotions or of defenses. Although there is fairly wide agreement that the function of a defense is to ward off an unbidden wish, action, or state (e.g., Freud, A. 1936; Vaillant, 1971, 1976, 1977), there is no comparable agreement on the function of the emotion. It is clear that KAM was angered by my brash confrontation. It is also clear that the thought of "permanently" hurting me confronted him with a dilemma about what to do. So, to use typical clinical terms, he compromised: He lost his "temper" and spoke sharply in his fantasies, but he remained silent. Whether he later repressed his angry wishes we shall never know, but he certainly inhibited them at the time.

The theory I shall outline will in the end allow us to understand not only common everyday events such as those in this anecdote but also the more subtle and complicated stories that patients tell when they come for psychotherapy or psychoanalysis. A fundamental presupposition of this theory is that emotions evolved as the primary means for our mammalian ancestors *to communicate to and understand fundamentally important intentions of other members of their own species.* In this sense, emotions constitute a basic *information processing system.* Moreover, emotions are the first language of every human infant before symbolic language is acquired.* And the commonsense knowledge that each of us has of our own and others' emotions underlies all our human interactions. What we need is a theory that accounts for the information-processing functions of emotions and explains our implicit knowledge of different classes of emotions that have radically different functions. I have presented the rationale, background, and support for such a theory (Dahl, 1978, 1979, 1991) together with an empirical classification of 400 emotion words (Dahl & Stengel, 1978) and a manual for classifying emotions in psychotherapy transcripts (Dahl, Hölzer, & Berry, 1992).

This summary of the theory is based on three basic propositions: (a) a 3-dimensional classification scheme for emotions, (b) the intentional concepts of *wishes and beliefs,*[†] and (c) the biologically rooted concept of *appetites.* The components are:

1. A three-dimensional classification scheme.
2. Basic definitions of *wish, belief, pleasure, unpleasure,* and *appetite.*
3. *Two major functional* classes of emotions.
4. A *causal feedback model* of the two classes.
5. The *relationship of the model to commonsense knowledge* of emotions.

## A THREE-DIMENSIONAL CLASSIFICATION
## OF EMOTIONS

I take for granted that any theory of emotions must include some account of both their similarities and their diversity; such an account implies, at a minimum, some system of classification. My system is an adaptation of the *n*-dimensional scheme that de Rivera (1962) used in his "decision" theory of emotions and the three dimensions are the same as the three polarities that Freud (1915) claimed are basic to mental life—Subject-Object, Pleasure-Unpleasure, and Active-Passive. My adaptation employs the following terminology.[‡]

---

*Searle (1983, p. 5) wrote: ". . . it seems to me obvious that infants and many animals that do not in any ordinary sense have a language or perform speech acts nonetheless have Intentional states. Only someone in the grip of a philosophical theory would deny that small babies can literally be said to want milk and that dogs want to be let out or believe that their master is at the door. . . . the causal basis of the animal's Intentionality is very much like our own, e.g., these are the dog's eyes, this is his skin, those are his ears, etc. Second, we can't make sense of his behavior otherwise." And, I would add, make sense of the dog's and the child's emotions in particular.

†These terms from our everyday common sense were first given a more formal status in Heider's (1958) "commonsense" or "naive" psychology and later in "folk" psychology (Stich, 1983) and intentional system theories (e.g., Dennett, 1978, 1987, 1988; Searle, 1983; and many others).

‡Among those who have proposed *n*-dimensional schemes only de Rivera, along with Descartes (see Stone, 1980) and Freud, has stressed the importance of the Subject-Object (IT-ME) dimension (cf.

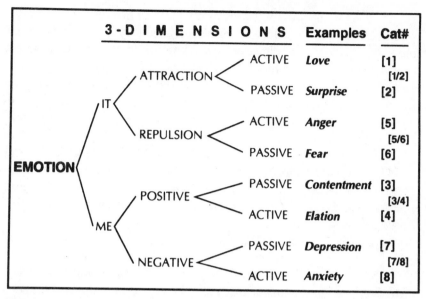

**Figure 5–1.** Emotion classification tree. A 3-dimensional decision tree—Orientation (IT-ME), Valence (Attraction-Repulsion/Positive-Negative), and Activity (Active-Passive)—yields 8 major categories of emotions, shown with typical emotion examples and arbitrarily assigned category numbers, and 4 intermediate categories of emotions (e.g. [½]), undecided on the Activity dimension.

| | |
|---|---|
| Orientation | IT-ME |
| Valence | Attraction-Repulsion or Positive-Negative |
| Activity | Active-Passive |

A classificatory tree showing the results of the intersections of these dimensions is illustrated in Figure 5–1 together with typical examples of emotion names for each of the eight ($2^3$) resulting categories.

If such a scheme has any validity it surely implies that ordinary people have some kind of internal representation of these dimensions and ought to be able to use them to classify emotions. In fact, in his dissertation, de Rivera showed that 20 judges could reliably classify 188 emotion words based primarily on their knowledge of definitions of these abstract dimensions. Stengel and I (Dahl & Stengel, 1978) replicated and extended his empirical classification using the preceding three dimensions. We

---

Wundt, 1907; Tolman, 1923; Schlosberg, 1954; Osgood, Suci, & Tannenbaum, 1957; Davitz, 1969). No theoretical (as distinguished from commonsense) rationale for this distinction is provided by any other major theory except perhaps that of Pribram and Melges (1969). "Orientation" (focus of attention on the object [IT] or the self [ME]), "valence," and "activity" (focus of control, i.e., whether the subject attributes control to the subject [Active] or to the object [Passive]) are abstract terms intended to capture the essential properties of the dimensions.

gave 58 judges definitions of each dimension and had the judges classify 400 emotion words to determine to what degree they shared both the implicit knowledge of the dimensions and knowledge of the internal states referred to by each emotion label.

The reliabilities (coefficient alphas) of these judgments by 58 judges for each of the three dimensions were .95, .99, and .97 respectively, and the intercorrelations among the dimensions were nil, providing important evidence for their empirical independence. Approximately 65% of the judged words were decided at $p < .05$ on all three dimensions; for 153 words, the choices were significant at $p < .001$ on each of the three dimensions. Moreover, the judges' ages and sex were uncorrelated with their choices.* Thus, despite the obvious fact that each person only has *direct* access to his own particular emotional states *and* in principle cannot have such access to another's internal state, and despite the fact that each person has a unique set of memories derived from his or her own developmental interactions, it seems necessary to assume substantial shared experiential referents to account for the judges' "shared variance" and agreement.

Even if we accept the tidy simplicity of this scheme, however, there is a certain arbitrariness to all classifications of emotions, as James (1890, p. 485) noted when he suggested that "the only question would be, does this grouping or that suit our purposes best?" For purposes of outlining the theory now, there were two results of special interest.

The first was that these abstract dimensions produced 12 major categories—8 main and 4 intermediate (as shown in Figures 5–1, 5–2, and 5–3)—which together appear to include most of the emotions that others have regarded as fundamental, based on a variety of criteria such as behavioral expressions (Darwin, 1872), instincts (McDougall, 1923), facial expressions (Ekman, 1973; Izard, 1971; Tomkins, 1970) and others (Davitz, 1969; Plutchik, 1962, 1980). For example, Dahl and Stengel's judges classified Izard's (1977) 10 designated "basic" (marked by *) and four "complex" (marked by †) emotions as follows: Love† [1]; Interest* [½]; Surprise* [2]; Joy* [¾]; Anger*, Contempt*, Hostility† [5]; Disgust* [⅚]; Fear* [6]; Shame*; Depression† [7], Guilt* [⅞]; Distress*, Anxiety† [8].

The second result was that the classification provided a *principled distinction* for two major *functional* classes of emotion: those about objects (IT) and those that are about one's own internal states (ME). Schwartz

---

*A complete list of the words along with the distribution of the judges' choices on each dimension appears in Dahl and Stengel (1978) and in Dahl et al. (1992).

and Trabasso (1984) produced evidence for the psychological reality of the IT-ME distinction in a study that showed 6-year-olds implicitly understand the classificatory dimensions as well as the implicit wishes and beliefs associated with the IT and ME emotions. Skeptics who find the $n$-dimensional classification implausible on other grounds should remind themselves that in the course of evolution just such $n$-dimensional computations were selected very early, allowing mobile animals with multiple senses to orient themselves in space and time by vision, smell, and sound. It is conceivable that evolution, having once selected whatever powerful computational methods underlay these capacities, might also use $n$-dimensional computational strategies for solving new problems such as the apparent need for conspecifics both to express and to recognize each other's intentions (i.e., wishes and beliefs). But first, some fundamental definitions.

## BASIC DEFINITIONS AND CHARACTERISTICS

### Wish, Belief, Pleasure, and Unpleasure

The theory of emotions as wishes and beliefs rests firmly on a definition of a *wish* as *an attempt to achieve perceptual identity and/or symbolic equivalence with a previous experience of satisfaction.* * A *belief* is an *"abstract concept" and/or perceptual experience "that is not disputed"* (Baars, 1988). *Pleasure,* in this model, is the *satisfaction of a wish* and *unpleasure* is the *nonsatisfaction of a wish.* These definitions have several decisive implications, some obvious, some not quite so. First, certain basic *initial experiences of satisfaction* are phylogenetically adapted, that is, they are wired in by evolution. As Deutsch and Deutsch (1966) put it:

> It is the taste of water, the feeling of satiety, the sensations from the genitalia that an animal finds rewarding. The connection of these sensations with need reduction is not one which is made by each individual animal. Such a connection . . . has been made by the process of natural selection. Only those animals which have found certain sensations rewarding have survived. Learning . . . has

---

*This definition is adapted from Freud's (1900) famous seventh chapter of the *Interpretation of Dreams* (cf. Dahl, 1965, 1978, 1979, 1983), in which he proposed two very different models of motivation: one based on wishes, a very modern-looking cognitive model, and the other on instinctual energy. It was the instinctual energy model that survived as the standard for psychoanalysis and has given rise to the current "crises" of theory. How different psychological history might have been had the cognitive model survived instead! I have been trying to resurrect it since 1965.

already occurred in the species; the individual need not recapitulate it. (pp. 143–144)

Second, memory is required to record the experiences. Third, memories, when activated by any means, serve as a *goal,* which is to repeat the
same experience of satisfaction (pleasure), that is, to achieve *perceptual
identity.* Freud (1900) even postulated that the initial activation might be
an hallucinatory fulfillment, an activation of the memory to hallucinatory intensity. Implausible as this may appear, Helen Keller (see Dahl,
1965) vividly described just such hallucinatory memories of previous experiences of satisfaction (e.g., the taste of ice cream) during the period
before she acquired language at about the age of six. The activation of
memories is the attempt to achieve perceptual identity; until then the
wish remains latent, that is, potential, or descriptively and/or dynamically unconscious.* Fourth, the inclusion of symbolic equivalence is to
provide for the well-known human capacity for finding and satisfying alternate wishes as substitutes for primary experiences of satisfaction.

And last, lest we be limited to highly restricted and stereotyped behavior, it is necessary to assume, with good evidence to support the assumption (e.g., Wolff, 1966; Sroufe & Waters, 1976; Nachman, Stern, &
Best, 1986), that novel experiences, for all their variety, are perceptually
identical in the sense of being classified on the property of their unex-
pectedness and the aroused emotion of mild surprise; novelty qua novelty
is an intrinsic experience of satisfaction. This attraction to novelty as-
sures a truly interesting creature, one with built-in opposing tendencies:
on the one hand to repeat the same old experiences of satisfaction, but on
the other to enlarge its repertoire, to satisfy its curiosity, and to expand
its range of experiences. Whereas once we were content with the taste of
milk alone, we can eventually acquire an appetite for such odd tastes as a
dry martini with onion.

## Appetite

There are four essential structural components to an *appetite:*

1. A *perception* of a specific internal (partly bodily) state (e.g., thirst
   or genital sensation).

---

*Koob and Bloom (1988, p. 720), as a result of their studies of "cellular and molecular mechanisms
of drug dependence," have in a sense reinvented the wheel (*wish* in this case) in their attempt to account for the intense craving experienced by opiate and cocaine addicts undergoing withdrawal.
They wrote, "If craving is defined as a memory for the pleasant aspects of the drug, then . . .
various external and internal signals can act as discriminative stimuli for eliciting the memory of
drug experiences and these memories may serve as motivational factors in drug recidivism."

2. An *implicit wish* to reinstate (achieve perceptual identity with) a *previous experience of satisfaction* (e.g., the taste of water or the sensations from copulation).
3. A *consummatory act* (e.g., drinking water or copulation).
4. A *reafferent perception* of the feedback from the consummatory act (e.g., the taste of water or the genital sensations and their motor accompaniments, which eventually terminate the act).

Lorenz (1965) emphasized the learning that takes place in the context of appetitive behavior through the "teaching function" of phylogenetically adapted motor patterns interacting with "the reafference which the organism produces for itself by performing the consummatory act in the adequate consummatory situation" (p. 88). In other words, the teaching is accomplished by the feedback that terminates a consummatory act (i.e., that satisfies the wish). As I wrote (Dahl, 1978; p. 389), "Using the model of infant feeding, we can say that the infant's consummatory act of sucking teaches it that the incoming fluid satisfies its appetites of hunger and thirst because that is the way the infant is built." And, I would now stress, built by natural selection in the course of evolution.

Appetites also have a number of conspicuous properties:

1. *Peremptoriness*—they function as *orders*.
2. *Selectivity* of objects—there are objects that are specifically necessary for their satisfaction.
3. *Displaceability* of objects—in the absence of the specific objects, substitutes may suffice.
4. A tendency of *self-stimulation* when satisfaction is possible.
5. A tendency to *expansion of range* and *refinement of discrimination* of experiences that will satisfy—in other words a tendency to acquire new "tastes."
6. Cyclicity.

## TWO MAJOR FUNCTIONAL CLASSES OF EMOTIONS

According to this theory, *emotions* are a special class of appetites, exhibiting the same structure as somatic appetites plus all but the last of the preceding properties of appetites. They function as *wishes* and *beliefs* in an evolutionarily given (phylogenetically adapted) nonverbal information feedback system, that is quintessentially *cognitive* in the sense of *knowing*. For the animal without symbolic language (which includes our evolutionary ancestors and every human before the acquisition of such symbolic language), emotions are the primary "intelligence" system for surviving in a complex world of many dangers and for communicating and recognizing the intentions of members of one's own species.

The essential difference of emotions from somatic appetites lies in the fact that two major classes of emotions, the IT and the ME emotions, are specialized to fulfill different structural components of appetites. The IT emotions include the functions of the first three structural components: (a) the *perception of a specific intentional state,* (b) an implicit *wish* toward an object, and (c) a *consummatory act;* the ME emotions function as the fourth structural component of an appetite, namely (4) the *reafferent perception* of the feedback information about satisfaction or nonsatisfaction accompanying the consummatory act. Thus we have the following definitions and examples:

- IT Emotions have objects, function as *appetitive wishes* about those objects, and can be represented as: "*P* wishes that *x*," where *x* is one of four formally definable classes of *consummatory acts,* defined by the intersection of two dimensions, *valence* (Attraction-Repulsion) and *activity* (Active-Passive). Figure 5–2 shows the four generic emotional appetites for objects (each with its generic wish and generic consummatory behavior, and typical example).

- ME Emotions do not have objects, function as *beliefs,* and can be represented as "*P* believes that *y*," where *y* is information about the status of *satisfaction* or *nonsatisfaction* of appetitive and other significant wishes. The satisfaction of wishes results in the experience of *pleasure,* while nonsatisfaction results in the experience of *unpleasure.* Four generic classes are defined by the intersection of the

| Cat# | Generic Wish | Generic GOAL: Consummation | Typical Emotion |
|------|--------------|----------------------------|-----------------|
| 1 | Active Attraction (to) **IT** | **Take Care of** It | *Love* |
| 1/2 | | | *Interest* |
| 2 | Passive Attraction (from) **IT** | **Behold/Explore** It | *Surprise* |
| 5 | Active Repulsion (to) **IT** | **Get Rid of** It | *Anger* |
| 5/6 | | | *Disgust* |
| 6 | Passive Repulsion (from) **IT** | **Escape from** It | *Fear* |

**Figure 5–2.** IT emotions. The four main IT emotion categories with arbitrarily assigned category numbers (cf. Figure 5–1) and two intermediate categories indicated by a slash for words undecided on the Activity dimension (i.e., [½] and [⅚]).

| Cat# | Generic Belief | Experience: GOAL | | Typical Emotion |
|------|----------------|------------------|---|-----------------|
| 3 | Passive Positive **ME** *Wishes have been satisfied* | | | Contentment |
| 3/4 | | **PLEASURE** [Repeat] | | Happiness |
| 4 | Active Positive **ME** *Wishes going well* | | | Elation |
| 7 | Passive Negative **ME** *Wishes can't be satisfied* | | | Depression |
| 7/8 | | **UNPLEASURE** [Get rid of] | | Guilt |
| 8 | Active Negative **ME** *Wishes not going well* | | | Anxiety |

**Figure 5–3.** ME emotions. The four main ME emotion categories with arbitrarily assigned category numbers (cf. Figure 5–1) and two intermediate categories indicated by a slash for words undecided on the Activity dimension (i.e., [3/4] and [7/8]).

two dimensions, *valence* (Positive-Negative) and *activity* (Active-Passive). Figure 5–3 shows the four generic ME emotions (each with its generic belief, unique experience, goal, and typical example).

## A CAUSAL FEEDBACK MODEL

Figure 5–4 is a schematic representation of a causal information feedback model. The solid black rectangles represent the relationships among four different motivational states:

1. IT emotions, which function as appetitive wishes about an object.
2. Somatic appetites—the wishes involved in hunger, sex, and thirst.
3. Positive ME emotions in which the experience of Pleasure functions as a belief that the wish *can* be satisfied and provides information feedback that facilitates further consummation.
4. Negative ME emotions in which the experience of Unpleasure functions as a belief that the wish *cannot* be satisfied and provides information feedback that inhibits and provokes defenses against the wish and/or the consummatory behavior and/or the negative ME emotion itself.

The different feedback functions of the positive and negative ME emotions reflect a difference long recognized in a behavioral context as positive and negative reinforcement.

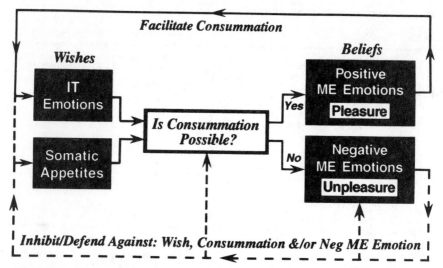

**Figure 5–4.** Emotions as an informational feedback system. The solid black rectangles represent four motivational states—IT emotions, which function as appetitive *wishes* about an object; somatic appetites, which are *wishes* involved in hunger, sex, and thirst; positive ME emotions in which the experience of Pleasure functions as a *belief* that the wish can be satisfied and provides feedback (solid arrows) that tends to facilitate further consummation; and negative ME emotions, in which the experience of Unpleasure functions as a *belief* that the wish cannot be satisfied and provides feedback (dashed arrows) that tends to inhibit and provoke defenses against the wish, the consummatory behavior, and/or the negative ME emotion itself. The center rectangle represents a decision process to determine the possibility of consummation of the wishes and whose result is a positive or negative ME emotion.

Note that the question in Figure 5–4, "Is consummation possible?" involves a computation that is assumed to be made automatically following the activation of *any* significant wishes including the wishes implicit in the IT emotions. The outcome of this computation, *Yes* or *No,* determines the resulting major category of ME emotion. It seems likely that many factors, historical and situational, influence the computation. Similarly, the consummatory act may or may not actually be carried out depending on many of the same factors. Part of a comprehensive program of research on emotions would have to include systematic investigation of these determinants.

It is a crucial premise of this theory that the causal effect (function) of the positive ME emotions is that of *facilitation* in the sense of helping to stabilize the memory of the experience of satisfaction, promoting both its reactivation under suitable conditions and fantasies about the objects involved. On the other hand, Frijda (1986; p. 38), a major emotion theorist, has claimed, "Joyful behavior has no function in the sense that angry or fearful behavior has. It has no purpose, it is just there." So here we have contradictory hypotheses.

Similarly, the causal effect of negative ME emotions is that of *inhibition* in the sense of a signal to invoke some kind of *defense* against (a) the wish itself, that is, the activation of the memory of the experience of satisfaction, (b) the consummation of the wish, and/or (c) the negative ME emotion itself. Needless to say, there is great variation in the success of such defenses, particularly against the negative emotion itself, often leading to auxiliary means such as alcohol and other drugs to get rid of the aversive quality of negative ME emotions.

## THE EMOTION THEORY AND
## COMMONSENSE KNOWLEDGE

Elsewhere (Dahl et al., 1992), I adapted a homely little scenario, created by Trabasso (1982), to illustrate an everyday commonsense application of the theory to a made-up story. But now if we apply the feedback model represented in Figure 5–4 to the KAM anecdote, we can understand several important features. First, it is clear that Menninger was taken aback by his student's abrupt challenge to his authority. It aroused wishes to permanently hurt and damage his student (Active Repulsion to IT). Second, he also made explicitly clear that he felt he had lost his temper and said some angry things in fantasy. So the answer to one question about consummation was yes, because he imagined doing serious harm. But in fact he was totally silent the entire time, so the answer to the other question about consummation was no, because he did not actually carry out the harmful actions. Thus, third, the yes enabled him to satisfy his rage in fantasy, but the no made him defend against acting out the consummation, and he ended up feeling guilty (Negative ME). Then he instituted another defense—this time directed at his guilt—and he tried to undo it by writing the note of apology, thereby in the same act also satisfying his angry wishes by letting the resident know what harmful wishes he had inhibited. A day's work all in a couple of hours! And the present theory offers a coherent explanation for KAM's observable ambivalent behavior.

One nonobvious advantage of this theory is that it fills an important theoretical niche in dual or multiple code models of mental representations such as Bucci's (1985) model, which posits separate, interacting verbal and nonverbal systems of mental representation but simply assigns emotions to the nonverbal system without specifying their structure and functions.

Another not necessarily self-evident advantage of these concepts lies in their *representation* of the *information content* of emotions as wishes and beliefs.* Since emotions can be systematically represented as propositional attitudes, (wishes and beliefs) (Dennett, 1987; p. 111), their propositional content can be incorporated into models and/or simulations of human cognitive processes, in particular, artificial intelligence models of cognition. Dyer (1983), for example, built commonsense knowledge of emotions into a computer program (BORIS) designed to understand emotions implicit in stories about everyday situations such as two people getting divorced.

Moreover one can systematically incorporate this model of the fundamental functions of emotions into intentional system theories that also use wishes and beliefs to predict and explain the behavior of complex bio-psycho-social systems. Both Dennett (1978, 1987, 1988) and Searle (1983), for example, claim that emotions are typical intentional states, yet neither has proposed or borrowed a theory of emotions that accounts for the inclusion of emotional states as wishes and beliefs. Among 48 states that Searle (p. 4) listed as potential intentional states were 38 explicit emotions including such obvious examples as anger, anxiety, contempt, depression, disgust, elation, fear, grief, guilt, hate, irritation, joy, love, shame, and sorrow.

## THE RELATIONSHIP BETWEEN EMOTIONS AND DEFENSES

A central prediction of this theory follows directly from the lower feedback loop shown in Figure 5–4 and states that negative ME emotions should tend to be followed by defenses more often than other states. In her doctoral dissertation, Sharir (1991) tested the hypothesis that the sequence IT emotion→Negative ME emotion should significantly more often be followed by a formal defense than the sequence IT emotion→Positive ME emotion. Using data from videotapes of 3 hours

---

*Even, or perhaps especially, among emotion researchers, there is still remarkable disagreement and unclarity over the cognition/emotion distinction. There are those who believe (e.g., Lazarus, 1984, following Arnold, 1960) that "appraisal" precedes emotional states and those who believe (e.g., Zajonc, 1980, 1984) that "preferences need no inferences." My position is clear and, I have always thought, simple. I regard emotions as just another given-by-evolution form of knowing, that is, of cognizing. Thus, for example, anger *just is* a computation by the nonverbal system (see Bucci, 1985) whose generic knowledge (read *cognitive*) content is "an active repulsion toward an object," and anxiety *just is* a computation whose generic cognitive content is "there is a probability, $p < 1$ and $>0$, that a relevant wish cannot be satisfied" and depression indicates $p = 1$ for nonsatisfaction. For the positive ME emotions, contentment indicates a computation of $p = 1$ that a significant wish has been fulfilled and elation a probability approaching 1 that a wish can be or is being satisfied.

each (early, middle, and late) of 26 different short-term psychotherapy cases, she had one group of judges reliably classify all expressions of emotions in each 3-minute segment and other judges independently classify all defenses using Vaillant's (1971, 1977) categories. She found, with a unique time-series analysis procedure, that the data strongly supported the hypothesis: Defenses do indeed appear sooner and more often after expressions of IT emotions that are followed by Negative ME emotions than those that are followed by Positive ME emotions.

The emotion theory implicitly claims that defenses serve two main and quite different functions. The first function includes restricting awareness of (a) the *experience* of the emotion, (b) knowledge of the *wish* implicit in the IT emotion, (c) knowledge of the *consummatory behavior,* and (d) knowledge of the *belief* implicit in the ME emotion. And the second function includes inhibition of wishes and acts and beliefs, as well as substituting actions while not restricting awareness. In the KAM example, the latter were most apparent.

The theory also assumes that appetites may be manifested in one or more of four major representations. To illustrate, let us first use an example from one of our better known somatic appetites, *thirst.* Here a wish for a drink of cold water might be represented (a) linguistically in some variation of the thought, "I want a drink of cold water," or (b) as an image (e.g. a taste of water, or a visualization of a cup of cold water or a water fountain), (c) as a sensation of thirst, or finally (d) as an appropriate consummatory act for the original appetitive wish (e.g., simply walking to a fountain and drinking the water).

Analogously, to take the example of the emotional appetite of anger, which, we have postulated, embodies an implicit wish *to get rid of the object of the anger,* the wish might be represented (a) as a conscious wish linguistically in some variation of the thought (read: appraisal), "I'd like to kill him." Or it might be represented (b) as an image of the person being hit by a fast car or getting killed in a drive-by shooting, or (c) as a feeling of rage. But (d) it might also be possible to carry out an assault (hitting, shooting, knifing) without the accompanying affect. In fact, under conditions of emergency, the latter representation of the wish in the behavior alone may sometimes be its clearest expression. To reiterate, there are at least four separate major ways in which a wish to get rid of an object may be represented: linguistically, as a nonverbal image, as an emotion, and as a consummatory act. That we often see such a wish represented in all four ways does not alter that we also see them represented separately or in various combinations. The important idea is that defenses may be directed at all or any combination of these expressions.

Odd as it may seem at first, it is also possible to think of the IT emotion itself (anger in the preceding example) occurring as a result of a defensive process if one presupposes that a linguistic (cognitive) representation is the basic form of representing the concept, as might be inferred from Arnold's and Lazarus's "appraisal" process (cf. preceding footnote). The problem with this possibility is that the appraisal process would still require the addition of a motive for the defense against the wish. And it is this motive that the information feedback theory provides in the function of the negative ME emotions. Although the wish may indeed become the primary object of the defense, the same wish may still manifest itself in one or more of the other representations.

To recapitulate, the IT emotion categories together with their four different possible representations appear to capture a wide range of clinically important behaviors. I believe that the most important of these is the inclusion of consummatory acts (implied or stated) that imply an emotion state even if it is not labeled or stated explicitly. A classification system of emotions that captures the emotions implicitly expressed in these actions is vital.

Beyond these first considerations, it is a commonplace that one emotion is substituted for another and inferably thus functions as a defense. For example, instead of experiencing (expressing) anger or irritation, the individual might offer phrases such as: "I was surprised at him," "I was taken aback," "I felt anxious all day," "I couldn't sleep last night," or "For some reason I can't concentrate." And this raises the interesting hypothesis that an unexpected emotion in a particular context might be an important clue to the operation of some defenses. It also follows that sudden changes in the kind of emotion expressed or in the manner of its expression are clues to the operation of a defense.

Common examples of the use of one emotion to defend against another are implicit in the different IT-ME emotion functions. For instance, if a person experiences a blind fury one moment and then shortly afterward no longer feels furious, but is intensely anxious, the feedback theory would claim that the anxiety expresses the person's *belief* that the fury could not be successfully consummated. In other words, acting on the furious wish would be futile (for whatever simple or complex reasons); and the information content of the anxiety would express that belief. Another commonplace example of a similar transformation that might indeed function defensively would be that of, say, an adolescent girl initially feeling intense love and infatuation with a boy classmate, but shortly thereafter finding herself acting timid and feeling bashful and shy. In a manner exactly analogous to the first example, we can reasonably infer from the theory that the girl's shyness expresses her belief that her love and infatuation cannot be consummated with that boy. In both instances—the anxiety replacing fury and the shyness replacing infatuation—the ME emotion can be understood as serving a defensive function in its expression of the belief that the IT wish could not be fulfilled. Of course, it is not accidental that the ME emotions in these examples (as well as implied by the theory) are negative ME emotions.

Differences in the intensity of emotional experience also might reflect the operation of defenses. For example, within the eight categories of emotions, a wide range of intensity is expressed by different emotion labels. We know that labels for emotions range in intensity from strong to moderate to minimal. The resulting emotion, depending on the context, may well be a clue to whether the emotional expression is proportionate to the situation (e.g., when rage is expectable, only mild irritation is expressed or when a major danger is met with slight worry). Here are a number of examples of emotion labels varying in intensity from strong to mild:

Category 1  Loving→Adoring→Devoted→Fond→Friendly

Category 5  Rage→Fury→Hate→Anger→Annoyance→Irritation→ Disinterest

Category 7  Despairing→Hopeless→Depressed→Gloomy→ Discouraged→Sad

Category 8  Panicky→Distressed→Anxious→Nervous→Upset→ Worried

Nonetheless, the idea that differences in intensity reflect defensive operations is only one of several possibilities. It is easy, for example, to point to people who almost never express "strong" emotions (or their implicit wishes), and it is easy to infer strong inhibitions (defenses) against such emotions. Moreover, it is certainly possible to infer that different intensities of the wish implicit in the emotions that we label with such different words are the result of some "control" or "inhibition" process that has different characteristics from those clinicians attribute to defenses. My point is simply that a judgment about which is which is a complex matter, requiring a large context to make a reliable and valid inference about the presence or absence of a defense.

This raises the central importance of context in assessing the appropriateness of any emotional expression in a given situation. A mere catalog of typical precipitants for particular emotional reactions will have only limited use because the consequent emotions are the result of the attribution of *meaning* to the occasion and this *meaning* will determine the emotion. For example, receiving an insult may, depending on the context, produce any of the following emotional states, represented linguistically:

| Emotion | Perception/Cognition |
|---------|---------------------|
| Anger | She insulted me so now I really hate her. |
| Fear | I can't counterattack, but I can escape. |
| Depression | I will never get what I want from her now. |
| Anxiety | What'll she do next? I'm not sure I can get her off my back. |
| Guilt | This is the punishment I deserve for what I did. |
| Love | Oh, she finally noticed me; thank God. |
| Surprise | That's amazing, I thought she was indifferent. |
| Joy | Oh great! Now I can really clobber her. |
| Contentment | Finally I've got her goat; now I can relax. |

Earlier I considered the possibility of an IT emotion itself serving a defensive function against its own implicit wish, and I pointed out that what was missing from this conception was a motivation for the defense such as that provided by negative ME emotions in the present theory. But it is also possible to imagine that negative ME emotions themselves might serve a defensive function despite my claim that defenses tend to be erected against the negative ME emotions because of their unpleasurable properties. However, we can speculate that, prior to instituting other defenses against the negative ME emotion, this emotion itself has one essential characteristic of many defenses, namely, to hide and/or inhibit the original wishes implicit in the IT emotions. If this speculation were true, then the closeness in time of a defense to a negative ME emotion (compared with a positive ME emotion) in Sharir's study (1992) might simply reflect the possibility that the classified defense and the negative ME emotion are merely redundant measures of the same defensive process. A careful retrospective examination of the kind of defenses and the kind of negative ME emotions in her sample of 78 sessions might shed light on this speculation.

It follows from the feedback model that unsatisfied wishes are the ultimate cause of negative ME emotions and therefore of defenses. But since defenses can operate against the wish, and/or the IT emotion, and/or it's consummation, and/or the resulting negative ME emotion, any expression (including an inappropriate emotion) that, in the context, appears unexpected given the situation, is a strong index of the operation of a defense. On the other hand, the absence of any significant defense would be marked by the expression of the wish, the IT emotion, and the appropriate ME emotion with its information content that the wish implied by the IT emotion either can or cannot be satisfied.

If, as I have claimed, an unsatisfied wish gives rise to a negative ME emotion, and this in turn tends to inhibit or provoke defenses against the wish and so on, how then can we account for the fact that most people have at least some unsatisfied wishes that do not leave them consciously anxious or depressed? It is clear that some such wishes need not be repressed or rendered unconscious; they may remain quite accessible to verbal expression, but are unaccompanied by either IT emotions or negative ME emotions. The quick answer to this question is that while growing up we can develop successful defenses against the emotional expression of wishes that we cannot satisfy. The most effective of these are presumed to be what Vaillant (1977) termed "mature" defenses such as altruism, humor, suppression, anticipation, and sublimation. The true answer to the question would lie in the results of longitudinal studies of the development of personality from birth to advanced maturity with careful assessments of both emotions and defenses at every stage. But that is another story beyond the scope of this chapter.

## CONCLUSION

The information feedback theory of emotions and defenses, though relatively simple, is not simplistic; it can explain very complex behaviors. Among its central strengths are the following factors:

1. It is a unified theory of motivation that includes both emotional and somatic appetites as well as emotions that signal the satisfaction or nonsatisfaction of basic wishes, and it attributes to emotions motivational roles that are independent of the somatic appetites.

2. It accounts for certain otherwise puzzling phenomena such as people seeking out danger and fear-arousing situations, but typically when their escape is assured (in fact or fantasy).

3. On the other hand, it also allows us to understand why anger and fear are so often thought of as aversive (produce unpleasure) because the exigencies of life often make satisfaction of these two appetites difficult or impossible.

4. The ME emotions conserve a major tenet of behaviorist theories, that of positive and negative reinforcement; negative emotions do indeed tend to inhibit appetitive behavior and positive emotions

tend to facilitate it. In common sense, these are the different consequences of hope and hopelessness.

5. It postulates that the most intense experiences might include satisfying several appetites at once, such as sexual attraction to, caring for, fascination with, and perhaps a slight flavoring of anger and fear.

6. It hypothesizes that a central task of growing up is the development of appetite controls that do not have the automatic properties of defenses, and so are "mature" defenses.

7. It offers a central hypothesis about change that explains two major facts from 5 decades of research. First, all treatments (including religious belief systems) help some people some of the time. Second, no single treatment helps all people all the time. The hypothesis is that the final common pathway in every treatment (psychological, pharmaceutical, social) is a reduction in negative ME emotions, a process that implies the alteration of some defenses.

A large-scale study now underway of transcribed sessions from 15 psychoanalyses should help shed new light on the information feedback theory's postulates as well as major hypotheses derived from it. The next few years ought to be fruitful.

## REFERENCES

Arnold, M. (1960). *Emotion and personality: Vol. 1. psychological aspects.* New York: Columbia University Press.

Baars, B. (1988). *A cognitive theory of consciousness* (p. 282). Cambridge: Cambridge University Press.

Bucci, W. (1985). Dual coding: A cognitive model for psychoanalytic research. *Journal of the American Psychoanalytic Association, 33,* 571–607.

Dahl, H. (1965). Observations on a "natural experiment": Helen Keller. *Journal of the American Psychoanalytic Association, 13,* 533–550.

Dahl, H. (1978). A new psychoanalytic model of motivation: Emotions as appetites and messages. *Psychoanalysis and Contemporary Thought, 1,* 375–408.

Dahl, H. (1979). The appetite hypothesis of emotions: a new psychoanalytic model of motivation. In C. E. Izard (Ed.), *Emotions in personality and psychopathology* (pp. 201–225). New York: Plenum Press.

Dahl, H. (1983). On the definition and measurement of wishes. In J. Masling (Ed.), *Empirical studies of psychoanalytical theories* (pp. 39–67). Hillsdale, NJ: Analytic Press.

Dahl, H. & Stengel, B. (1978). A classification of emotion words: A modification and partial test of de Rivera's decision theory of emotions. *Psychoanalysis and Contemporary Thought, 1,* 269–312.

Dahl, H. (1991). The key to understanding change: Emotions as appetitive wishes and beliefs about their fulfillment. In J. Safran & L. Greenberg (Eds.), *Emotion, psychotherapy and change* (pp. 130–165). New York: Guilford Press.

Dahl, H., Hölzer, M., & Berry, J. W. (1992). *How to classify emotions for psychotherapy research.* Ulm, Ger: Ulmer Textbank.

Darwin, C. (1872). *The expression of the emotions in man and animals.* London: John Murray.

Davitz, J. (1969). *The language of emotion.* New York: Academic Press.

Dennett, D. (1978). *Brainstorms: Philosophical essays on mind and psychology* (pp. 3–22). Cambridge: MIT Press.

Dennett, D. (1987). *The intentional stance.* Cambridge: MIT Press.

Dennett, D. (1988). Précis of The Intentional Stance. *Brain and Behavioral Sciences, 11,* 495–546.

de Rivera, J. (1962). A decision theory of emotions. *Dissertation Abstracts International* (University Microfilm # 62-2356).

Deutsch, J. A., & Deutsch, D. (1966). *Physiological psychology.* Homewood, IL: Dorsey Press.

Dyer, M. (1983). *In-depth understanding: A computer model of integrated processing for narrative comprehension.* Cambridge, MA: MIT Press.

Ekman, P. (Ed.). (1973). *Darwin and facial expression: A century of research in review.* New York: Academic Press.

Freud, A. (1946). *The ego and the mechanisms of defence.* New York: International Universities Press. (Original work published 1936)

Freud, S. (1953). The interpretation of dreams. In J. Strachey (Ed. and Trans.), *The standard edition of the complete psychological works of Sigmund Freud,* (Vols. 4 & 5). London: Hogarth Press. (Original work published 1900)

Freud, S. (1957). Instincts and vicissitudes. In J. Strachey (Ed. and Trans.) *The standard edition of the complete psychological works of Sigmund Freud,* (Vol. 14, pp. 117–140). London: Hogarth Press. (Original work published 1915)

Frijda, N. (1986). *The emotions: Studies in emotion and social interaction.* Cambridge: Cambridge University Press.

Heider, F. (1958). *The psychology of interpersonal relations.* New York: Wiley.

Izard, C. (1971). *The face of emotion.* New York: Appleton-Century-Crofts.

Izard, C. (1977). *Human emotions.* New York: Plenum Press.

James, W. (1950). *The principles of psychology* (Vol. 2). New York: Dover. (Original work published 1890)

Koob, G., & Bloom, F. (1988). Cellular and molecular mechanisms of drug dependence. *Science, 242,* 715–723.

Lazarus, R. (1984). On the primacy of cognition. *American Psychologist, 39,* 124–129.

Lorenz, K. (1965). *Evolution and modification of behavior.* Chicago: University of Chicago Press.

McDougall, W. (1923). *Outline of psychology.* New York: Scribners.

Nachman, P., Stern, D., & Best, C. (1986). Affective reactions to stimuli and infants' preferences for novelty and familiarity. *Journal of the American Academy of Child Psychiatry, 25,* 801–804.

Osgood, C., Suci, G., & Tannenbaum, P. (1957). *The measurement of meaning.* Urbana: University of Illinois Press.

Plutchik, R. (1962). *The emotions: Facts, theories and a new model.* New York: Random House.

Plutchik, R. (1980). A general psychoevolutionary theory of emotion. In R. Plutchik & H. Kellerman (Eds.), *Emotion: Theory, research, and experience* (pp. 3–33). New York: Academic Press.

Pribram, K., & Melges, F. (1969). Psychophysiological basis of emotion. In P. Vinken & G. Bruyn (Eds.), *Handbook of clinical neurology* (pp. 316–342). Amsterdam: North-Holland.

Schlosberg, H. (1954). Three dimensions of emotion. *Psychological Review, 61,* 81–88.

Schwartz, R., & Trabasso, T. (1984). Children's understanding of emotions. In C. Izard, J. Kagan, & R. Zajonc (Eds.), *Emotions, cognition and behavior* (pp. 409–437). Cambridge: Cambridge University Press.

Searle, J. (1983). *Intentionality: An essay in the philosophy of mind.* New York: Cambridge.

Sharir, I. (1992). *The relationship between emotions and defenses in the psychotherapeutic process.* Unpublished doctoral dissertation, Department of Psychology, New York University.

Sroufe, L., & Waters, E. (1976). The ontogenesis of smiling and laughter: A perspective on the organization of development in infancy. *Psychological Review, 83,* 173–189.

Stich, S. (1983). *From folk psychology to cognitive science: The case against belief.* Cambridge, MA: MIT Press.

Stone, M. (1980). Modern concepts of emotion as prefigured in Descartes' "Passions of the Soul." *Journal of the American Academy of Psychoanalysis, 8,* 473–495.

Tolman, E. (1923). A behavioristic account of the emotions. *Psychological Review, 30,* 217–227.

Tomkins, S. (1970). Affect as the primary motivational system. In M. Arnold (Ed.), *Feelings and emotions: The Loyola symposium* (pp. 101–110). New York: Academic Press.

Trabasso, T. (1992). The importance of context in understanding discourse. In R. Hogarth (Ed.), *Question framing and response contingency: New directions for methodology of social and behavioral sciences* (pp. 77–89). San Francisco: Jossey-Bass.

Vaillant, G. (1971). Theoretical hierarchy of adaptive ego mechanisms. *Archives of General Psychiatry, 24,* 107–118.

Vaillant, G. (1976). Natural history of male psychological health. V. The relation of ego mechanisms of defense to adult adjustment. *Archives of General Psychiatry, 33,* 535–545.

Vaillant, G. (1977). *Adaptation to life*. Boston: Little Brown.

Wolff, P. (1966). The causes, controls and organization of behavior in the neonate. *Psychological Issues, 17*. New York: International Universities Press.

Wundt, W. (1907). *Outlines of psychology* (C. Judd, Trans.). New York: Strechert.

Zajonc, R. (1980). Feeling and thinking: Preferences need no inferences. *American Psychologist, 35*, 151–175.

Zajonc, R. (1984). On the primacy of affect. *American Psychologist, 39*, 117–123.

# 6

# A Developmental View of Defenses
## Empirical Approaches

ANDREW W. SAFYER AND
STUART T. HAUSER

In this chapter, we explore the use of defenses from a developmental perspective. The idea that defenses may follow a developmental course, in terms of their emergence and relation to other ego functions has been implicit in numerous clinical, theoretical, and, increasingly, empirical writings (Cramer, 1991a). Despite these contributions, important questions remain unanswered. Are defenses necessarily pathological? What is the relation between defense use and psychological maturity? Does the use of certain defenses require specific levels of cognitive and ego development? To what extent do developmental advances depend on, or require, the availability of other personal resources (e.g., intelligence)? An observation made by Anna Freud (1936) (as cited by Vaillant, 1986) is still relevant today: ". . . a chronology of psychic processes is one of the most obscure fields of analytic theory" (p. 53).

## HISTORICAL PERSPECTIVE

The concept of defense was described in the early phase of Freud's writings as a means of preventing painful affects associated with traumas from entering awareness (Freud, 1894). For the next 20 years, Freud's interest in ego functions receded as he focused more on drives—their vicissitudes and their derivatives (Freud, 1915/1957). With the introduction of the structural model, Freud began to concentrate more on the ego and its processes (Freud, 1923/1961). The motive

Preparation of this chapter was supported in part by NIMH Faculty Scholar Award MH 19144 to the first author, and NIMH Research Scientist Award K-05 70178-07 to the second author.

for defense use, anxiety, became more articulated, and he also made explicit specific methods of defenses (e.g., repression, reaction formation, undoing) suggesting that they can serve adaptive purposes (Cooper, 1989; Vaillant, 1992).

Anna Freud deepened and extended the discussion of defenses. Besides defining a large number of defense mechanisms, she speculated that they might be arranged along a developmental continuum that links them to the origin of anxiety (e.g., superego) (Cooper, 1989; A. Freud, 1936). Certain defenses, for example, evolve to master a specific instinctual urge (repression of sexual wishes during the oedipal period). Relevant to our developmental theme is the idea that particular defenses cannot be employed until certain levels of psychic organization have been achieved: "The expulsion of ideas or affects from the ego and their relegation to the outside world would be a relief to the ego only when it had learned to distinguish itself from that world" (A. Freud, 1936, p. 51).

A central concern for Hartmann (1939, 1950) was the ego's role in adaptation, marking the emergence of psychoanalysis as a general theory of human development. In doing so, he greatly expanded the psychoanalytic concept of the defense as a normative process used by individuals in their adaptation to reality. Specifically, he postulated that behaviors that originally evolved through coping with conflict could become transformed, or "autonomous" from the original conflicts from which they arose, and could become engaged in other adaptive activities. For example, while the initial defensive function of intellectualization may be evoked by conflicts over sexual or aggressive impulses possibly involving superego prohibitions (e.g., masturbation), this ego process may subsequently be reflected as intellectuality (Haan, 1977). Regression may also be adaptive, as exemplified by the expression of feelings and fantasies associated with earlier development in creative writing and visual products ("regression in the service of the ego"). Hartmann refers to such transformations as "secondary autonomy." Thus, from Hartmann's perspective, psychological adaptation arises from two sources, innate adaptive capacities (the conflict-free realm) and transformed psychic functions, previously associated with the resolution of psychic conflict.

In the next decades, there emerged increasingly sophisticated theoretical and clinical contributions regarding defenses in terms of their development and their role in adaptation and psychopathology (e.g., Bellak, Hurvich, & Gediman, 1973; Engel, 1962; Prelinger & Zimet, 1964; Schafer, 1968; Spitz, 1961). In comparison, there have been few systematic empirical studies examining defense development. In part, this discrepancy may reflect several dilemmas that continue to be central for investigators. Difficulties include the failure by researchers to arrive at a consensually validated list of defenses and then to develop methodologies to measure them reliably.

## CONCEPTUAL DILEMMAS

It is generally agreed that defenses are inferred mental processes that mediate between individuals' impulses, cognitions, and affects on the one hand, and internalized prohibitions or external reality on the other (Hauser, 1986, p. 91). Yet there are major questions regarding the systematic classification of defenses: What is the universe of defense mechanisms? What is the most theoretically meaningful way to classify them? Various researchers generate different lists of defenses, and then use contrasting classification principles to order them (e.g., Bellak et al., 1973; Valenstein, in Bibring, Dwyer, Huntington, & Valenstein, 1961; Vaillant, 1971). A closely related problem is that these investigators then treat defenses differently with respect to how they align with aspects of individual development (Hauser, 1986). Not surprisingly, these differences can almost always be traced to varied underlying assumptions, based on differing theoretical perspectives and sometimes different research populations (Vaillant, 1986).

These conceptual problems, lurking in the most general theoretical frameworks and at specific definitional levels, lead to a second set of problems that interfere with the task of deriving crisp empirical (operational) definitions. Empirical definitions of defenses frequently differ among investigators, even when the defense is one so commonly discussed as denial (Jacobson, Beardslee, Hauser, Noam, & Powers, 1986a; Vaillant, 1971; Valenstein, in Bibring et al., 1961). Whereas Vaillant (1986) argues that this lack of perfect convergence among researchers must be viewed in light of the "elusiveness" of intrapsychic variables, our more optimistic stance is to see these nonalignments as understandable consequences of the conceptual dilemmas we review here.

## MEASUREMENT DILEMMAS

There are two basic approaches to measuring defenses: self-report questionnaires and ratings derived from clinical interviews. A number of assets and liabilities are associated with each method (see Hauser, 1986; Jacobson et al., 1986a). Self-report measures rely on the subjects' recognition of their own behaviors. For example, one of the most widely used paper-and-pencil tests is the Defense Mechanism Inventory (DMI) (Gleser & Ihilevich, 1969). Based on subjects' responses to hypothetical interpersonal conflicts, the DMI generates scores on five defense clusters: turning against the self, projection, principalization, turning against the object, and reversal. This type of approach has the virtue of avoiding problems of interrater reliability, assessment time, and professional participation in the evaluation process. Its disadvantage is that data derived from this method are susceptible to a number of serious response distortions. They include biases that result from respondents' defensive denial, or social stereotypes reflecting what they believe a person is supposed to say in a given situation. Moreover, they offer subjects a limited number of standardized statements that individuals can evaluate and from which they may consciously choose (Jacobson et al., 1986a).

Clinical ratings or judgments of defenses have been utilized by several researchers (Beardslee et al., 1986; Haan, 1977; Perry & Cooper, 1989; Semrad, Grinspoon, & Feinberg, 1973; Vaillant, 1971). For example, Jacobson et al. (1986a) devised a coding system for evaluating defenses from in-depth clinical research material. Twelve defenses (e.g., acting out, altruism, turning against the self) that are believed to be pertinent to adolescent developmental processes are assessed, as well as an overall defensive score. The major value of this approach is the richness of the data, providing the opportunity to detect more subtle dimensions that are present but may be out of the subject's awareness. The limitations of this approach include difficulty in developing good interrater reliability, reliable ratings, and the time-consuming and complex nature of the rating process.

## DEVELOPMENTAL INVESTIGATIONS

This section highlights empirical approaches to the study of defense use from a developmental perspective. They will be described in terms of two types of studies (Cramer, 1991a; Hauser, 1986). One type attempts to arrange defenses along some kind of developmentally related hierarchy, such as level of maturity or degree of pathology. Such hierarchies provide mutually exclusive definitions and describe methodologies for their assessment. The other type of study does not necessarily cluster defenses into levels, ". . . leaving the issue open, to be studied through the developmental evidence itself" (Hauser, 1986, p. 98). Instead, they investigate the linkage between defense use and such developmental constructs as chronological age, gender, and cognitive or ego development level of an individual.

## Developmental Hierarchies

### Norma Haan

Haan's (1977) model of coping reflects one of the earliest empirical attempts to conceptualize ego processes from a developmental perspective. This approach conceptualizes ego processes as the regulators with which individuals mediate stress, accommodate to change, and assimilate new information about themselves and others (Haan, 1977). Because these processes refer to the way people interact in specific situations, Haan emphasizes that the particular strategy they use is determined by both personal preference and environmental circumstances (Morrissey, 1977).

Haan distinguishes 10 generic processes that have been identified; each can be expressed through coping, defensive, or fragmenting modes. These three modes differ from one another with respect to a set of formal properties. Coping allows choice, is reality oriented, and enables the individual to experience a wider range of affective and cognitive expression; defenses are rigid, compelled, and distort or misdirect an individual's experiences and reactions; fragmentation is automated, ritualistic, and irrationally expressed (Haan, 1977). For example, the generic dimension of sensitivity includes the processes of empathy (coping mode), projection (defensive mode), and ideas of reference (the fragmentary mode). These processes can be further classified in terms of general functions: cognitive, self-reflective (whereby people interact with their own feelings and thoughts), attention focusing, and emotion regulating.

Haan's conclusions are derived mostly from a normative, longitudinal sample (the Oakland Growth study) based on extensive clinical interviews. Her method for identifying coping processes is based on a $Q$-sort procedure that could be applied to these interviews. Trained coders sort cards representing coping and defending processes in a forced distribution (most uncharacteristic to most characteristic), in terms of their accuracy in portraying the individual as he or she appears in a clinical interview. Coping and defense processes have been found to be meaningfully related to intelligence and its pattern of change (Haan, 1963), socioeconomic status (Haan, 1964), and gender (Haan, 1977).

While the processes that Haan identifies are important, the distinction between coping and defensive process is not as helpful. These terms tend to confound coping efforts with their outcomes, by implying that certain processes are inherently more adaptive than others (Cohen & Lazarus, 1983). Such confounding obscures other important questions: Which strategies are connected to varied outcomes? What influences these coping-outcome connections (Hauser & Bowlds, 1990)? In their studies of developmental processes during adolescence, Hauser and colleagues (Hauser, Borman, Bowlds et al., 1991; Hauser, Borman, Jacobson, Powers, & Naom, 1991) propose a distinction between differentiated/engaging and constricted/detaching processes. In other words, the perspective taken is that both coping and defending can be adaptive, depending on the context and individual (developmental, personality) variables. At one pole of the proposed theoretical coping strategies continuum are those ways that individuals narrow their affective and cognitive responses to conflict and rigidly detach from confronting difficulties at hand. At the other pole are differentiated and flexibly engaging ways that individuals may use to handle specific problems, involving such matters as developmental conflicts (bodily changes) or situational difficulties (family conflicts over emergent independence strivings).

## Elvin Semrad

Concurrent with Haan's work, Elvin Semrad (Semrad, 1967; Semrad et al., 1973) studied defenses in a developmental longitudinal context by observing acute schizophrenics during states of regression and then as they returned to more optimal functioning (Vaillant, 1992). During decompensation, Semrad observed that patients employ narcissistic defenses (projection, denial, and distortion) to preserve the integrity of the ego organization and to exclude external objects. As they recover, patients utilize fewer pathological defenses. Defenses that are more interpersonally oriented and elicit the support and encouragement of others are first utilized. Patients then use defenses that eventually enable them to experience "relatively unmodified sadness and anxiety" (Semrad et al., 1973, p. 71).

Based on these observations, Semrad and colleagues developed the Ego Profile Scale, consisting of 45 questions that assess the degree to which nine defenses are present, grouped in three levels: (a) narcissistic defenses (denial, projection, and distortion); (b) affective defenses (compulsive, obsessive, hypochondriacal, and neurasthenic patterns); and (c) neurotic defenses (dissociation, somatization, and anxiety patterns). The scale items were selected from a pool of 200 items by 25 senior psychiatrists who were asked to assign each item to one of the nine ego defense categories. Semrad believed that categorizing patients' defenses would "allow more meaningful understanding of clinical states than do such concepts as diagnosis and symptom cluster" (Semrad et al., 1973, p. 70).

In order to start determining the measure's utility, the questionnaire was completed by the therapists for 63 patients (31 acute schizophrenics and 32 other individuals diagnosed with a variety of other disorders), during the week following their admission to the hospital and then throughout the entire period of hospitalization. Interrater reliability was reported as relatively high. Factor analysis of the 45-item scores indicated that the scale did not distinguish between hypochondriasis and somatization. The authors also described the case of one patient during the period of recovery from an acute psychotic episode as she moved away from more narcissistic defenses, toward more affective defenses, and then toward the use of neurotic defenses as she recovered sufficiently to be discharged.

While the Ego Profile Scale has never been adequately validated, it has served as the basis for the development of other hierarchies (e.g., Meissner, 1980; Vaillant, 1971, 1992). In addition, it has been employed in a study longitudinally exploring ego defense patterns in 36 hospitalized manic-depressive patients (Ablon, Carlson, & Goodwin, 1974). The authors concluded that the Ego Profile Scale was a helpful measure for assessing defenses in affective disorders and was capable of indicating changes in ego function. During clinical improvement, there was a change from immature defenses to more interpersonally oriented defenses.

### George Vaillant

Building on Semrad's and Haan's work, George Vaillant (Snarey & Vaillant, 1985; Vaillant 1971, 1976, 1977, 1986, 1992; Vaillant, Bond, & Vaillant, 1986; Vaillant & McCullough, 1987; Vaillant & Vaillant, 1990) reliably identified a group of 18 defenses that could be classified in terms of maturity and level of psychopathology. An underlying assumption of Vaillant's hierarchy is that people using mature defenses are happier and enjoy more optimal mental health than individuals who rely on the less mature mechanisms (Vaillant, 1992). In addition, he created methodologies for their assessment. Numerous indicators of psychosocial functioning and physical health are linked to his proposed paradigm.

Vaillant's hierarchy includes three levels of defenses: The immature defenses (projection and acting out) are observed in youngsters, as well those individuals diagnosed with personality and mood disorders. At the intermediate level, such defenses as repression, displacement, and reaction formation predominate, and are found among individuals with neurotic disorders. The mature defenses (altruism and humor) are most common among healthier, more mature adults (Vaillant, 1976, 1977; Vaillant & Vaillant, 1990).

This hierarchy of defenses draws from the longitudinal analyses of two male cohorts: college men who were selected on the basis of psychological and physical health (referred to as the Grant sample) (Vaillant, 1971, 1977) and economically disadvantaged inner-city boys who had initially served as the control group in an investigation of juvenile delinquency (referred to as the Glueck sample) (Vaillant, 1976). Vignettes about the men's reactions to crises and conflicts were drawn from these interviews and biographical data. Coders then rated the vignettes in terms of specific defenses as well as an overall defense maturity score, derived from a ratio of immature versus mature defenses (Vaillant, Bond, & Vaillant, 1986).

With respect to developmental dimensions, Vaillant traces defense usage in the Grant sample over a period of 40 years (Vaillant, 1977). Comparisons of vignettes obtained during late adolescence (before age 20), young adulthood (from age 20 to 35), and midlife (over age 35) revealed that use of mature defenses (sublimation, anticipation) tended to increase with age, whereas immature defenses (e.g., projection) decreased (Vaillant, 1977). Moreover, emotional health in childhood was associated with higher levels of mature defense use in adulthood.

Most recently, Vaillant and Vaillant (1990) explored late life adjustment among the Grant sample. A total of 173 men were still active members of the study (six had dropped out in college, 23 men had died before age 60, and two had incomplete data sets. Findings indicated that five "overarching" variables were important to late life adjustment. They were "long-lived ancestors (for physical health only), sustained familial relationships (prior closeness to parents was important in young adulthood; prior closeness to siblings loomed more important in late midlife), maturity of defenses, and absence of alcoholism and depressive disorder" (Vaillant & Vaillant, 1990, p. 36). "Paradoxically, a warm childhood environment made an important independent contribution to predicting physical—not mental health" (Vaillant & Vaillant, 1990, p. 31).

In an intriguing study exploring how investigating defenses can contribute to the understanding of resiliency as well as pathological developmental pathways, Snarey and Vaillant (1985) explored which members of the Glueck sample were able to defy the odds and become members of the middle and upper classes. These authors found that three defense mechanisms—intellectualization, altruism, and anticipation—strongly predicted upward social mobility, even after accounting for IQ, boyhood ego strengths, and parent education and occupation.

## Linkages of Defense Mechanisms to Chronological Age, Cognition, Gender, and Ego Development

### Chronological Age

One group of studies examining age differences in defense use has focused on the frequency with which people fail to acknowledge intense or negative emotions (referred to as psychological defensiveness) (Brody, Rozek, & Muten, 1985). Strategies utilized to measure psychological defensiveness include social desirability scales (Crandall, Crandall, & Katkovsky, 1965; Walsh, Tomlinson-Keasey, & Klieger, 1974) and projective measures (Brody et al., 1985; Glasberg & Aboud, 1982). Social desirability scales measure the propensity of an individual to give socially desirable responses. Such responses are believed to reflect an individual's desire to deny culturally unacceptable affects, ideas, and behaviors (Brody et al., 1985). Projective measures present subjects with conflict-laden stories and then ask about the feelings they and others might feel in the situation (Brody et al., 1985; Glasberg & Aboud, 1982).

The majority of these studies have focused on the developmental onset of psychological defensiveness in young children (e.g., Ames, Learned, Metreaux, & Walker, 1974; Brody et al., 1985; Glasberg & Aboud, 1982; Walsh et al., 1974). They suggest that children begin to deny socially undesirable feelings as early as age 2 years and increasingly during the preschool years. After age 8, psychological defensiveness decreases when children begin to employ more psychologically sophisticated defenses (e.g., intellectualization) (Brody et al., 1985). Brody et al. (1985) for example, found that 6-year-olds are more defensive than 4-year-olds in terms of attributing less frequent negative emotions and less intense emotions to themselves and others. Crandall et al. (1965) demonstrated that social desirability responses were more frequently given by younger children than older children among subjects in grades 3 through 12.

Another approach to examining the relation between defense use and chronological age focuses on describing specific defenses that characterize particular age periods. Ames et al. (1974) demonstrated from Rorschach responses in young children (ages 2 to 10) that denial decreased with age. In terms of other defenses, Cramer (1987) studied age differences in the use of denial, projection, and identification in four groups of children (preschool, elementary school, early adolescent, and late adolescent). She found that denial was used most frequently by the youngest children and decreased steadily thereafter. Projection was most frequently employed in the middle age groups, whereas identification increased during adolescence. In another study designed to investigate the effect of experimentally induced anger on defense use among college students, Cramer (1991b) demonstrated that the predominant defenses of late adolescents are projection and identification.

Ihilevich and Gleser (1986) make the important observation that few studies have explored defense use at the opposite end of the lifespan. McCrae (1982) suggests that there are at least two very different theoretical positions concerning defense use in later life. One perspective suggests that older people tend to regress to more primitive forms of defense use. The other perspective suggests that as people mature, they are less likely to use defenses that distort reality. In two cross-sectional studies assessing 28 coping mechanisms, McCrae (1982) found that most older people use defenses similar to those of younger people. When differences were observed, they were the result of the kinds of struggles that challenged them in their lives. In his most recent follow-up of the Grant sample, Vaillant (Vaillant & Vaillant, 1990) found that those individuals who demonstrated good late life adjustment used more mature defenses.

*Cognition*

A cognitive approach to defense use is one way in which researchers have explained differences in the kinds of defenses that characterize particular age groups (Cramer, 1991a). From this point of view, the use of a particular defense is determined by both the cognitive level of the child and the logical complexity inherent in the particular defense (Chandler, Paget, & Koch, 1978; Cramer, 1983, 1987, 1991a). For example, cognitively simple defenses (denial and repression) would be effective for younger children because they do not yet understand them (Cramer, 1983). Eventually, these defenses become less effective and give way to cognitively more sophisticated defenses (e.g., projection and identification). "Thus the use of a defense must precede its understanding, since understanding destroys its function" (Cramer, 1991a, p. 31).

Several studies (Chandler et al., 1978; Dollinger & McGuire, 1981; Whiteman, 1967) were influential in conceptualizing this cognitive approach. Chandler et al. (1978), for example, identified the cognitive development level of 10 preoperational, concrete operational, and formal operational children and their success or failure in explaining each of eight commonly described defense mechanisms. The results indicated that preoperational children fail to decode any defenses. Subjects at the concrete operational stage could explain defenses involving simple inversions (e.g., repression and denial) and reciprocal operations (e.g., displacement and reaction formation). Formal operational subjects were able to decode defenses involving second-order propositions (e.g., projection and introjection).

To explore the relation between defense use and cognition, Cramer (1987) used a projective measure based on the Thematic Apperception Test (TAT). She believed that children's ability to explain the motivation behind the defense strategies that story characters employed would predict the ages at which specific defense mechanisms would emerge and predominate. Denial (a less sophisticated defense that involves negation of the frightening stimulus) was most frequently used during early childhood and decreased in use thereafter. During adolescence, projection (a more complex defense that requires the ability to differentiate between internal and external stimuli) predominated. The most cognitively complex defense, identification (requiring the ability to form mental internal representations) increased in frequency during the adolescent years. In a related study exploring defense use among 7- and 10-year-olds, Cramer (1983) observed that there were no significant age differences, except for the greater use of turning against the self among the younger children. Cramer (1991a) suggests that the failure to find differences between these two age groups within latency is consistent with the ". . . theoretical position of Anna Freud who discusses middle childhood as a period of time in which there are no new psychological upheavals, and thus less need for defense utilization" (p. 90).

## Gender

Gender differences in psychological defensiveness are based on the belief that girls are more willing to report their feelings than boys due to differential socialization pressures (Brody, 1985). Brody et al. (1985) speculate that boys "modulate the intensity of their emotional expression which may alter ways in which (they) communicate or verbalize feelings" (p. 136). Empirical studies that have examined this theoretical assumption have revealed contradictory findings. Using an emotional attribution task with 4- and 6-year-old children, Brody et al. (1985) found that defensiveness was more common among boys. In contrast, no gender differences in defensiveness were found among fifth- and sixth-graders using a self-report anxiety measure (Douglas & Rice, 1979).

In terms of gender differences in defense strategies, the most consistent findings have been along the internalizing and externalizing dimensions (Cramer, 1991a; Ihilevich & Gleser, 1986). Boys utilize more outer-directed defenses (e.g., projection), whereas girls use more inner-directed defenses (e.g., turning against the self) (Brody, 1985). Such findings are consistent with both gender role prescriptions (e.g., Hoffman, 1977; Maccoby & Jacklin, 1974) and psychodynamic formulations (Deutsch, 1944), which suggest that girls demonstrate greater self-blame and less preference for direct expression of hostility than do boys.

Most of the studies exploring gender-related differences in defense use have been carried out with subjects who are college age or older (see Ihilevich & Gleser, 1986). Research studies with children and adolescents have yielded less consistent gender differences than those observed in adults. Cramer (1979), for example, found that a tendency for such differences in defense choice is evident in young adolescents (mean age = 14.2) and becomes firmly established by the final two years of high school (mean age = 16.2), suggesting that sex-related choices of defense mechanisms become stronger during the adolescent period. Jacobson, Beardslee, and Hauser et al. (1986b) reported that with their adolescent sample, girls were significantly higher in altruism and lower in acting out than boys. In a study among 7- and 10-year-olds, Cramer (1983) found no significant gender differences in the use of external versus internal defenses for the older children. They did, however, for the younger children. In her study of defense use among late adolescents, Cramer (1991b) showed that boys used more projection than did girls. Noam and Recklitis (1990) did not observe any gender differences in their sample of adolescent inpatients.

It may be that defense preferences are influenced not only by gender, but also by the sex role orientation of an individual (Evans, 1982). At least two studies have looked at the relation between gender identity and defense use. In a sample of undergraduates, Cramer and Carter (1978) demonstrated that males who were particularly prone to use projection demonstrated a tendency toward a stronger masculine gender identity than males who were unlikely to employ this defense. Those females who were especially likely to handle conflict by avoiding external conflict, tended to have an especially strong feminine gender identity. In a study of female college students, Evans (1982) demonstrated that high masculine subjects were less likely to turn the aggression inward. There were no differences, however, between high and low masculine subjects with regard to the outward expression of aggression. This unexpected finding was believed to reflect the willingness of low masculine identity subjects to attack objects of their frustration only through fantasy, but not in their actual behavior (Evans, 1982).

## Ego Development

Several studies have explored the relation between defenses and Loevinger's model of ego development, suggesting that individuals at higher ego levels will utilize more mature defenses. According to Loevinger, ego development refers to the framework of meaning that individuals impose on their inner experience and perceptions of people and events (Hauser with Powers, & Noam, 1991; Loevinger, 1976, 1979). In general, early stages of ego development are characterized by impulsivity, self-absorption, and stereotypic thinking. Later stages reveal an emerging capacity for introspection, a growing appreciation for individual differences, and greater conceptual complexity.

Although Loevinger's model of ego development does not assume or predict any relation between ego development and defense use, her descriptions of the personality (or character) patterns unique to each stage imply that it should be possible to find such coping correlates of these patterns. Hauser et al. (1991a, 1991b) argue that the stages define the range and nature of the available coping strategies. It is an empirical question whether such a model is tenable or whether changes in coping strategies, occurring because of specific experiences, can in turn lead to ego development progressions or regressions. For example, individuals at the lowest levels of ego development where impulses are not experienced as one's own, are more likely to use strategies such as regression or projection. At the highest stages, where mutuality and appreciation of individual differences are prized, increased use of empathy is to be expected, a prediction supported by findings of Carlozzi, Gaa, and Liberman (1983).

Haan, Stroud, and Holstein (1973) examined relations between defenses and moral and ego development in a sample of "hippies." With respect to ego development, two defenses—projection and intellectualization—were found to be more frequent among individuals at higher levels. The use of projection (a relatively immature defense) by individuals at higher levels of ego development may be due to the idiosyncratic nature of the sample. The authors did not find any significant correlations between defenses and moral development. In contrast, Vaillant and McCullough (1987) failed to find any significant relation between ego development and maturity of defense style among the Grant sample. Ego level, however, was related to their measure of psychosocial development based on Erikson's model, to number of postgraduate visits to a psychotherapist, and perhaps, to creativity. The authors speculated that Loevinger's test may be measuring something "more limited than global ego maturity" (p. 1194). Instead, it may be an indicator of psychological mindedness and creativity.

To date, the most extensive research that links ego development with defense mechanisms is the work of Hauser and colleagues (e.g., Beardslee et al., 1986; Hauser et al., 1991a, 1991b; Jacobson et al., 1986a, 1986b). These authors approach the developmental nature of defenses by viewing these mechanisms within the spectrum of ego processes and examining their relationship to ego development during adolescence. Guiding this research program about adolescent development is the assumption that individuals can use defenses in adaptive as well as maladaptive ways. These studies represent one aspect of a longitudinal project that is considering the interplay of adolescent and young adult development with family processes.

In one series of studies, Hauser et al. (1991a) applied Haan's assessment of coping and defending to clinical research interviews of adolescents who were psychiatrically hospitalized and likely to be developmentally impaired. Numerous theoretically expected and substantial correlations between adolescent ego development and all but one ego process (reaction formation) were observed, with individuals at higher levels of ego development using differentiated/engaging coping processes. Another set of observations address relations between parental ego development and adolescent coping strategies, highlighting links between parenting characteristics (ego development) and developmentally relevant aspects of adolescent functioning (coping strategies) (Hauser et al., 1991b). It was observed that parents (particularly the mother) functioning at higher levels of ego development were more likely to use differentiating/engaging coping and were less likely to cope through constricting/detaching strategies.

In another series of studies, Hauser and colleagues (Beardslee et al., 1986; Jacobson et al., 1986a, 1986b) applied their interview-based measure of ego processes among three groups of early adolescent subjects: diabetic adolescents, nonpsychotic psychiatric patients, and high school students. Comparisons between the groups revealed that the psychiatric patients were rated higher in acting out, projection, and displacement and lower in the use of altruism, intellectualization, and suppression than the other two groups. Moreover, intellectualization, altruism, and suppression and successful use of defense were positively correlated with higher levels of ego development, whereas several of the more immature defenses (e.g., acting out, projection, repression) were positively correlated with lower levels of ego development.

## CONCLUSION

An increasing body of empirical evidence supports the idea that a developmental framework is a useful approach to understanding defenses. Researchers continue to debate the relative strengths of the various proposed hierarchies and the methodologies that have been used to measure them (see Vaillant, 1992). Unfortunately, this research has been hampered by the failure of investigators to arrive at a common list of defenses based on conceptual and empirical consensus.

It does appear that the emergence and use of certain defenses is affected by the age, gender, and ego and cognitive level of an individual. More longitudinal studies performed on the same subjects are needed, however, to further evaluate causal links. Such analyses would also help increase our understanding as to how these relations change over time. An additional challenge for researchers is to begin to establish whether these relationship patterns are moderated by other constitutional factors (e.g., temperament) and other individual differences (e.g., family and peer context experiences).

## REFERENCES

Ablon, S., Carlson, G., & Goodwin, F. (1974). Ego defense patterns in manic-depressive illness. *American Journal of Psychiatry, 131,* 803–807.

Ames, L., Learned, J., Metreaux, R., & Walker, R. (1974). *Child Rorschach responses: Developmental trends from 2 to 10 years.* New York: P. B. Hoeber.

Beardslee, W. R., Jacobson, A. M., Hauser, S. T., Noam, G. G., Powers, S., Houlihan, J., & Rider, E. (1986). An approach to evaluating adolescent adaptive processes: Validity of an interview-based measure. *Journal of Youth and Adolescence, 15,* 355–376.

Bellak, L., Hurvich, M., & Gediman, H. K. (1973). *Ego functions in schizophrenics, neurotics and normals: A systematic study of the conceptual, diagnostic, and therapeutic aspects.* New York: Wiley.

Bibring, G., Dwyer, T., Huntington, D., & Valenstein, A. (1961). A study of the psychological processes in pregnancy and of the earliest mother-child relationship. *Psychoanalytic Study of the Child, 16,* 9–72.

Brody, L. R. (1985). Gender differences in emotional development: A review of theories and research. *Journal of Personality, 53,* 102–145.

Brody, L. R., Rozek, M. K., & Muten, E. O. (1985). Age, sex, and individual differences in children's defensive styles. *Journal of Clinical Child Psychology, 14,* 132–138.

Carlozzi, A. F., Gaa, J. P., & Liberman, D. B. (1983). Empathy and ego development. *Journal of Counseling Psychology, 30,* 113–120.

Chandler, M. J., Paget, K. F., & Koch, D. A. (1978). The child's demystification of psychological defense mechanisms: A structural developmental analysis. *Developmental Psychology, 14,* 197–205.

Cohen, F., & Lazarus, R. (1983). Coping and adaptation and health and illness. In D. Mechanic (Ed.), *Handbook of health, health care, and the health professions.* (pp. 608–635). New York: Free Press.

Cooper, S. (1989). Recent contributions to the theory of defense mechanisms: A comparative view. *Journal of the American Psychoanalytic Association, 37,* 865–893.

Cramer, P. (1979). Defense mechanisms in adolescence. *Developmental Psychology, 15,* 476–477.

Cramer, P. (1983). Children's use of defense mechanisms in reaction to displeasure caused by others. *Journal of Personality, 51,* 78–94.

Cramer, P. (1987). The development of defense mechanisms. *Journal of Personality, 55,* 597–614.

Cramer, P. (1991a). *The development of defense mechanism.* New York: Springer-Verlag.

Cramer, P. (1991b). Anger and the use of defense mechanisms in college students. *Journal of Personality, 59,* 39–55.

Cramer, P., & Carter, T. (1978). The relationship between sexual identification and the use of defense mechanisms. *Journal of Personality Assessment, 42,* 63–73.

Crandall, V. C., Crandall, V. J., & Katkovsky, W. (1965). Children's beliefs in their control of reinforcements in intellectual academic achievement situations. *Child Development, 36,* 91–109.

Deutsch, H. (1944). *The psychology of women.* New York: Grune & Stratton.

Dollinger, S. J., & McGuire, B. (1981). The development of psychological-mindedness: Children's understanding of defense mechanisms. *Journal of Clinical Child Psychology, 10,* 117–121.

Douglas, J., & Rice, K. (1979). Sex differences in children's anxiety and defensiveness measures. *Developmental Psychology, 15,* 223–224.

Engel, G. (1962). *Psychological development in health and disease.* Philadelphia: Saunders.

Evans, R. (1982). Defense mechanisms in females as a function of sex-role orientation. *Journal of Clinical Psychology, 38,* 816–817.

Freud, A. (1936). *The ego and the mechanisms of defense.* New York: International Universities Press.

Freud, S. (1894). The justification for detaching from neurasthenia a particular syndrome: The anxiety-neurosis. *Collected papers* (Vol. 1, pp. 76–106). New York: Basic Books.

Freud, S. (1957). Instincts and their vicissitudes. In J. Strackey (Ed. and Trans.) *The standard edition of the complete psychological works of*

*Sigmund Freud* (Vol. 14, pp. 117–140). London: Hogarth Press. (Original work published 1915)

Freud, S. (1961). The ego and the id. In J. Strackey (Ed. and Trans.) *The Standard Edition of the complete psychological works of Sigmund Freud (Vol. 19).* London: Hogarth Press. (Original work published 1923)

Glasberg, R., & Aboud, F. (1982). Keeping one's distance from sadness: Children's self-reports of emotional experience. *Developmental Psychology, 18,* 287–293.

Gleser, G. C., & Ihilevich, D. (1969). An objective instrument for measuring defense mechanisms. *Journal of Consulting and Clinical Psychology, 33,* 51–60.

Haan, N. (1963). Proposed model of ego functioning: Coping and defense mechanisms in relationship to IQ change. *Psychological Monographs, 77* (8), 1–23.

Haan, N. (1964). The relationship of ego functioning and intelligence to social status and social mobility. *Journal of Abnormal and Social Psychology, 6,* 594–605.

Haan, N. (1977). *Coping and defending.* New York: Academic Press.

Haan, N., Stroud, J., & Holstein, C. (1973). Moral and ego stages in relationship to ego processes: A study of "hippies." *Journal of Personality, 41,* 569–612.

Hartmann, H. (1939). *Ego psychology and the problem of adaptation.* New York: International Universities Press.

Hartmann, H. (1950). Psychoanalysis and developmental psychology. In H. Hartmann (Ed.), *Essays on ego psychology* (pp. 99–112). New York: International Universities Press.

Hauser, S. T. (1986). Conceptual and empirical dilemmas in the assessment of defenses. In G. E. Vaillant (Ed.), *Empirical studies of ego mechanisms of defense* (pp. 89–99). Washington, DC: American Psychiatric Press.

Hauser, S. T., & Bowlds, M. K. (1990). Stress, coping, and adaptation within adolescence: Diversity and resilience. In S. Feldman & G. Elliot (Eds.), *At the threshold: The developing adolescent* (Carnegie Foundation Volume on Adolescence). Cambridge, MA: Harvard University Press.

Hauser, S. T., Borman, E. H., Bowlds, M. K., Powers, S., Jacobson, A., Noam, G., & Knoebber, K. (1991). Understanding coping within adolescence: Ego development trajectories and coping styles. In A. L. Greene, E. M. Cummings, & K. Karraker (Eds.), *Life-span developmental psychology: Perspectives on stress and coping.* Hillsdale, NJ: Erlbaum.

Hauser, S. T., Borman, E. H., Jacobson, A. M., Powers, S. I., & Noam, G. G. (1991). Understanding family contexts of adolescent coping: A study of parental ego development and adolescent coping strategies. *Journal of Early Adolescence, 11,* 96–124.

Hauser, S. T., with Powers, S. I., & Noam, G. G. (1991). *Adolescents and their families: Paths of ego development.* New York: Free Press.

Hoffman, M. L. (1977). Sex differences in empathy and related behaviors. *Psychological Bulletin, 84,* 712–722.

Ihilevich, D., & Gleser, G. (1986). *Defense mechanisms,* Owosso: DMI Associates.

Jacobson, A. M., Beardslee, W. R., Hauser, S. T., Noam, G. G., & Powers, S. (1986a). An approach to evaluating ego defense mechanisms using clinical interviews. In G. Vaillant (Ed.), *Empirical studies of ego mechanisms of defense* (pp. 47–59). Washington, DC: American Psychiatric Press.

Jacobson, A. M., Beardslee, W., Hauser, S. T., Noam, G. G., Powers, S., Houlihan, J., & Rider, E. (1986b). Evaluating ego defense mechanisms using clinical interviews: An empirical study of adolescent diabetic and psychiatric patients. *Journal of Adolescence, 9,* 303–319.

Loevinger, J. (1976). *Ego development: Conceptions and theories.* San Francisco: Jossey-Bass.

Loevinger, J. (1979). Construct validity of the sentence completion test of ego development. *Applied Psychological Measurement, 3*(3), 281–311.

Maccoby, E., & Jacklin, C. (1974). *The psychology of sex differences.* Stanford: Stanford University Press.

McCrae, R. (1982). Age differences in the use of coping mechanisms. *Journal of Gerontology, 37,* 454–460

Meissner, W. W. (1980). Theories of personality and psychopathology: classical psychoanalysis. In H. Kaplan, A. Freedman, & B. Sadock (Eds.), *Comprehensive textbook of psychiatry* (3rd ed., Vol. 1). Baltimore: William & Wilkins.

Morrissey, R. (1977). The Haan model of ego functioning: An assessment of empirical research. In N. Haan, *Coping and defending.* New York: Academic Press.

Noam, G. G., & Recklitis, C. (1990). The relationship between defenses and symptoms in adolescent psychopathology. *Journal of Personality Assessment, 54,* 311–327.

Perry, J., & Cooper, S. (1989). An empirical study of defense mechanisms. *Archives of General Psychiatry, 46,* 444–452.

Prelinger, E., & Zimet, C. (1964). *An ego psychological approach to character assessment.* Glencoe, IL: Free Press.

Schafer, R. (1968). The mechanisms of defence. *International Journal of Psychoanalysis, 49,* 49–61.

Semrad, E. (1967). The organization of ego defenses and object loss. In D. M. Moriarity (Ed.), *The loss of loved ones.* Springfield, IL: Charles C. Thomas.

Semrad, E., Grinspoon, L., & Feinberg, S. (1973). Development of an Ego Profile Scale. *Archives of General Psychiatry, 28,* 70–77.

Snarey, J., & Vaillant, G. (1985). How lower- and working-class youth become middle-class adults: The association between ego defense mechanisms and upward social mobility. *Child Development, 56,* 899–910.

Spitz, R. (1961). Some early prototypes of ego defenses. *Journal of the American Psychoanalytic Association, 9,* 626–651.

Vaillant, G. E. (1971). Theoretical hierarchy of adaptive ego mechanisms. *Archives of General Psychiatry, 24,* 107–118.

Vaillant, G. E. (1976). Natural history of male psychological health. V. The relation of choice of ego mechanisms of defense to adult adjustment. *Archives of General Psychiatry, 33,* 535–545.

Vaillant, G. E. (1977). *Adaptation to life.* Boston: Little Brown.

Vaillant, G. E. (Ed.). (1986). *Empirical assessment of ego mechanisms of defense.* Washington, DC: American Psychiatric Press.

Vaillant, G. E. (Ed.). (1992). *Ego mechanisms of defense.* Washington, DC: American Psychiatric Press.

Vaillant, G., Bond, M., & Vaillant, C. (1986). An empirically validated hierarchy of defense mechanisms. *Archives of General Psychiatry, 43,* 786–794.

Vaillant, G. E., & McCullough, L. (1987). The Washington University sentence completion test compared with other measures of adult ego development. *American Journal of Psychiatry, 144,* 1189–1194.

Vaillant, G. E., & Vaillant, C. (1990). Natural history of male psychological health, XII: A 45-year study of predictors of successful aging at age 65. *American Journal of Psychiatry, 147,* 31–37.

Walsh, J., Tomlinson-Keasey, C., & Klieger, D. (1974). Acquisition of the social desirability response. *Genetic Psychology Monographs, 89,* 241–272.

Whiteman, M. (1967). Children's conception of psychological causality. *Child Development, 38,* 143–156.

# 7

# The Evolved Function of Repression and the Adaptive Design of the Human Psyche

MALCOLM OWEN SLAVIN AND
DON GREIF

Someone once commented to Talcott Parsons, the noted sociologist, that it was unfortunate that Freud had been so biological in his thinking. Parsons is reported to have quipped, "Psychoanalysis is not *too* biological, it is not biological *enough!*" What did he really mean?

The great social theorist (who, incidentally, was analytically trained in Boston) did not, of course, mean that human psychological and social experience could or should be reduced to somatic or genetic variables. On the contrary, Parsons was a consummate cultural determinist. Yet he recognized that psychoanalysis needed not only a more accurate biological foundation than existed in the classical metapsychology, but, more significantly, it would benefit greatly from a *different,* broader biological emphasis that focused on the functions and purposes of whole organisms in adaptation to a complex, interactive environment. This would correct the overemphasis in the classical psychoanalytic metapsychology on the inner workings of universal, intrapsychic mechanisms operating outside a larger adaptive context (Parsons, 1963).

The aim of this chapter is to show what might happen if—using the conceptual tools of contemporary evolutionary biology—such a broader, functional, biological perspective were brought to bear on the concept of repression (as well as other defenses), and then by extension, on an issue

This chapter is an extension and elaboration of views originally presented in "The Dual Meaning of Repression and the Adaptive Design of the Human Psyche, by M. Slavin, 1992, *The Journal of the American Academy of Psychoanalysis, 18*(2), 307–341, and sections of *The Adaptive Design of the Human Psyche: Psychoanalysis, Evolutionary Biology, and the Therapeutic Process,* by M. Slavin and D. Kriegman, 1992, New York: Guilford Press.

that is arguably the main point of controversy in current psychoanalytic thought—the paradigmatic clash between the classical tradition of drive theory (including its Kleinian versions and ego psychological revisions) on the one hand, and the relational tradition represented by Winnicott, Kohut, and various American interpersonalists on the other (Eagle, 1984; Greenberg & Mitchell, 1983; Slavin & Kriegman, 1992).

## WHAT DO WE REPRESS AND WHY: ENDOGENOUS DRIVES OR VITAL ASPECTS OF THE SELF?

We shall begin in the way that, as clinicians, we find most compelling: by identifying a problem with palpable, everyday, treatment implications for psychoanalysis that, nevertheless, has eluded a good solution within the customary range of psychoanalytic discourse. The problem begins with the concept of repression and its different, even contradictory meanings in different psychoanalytic traditions. We shall attempt to reframe this controversy in light of contemporary evolutionary biology, and then spell out some of the broader consequences of the evolutionary perspective for psychoanalysis.

Most of us would probably agree that, broadly defined, the concept of repression is at the heart of psychoanalytic theory. We shall define repression in the generic, almost phenomenological fashion alluded to by Greenberg and Mitchell (1983): a state in which something is missing in a person's "experience of him- or herself." Some "crucial dimension of meaning is absent in his account of his own experience" (p. 15). As Freud (1915/1961) put it, it is in *"ein andere Platz"*—another place—missing, but *not* lost.

If we take this "other place" absolutely figuratively, without specifying the content of what is "missing" from focal awareness, we remain on fairly consensual psychoanalytic ground. Although the actual term *repression* per se is not always emphasized in all psychoanalytic traditions (the notion of split-off, or disavowed, aspects of the psyche is more compatible with many nonclassical approaches), the underlying notion that there is some important set of desires or perceptions missing from the central conscious personality is, almost by definition, a universal psychoanalytic observation. Accordingly, the clinical task of the analyst—from the classical drive theorist, to the object relations theorist, to the self psychologist—always includes a significant effort to identify and understand that missing dimension, to bring it into greater awareness and thereby—in the context of the treatment relationship—promote greater continuity and integration within the psyche (Schafer, 1983).

At this point, however, the psychoanalytic consensus completely breaks down. The conception of *what* is missing, repressed, or split off, and *why* it is repressed, is a matter of considerable controversy. Although specific psychoanalytic positions on repression range all over the theoretical map, it is possible to organize these individual perspectives into a comparative psychoanalytic framework that is relevant to contemporary clinical and theoretical concerns. Such a comparative approach can illuminate the implicit "narrative structures" (Schafer, 1983) or "basic visions of human nature" (Greenberg & Mitchell, 1983) that underlie the vast field of specific psychoanalytic perspectives. Painted with, admittedly, very broad strokes, such a comparative framework yields views of repression that fall into two camps.

## The Classical Position

One camp sees the role of repression as lying in the need to manage the tensions that are ultimately attributable to the clash between the endogenous, bodily based driving forces within the individual and the norms and limits that realistically exist in ordinary social reality (the "average expectable environment"). Repression is seen, essentially, as regulating the conflicts that inevitably arise as the inherently more selfish, less organized, self-centered motivations and cognitions of the child struggle with the complex, ordered, differentiated, relatively realistic world of the parental (average expectable) environment. Classical drive theory, Kleinian theory, as well as their innumerable permutations into modern ego and developmental psychology (A. Freud, 1936; Hartmann, 1958; Jacobson, 1964; Kernberg, 1980; Mahler, Pine, & Bergman, 1975) start with this conception of an innate dividedness and tension at the core of human nature and the human condition.

In the course of development, normal growth necessitates the shifting of the child's less organized, more selfish and self-centered modes of construing reality away from their central place in the organization of subjective experience. These motivations and perceptions are, at least in part, repressed in order not to disrupt the conscious process of subjectively organizing experience and behavior in a way that would otherwise conflict with the child's adaptation to the realities of the family. On the whole, a significant part of what is repressed can be said to be disguised in a fashion that is intrinsically deceptive to the individual and others (Freud, 1915/1961).

The continued presence of, indeed fixation on, repressed aspects of the self, albeit in deceptively disguised form, represents a continuing threat to the accommodation the child has made to external (largely parental) reality. Moreover, the classical tradition assumes that there is actually an inherent tendency of the repressed to return, to seek expression in ever-changing, deceptive guises. This "unbidden return of the repressed" is one major source of the repetition compulsion: the tenacious, often painful repetition of archaic patterns that is at the heart of the classical Freudian and Kleinian conceptions of psychopathology (Fenichel, 1945; Segal, 1964), and has been conceptually tailored to fit the altered premises of modern ego psychology (see Kriegman & Slavin, 1989, for an extended discussion of classical and relational views of the "compulsion to repeat").

## The Relational Position

In contrast, the other psychoanalytic camp sees the process of repression as lying in a fundamentally different type of tension, namely, the tension between a unique, perhaps innate configuration of individual needs, identity elements, or vital experiences of self on the one hand and a social environment that is insufficiently or inadequately attuned, matched, or invested in the recognition and cultivation of these innate, individual elements, on the other. Certain of the interpersonalist theorists (e.g., Fromm, 1941; Sullivan, 1953), the British object relationists (see Winnicott, 1965; Guntrip, 1971) as well as the self psychologists and current intersubjective theorists (e.g., Kohut, 1982, 1984; Stolorow, Brandchaft, & Atwood, 1987) emphasize this alternative view of repression. They represent a radically different sensibility within psychoanalysis in which repression is viewed as the means of hiding a true, spontaneous, or authentic self from a social world that, in some basic fashion, fails to coordinate itself with these vital dimensions of inner, individual experience.

In this tradition, repression is seen as sheltering, or protecting parts of the self; often this is seen as taking place to enhance the possibilities for future growth and development. Patterns of reliving and repeating are viewed—particularly in the work of Winnicott as well as Kohut and his school—less as an "unbidden return" or "compulsion to repeat" than as an attempt to reactivate and reinitiate thwarted growth (Kriegman & Slavin, 1989).

Depending on which of these paradigms—or competing metapsychological views—a person adheres to, the view of what is repressed will characteristically be either (a) that some variety of egocentric, forbidden, ultimately selfish or dangerous aim or wish is *deceptively disguised* to avoid inner conflict; or (b) that, at root, a striving to express, validate, or actualize some aspect or version of the self cannot find inclusion in the relational environment and becomes *split off and/or walled off* into some covert place where it is sequestered from the overt accommodation made with the external world. Whenever symptoms and repetitive patterns are experienced without what is judged to be an adequate awareness of their underlying meaning, that crucial dimension of missing meaning turns out to be interpretable in terms of one or the other of these two alternative metaphors. These metaphors can also be seen in hermeneutic terms as alternative narrative themes (Schafer, 1983; Spence, 1982).

Many readers will no doubt object that few of us work in such a dichotomous way: that the either/or quality of our two paradigms of repression has long since been intricately integrated theoretically in the psychoanalytic literature (e.g., Loewald, 1965/1980; Modell, 1984; Pine, 1985) as well as continually combined and blended in the rich tapestry of real clinical work. No doubt there is some truth in this objection. But although this is not the place to debate this issue at length, we believe that the overwhelming evidence from our actual practice shows that when the individual's overall orientation is viewed as a whole, contemporary clinicians and clinical settings strongly tend to polarize around one or the other basic view of the primary nature and origin of the conflicts we must repress, and, consequently, of the very meaning of repression (and repetition) itself. Greenberg and Mitchell (1983) have called a similar range of deep and pervasive psychoanalytic beliefs "paradigmatic loyalties," and while moment to moment, or phase to phase, some analytic treatments may shift between the two narrative emphases, the deeper trends, the basic metaphors, and narrative structure of a given treatment will tend to coalesce around one or the other of these organizing perspectives. On a still broader scale, the *historical* trends within psychoanalytic theory—starting with Freud's radical rejection of his early seduction theory—have moved like a pendulum from one side to the other of this basic divide (see Erikson, 1964a; Lawner, 1985; Rapaport, 1960).

Let this suffice as our depiction of the issue in psychoanalytic theory. How might it be illuminated by evolutionary biology?

## PARENT-OFFSPRING CONFLICT THEORY: THE BIOLOGICAL BASIS OF CONFLICT IN EARLY DEVELOPMENT

### Psychoanalytic Theory and Modern Evolutionary Biology

The essential principle in evolution is that all life forms represent structures that enhance the survival and replication of copies of their underlying genetic codes. Those that succeed become more common, eventually characterizing the species as a whole. Those that fail disappear. All life forms and structures (physical as well as mental, as well as behavioral inclinations) can be understood in terms of the benefits they provide to the genetic material underlying them (Kriegman & Slavin, 1989; Mayr, 1983) (see Figure 7–1).

To be sure, we shall not ask the reader to assume a simplistic evolutionism in which complex dynamic processes such as repression are seen as operating solely as an unfolding of prerecorded genetic instructions. Such overly deterministic attempts to explain the psyche in terms of genes (such as the early "sociobiology" of E. O. Wilson (1975), which is

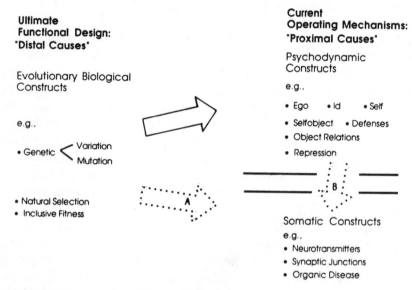

**Figure 7–1.** The question of "reductionism" in evolutionary explanations. An evolutionary biological analysis is primarily an attempt to understand *distal* or *ultimate* causes, that is, the selective pressures in the evolutionary experience of the species (the left-hand column). These are the historical, functional pressures that shaped the phenotypes we see today. In the right-hand column are the *proximal* mechanisms, the current structures and processes that control the ongoing expression of the phenotype. An evolutionary biological analysis of psychological phenomena basically consists of an attempt to find the ultimate causes (or functional rationales) for those proximal mechanisms involved in the functioning of the psyche. This relationship is represented by the *solid arrow*. The *dotted arrows* refer to other types of evolutionary and nonevolutionary biological explanations that are *not* pursued in the current study: (A) evolutionary biological explanations of molecular mechanisms that represent the biochemical substrate of higher level adaptive structures; (B) neurobiological (reductionist) descriptions of mechanisms that represent the somatic substrate for higher level psychological phenomena. Adapted from "Self Psychology from the Perspective of Evolutionary Biology: Toward a Biological Foundation for Self-Psychology" by D. Kriegman, 1988, in A. Goldberg (Ed.), *Progress in Self-Psychology*, Vol. 3, Hillside, NJ: Analytic Press. Copyright 1988 by Analytic Press. Reprinted by permission.

often equated with the field of sociobiology as a whole) bypass the construct of mind and eliminate psychodynamics (Kriegman & Slavin, 1989; Tooby & Cosmides, 1989). In so doing, these approaches add little of interest or utility to a psychology of human inner life and especially little of dynamic or clinical interest. Moreover, evolutionary biological explanations are at such a level of theoretical abstraction—are so removed from the "language of the psyche"—that they cannot, themselves, be used to derive a psychology (Tooby & Cosmides, 1989). As we have argued elsewhere (Kriegman & Slavin, 1989, 1990), the development of a model of the psyche still remains squarely within the province of psychoanalysis (see Figures 7–1 and 7–2).

## Adaptation and Inclusive Fitness

The term *adaptation* has a long, complicated history both within and outside psychoanalysis, some of which will be alluded to later. This section

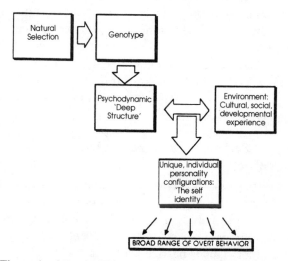

**Figure 7–2.** The path of determinism in evolutionary explanations. Psychodynamic "deep structure" represents the crucial set of complex, overarching proximal mechanisms that mediate between the genes and our inner experience. Evolutionary biology can provide a perspective on the nature of the relational world in which the basic functional design of the psyche was shaped over evolutionary time. An understanding of this functional "architecture" can allow us to evaluate and compare different psychoanalytic paradigms, each of which contains specific assumptions not only about the design features of the psyche per se but, more fundamentally, about the nature of the object world in which the human psyche must function. Adapted from "The Myth of the Repetition Compulsion and Negative Therapeutic Reaction: An Evolutionary Biological Analysis" by D. Kriegman and M. O. Slavin, 1989, in A. Goldberg (Ed.), *Progress in Self-Psychology,* Vol. 6, Hillsdale, NJ: Analytic Press. Copyright 1989 by Analytic Press. Reprinted by permission.

will focus on its evolutionary biological meaning. As we noted, whenever anything (a structure or behavior) about an organism is called adaptive in contemporary evolutionary theory, we mean it is organized to maximize the pursuit of ends that are advantageous to its *individual genotype* (Mayr, 1983; Trivers, 1985). Although most of us are familiar with this idea in terms of the Darwinian metaphor of survival of the fittest (or, natural selection helps those genes that help themselves), there is an important extension of this idea in contemporary evolutionary thought (Badcock, 1985).

Since our genotype is, literally, shared with kin (as well as potentially linked reciprocally with the genotypes of nonkin) the *phenotypic* (or overt observable) behavior that is actually most advantageous to it will necessarily include the welfare of these other individuals—albeit always in somewhat discounted form relative to our own interests. Hence the current use of the term *inclusive fitness* (Hamilton, 1964). Inclusive fitness is based on the recognition that the survival of copies of an organism's genes in other individuals, and eventually in the future gene pool of the species, is the only real measure of evolutionary success or ultimate fitness. What is adaptive is what ultimately maximizes inclusive fitness, not simply personal fitness (Hamilton, 1964; Trivers, 1985). Let us now look more closely at the implications of this whole view of adaptation as it applies to the interactive dynamics that occur during the prolonged period of human child development.

### The Genetics of Self and Other and the Essence of Relational Conflict

Because of the very close genetic relationship between parents and offspring in all species, there is a large degree of overlap between the individual self-interests of parent and child. They inherently share many of the same aims; in many respects, what is advantageous to one is advantageous to the other. This is particularly obvious from the parents' point of view. We need little biological sophistication to appreciate that the parents' own reproductive success, their inclusive fitness, is intimately tied to the future reproductive success—the inclusive fitness—of their offspring.

This is also true, to some extent, in terms of the child's tie to the parent. Not only is the child tied to the parent for more obviously selfish, or individual, reasons but also because the child derives distinct benefits to his or her inclusive fitness from the parents' successful pursuit of their own fitness; remember, the average parental genome includes half of the child's own genetic material.

In this sense, the parent-child dyad is, in part, a *phenotypic illusion,* so to speak (see Figure 7–3): parts of the child's genetic "self" are, literally, included within the parental "self" and vice versa.

Though this may, indeed, look like a psychotic version of reality (a fusion or primitive merger of identities), it is, at root, nothing other than the actual biological reality that underlies Winnicott's (1965) telling aphorism, "There is no such thing as an infant, only a nursing couple." In this important biological sense, the notion of the child's individuality is, in some respects, an illusion based on our conscious overestimation of the phenotypic (overt, observable) physical separateness of the two organisms. At some level, this fundamental biological truth can be seen to underlie the basic metaphors, or visions of human nature, that underlie the relational tradition in psychoanalysis. It is implicit in the notion of the "selfobject" in Kohut's (1984) work.

Now, however, we shall emphasize a second biological fact: Despite the overlap in their interests, parents and offspring are genetically distinct, unique, separate individuals. Thus, to some degree, from the moment of conception onward, their interests necessarily diverge as well as potentially compete and conflict. Dr. Winnicott notwithstanding, we must affirm that, in a fundamental, psychologically relevant sense, there definitely *is* such a (separate) thing as a baby; and a (separate) nursing mother. There is, genetically, a baby with a distinct, unique self from the very beginning of life, and there is a (average, good-enough, devoted)

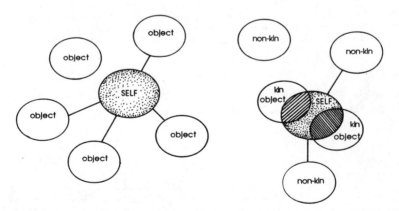

**Figure 7–3.** The "Self": Phenotypic and genotypic perspectives. From "The Myth of the Repetition Compulsion and Negative Therapeutic Reaction: An Evolutionary Biological Analysis" by D. Kriegman and M. O. Slavin, 1989, in A. Goldberg (Ed.), *Progress in Self-Psychology,* Vol. 6, Hillside, NJ: Analytic Press. Copyright 1989 by Analytic Press. Reprinted by permission.

mother with interests, aims, and views that are *intrinsically different from her baby's* aims and interests.

The universality of this basic biological matrix has the following major implications: On virtually every crucial psychological issue in the course of development (indeed of the full life cycle), the parent as a functioning biological organism is likely to have been psychologically designed to operate with a subjective interpretation of reality that is consistent with its own inclusive fitness, that is, derived in a self-interested fashion from its own subjective experience and biased toward those individuals (usually kin) to whom it is most closely, reciprocally tied. We shall call this the parent's *inclusive self-interest;* it is the essence of what, in a biologically consistent fashion, we can also call, borrowing from Erikson's (1956) apt term, the parental psychosocial identity.

Thus, because the inclusive fitness of parent and child are only in part the same, there is a basic biological reason to assume, as Robert Trivers (1974), the leading theorist in contemporary social biology, put it, that

> conflict is . . . an expected feature of such [parent-offspring] relations . . . in particular, over how long the period of parental investment should last, over the amount of parental investment . . . and over the altruistic and egoistic tendencies of the offspring. (p. 249)

Put more broadly, at the level of the psychological phenotype, we expect normative (as opposed to simply pathological) conflict to occur in the complex developmental process by which the child's identity is formed. Conflict should also be a regular, ongoing feature of the interaction between the identities of parent and child. Our hypothesis is that, over vast evolutionary time, the realities of this "universal relational matrix" represent the chief selection pressure that shaped important aspects of the psychodynamic "deep structure" (Chomsky, 1972) of our mind.*

---

*The term "psychodynamic deep structure" is inspired by Chomsky's (1972) notion of linguistic deep structure, the complex innate, universal mechanisms that enable individuals to learn and use specific, culturally determined languages. In this context, we are referring to those innate, universal psychodynamic structural features (e.g., a self, an ego, repression, primary object attachments) that, similarly, enable our psyche to process interactive, developmental experience and use it to build a functioning, adult identity.

## THE ADAPTIVE DILEMMA OF THE HUMAN CHILD

### A Few Facts Concerning Human Adaptation

The following are a few facts concerning human adaptation:

1. The prolonged childhood of the human species entails a period of extreme dependency and immaturity in which an enormous amount of innate, hard-wired responsiveness has been sacrificed in the course of human evolution to create the flexibility in the child's capacity for constructing an identity through social interactions. This plasticity in the psychosocial representation of the child's own inclusive self-interest can thus permit an exquisite attunement to the complex, changing realities of the sociocultural world into which he or she is born (LaBarre, 1954; Mayr, 1983).

2. The long developmental period of parent-child interaction (as well as the interactions between the child and the wider social environment) is one in which most interpersonal transactions—arguably the most important ones—take place through language and other forms of symbolic communication. Much that is communicated and learned is *not* rooted in direct observation, but rather comes through symbolic communication. Language and other forms of symbolism enable the child to construct a map of the relational world that far exceeds (and differs in quality from) anything that could be created from direct experience (Konner, 1982).

3. Yet, as numerous theorists have increasingly noted (Mitchell, 1985; Trivers, 1985), deception is a pervasive, universal intrinsic feature of all animal communication. In the pursuit of their own inclusive fitness, organisms do not simply communicate to convey a truth about reality to others, but rather to convey a "presentation of self": to hide certain features and selectively accentuate others that they need or desire others to perceive. The unique feature of human symbolic communication—its displacement from direct observation—greatly amplifies this power both to convey realities accurately and to hide them.

### Psychological Implications of Human Prolonged Childhood, Language, and the Role of Deception

With the factors of prolonged childhood, learning, and language in mind, we can try to formulate the central adaptive dilemma of the human child, that is, the essence of what he or she must accomplish psychologically to know and enhance his or her own inclusive fitness. Biologically, we know the child must maximize the amount of investment (time, interest, love, guidance) given by the parental environment. This is critical to basic survival and, equally, to the maximization of fitness. Psychologically, we know that the child must incorporate from the parents whatever is in the child's own interest to learn accurately (about self and the world) as this is transmitted through the parents' vision of reality. This aspect of the problem is well known and is essentially the sole focus of theories of attachment (e.g., Bowlby, 1969) that have accurately stressed the motivational significance of attachment but have viewed it in isolation, outside the context of the inherently competing interests that characterize the kin environment.

The adaptive problem of the human child is far more complex than has ever been dealt with by attachment theories. The child is almost totally dependent on direct investment from an environment that only partially shares that self-interest. More problematically still, the only chance for the child to develop an internalized map of reality—a well-structured inner guide to the relational world—is to have a way of dealing adequately with the inherent, often covert, biases in the parental environment by correcting or compensating for them so as to use the parents' interpretations of reality to define and build crucial aspects of his or her own self. In short, the human child is dependent on self-interested parental figures not only to survive, learn, and grow, but also as objects to internalize in the very process of forming a self and a defined sense of its own self-interest. How, then, does the child maintain and promote a sufficiently unbiased sense of its own self-interest throughout the developmental process?

The evolutionist asks, "How did the human child evolve the basic structural-dynamic capacity, as it were, to accomplish this task? In functional turns, how would one want to "design" a child to be capable of developing a viable, internalized self derived through interactive relationships while, simultaneously, successfully looking out for his or her own specific interests under such conditions?" We suggest that the concept of repression provides a basic clue as to how this took place.

## REPRESSION AS THE CORNERSTONE OF AN EVOLUTIONARY-ADAPTIVE SOLUTION

### A Functional Redefinition of Repression

Repression is a psychological process in which attention or conscious awareness is structurally diverted, as it were, from certain wishes, aims, affects, or images of self and others. Into the more conscious realm go those wishes and aims that are overtly more acceptable to, and internally more congruent with, the close kin environment of the family (including parental identities and views of reality). At the same time, however, the dynamic conception of repression ensures that many of the child's aims and views less acceptable to or less congruent with parental views will not be lost as potential representations of, or guidelines for, the pursuit of the child's own narrower (in the sense of more purely individual) interests. Unlike a simple model in which behavioral responses are learned and unlearned, the process of repression ensures that these aims, as well as related self and object representations, can be put away, out of consciousness, but held in reserve, to return or be retrieved when it may well be in the child's long-range interests to do so (Slavin, 1985).

We are saying, in effect, that, from an evolutionary perspective, what may be the *most* critical function of repression is *not* its more obvious diversion of conscious subjective experience, but rather, its use of such a diversion to preserve access to temporarily unacceptable but potentially vital aims and needs. Indeed, the evolutionary biology of parent-offspring conflict theory (Trivers, 1974) predicts precisely that such potentially conflictual, individually self-interested aims will surface when (a) conditions of direct parental investment decrease or threaten to decrease, and/or (b) the parents' control over and view of reality is less closely aligned with the child's interests than it was when the repression took place.

Repression thus can be seen as a central psychological process that makes possible a certain innate skepticism—a normative resistance to oversocialization into the family culture (Slavin, 1985). This dynamically accessible storage then actually permits the child to risk being far more open to and influenced by the culture of that environment. The relational world can be "used" (in Winnicott's sense of "the use of an object" and Kohut's sense of the selfobject) as a means of self-structuralization far more readily than would otherwise be possible given the potential costs to fitness incurred by overt conformity—let alone internal accommodation—to a psychosocial world biased toward parental (and other social or group) interests (Kohut, 1984; Winnicott, 1965). And, given the intrinsic relational conflicts of interest within the family itself, such a biased outcome would virtually always be the result of *normative* socialization pressures. This, we should remember, is distinct from whatever further distortions may be introduced by parental pathology.

Slavin and Kriegman (1992) stated the following:

> In terms of the "design problem" we are considering, repression represents an evolved strategy, part of an overall adaptive design,

that allows the child to identify with, to optimally internalize major components of the parents' psychosocial identities without sacrificing the child's own long-term interests. Repression permits the child to "plan" for—to be more fully equipped to deal with—future developmental contingencies some of which are predictable parts of the life cycle, others of which are not. What is crucial in this regard is that the process of repression actually ensures that aspects or versions of the child's self will never be irretrievably lost. Rather, they will be "put away" out of consciousness, but held in reserve, "pressing to return," not in a blind mechanical sense but functionally available under altered relational conditions.

From the evolutionary-adaptive perspective, what may be the most critical aspect of the classical concept of repression is that it signifies or alerts us to the fact that at the very center of psychic organization lies an organized inner system that enables us to use a diversion of awareness, an alteration of consciousness—in effect an act of "intentional" or strategic self-deception—while simultaneously preserving the possibility of access to temporarily unacceptable but potentially vital versions of the self. Repression is a central aspect of our deep structure, one that makes it possible that a certain innate skepticism can exist in the child, a skepticism vis-à-vis the whole developmental process; this capacity allows the child to *temporarily* shape itself to fit into the family (or other social environment) while preserving (as an existing unconscious potential) parts of the self that serve as a check on "over-socialization" (Wrong, 1963) into the family culture. (pp. 158–159)

The dynamic process we refer to as repression thus can be seen as an evolved, functional strategy that has become built into the psyche in the form of an inner force that generates altered experiential states. In response to the blind, mechanistic, overly physicalistic view of repression in the classical model, Mitchell (1988) argued that repression must be viewed as a state rather than a force in order to be compatible with the relational perspective. Yet the evolutionary-adaptive view depicts the way in which a mechanistic force can operate as a *means* of achieving broader relational ends.

## Development as an Intrapsychically Regulated Negotiation Process

We are suggesting that it may be useful to view the human child, during development, as centrally involved in the negotiation of a kind of provisional identity. This provisional psychic structure represents a kind of working compromise between the child's interests and the interests of the kin environment. It allows the child to keep alternative impulses, affects, and narcissistic and creative elements in reserve, out of awareness, perhaps, but not out of the realm of future renegotiated possibility (Slavin & Slavin, 1976).

What are the future events that may require renegotiation? There are expectable but unpredictable changes in parental and kin investment (e.g., the birth of siblings, the health and emotional state of parents, as well as the myriad ways in which family fortunes and dynamics can drastically change over time). We know that there are usually substantial shifts in the quality and attunement of most interpersonal environments at different periods of development (Erikson, 1964b).

More significantly, however, there is a major *predictable* change built into every child's life cycle—adolescence. A prolonged childhood in the context of primarily very close kin relations is, to be sure, an excellent environment in which to develop. Although we have emphasized intrafamilial conflicts of interests, biases, and normal deceptions, "kin altruism"—the motivation to identify with the interests of kin, based on highly overlapping self-interests—is real and adaptively indispensable. No one but parents and close kin could conceivably be counted on, in any regular, predictable way, to make the degree of investment necessary to ensure a human child's present and future development (Kriegman, 1988).

There is, however, a radical shift at adolescence. The biological change that takes place at adolescence is not only the well-known physiological maturation of the body, the brain, and the capacity for reproduction. It is also an equally fundamental—equally biological—shift from an environment composed primarily of interactions between close kin to an environment of more distant kin and unrelated individuals bound together primarily by ties of reciprocity and exchange.

Although there are vast differences (between social classes, cultures, and historical eras) in the degree to which adolescents are expected to move away from the family in the process of establishing an adult life, there is, nevertheless, always a *relative* movement away from primary relationships with close kin toward more distant and unrelated individuals (for mating and exchange relationships) in virtually every human society. Biologically, there are vast differences in the meanings of relationships with different degrees of relatedness (Trivers, 1985).

We would expect, therefore, that a major developmental mechanism would have to exist by which those elements of individual identity developed in the context of kin investment and kin altruism can be reevaluated and renegotiated in the context of the drastically different conditions of reciprocal exchange outside the nuclear family.

The ubiquity of regression in adolescence that has long fascinated psychoanalytic theorists (see Blos, 1979; Erikson, 1964a, 1964b; Freud, 1958) may be understood within the evolutionary framework as an adaptive process that has been prepared for by the operation of repression in childhood. In this view, adolescent regression represents the process by which selectively repressed aims and identity elements that did not fit the family environment are retrieved at a later point in development when they may provide a uniquely valuable means with which to renegotiate what is essentially a new compromise between individual interests and the new parameters and possibilities of an altered environment. Inclusive self-interest—provisionally internalized in a childhood identity—is thus reopened and, in the course of interaction with new objects, redefined into its adult form (Slavin, 1994; Slavin & Slavin, 1976).

## REPRESSION AS DECEPTIVE TACTIC AND DEVELOPMENTAL STRATEGY

Repression has been described (Alexander, 1979; Nesse, 1990; Slavin, 1974; Slavin & Slavin, 1976; Trivers, 1976, 1985) as a mechanism by which the individual engages in a complex form of self-deception to deceive others into greater investment and reciprocity than would obtain if the person's true intentions were known. The self- (or inner) deception presumably makes the social (or external) deception far more believable by convincing others that what is overtly expressed represents the true experiential state and intentions of the individual who is engaged in the self-deceptive strategy (that he or she really believes it and means it). However, such a strategy exists at potentially considerable costs to the actor in divorcing him or her even temporarily from a more complete or accurate perception of reality (Trivers, 1976, 1985). The cost of repression—the structural distortion of reality and the loss of crucial dimensions of meaning—is quite real. Traditionally, it is what overwhelmingly impresses the clinician in considering the workings of repression, and has created the common tendency to equate repression and psychopathology.

While at the overt, behavioral level, the description of repression as a self-deception in the service of deception is, no doubt, valid, this conceptualization does not adequately explain how its benefits outweigh its costs, nor does it convey several of the important human developmental and dynamic functions of repression we have discussed. We need a broader conception of repression that is compatible with these deceptive functions but also captures the full range of adaptive functions that re-pression may have evolved to serve. Such a view needs to embrace those aspects of repression that sequester and safeguard individual interests so as to enable the individual to become truly an integral part of the rela-tional world; such functions, while safeguarding individual interests, also promote empathy, mutual identification, and cooperative action.

In certain cases where (a) the welfare of the other individual is be-lieved to supersede the costs to self (such as many parental and certain other close kin interactions), or (b) there are likely to be long-term recip-rocal benefits to self or kin from altruistic action, we have probably been designed to experience quite genuine, subjective altruistic impulses; that is, not reducible to other more selfish aims (Trivers, 1971). While such altruistic behavior is, by definition, self-interested (in that it "ulti-mately" benefits the individual's own genes), as Kriegman (1988) has shown, there is no reason to believe that genuinely altruistic motivations cannot exist at the level of the proximal mechanisms (the affective sig-nals and perceptions that actually provide the inner push to motivate hu-man action). No doubt, it is sometimes necessary to repress more self-interested aims and egocentric aspects of identity to act in accord with such altruistic intent.

### Repression as Behavioral Tactic versus a Developmental, Dynamic Strategy

The notion (found especially in the biological and nonpsychoanalytic psychological literature) that repression has been selected as a self-deception in the service of deception may thus need to be expanded. It must embrace not only the altruistic or prosocial dimension of the proc-ess but, more significantly, move it beyond the level of a simple, decep-tive "behavioral tactic" to include its broader, "strategic," developmental functions. These functions provide for a "provisional identity" in the parent-offspring environment as well as its renegotiation under condi-tions of changed investment.

The capacity to suspend access to parts of one's inner experience—indeed to vital aspects of the self—and later to make use of this reserve in negotiations with the environment can also serve as a major fulcrum for dynamic change throughout the entire life cycle (Slavin, 1994; Slavin & Slavin, 1976). It is an internal mechanism that governs current adapta-tion as well as future change, rather than simply a set of self-deceptive and deceptive behavioral tendencies as has been described by certain bio-logical authors (Lockhard, 1980). Indeed, it is possible that given the high cost of self-deception, a mechanism such as repression could *only* have conferred a sufficiently large, net selective benefit if, in fact, it served *all* these complex, far-ranging functions.

## A Functional Redefinition of the Traditional Analytic Concept of Endogenous, Instinctual Drives

Parallel to this functional reinterpretation of repression, the evolutionary perspective also suggests a corollary function for the role of endogenous, instinctual drives. The evolutionary view of repression represents a solution to one aspect of what we have called the dilemma of human adaptation: how the human child took the enormous historical risk, as it were, of sacrificing a huge amount of innate, hard-wired adaptedness in favor of evolving a psyche that needs to take on most of its own identity through internalized interactions with a relational environment that is inevitably somewhat biased toward the self-interest of others. How have we risked evolving a long, complex program of development that is dependent on symbolic, deception-prone interactions with powerful, needed objects whose own interests will inevitably lead them to try to shape our identity to conform more closely to their interests?

If the dynamics of repression do represent a significant way in which we are internally equipped with a strategy for hiding, preserving, and retrieving those aspects of our aims and experience that cannot fit with the developmental environment, we still need to explain how such uniquely personal aims ever arise in the first place. Enter the notion of the endogenous (or instinctual) drive.

As Bateson said, "The concept of instinctual drive explains nothing but it does point to something that needs explaining" (Modell, 1987). What "needs explaining" from an evolutionary-adaptive perspective is how we can conceive the origins of those affect states or emotional signals that press us to act in intensely self-interested ways if, on the whole, the self is defined entirely as a social, relational product, a configuration built up of interactional meanings (Kernberg, 1980; Stolorow et al., 1987), introjected objects (Jacobson, 1964), or internalized self-object functions (Kohut, 1984). Can it be expected that a socially, or relationally constructed self, totally built out of familial-cultural meanings, could be counted on to generate and insist on the pursuit of a whole range of passionately individual aims? As Dennis Wrong (1963) pointed out, theories that do not adequately address this question will always present us with an "oversocialized image of man," an incomplete and unrealistic picture of human motivation. Thus there need to be other sources of experience that will activate and sustain the emotional salience of those subjective states likely to lead to self-interested actions (Lloyd, 1984). In other words, we need to have a guaranteed access to some types of motivation that arise from nonrelational sources and are, in a sense, totally dedicated to the promotion of our individual interests.

The single, unique functional feature of endogenous drives—conceived as a type of motivation rooted in our bodily nature—is the way in which they will protect our genetic self-interest from being usurped by the social influence of important others, notably those serving as models for introjection and identification in the course of development. Thus evolutionary theory suggests that a type of motivation that, at least in this respect, resembles the instinctual drives of the classical model may need to exist as one type of proximal mechanism that provides a unique source of adaptively relevant information operating within the larger functional organization of the aims of the individual. Yet simply because such endogenous motives must be closely linked to bodily—as distinct from relational or environmental—sources of input, there is no need to equate them with what is animal or biological in our nature, nor, certainly, do they exist in basic opposition to something that is presumably nonbiological, or social, in our nature. From an evolutionary perspective, this is a completely false, misleading dichotomy (Mayr, 1974).

This conception of the balancing function of the drives in relation to social influences echoes Rapaport's (1960) notion of the way in which the drives guarantee a certain "autonomy from the superego" or, as Eagle (1984) more recently put it, the instincts serve to resist the individual's "enslavement by society." It is critical to note, however, that the evolutionary argument for the adaptive function of the drives differs radically from its ego psychological predecessors (e.g., Rappaport). Beyond any of the modifications introduced by ego psychology, the evolutionary paradigm revises the assumptions of classical theory in several ways: (a) It puts the drives and their role into a clearly subsidiary position in relation to other, superordinate relational principles of motivation; (b) it emphasizes the existence of pervasive biases in the motives and aims of adults within the thoroughly good-enough environment—the essentially nonpathological, yet profoundly self-interested, environmental influences that the child must be equipped both to internalize *and* resist in the course of normal development.

The basic nature of the drives themselves has thus been profoundly shaped over our evolutionary history by its social, development functions as part of a larger, superordinate intrapsychic system that generates individual identity and safeguards inclusive fitness. In a profound sense, for our social self to be viably constructed from a culture of intersubjective meanings (Ricoeur, 1970), it must be equally rooted in and continuously informed by our biological nature.

### Repression: The Prototype of All Defenses

Freud (1926/1961) came to view defenses as designating the various methods that the ego employs to deal with conflicts, and he saw repression as a specialized form of defense. Anna Freud (1936) viewed repression as having an elevated status among the defenses. She saw it as unique in its efficacy, as "capable of mastering powerful instinctual impulses, in face of which the other defensive measures are quite ineffective" (p. 49). Anna Freud was interested in understanding what factors determine the ego's choice of defense. On this question, she made various speculations but ultimately expressed uncertainty. She considered the possibility that repression functions best to combat sexual wishes whereas other methods of defense function best against different kinds of instinctual forces, mainly aggressive impulses. She also raised the possibility that other methods of defense function "to complete what repression has left undone or to deal with such prohibited ideas as return to consciousness when repression fails" (p. 51). Finally she tried to link the various defenses to specific developmental periods and the instinctual urges associated with those periods.

Within the evolutionary-adaptive framework, repression can be seen as a generic defensive process that underlies all the other defenses. According to this view, the overarching function of all defensive strategies is simultaneously to keep out of awareness yet preserve the possibility of retrieving subjective experiences (motives, strivings, impulses, perceptions, etc.) that jeopardize the vital interests of the self. In childhood, the primary interest of the self is to maximize parental investment. The various defenses are seen here, as Nesse (1990) put it, as "specialized strategies for deception" (p. 279). Why, though, would we need specialized strategies? We can speculate that the tremendous variations in the relational environment partly account for the specialization of functions implied by the multiplicity of defenses. In wars, military leaders employ an array of strategies for the purpose of dissimulation. The specific strategies they choose depend on a variety of factors, including the enemies' strengths and weaknesses, their own strengths and weaknesses, and the existing environmental conditions. Similarly, an individual's choice of strategy for deception or defense is likely to be based on a number of different variables, including the individual's constitutional and temperamental predispositions, the prevailing deceptive strategies or defensive methods available to be learned and the specific relational conditions, which may call for one defense rather than another. This last notion is one that Nesse (1990) elaborated.

## The Case of Peter

The following clinical material serves to illustrate the role of defenses as viewed from within an evolutionary-adaptive framework.

Peter, a 29-year-old married man, entered therapy in response to marital conflict emanating from his wife's angry reactions to what she saw as his minimal degree of involvement and investment in her (his insufficient attention, consideration, and affection). After several years of therapy, it became clear that Peter felt, in his mother's eyes, that he was less important than his older brother. He felt that his brother was treated as very special while he was treated as simply a body that had to be fed and clothed. He felt like an "afterthought." To elicit as much parental investment and interest in him as was possible, Peter developed a system of relating that was geared toward fulfilling his parents' wishes. He strived to do whatever he could to make them happy. This meant living up to the family ideals, which involved behaving in accord with certain narrowly construed moral norms and making lifestyle choices, including the timing of decisions about career, marriage, and buying a home, based on his family's expectations. It also meant fulfilling his mother's wishes for him to stay close to her and not to upset her by being critical or angry at her. He recalled the occasions when his mother became upset as terribly frightening—she became explosive and chastised whichever one of her four children had "upset" her. Peter's capacity for perceiving what his mother needed of him became highly developed.

His dilemma became evident in the transference as well. He was often greatly concerned with the impact of his needs on the therapist's needs. For example, if he needed to cancel an appointment because of a business trip (he was not charged for these cancellations), he worried about the effect on the therapist of the lost fee. He worried too about the effect of arriving late for a session on the therapist, specifically whether the therapist would be angry with him for what he felt was his failure to meet his therapist's need for him to arrive on time. Whenever he chose to take care of himself, he was very wary of displeasing his therapist. The result was that the therapist felt exceptionally unthreatened, and that he was being treated in a respectful and careful manner.

During his childhood when Peter tried his own unique way of doing things, his parents let him know that any deviation from their ways was wrong and would inevitably result in failure. When Peter disappointed his parents (and they were sure to let him know of this), he felt that he had failed as a son. Peter's parents were highly adroit, and successful, in encouraging a perception of themselves as self-sacrificing (putting their children's interests above their own). Peter grew up accepting, at least manifestly, this view of his parents.

The cost of Peter's adaptation to his family environment was that he grew up with little access to his own wants and needs. His attempts at self-assertion and separation were effectively hampered. During the course of therapy, Peter's use of dissociation as a strategy designed to keep his self-interested aims, motives, and wishes out of awareness emerged with increasing clarity. In spite of an increase to twice-weekly sessions after a year of once-a-week therapy, Peter regularly forgot what had been discussed in the previous session. Gradually, aided by a minimal amount of reminding by the therapist, Peter was able to recall a great deal of what he had forgotten and, more importantly, he was able to regain access to perceptions, feelings, and strivings from which he had so radically disconnected. An understanding of why he had become dissociated from his experience also emerged. Usually it had to do with the threat to his relationships that he experienced when he was in touch with his own feelings. These feelings were inevitably connected to his own unique and self-interested strivings and aims. The threat that he felt usually involved his fear of disappointing or angering his mother, his wife, his boss, or his therapist. Over time, Peter came to perceive his parents as having deceived him into thinking that they had only his best interests in mind. He also came to see his own self-interested aims, wishes, and strivings as highly discrepant with theirs. This newfound awareness brought with it a stronger, more vibrant, and buoyant experience of himself. He was able to differentiate himself further from his parents and to make choices for himself and his marriage based not on his family's moral code but on his own uniquely self-interested wishes. This also involved a greater investment in and commitment to his wife and to their marriage. Some of his choices in this regard came at the cost of an increased sense of isolation from his parents and a fear of alienating or hurting them.

As he has increasingly differentiated his own aims from those of his parents and invested himself more fully in his marriage, Peter's tendency to subordinate his own wishes to those of his wife, and his fear of displeasing her, have emerged as salient issues within the treatment. It has become clear that he feels a tremendous sense of responsibility for her well-being and that he tends to have feelings of inadequacy and worthlessness whenever she expresses her displeasure toward him. At these times, he automatically assumes that he has failed to please her and is, therefore, an inferior husband. He typically responds by trying to atone or repent through a self-punitive or self-depriving mode, and then he redoubles his efforts to please her, usually at the cost of sacrificing his own interests. Peter's use of dissociation to keep out of awareness his self-interested aims and motives can be seen as having served simultaneously to maximize his parents' investment in him while growing up and to hold in abeyance, or keep in a dormant state, his autonomous and self-interested strivings until relational conditions changed, which they did most definitely as a result of getting married. Dissociation for Peter seemed to be a defense based on a style that was modeled by his father and brother. Moreover, given the pressures on him to disavow his self-interest to accommodate to his parents' rigid worldview, a radical defensive strategy was perhaps necessary for him to make the required adaptation.

## CONCLUSIONS: THE BIOLOGY OF PARENT-OFFSPRING CONFLICT VERSUS THE METAPSYCHOLOGIES OF CLASSICAL AND RELATIONAL MODELS IN PSYCHOANALYSIS

Let us now reapproach the problem with which we started, the two contrasting psychoanalytic views of repression: the classical and relational paradigms. First, we shall show how the evolutionary perspective fundamentally alters our understanding of the average expectable or good-enough environment in a fashion that shares features with both these models yet reassembles them in a way that diverges significantly from each. Second, we shall show how evolutionary reasoning suggests an altered conception of what is primary in our basic motivational aims and why these aims inherently conflict. Finally, we shall discuss what the new evolutionary paradigm implies about the meaning of repression and clinically observed patterns of repetition.

### The Psyche as an Evolved Adaptation That Has Been Structured by Relational Conflict

Evolutionary social theory in general, and parent-offspring conflict theory in particular, radically change our overall picture of what actually comprises normal developmental interactions—whether this is cast in ego-psychological terms as the average expectable environment or, more relationally, as good-enough, and ordinary devoted parental concern. Congruent with the relational tradition (e.g., aspects of the interpersonalists, Fairbairn, Winnicott, self-psychology), the evolutionary perspective suggests that we take a fundamentally holistic, relational view of object relations. Such a view implies that we are innately social beings in whom the basic structure of mind, object ties, and attachments ultimately derives from forces inherent in the world of interpersonal interactions. This view differs from the highly individualistic, classical perspective in which the vicissitudes of endogenous drive gratification and frustration are seen as the primary forces that create and organize all aspects of the psyche (Greenberg & Mitchell, 1983).

In other words, the basic patterning of our psychic structure is ultimately explainable as an evolved, deep structural adaptation that has been shaped over vast evolutionary time to regulate the inherently conflicting pressures of the relational world. Significant universal (or psychodynamically invariant) aspects of our psyche are, indeed, seen as patterned by an "interpersonal field" as Greenberg and Mitchell (1983) have characterized the relational perspective. But this field is, in good part, not equated with the individual developmental experience of each individual. Rather, it is the relational world of countless life cycles, in which hundreds of thousands of generations of our ancestors (and their unsuccessful competitors) strove to maximize their inclusive fitness.

As noted earlier, endogenous or physiologically rooted (instinctual) drives probably represent a functionally necessary type of motivation within the deep structure of such a system that helps to safeguard individual self-interest in face of the enormous defining and shaping power of the relational world during individual development. Yet, although such a paradigm is consummately relational in character (even its drive mechanism is seen as shaped over evolutionary time by the interactions in the relational field), it sharply differs from all existing psychoanalytic relational theories in two ways:

1. It does not dichotomize what is innate (or endogenous) and what is derived from relational interactions—selectively advantageous past relational strategies *become* innate dynamics and endogenous inputs.
2. The narrative account it gives of the normative developmental interactions within the relational world (past and present) is quite different from the underlying narratives found in existing relational models.

### Intrinsic Relational Conflict in the Expectable, Good-Enough Environment

The evolutionary perspective depicts an environment that universally consists of distinct, unique individuals whose interests necessarily diverge and, to some degree, inevitably compete. This evolutionarily based conception of conflict is at marked variance with the tendency of existing relational theories to attribute virtually all psychologically significant conflict to inadequacy, pathology, or abnormal lack of attunement in the caregiving environment (Kriegman & Slavin, 1990). In other words, the evolutionary perspective suggests that conflict and its accompanying strategic deceptions and self-deceptions are intrinsic features of all object relations and interactions. The conflictual dimension—Winnicott, Kohut, Sullivan, and others notwithstanding—is understood to be absolutely normative in the fully good-enough environment.

There are huge variations in the degree to which parents (and the caregiving environment as a whole) are able to recognize and respond to the child's own intrinsic self-interest and this, to be sure, will profoundly affect the child's capacity to manage and integrate those intrinsic, universal tensions and inner divisions that we are depicting as an inherent part of the relational reality itself. The ways and the amount that these normative conflicts influence the development patterns we call psychopathological may be more of an open question than is usually recognized, particularly by retrospective analyses in which early experience is assumed to be the sole factor in shaping later pathology (see Mitchell, 1988). It may make a real difference in our eventual understanding of pathology whether we think about the normal relational world as an inherently mutualistic reality of convergent interests, or one of mutuality as well as (ambiguously) divergent interests and subjective biases. Might it not be the case that the dilemmas and conflicts of development are sufficiently complex, ambiguous, at times wrenchingly painful—and only partially soluble—to necessitate enduring patterns of self-deception? Do not such universal, relational dilemmas remain, for many individuals, very deeply and elusively entwined with other facets of psychopathology?

## Primary Relational Conflict

This perspective yields a view of our intrapsychic struggles characterized by a primary relational conflict (as distinct from the drive-based conflict depicted in the classical model or the environmentally induced conflict of the relational perspective). In other words, both the harmony and conflict that exist in human relations are found in the interactive dynamics of the relations themselves, as opposed to being something that is, in a sense, imposed on them by drive demands or environmental pathology. Certainly, relational dynamics are influenced by the adaptively relevant information provided by endogenous drives (as *one* source of input on the more selfishly individual side) as well as profoundly shaped by the character and reliability of the particular relational world into which we are born; our selves are nevertheless normally divided, rather than unified, entities. This inherent dividedness is embodied in the fact that our primary motivational structure is very likely to be broadly organized around two simultaneous, yet inherently competing, sets of aims:

1. The first is a relatively altruistic set of social aims and related affects that represent adaptations to the realities of our shared, overlapping interests (the realities of the extended self). Such motives—object love, altruism, and all the attachment-based affects—are as real, primary, and innate as the aggressive and libidinal instinctual aims that the classical model views as motivational bedrock. In the classical view, such social motives have been characterized as a complex, layered—yet ultimately defensive and reactive—overlay on aggressively self-interested aims (Kriegman, 1988).

2. The second is a competing set of shorter term, more aggressively self-interested, "driven" aims that represent the unique, inherently selfish, needs of the individual. Such aims are, in part, sustained and guaranteed to operate in the interests of the individual by virtue of their making use of endogenous drives—or nonrelationally based motives—as vital, imperative signals of adaptively relevant information, or peremptory pushes, that will effectively counter the powerful, inherently biased forces (of others' self-interests) in the normal relational environment.

Intrapsychic conflict thus represents an "archaic heritage," as Freud (1939/1961) put it, by which is meant an ancient, inner structural legacy that is our inherited capacity to organize and cope with the incredibly complex realities of divergent interests, conflict, and bias in the relational world.* Such a model echoes Bakan's (1966) conception of the inherent opposition between "agentic" (individualistic, selfish) aims and "communal" (other-directed or group-oriented) aims in human motivation. The emphasis in this evolutionary model is similar to Klein's (1976) effort to reformulate the universal basis for inner conflict in terms of a clash between "inherently irreconcilable human aims" in preference

---

*The term "archaic heritage" was used by Freud many times to refer to psychological dispositions (e.g., guilt) or structures (e.g., the superego) that he believed had, at least in part, universal, evolutionarily based, inherited features. Freud had no grasp of the genetic mechanism of natural selection and did not fully appreciate the possible functions of such innate, functional designs. He substituted his own, somewhat naive speculations in place of this theoretical knowledge. Consistent with modern evolutionary theory, however, he recognized that a broader, evolutionary perspective would shed light on virtually all psychodynamic mechanisms (especially the ones concerning conflict; see Slavin & Kriegman, 1988).

to the ego psychological notion of an inherent clash between ego and id (Eagle, 1984). The reinterpretation of instinctual drives in functional, evolutionary terms as a means—subordinate to and operating in the service of broader, relational ends—resembles Fairbairn's (1952) attempt to recast the libido theory in an object relational context. Yet, in clear distinction to all such previous attempts at reformulating the nature of inner conflict, the evolutionarily based model is rooted in a general theory of the inherently conflictual relationship between individuals and their relational environment. It is supported by a broad conception of how the overall functional architecture of the psyche has been selectively shaped by the adaptive requirements of developing and functioning within that relational context.

## The Dual Meaning of Repression (and Clinically Observed Repetition)

From the evolutionary perspective, conflicts of interest and the occurrence of deception and self-deception have an inherent place in the relational world, and development is understood as an inherently conflictual process of constructing and negotiating the inner experiential structures, the configurations of personality that represent the individual's "inclusive self-interest" in such an environment.

### The Classical View

*Selfishness, Distortion, and Deception in the Child.* In qualified agreement with the classical view, the evolutionary conception of repression depicts a developmental strategy that consists of a significant degree of thoroughly normal, adaptively necessary deception and self-deception that must be sustained by mechanisms designed to hide from awareness motives and perceptions that are distinctly biased toward the child's own interest, the completely natural, yet undeniably self-centered and selfish pursuit of his or her own aims. These repressed aims are, by their very nature, at times in phenotypic (openly observed) competition with the aims and needs of even the child's closest (kin) objects. The individual's assertion of such aims will, under some conditions, inevitably impede, diminish, and often harm the interests of others.*

---

*The aggressive component of these aims is viewed as essentially self-assertive in nature rather than emanating from a central reservoir of inherently destructive or sadistic energies as the Freudian, and particularly the Kleinian, metapsychologies would have it. From an evolutionary perspective, the existence of an overriding destructive drive energy that requires discharge would be a costly, unnecessary way for natural selection to have designed us.

Yet the evolutionary view only partially resembles the familiar notion that aggression is a response to relational frustration or a more contemporary relational "systems" view (e.g., Stechler

*Repression as the Defensive Disguise of Intrinsically Selfish Aims.* We can also find a more functional explanation of the classical view that the dynamic basis for the development of individuals as social beings revolves around the repression of their instinctual aims. Over and above its subjective role in attenuating inner pain or simply managing the inner psychic economy, repression self-deceptively and deceptively disguises motives that do not fit within the needs, interests, and biases of the family environment. Such motives do—in many, if not all, developmental environments—threaten to decrease parental investment and compromise individual fitness. However elemental, fragmentary, and costly this process of regulating awareness and managing self-presentation may end up to be, it is basically an adaptive effort to hypercathect and resist the relinquishment of aims and identity elements that are distinctly biased toward the child's own interests. Though it is cast in very different terms, this appears to be the adaptive reality that is referred to in the classical Freudian as well as Kleinian metaphors about the need to repress threatening libidinal and aggressive drives and their derivatives. This fact supports some of the stress placed in the classical and, especially, the ego psychological traditions (e.g., Hartmann, 1958; Kernberg, 1980) on the critical importance of the "successful" operation of repression in making development and inner integration (i.e., socialization) possible.

## The Relational View

*Altruism and Self-Knowledge in the Child.* There is however, a fundamental problem with the classical view. The classical perspective depicts a psyche in which the child's drives push selfishly toward individual advantage and operate through endogenous (bodily) impulses. Yet it misses the larger picture of how the psyche is functionally organized, viewing these motives as blind bodily forces exercising an ultimate kind of primal pressure on the mind to seek gratification. Not only are they taken out of context, but such patently selfish aims do not necessarily represent any

---

& Halton, 1987) that healthy self-assertiveness becomes "contaminated" with destructive rage in an unresponsive environment. From the evolutionary perspective, the whole notion of environmental "frustration" and "unresponsiveness" is basically altered by the recognition that frustrating conflicts of interest and biased responsiveness are thoroughly expectable features encountered by an innately self-interested, self-promoting individual developing in the normally biased object world. Our overarching tendency to experience the world in a self-interested manner, and to act aggressively on this experience, will lead in the thoroughly good-enough environment—from earliest infancy onward—to certain major clashes between our aims and those of even our most intimate objects. The proximal mechanisms that equip us to deal with a biased, self-interested relational world may well include the capacity to mobilize—under certain conditions—urges and desires to harm others in the pursuit of our own advantage.

more basic or primal part of the motivational systems as a whole than do social, cooperative, and altruistic impulses (Kriegman, 1988).

On the contrary, even as we acknowledge the gap between certain of the child's wishes and realities of the external world, we must recognize that—given the expectable biases and self-interested (self-protective) motives of the caretaking environment—the child's subjective version of his or her own needs is likely to have been selected (and intricately designed) to be an extremely reliable guideline as to the realities of the child's own interests. Not only are so-called infantile impulses likely to include a substantial component of innate altruism, or attunement to the real interests of related others, but often so-called primitive perceptions (e.g., of parental motives and intent) and preverbal longings (for self-object merger) will express something closer to a "gene's eye" view of the realities of competing and overlapping interests that have been largely lost to the adult parental phenotypic perspective.

*Repression as the Sequestering of Vital Developmental Needs.* In agreement with the emphasis of the major relational theorists, the evolutionary perspective implies that we have been designed, as it were, to repress certain aspects of our affects, aims, and true identity in order to sequester them safely, to protect them from the inevitable side of the parental environment or family culture that is geared more closely to its interests than to the child's.

Implicitly, the evolutionary biological paradigm suggests the crucial adaptive need for an innate, subjective sense of our "true" (Winnicott, 1965), "authentic" (Fromm, 1941), or "nuclear" (Kohut, 1984) self. Moreover, it suggests that we have been designed to ensure that this vital configuration of impulses, aims, and fantasies is effectively held in reserve in order to be retrieved and reactivated under altered relational conditions. Such an overall structural design for the psyche is consistent with the basic meaning of repression in the later work of Kohut (1977, 1984) and Winnicott (1965).

## The Compulsion to Repeat versus the Capacity to Repeat

From a clinical vantage point, however, we rarely, if ever, see repression operate in a direct way. Instead, we see repetition. That is to say, the operation of repression is inferred from repeated patterns of behavior in which we assume that repressed aspects of the self are being expressed in restricted, indirect ways—usually in the form of certain actions or symptoms. Thus the meaning that is given to clinically observed patterns of repetition will derive in good part from our underlying assumptions about why and how repression operates.

From the classical perspective, problems in adaptation arise because the exclusion of repressed needs from awareness cannot be maintained (Brenner, 1976; Fenichel, 1945; Freud, 1936). The frustration, fixation, or traumatic overstimulation of infantile aims creates an imperative, continuous need to seek new arenas for their expression—albeit in distorted, disguised form. Caught in a web of continuing conflict (essentially over the selfishly aggressive character of these primary needs), individuals are driven to enact painful repetitions of their original failures to find acceptable ways of fulfilling their aims. This is the essence of the so-called compulsion to repeat (Freud, 1920/1961) or "repetition compulsion" (Bibring, 1943; Fenichel, 1945; Glover, 1955). It is a motivational concept that goes hand-in-hand with the classical view of repression and invariably plays an absolutely central role in the classical and ego-psychological definition and basic understanding of psychological disorder (Kriegman & Slavin, 1989).

Symptoms, transference repetitions, the persistence of subjectively painful, otherwise inexplicable actions are ultimately described as extended ways of reliving the past without consciously experiencing or knowing it. Most clinically observed repetitions are thus regarded not as persistent efforts at accomplishing something new, but rather as deceptive strategies for maintaining or restoring something old, some prior state of equilibrium, or status quo ante (Bibring, 1943). The emphasis is thus on repetition as signaling self-deception—as a way of keeping the connection alive but out of awareness. In effect, it becomes a way of *not* remembering, of *not* changing, of distorting meanings, of *not knowing*.

As we have seen, the evolutionary perspective suggests that the process of repression is indeed based, in part, on a kind of functional self-deception that diverts awareness from certain highly conflictual aims in a fashion that will ensure their later return as part of an ongoing, relational negotiation process. Thus we would expect that a whole range of earlier developmental experiences—particularly those relating to the individual's personal self-interest—will be readily revived and repeated at other points in development; it is assumed that the need to conceal and distort some of their more conflictual meanings will certainly continue to operate during the whole repetitive process of retrieving, reliving, and renegotiating both the internal and the interpersonal dimensions of the individual's identity or inclusive self-interest.

Thus the elements of overlap with the classical model are apparent: There is assumed to be a certain built-in tendency to return to and relive aspects of the past—particularly those in which conflicts over the expression and pursuit of personal self-interest is involved—and there is a persistent emphasis on the need to alter the subjective experience of reality in ways that would conceal certain selfish and aggressive aims that are likely to diverge and compete with those of needed others.

However, the differences between the evolutionary paradigm and the classical model are also significant, perhaps, ultimately, farther reaching. From the evolutionary perspective, the most important dynamic aspect of clinically observed repetitions—and the whole range of phenomena that are readily referred to as manifestations of the repetition compulsion—is the fact that they cannot be understood apart from the larger adaptive context in which they occur (Kriegman & Slavin, 1989), (Slavin & Kriegman, 1990).

Specifically, this means that the universal salience of early experiences, and the persistence of infantile attachments, is understood not primarily as a function of the inherent conservatism of the instincts or the persistence of the child's immature distortions of adult reality; rather, it is seen as one element in a far broader adaptive system designed to preserve repressed early experiences because, given the assumed biases in the familial version of reality, they represent a version of reality that contains substantial subjective truth. It is a version of reality that is particularly crucial for the process of redefining self-interest and thus adaptively reorganizing the self.

The repetitive enactment of repressed meanings is thus, ultimately, less accurately understood as an effort at self-deception and distortion of reality—though it inevitably includes this—than as a striving to make use of certain highly subjective meanings for the adaptively relevant information they contain, and to use them as renewed developmental guidelines. There is always an effort to communicate them in some form to others and (to the extent that the new environment is reliably different from the old one) to renegotiate their place in the structure of the self. Repression confers, in effect, a capacity for future repetition that may well appear to be (or even be experienced as) a compulsion. Unlike the repetition compulsion, it is not fundamentally in the service of restoring and maintaining an inner equilibrium, in the sense of a status quo, but rather of promoting developmental repair and change.

In this way, the evolutionary perspective profoundly validates the view of Winnicott and Kohut that developmental strivings toward the resumption of thwarted growth must play a central, perhaps superordinate, role in the organization of the psyche (Kriegman & Slavin, 1988, 1989). It supports recent efforts such as Stolorow and Lachmann's (1984) to increase our basic appreciation of the critical subjective truths entailed in the phenomena of transference, as well as efforts (e.g., Hoffman, 1983) to recast the meaning of transference in terms of a social exchange. It broadens and lends considerable weight to constructs such as the "curative fantasy" (Ornstein, 1984) in which many of the so-called misperceptions and distortions of reality in the transference are seen as expressions of patients' overarching efforts to generate the interactive conditions in which, for them, a cure may be possible.

## THE EVOLUTIONARY RAZOR CUTS BOTH WAYS

Thus, overall, the evolutionary view of the average expectable environment and the conflicts within it differs from both the classical and the relational traditions. It echoes aspects of both views—the centrality of conflict in the classical view and the innate sociality, the "primary object love" (Balint, 1965), if you will, of the relational perspective. Yet, it is really a new, unique paradigm in that it enables us to steer a conceptual course that avoids the following more problematic assumptions of each tradition:

1. The classical paradigm's overemphasis on the mechanics of drive discharge as the ultimate organizer of psychic structure, as well as that tradition's unsupportable assumptions about the primacy of a limited set of asocial, animal drives in human nature (Eagle, 1984; Holt, 1976; Klein, 1976).

2. The dubious underlying assumption in virtually all versions of relational theories (American interpersonalist, Kohutian, British object relationist) that convergence, harmony, or mutuality in aims and interests is what primarily characterizes the normal, good-enough environment and the related tendency to downplay the role of endogenously derived, inner conflict in the creation of psychic reality (Cooper, 1983; Wallerstein, 1983).

To the extent that we read the classical analytic agenda as synonymous with drive theory, the structural model, and many of its ego psychological revisions, the evolutionary perspective does not support it. From an evolutionary perspective, drives, and the structural model of drive-defense conflict, assume a secondary place within a larger, relationally designed and configured psyche. But, to the extent that the classical agenda is read as a narrative of conflict, it alone in the psychoanalytic realm captures certain major, significant features of the relational world and the inherently divided way we are adapted to it. Its metaphors depict the deep divisions and tensions within the self that are indispensable concomitants of an adaptation to the conflictual relational world.

Conversely, to the extent that the relational tradition has as its agenda the replacement of the narrative of conflict with a view of the normal relational world as consisting of individuals whose motives primarily converge and mutually harmonize, it finds little validation from an evolutionary perspective. If instead, however, we read it as a vision of human nature in which the overall functional architecture of our psyche is understood as holistically organized around motives and capacities for conducting our social relationships in the service of optimal, authentic self-development, the relational model finds a strong, clear echo in evolutionary biological thought.

An evolutionarily based metapsychology thus depicts us as innately individualistic *and* innately social, as endowed with inherently selfish, aggressively self-promoting aims *as well as* an equally primary, innately altruistic disposition toward those whose interests we share. We are, in short, never destined to attain the kind of highly autonomous individuality enshrined in the classical tradition, nor are we the completely social animal of the relational vision. We are essentially semisocial beings whose nature—or self structure and motivational system—is inherently divided between eternally competing aims.

The evolutionary biological paradigm permits us to embrace *both* classical and relational traditions as valid parts, indeed complementary parts—but *only* parts—of a larger, broader picture of human psychodynamic adaptation. This chapter has been an attempt to point us in the direction of such a new paradigm.

## REFERENCES

Alexander, R. D. (1979). *Darwinism and human affairs.* Seattle: University of Washington Press.

Badcock, C. (1985). *The problem of altruism.* Oxford: Basil Blackwell.

Bakan, D. (1966). *The duality of human existence: An essay on psychology and religion.* Chicago: Rand-McNally.

Balint, M. (1965). *Primary love and psychoanalytic technique.* New York: Liverwright.

Bibring, E. (1943). The conception of the repetition compulsion. *Psychoanalytic Quarterly, 12,* 486–519.

Blos, P. (1979). *The adolescent passage.* New York: International Universities Press.

Bowlby, J. (1969). Attachment. In *Attachment and loss.* New York: Basic Books.

Brenner, C. (1976). *Psychoanalytic technique and psychic conflict.* New York: International Universities Press.

Chomsky, N. (1972). *Language and mind.* San Diego: Harcourt Brace.

Cooper, A. (1983). The place of self psychology in the history of depth psychology. In A. Goldberg & P. Stepansky (Eds.), *Kohut's legacy: Contributions to self psychology* (pp. 3–17). Hillsdale, NJ: Analytic Press.

Eagle, M. (1984). *Recent developments in psychoanalysis.* New York: McGraw-Hill.

Erikson, E. (1956). The problem of ego identity. *Journal of American Psychoanalytic Association, 4*, 56–121.

Erikson, E. (1964a). *Identity youth and crisis.* New York: Norton.

Erikson, E. (1964b). *Insight and responsibility.* New York: Norton.

Fairbairn, W. R. D. (1952). *An object-relations theory of the personality.* New York: Basic Books.

Fenichel, O. (1945). *The psychoanalytic theory of the neurosis.* New York: Norton.

Freud, A. (1936/1966). *The ego and the mechanisms of defense.* New York: International Universities Press.

Freud, A. (1958). Adolescence. *Psycholanalytic study of the child, 13*, 255–278.

Freud, S. (1961). Repression. In J. Strachey (Ed. and Trans.), *The standard edition of the complete psychological works of Sigmund Freud* (Vol. 14, pp. 141–158). London: Hogarth Press. (Original work published 1915)

Freud, S. (1961). Beyond the pleasure principle. *The standard edition of the complete psychological works of Sigmund Freud* (Vol. 18, pp. 3–64). London: Hogarth Press. (Original work published 1920)

Freud, S. (1961). Inhibitions, symptoms, and anxiety. *The standard edition of the complete psychological works of Sigmund Freud* (Vol. 20, pp. 77–175). London: Hogarth Press. (Original work published 1926)

Freud, S. (1961). Moses and monotheism. *The standard edition of the complete psychological works of Sigmund Freud* (Vol. 23, pp. 7–140). London: Hogarth Press. (Original work published 1939)

Fromm, E. (1941). *Escape from freedom.* New York: Avon.

Glover, E. (1955). *The technique of psychoanalysis.* New York: International Universities Press.

Greenberg, J., & Mitchell, S. (1983). *Object relations and psychoanalytic theory.* Cambridge, MA: Harvard University Press.

Guntrip, H. (1971). *Psychoanalytic theory, therapy, and the self.* New York: Basic Books.

Hamilton, W. D. (1964). The genetical evolution of social behavior. *Journal of Theoretical Biology, 7*, 1–52.

Hartmann, H. (1958). *Ego psychology and the problem of adaptation.* New York: International Universities Press.

Hoffman, I. (1983). The patient as interpreter of the analyst's experience. *Contemporary Psychoanalysis, 19*(3), 389–442.

Holt, R. (1976). Drive or wish? A reconsideration of the psychoanalytic theory of motivation. In M. Gill & P. Golzman (Eds.), *Psychology versus metapsychology: Essays in memory of George S. Klein. Psychological Issues* [Vol. 9, No. 4, Monograph 36]. New York: International Universities Press.

Jacobson, E. (1964). *The self and the object world.* New York: International Universities Press.

Kernberg, O. (1980). *Internal world and external reality.* New York: Jason Aronson.

Klein, G. (1976). *Psychoanalytic theory.* New York: International Universities Press.

Kohut, H. (1977). *The restoration of the self.* New York: International Universities Press.

Kohut, H. (1982). Introspection, empathy and the semicircle of mental health. *International Journal of Psychoanalysis, 63,* 395–407.

Kohut, H. (1984). *How does analysis cure?* Chicago: University of Chicago Press.

Konner, M. (1982). *The tangled wing: Biological constraints on the human spirit.* New York: Harper & Row.

Kriegman, D. (1988). Self psychology from the perspective of evolutionary biology: Toward a biological foundation for self psychology. In A. Goldberg (Ed.), *Progress in self psychology* (Vol. 3, pp. 253–274). Hillsdale, NJ: Analytic Press.

Kriegman, D., & Slavin, M. (1989). The myth of the repetition compulsion and the negative therapeutic reaction: An evolutionary biological analysis. In A. Goldberg (Ed.), *Progress in self psychology* (Vol. 5, pp. 209–253). Hillsdale, NJ: Analytic Press.

Kriegman, D., & Slavin, M. (1990). On the resistance of self psychology: Clues from evolutionary biology. In A. Goldberg (Ed.), *Progress in self psychology* (Vol. 6). Hillsdale, NJ: Analytic Press.

LaBarre, W. (1954). *The human animal.* Chicago: University of Chicago Press.

Lawner, P. (1985). *Sincerity, authenticity, and the waning of the Oedipus complex.* Paper presented to the Manhattan Institute for Psychoanalysis, New York.

Lockhard, J. (1980). Speculations on the adaptive significance of self-deception. In *The evolution of human behavior.* New York: Elsevier.

Lloyd, A. (1984). *On the evolution of the instincts: Implications for psychoanalysis.* Unpublished manuscript.

Loewald, H. (1980). Some considerations on repetition and the repetition compulsion. In *Papers on psychoanalysis.* New Haven: Yale University Press. (Original work published 1965)

Mayr, E. (1974). Behavior programs and evolutionary strategies. *American Scientist, 62,* 650–659.

Mayr, E. (1983). *The growth of biological thought.* Cambridge, MA: Belknap Press of Harvard University Press.

Mahler, M., Pine, F., & Bergman, A. (1975). *The psychological birth of the human infant.* New York: Basic Books.

Mitchell, R. (1985). *Deception: Perspectives on human and non-human deceit.* New York: State University of New York Press.

Mitchell, S. (1988). *Relational concepts in psychoanalysis: An integration.* Cambridge, MA: Harvard University Press.

Modell, A. (1984). *Psychoanalysis of a new context.* New York: International Universities Press.

Nesse, R. (1990). The evolutionary functions of repression and the ego defenses. *The Journal of the American Academy of Psychoanalysis, 18*(2), 260–285.

Ornstein, A. (1984). Psychoanalytic psychotherapy: A contemporary perspective. In P. E. Stepansky & A. Goldberg (Eds.), *Kohut's legacy* (pp. 171–181). Hillsdale, NJ: Analytic Press.

Parsons, T. (1963). Social structure and the development of personality: Freud's contribution to the Integration of psychology and sociology. In N. Smeltser & W. Smeltser (Eds.), *Personality and social systems* (pp. 33–54). New York: Wiley.

Pine, F. (1985). *Developmental theory and clinical process.* New Haven: Yale University Press.

Rapaport, D. (1960). The structure of psychoanalytic theory. *Psychological Issues* [Vol. II, No. 2, Monograph 6]. New York: International Universities Press.

Ricoeur, P. (1970). *Freud and philosophy.* New Haven: Yale University Press.

Schafer, R. (1983). *The analytic attitude.* New York: Basic Books.

Segal, H. (1964). *Introduction to the work of Melanie Klein.* New York: Basic Books.

Slavin, M. (1974). *An evolutionary perspective on the mechanism of repression and the function of guilt.* Paper presented to the Graduate Seminar on Social Behavior, Department of Biology, Harvard University, Cambridge, MA.

Slavin, M. (1985). The origins of psychic conflict and the adaptive function of repression: An evolutionary biological view. *Psychoanalysis and Contemporary Thought, 8*(3), 407–440.

Slavin, M. (1992). The dual meaning of repression and the adaptive design of the human psyche. *The Journal of the American Academy of Psychoanalysis, 18*(2), 307–341.

Slavin, M. (1994). *Adolescence and the problem of human adaptation: The work of Anna Freud, Blos, and Erikson in the perspective of contemporary evolutionary biology.* Manuscript in preparation.

Slavin, M., & Kriegman, D. (1990). Toward a new paradigm for psychoanalysis: An evolutionary biological perspective on the classical-relational dialectic. *Psychoanalytic Psychology, 7* (Suppl.), 5–31.

Slavin, M., & Kriegman, D. (1988). Freud, biology, and sociobiology. *American Psychologist, 8,* 658–661.

Slavin, M., & Kriegman, D. (1992). *The adaptive design of the human psyche: Psychoanalysis, evolutionary biology, and the therapeutic process.* New York: Guilford Press.

Slavin, M., & Slavin, J. (1976). Two patterns of adaptation in late adolescent borderline personalities. *Psychiatry, 39,* 41–50.

Spence, D. (1982). *Narrative truth and historical truth: Meaning and interpretation in psychoanalysis.* New York: Norton.

Stechler, G., & Halton, A. (1987). The emergence of assertion and aggression in fancy: A psychoanalytic systems approach. *Journal of the American Psychoanalytic Association, 35*(4), 821–839.

Stolorow, R., Brandchaft, B., & Atwood, G. (1987). *Psychoanalytic treatment: An intersubjective approach.* Hillsdale, NJ: Analytic Press.

Stolorow, R., & Lachmann, F. (1984). Transference: The future of an illusion. In *The annual of psychoanalysis* (Vol. XII/XIII). Madison, CT: International Universities Press.

Sullivan, H. S. (1953). *The interpersonal theory of psychiatry.* New York: Norton.

Trivers, R. (1971). The evolution of reciprocal altruism. *Quarterly Review of Biology, 46,* 35–57.

Trivers, R. (1974). Parent-offspring conflict. *American Zoologist, 14,* 249–264.

Trivers, R. (1976). Foreword to *The selfish gene* by R. Dawkins. New York: Oxford University Press.

Trivers, R. (1985). *Social evolution.* Menlo Park, NJ: Benjamin Cummings.

Tooby, J., & Cosmides, L. (1989). Evolutionary psychology and the generation of culture, Part I: Theoretical considerations. *Ethology and Sociobiology, 10,* 1–3, 29–51.

Wallerstein, R. (1983). Self psychology and "classical" psychoanalytic psychology: The nature of their relationship. In A. Goldberg (Ed.), *The future of psychoanalysis* (pp. 19–64). New York: International Universities Press.

Wilson, E. O. (1975). *Sociobiology: The new synthesis.* Cambridge, MA: Belknap Press of Harvard University Press.

Winnicott, D. W. (1965). *The maturational processes and the facilitating environment.* London: Hogarth Press.

Wrong, D. (1963). The oversocialized conception of man in modern sociology. In N. Smeltser & W. Smeltser (Eds.), *Personality and social systems* (pp. 68–79). New York: Wiley.

# PART II
# Measurement

# 8

# The Life Style Index
## A Self-Report Measure of Ego Defenses

HOPE R. CONTE AND
ALAN APTER

The concept of ego defenses represents one of the most important contributions made by psychoanalysis to personality theory and to the theory of psychological adaptation. The two essential points in the Freudian conception of defenses are (a) they are unconscious; and (b) their function is to keep out of awareness impulses, desires, or affects that would be unacceptable or painful to the ego. In her work describing 10 methods of functioning that the ego uses to ward off dangerous drives or wishes, Anna Freud (1936) explicated these features. Since that time, the idea that external events as well as internal stimuli may trigger defenses because they too may stimulate intrapsychic conflict (Fromm, 1947; Sullivan, 1947) has become well accepted. More recently, investigators such as Vaillant (1971) and Horowitz (1988) have broadened the field even further. In addition to unconscious mechanisms directed at internalized prohibitions on the one hand and external reality on the other, they include mechanisms that are conscious. In general, there is substantial agreement among psychoanalysts and other clinicians on at least three aspects of defense mechanisms, in addition to their being unconscious and serving the function of dealing with potentially dangerous drives:

1. Although a patient may be characterized by his or her most prominent defense, each individual uses several defenses.
2. Defenses are dynamic and reversible.
3. Defenses may be adaptive as well as pathological (Perry & Vaillant, 1990; Sackeim, 1983).

However, considerably less agreement exists over how many defenses there are and what should or should not be considered a defense mechanism. In terms of numbers, Anna Freud (1936) originally described 10, Vaillant's (1971) glossary defines 18, DSM III-R (American Psychiatric

Association Committee, 1987) identifies 18, and Wong (1989) defines 32. The decision to include or exclude a mechanism as an ego defense appears to depend largely on an investigator's willingness to admit the more conscious mechanisms. For example, Brenner (1973); Plutchik, Kellerman, and Conte (1979); Conte and Plutchik (1993); and Perry and Cooper (1989) do not include "suppression" as a defense mechanism, considering it to be a conscious activity. In contrast, it is included by Andrews, Pollock, and Stewart (1989); Bond, Gardner, Christian, and Sigal (1983); Meissner, Mack, and Semrad (1975); and Vaillant, Bond, and Vaillant (1986); as are humor and other more clearly conscious mechanisms such as altruism. The authors of the Life Style Index (Plutchik et al., 1979) remain closer to the original Freudian notion of defenses as unconscious mechanisms, preferring to label the more conscious adaptive processes as "coping styles" (Plutchik & Conte, 1989).

There is also little agreement concerning how best to measure the presence and extent of defensive functioning in an individual. The most widely used approach has been the clinical, which includes the techniques and instruments developed by such investigators as Ablon, Carlson, and Goodwin (1974); Hackett and Cassem (1974); and Vaillant (1976). These methods require the judgment of interviewers, usually working with explicit definitions of the ego defenses and employing rating scales. These, of course, present the problem of interrater reliability as well as that of validity.

Other techniques of measurement derive from projective testing. For example, Kragh's Defense Mechanism Test (1969, 1985), which has been used extensively in Europe, utilizes subliminal perception. However, the validity of this type of assessment has been questioned (Cooper & Kline, 1986; Kline, 1987). Still other approaches depend on self-reports (e.g., Bond et al., 1983; Gleser & Ihilevich, 1969; Kreitler & Kreitler, 1972; Marshall, 1982). These have the advantage of potentially enhanced reliability by avoiding the issue of interrater agreement, but raise the question of how a self-report instrument can be used to measure unconscious processes. Despite their individual advantages and disadvantages, what all these defense mechanism tests have in common is the lack of a theoretical framework for explicating the relations among the defenses and related constructs.

The Life Style Index (Plutchik et al., 1979) does provide such a theoretical framework. Based on Plutchik's general theory of affect (1962, 1980), what this model does is to provide a rationale for the choice of defenses to be measured. At the same time, it helps to define the relations among these defenses. Little attention has been paid to the fact that defenses vary in their similarity to one another. It has been shown, for example, that displacement and projection are more similar to one another than they are to denial. In a similar fashion, repression and denial are more alike than either one is to intellectualization (Plutchik et al., 1979). These similarities imply that a circumplex, or circular, structure is appropriate for describing the relative similarities among the defenses. The circumplex also demonstrates that in addition to similarity, defense mechanisms are characterized by the property of polarity (see Figure 1–2, Chapter 1). The rationale for the proposed relations among the ego defenses, as well as the proposed relations among ego defenses, emotions, and diagnostic constructs, is presented more fully in Chapter 1.

The following sections will describe the Life Style Index and its properties and its use in clinical research, both in English and in translations, and will discuss some important issues requiring further research.

## THE LIFE STYLE INDEX

On the basis of a review of a large number of psychoanalytic, psychiatric, and psychological sources, 224 items were constructed to represent 16 defense mechanisms. Over the course of several studies designed to determine the psychometric properties of the test, the number of items was systematically reduced to 97. Also, a factor analysis indicated considerable overlap among the defenses. Thus, on the basis of empirical data as well as psychoanalytic theory, which holds that anxiety is at the core of the development of any defense, the items were regrouped into eight scales: compensation (including identification and fantasy), denial, displacement, intellectualization (including sublimation, undoing, and rationalization), projection, reaction formation, regression (including acting out), and repression (including isolation and introjection). Detailed definitions of these defenses are presented in Chapter 1.

Each scale contains between 10 and 14 items, designed to represent the conscious derivatives of the eight defense mechanisms. For each item, respondents are asked to indicate whether or not it describes them by checking "Yes" or "No." Internal consistency of the LSI (alpha coefficients for each of the scales obtained from the data of a sample of psychiatric inpatients and a sample of college students) is shown on Table 8–1. Also shown are those items ranking highest on relevancy for each of the defense scales as rated by 17 clinicians with an average of 13 years' experience (Plutchik et al., 1979). The median alpha for the patients is .62; for the students it is .54.

**TABLE 8–1**
**Alpha Coefficients and Items Ranking Highest on**
**Relevancy for the Eight Ego Defense Scales**

| | Alpha Coefficients | | Test-Retest Norwegian |
|---|---|---|---|
| | Inpatients (N = 60) | Students (N = 75) | Adults (N = 39) |
| *Compensation, Identification, Fantasy* In my dreams I'm always the center of attention. | .59 | .43 | .61*** |
| *Denial* I am free of prejudice. | .54 | .52 | .55*** |
| *Displacement* If someone bothers me, I don't tell it to him, but I tend to complain to someone else. | .69 | .62 | .76*** |
| *Intellectualization, Sublimation, Undoing, Rationalization* I am more comfortable discussing my thoughts than my feelings. | .58 | .30 | .61*** |
| *Projection* I believe people will take advantage of you if you are not careful. | .86 | .75 | .75*** |
| *Reaction Formation* Pornography is disgusting. | .73 | .63 | .76*** |
| *Regression* I get irritable when I don't get attention. | .65 | .56 | .38* |
| *Repression, Isolation, Introjection* I rarely remember my dreams. | .55 | .38 | .48** |

*$p < .02$.
**$p < .01$.
***$p < .001$.

The higher alpha coefficients for the patients than for the students probably reflect the fact that for each of the scales, scale variance was higher for the patients, thereby increasing the magnitude of the correlations. The considerable variation in internal consistency among the scales themselves is harder to explain. Defense mechanisms are difficult, abstract concepts about whose definitions there is much difference of opinion, even among experts. Inspection of Table 8–1 suggests that when combining several abstract concepts into a single, relatively short scale (even when there are both empirical and theoretical reasons for so doing), the researcher is bound to sacrifice a certain amount of internal consistency for that scale. The scale combining intellectualization, sublimation, undoing, and rationalization is a case in point.

Table 8–1 also presents test-retest correlations obtained on a sample of Norwegian normal adults who were administered the Norwegian translation of the LSI (Endresen, 1991) and then completed it again after an interval of 5 months. These values indicate that, with the possible exception of regression, the various defense mechanisms as measured by the LSI remain highly stable over time. Thus they more nearly resemble traitlike characteristics of an individual than transient states.

In addition to the data dealing with reliability, a number of studies have demonstrated evidence for the validity of the LSI. For example, in a study comparing the use of ego defenses by 29 hospitalized schizophrenic patients and 70 college students, the patients scored significantly higher than the students on seven of the eight defenses (Plutchik et al., 1979). Insofar as increasing psychiatric symptomatology leads to increasing anxiety, which in turn leads to a greater use of ego defenses, these findings provide a measure of discriminative validity for the LSI. The results of this same study also provided some evidence for the test's construct validity when it was shown that all but one of the scales correlated positively with the Taylor Manifest Anxiety Scale (Bendig, 1956) and that there were significant negative correlations between five of the eight defenses and a test of self-esteem based on the Tennessee Self-Concept Scale (Fitts, 1965).

Additional evidence for the construct validity of the scales of the LSI may be found in a study that investigated the relations between the use of defense mechanisms and the potential risk or probability of suicide and violence (Apter et al., 1989). Sixty psychiatric inpatients were administered a battery of tests that included the LSI, a Suicide Risk Scale (SR), and an Acts of Violence scale (PFAV) (Plutchik, van Praag, & Conte, 1989). Both the SR and the PFAV have been shown to have high internal consistency (coefficient alpha = .84 and .77, respectively) and have shown evidence for both concurrent and discriminant validity (Plutchik & van Praag, 1990; Plutchik, van Praag, Conte, & Picard, 1989). Of the 60 patients in Apter et al.'s (1989) study, 30 had been admitted subsequent to a suicide attempt. These were matched for age, sex, and diagnosis with nonsuicidal patients. Of the 30 suicidal patients, 20 had to be secluded or restrained for assaulting a staff member or fellow patient. These constituted the violent group and were compared with the other 40 patients.

Suicide risk was found to be significantly and positively related to regression and displacement (.48 and .47, $p < .001$, respectively), and to be significantly and negatively related to denial ($-.42$, $p < .001$). These relations make both intuitive and clinical sense. Patients who are able to successfully deny anxiety-provoking feelings and situations would be less likely to attempt suicide, whereas those utilizing regression to a marked degree might also be prone to severe self-destructive acting-out behavior. The high positive correlation with displacement suggests that these patients, rather than displaying their anger and behaving destructively toward others, turn these negative emotions back toward themselves.

Risk of violence was positively correlated with two of the ego defenses: projection (.46, $p < .000$) and denial (.32, $p < .01$). These findings are not unexpected, since a person's denial of unacceptable aggressive impulses and projection of them away from the self and onto others is highly likely to lead to acts of violence. The negative correlation of denial with risk of suicide in contrast to its positive correlation with violence risk suggests that the defense of denial may be used in a number of different ways. Depending on what other defenses are high in an individual's repertoire, it can lead to either potential aggression toward self or others.

There is also evidence for the predictive validity of the scales of the LSI. Thirty schizophrenics completed the LSI at their admission to a municipal hospital. After discharge, these patients were followed for 2 years, and it was found that 14 out of the 30 were rehospitalized sometime during those years. Significant positive point-biserial correlations were found between readmission and the use of repression ($r = .40$, $p < .03$), displacement ($r = .36$, $p < .05$), and denial ($r = .35$, $p < .05$) (Conte, Plutchik, Schwartz, & Wild, 1983). It is interesting to note that repression and denial have been considered to be primitive or immature defenses (Bond et al., 1983; Plutchik et al., 1979; Wong, 1989) and displacement has at best been termed "intermediate" or "neurotic" (Vaillant & Drake, 1985; Wong, 1989). Thus, although rehospitalization undoubtedly has multiple causal factors, it appears that patients high in the use of these relatively immature defense mechanisms are more likely candidates for rehospitalization than those who report lower levels of their usage.

## RECENT STUDIES USING THE LIFE STYLE INDEX

Since the publication of the original 1979 chapter describing the LSI (Plutchik et al., 1979), normative data, derived from test data of 147 normal adults (no history of psychiatric difficulties), have been constructed. They are available both as percentiles and as $T$-scores. In addition, the LSI has been translated into Norwegian (Endresen, 1991), Dutch (Olff & Endresen, 1991), Russian, and Hebrew. The following sections of this chapter will report the findings of some recent studies using both the

English and translated versions of the LSI. In general, the purpose of these studies is to investigate the use of the defense mechanisms in various populations and to further assess the scales' psychometric properties and relations to other variables.

## Use of Ego Defenses by Patients with Major Depressive Disorders

Twenty-four outpatients attending an Anxiety and Depression Clinic participated in this study, which was part of a larger investigation concerned with the use of ego defenses by depressed patients with and without mood reactivity (Plutchik, 1991). There were 12 males and 12 females with a mean age of 40.31 ($SD = 13.00$) years who were diagnosed through Schedule for Affective Disorders and Schizophrenia (SADS) or Structured Clinical Interview for DSM-III-R (SCID) interviews as having a current major depressive disorder without psychotic features.

All patients completed the LSI as well as an Ego Strength Scale (ES Scale). This latter scale is based on the work of Bellak, Hurvich, and Gediman (1973) and is described more fully in Conte, Plutchik, Buck, Picard, and Karasu (1991). It is a brief self-report questionnaire composed of 10 questions designed to measure overall ego strength. Examples of questions, rated on a 4-point scale ranging from "Never" to "Often" are "Do you remain calm under pressure?" and "Do you enjoy competition?" A total score is obtained. The ES Scale has been shown to have good reliability (coefficient alpha = .82), and its relations to depression, passivity, and submission ($-.63$, $-.56$, $p < .001$ and $-.53$, $p < .01$, respectively) are what would be expected clinically, thus giving it a measure of construct validity (Conte et al., 1991).

Mean LSI scores for the 24 patients are shown on Table 8–2. Compared with the norm group, whose means would be at the 50th percentile, there are a number of marked differences. The patients score much higher on regression, repression, reaction formation, and projection. Their total score is also considerably above the norm. What these data imply is that, on the average, depressed patients are more defended than are nonpatients. The depressed patients' high scores on regression and projection indicate also that they tend to use primarily primitive or immature defenses (Bond et al., 1983; Plutchik et al., 1979; Vaillant, Bond, & Vaillant, 1986; Wong, 1989) or those ranked at an intermediate level (reaction formation and repression).

Significant correlations were found between ego strength and the LSI scales of intellectualization ($r = +.48$, $p < .05$), displacement ($r = -47$, $p < .05$), and denial ($r = -.39$, $p < .10$). Inasmuch as intellectualization

**TABLE 8–2**
**Life Style Index—Means and Standard Deviations**
**(Percentiles)**

| | Major Depressive Disorder (Outpatients) (N = 24) | | Normal Elderly (N = 55) | | Hospitalized Male Alcoholics (N = 74) | |
|---|---|---|---|---|---|---|
| | $\overline{X}$ | SD | $\overline{X}$ | SD | $\overline{X}$ | SD |
| Denial | 43.62 | 35.44 | 54.33 | 30.73 | 58.14 | 27.25 |
| Repression | 73.65 | 24.82 | 61.14 | 28.23 | 72.34 | 25.61 |
| Regression | 64.14 | 28.43 | 29.81 | 26.54 | 58.58 | 29.81 |
| Compensation | 45.82 | 29.46 | 41.30 | 25.36 | 47.42 | 29.01 |
| Projection | 58.17 | 35.13 | 55.50 | 33.39 | 58.92 | 27.97 |
| Displacement | 50.41 | 31.11 | 31.65 | 23.40 | 46.15 | 26.85 |
| Intellectualization | 57.39 | 31.68 | 65.09 | 29.42 | 67.27 | 29.48 |
| Reaction Formation | 73.87 | 22.42 | 66.49 | 27.35 | 52.86 | 24.71 |
| Total Score | 61.80 | 33.15 | 34.90 | 10.48 | 54.11 | 31.47 |

is considered to represent a higher level of defense than the other two, its positive correlation with ego strength as opposed to the negative correlations of denial and displacement speaks to the construct validity of the scales, as does ego strength's negative correlation with total LSI score ($-.35, p < .01$). This indicates that the more highly an individual is defended in general, the lower is his or her ego strength, a notion that is consistent with Bond et al.'s (1983) findings that maladaptive ego defense styles showed significant negative correlations with a measure of ego development based on Loevinger's work (Loevinger, 1976; Loevinger & Wessler, 1970) and also with an independent ego strength scale.

## Relations between Use of Ego Defenses and Life Problems in the Elderly

To explore the relations between the use of defense styles and symptoms or problems likely to produce stress, 55 normally functioning elderly people were recruited at two senior citizen centers where they had gone to participate in such activities as handicrafts, dancing, and socializing. Thirty-two men, with an average age of 71.43 years ($SD = 5.8$) and 23 women whose average age was 70.60 years ($SD = 7.08$) volunteered. This particular population was chosen primarily because little is known about the use of defense mechanisms by individuals at this end of the developmental spectrum but also because of an interest in knowing specifically whether men and women in this age range would have a different pattern in their use of defense mechanisms (M. B. Weiner & Robert Plutchik, personal communication, April 1992).

All subjects completed the LSI and a Problem Checklist (Plutchik, Hyman, Conte, & Karasu, 1977). This instrument consists of 66 items describing relatively common problems or feelings indicative of stress in five areas: job problems, intrapersonal and interpersonal problems, family problems, and physical problems. Respondents rate each problem as not relevant to them, as a small problem, or as a large problem. A total score is obtained.

Table 8–2, which shows the means and standard deviations for the elderly group as a whole, highlights a number of interesting findings. On five out of eight defense mechanisms, these well-functioning elderly individuals scored, on the average, the same as or lower than the normative group. In addition, they were considerably lower than the norm on total score. In contrast, their scores on reaction formation ($\overline{X} = 66.49$), intellectualization ($\overline{X} = 65.09$), and repression ($\overline{X} = 61.14$), all defenses considered to be at a high or intermediate level of maturity, are well above the norm. They are also a much less defended group than the patients with major depressive disorders. It would appear that psychopathology is a more crucial determinant of the use of ego defenses than is advanced age.

When the males and the females were compared on their use of defenses, three significant differences were found. The females' use of reaction formation ($\overline{X} = 81.65$, $SD = 17.80$) was considerably greater than that of the males ($\overline{X} = 55.59$, $SD = 27.83$, $t = 3.87$, $p < .001$). The females' score on regression ($\overline{X} = 40.69$, $SD = 27.97$) was also significantly higher than the males ($\overline{X} = 22.00$, $SD = 22.40$, $t = 2.69$, $p < .01$). The females were also higher on total score ($\overline{X} = 38.65$, $SD = 9.34$ versus $\overline{X} = 32.21$, $SD = 10.43$, $t = 2.31$, $p < .05$).

Thus the females appear to be more defended, which is interesting because they also reported experiencing a greater degree of life problems or stresses ($\overline{X} = 11.22$, $SD = 8.37$ versus $\overline{X} = 6.88$, $SD = 5.79$, $t = 2.23$, $p < .05$). For all 55 subjects combined, the correlations between all ego defense scales, except intellectualization and denial, with total life problems were significant and positive (range $= .30$ to $.56$). Problems and total LSI score correlated $.56$ ($p < .001$). These findings imply additional evidence for the construct validity of the LSI.

### Defense Mechanisms, Personality Style, and Risk of Suicide or Violence in Alcoholic Males

To investigate predictors of aggressive expression, directed inwardly or outwardly, male subjects were recruited from two New York State alcoholism rehabilitation units and one alcohol detoxification program at a New York City municipal hospital (Greenwald, 1991). One aim of the study was to investigate the magnitude of the correlations between defense mechanisms and personality styles that would be predicted by Plutchik's theoretical model (Plutchik et al., 1979); a second aim was to determine the extent to which various types of defenses might differentially characterize those individuals at risk for suicide and those at risk for violence.

Seventy-four males with a mean age of 38.6 years ($SD = 9.43$) and a primary diagnosis of alcoholism volunteered. Approximately 50% were black, with the remaining subjects divided about equally among whites and Latinos. All subjects completed a Suicide Risk Scale (SRS), a Violence Risk Scale (PFAV) (Plutchik et al., 1989), the LSI, and the Millon Clinical Multiaxial Inventory-II (MCMI-II) (Millon, 1987). The MCMI-II (Millon, 1987) consists of 175 true-false items considered to be consistent with the DSM-III-R categories of personality disorders and clinical syndromes. Psychometric and normative data are available on a sample of 1,292 male and female clinical subjects.

Table 8–2 presents the means and standard deviations of the alcoholic subjects on the LSI scales. As may be seen, they score well above the norm on repression and intellectualization, but for the most part they are not markedly different from the normative group; in terms of total score, they are almost identical. One possible interpretation of these findings is that these individuals have habitually used alcohol to insulate themselves from anxiety and have not, therefore, needed excessive recourse to psychological mechanisms to ward off unacceptable thoughts and feelings.

The correlations obtained between the alcoholics' scores on the LSI scales and Millon's personality disorder and clinical syndrome categories provided partial confirmation of Plutchik's structural model (Plutchik et al., 1979). Table 8–3 presents the magnitude of the predicted relations.

Denial and histrionic and repression and passive-aggressive (passive type) showed a tendency to be associated ($p < .10$). The next four ego defenses were, however, significantly correlated with their predicted personality style or clinical syndrome ($p < .001$). Those individuals scoring high in regression also scored high on the MCMI-II scale depicting antisocial personality. Similarly, those scoring high on compensation, projection, and displacement also scored high on the clinical scale for dysthymia and the personality styles of paranoid and passive-aggressive, respectively. These data provide support for the structural model as well as support for the construct validity of the scales. Denial showed a tendency to be associated with a histrionic personality style ($p < .10$) as did repression with the syndrome of passive-aggressive (passive type)

**TABLE 8–3**
**Relations between Ego Defenses and Predicted**
**Personality Styles and Clinical Syndromes**
**for 74 Hospitalized Male Alcoholics**

| Ego Defense | Personality Style/ Clinical Syndrome | Pearson r |
|---|---|---|
| Denial | Histrionic | .20* |
| Repression | Passive-Aggressive (Passive) | .22* |
| Regression | Antisocial | .44** |
| Compensation | Dysthymic | .49** |
| Projection | Paranoid | .52** |
| Displacement | Passive-Aggressive (Aggressive) | .49** |
| Intellectualization | Compulsive | .13 |
| Reaction Formation | Manic | .06 |

*$p < .10$.
**$p < .001$.

($p < .10$). The remaining two ego defenses—intellectualization and reaction formation—were not, as predicted, significantly correlated with a compulsive personality style or a diagnosis of mania, respectively.

Because suicide risk and violence risk were found to be significantly correlated in this sample of patients ($r = .23$, $p < .05$), partial correlations were used to assess the relations between the ego defense scales and risk for suicide or violence. When the association between the two was removed by partial correlation, the only ego defense that was significantly related to violence was displacement ($r = .39$, $p < .001$). This fact confirms the clinical impression that many acts of violence are symbolic of displaced aggression from primary objects onto representations of or substitutes for those objects.

In contrast, significant partial correlations were found between risk of suicide and four ego defenses: regression ($r = .49$, $p < .001$); compensation ($r = .33$, $p < .001$); and intellectualization and reaction formation ($r$'s $= .29$ and $.26$, $p < .05$, respectively). The significant positive correlation between suicide risk and regression replicates the results of Apter et al. (1989) and is consistent with the clinical observation that suicidal patients show a tendency toward severe acting-out behavior. It is well known that suicide risk is highly correlated with depression. From a theoretical point of view, the ego defense of compensation is related to the personal experience of loss or inadequacy. Therefore, the connection between suicide risk and compensation is understandable. Interpretation of the relations between risk of suicide and intellectualization and reaction formation is less clear.

## TRANSLATIONS OF THE LIFE STYLE INDEX

In discussions of psychological constructs like ego defense mechanisms, scientists rely on the assumption that what is measured in one culture or one language is translatable into other languages or cultures. For questionnaires, the usual procedure is to translate the test, backtranslate, and then analyze the psychometric properties of the test. This is usually successful from a linguistic standpoint. However, in spite of diligence on the part of translators, problems may arise.

### Russian Translations

The LSI has been translated into Russian at the Moscow State Educational University, and it was observed that some items became less discriminative in translation (Leonid R. Grebennikov, personal communication, September 28, 1991; June 17, 1992). The suggestion was made that this was due primarily to a different social reality, and over the course of four adapted versions, several items were reformulated. The fourth version now appears to have acceptable psychometric properties, norms in percentiles have been developed, and the Russian LSI is presently being used to study the differences in the way in which maladapted individuals (addicts, delinquents) and "normal" individuals use defense mechanisms.

Another Russian version of the LSI has been used at the St. Petersberg Bekhterev Psychoneurologica Research Institute. They investigated the personality, cognitive characteristics, and use of defense mechanisms of 100 inpatient male alcoholics (Elena Clubova, PhD, personal communication, 1992). Results showed no significant differences between these patients and a control group of 104 healthy males on any of the LSI subscales (total score was not used). These findings are interesting because they are similar to those of a recent study conducted at an inpatient alcohol detoxification unit of a New York City hospital (Conte, Plutchik, Picard, Galanter, & Jacoby, 1991). That study found no significant difference in personality traits between 23 hospitalized alcoholics and a normal comparison group and only one out of a possible eight significant differences between the two groups in terms of coping styles (the alcoholics scored higher on the coping style of "blame," which can be considered the counterpart of the ego defense "projection"). What these studies suggest is that constructs such as ego defenses may have some generality across cultures.

### Dutch and Norwegian Translations

This viewpoint is not supported by the work of Olff and Endresen (1991) who describe the use of the Dutch and Norwegian translations of the LSI.

Comparison of data obtained from the use of the two translations with that from two groups of college students ($N$'s = 70 and 50) who took the original U.S. version (Plutchik et al., 1979) showed more similarities between the Dutch ($N = 679$) and the Norwegian ($N = 704$) populations than between either of the two translations and the U.S. material. The authors suggest that this may indicate cultural differences between the United States and Europe on some of the parameters measured by the scales. It should also be noted, however, that the U.S. sample is considerably smaller than the other two and that this might have influenced the results.

Both the subscales and total score of the Norwegian translation of the LSI (Endresen, 1991) have shown interesting relationships with other variables. One investigation concerned psychological stress factors and levels of immunoglobulins and complement components in Norwegian nurses (Endresen et al., 1987). A second study investigated the relations among stress, psychological factors, health, and immune levels among 64 military aviators (Vaernes, Myhre et al., 1991). Both confirmed that "immunological parameters may be used as psychological stress indicators, but the relationships are complex and can be best understood if individual coping and defense strategies are considered" (p. 5). Further support for this hypothesis is provided by a study also conducted by Vaernes and his colleagues (Vaernes, Knardahl et al., 1988) of 89 shift workers in a Norwegian petroleum refinery. Results of this investigation showed that approximately 25% of the variance in the immunological measures was explained by a combination of LSI subscale scores and those of perceived health and work problems.

## Hebrew Translation

The LSI has also been translated into Hebrew and administered to 130 adolescent inpatient psychiatric patients at the Geha Psychiatric Hospital of the Tel Aviv Medical School, Israel, as well as to a comparison group of 78 adolescent Israeli high school students (Alan Apter, MD, personal communication, June 1992).

Of these patients, 47% were male and 53% were female. Their mean age was 16.05 years ($SD = 1.70$), and they had an average of 9.71 years ($SD = 1.67$) of education. Neither the sex distribution of the comparison group (41% male; 59% female), nor their mean age (15.23 years, $SD = 1.80$) nor their average years of education ($\overline{X} = 9.59$, $SD = 1.74$) were significantly different from those of the patients. Forty of the 130 patients were admitted subsequent to a suicide attempt. Ratings on whether or not a patient was also considered destructive at admission were made for 108 of the patients.

All patients at admission were diagnosed according to DSM-III-R criteria following an extensive diagnostic evaluation that included a structured interview (K-SADS). Twenty percent were given the diagnosis of schizophrenia, 20% were diagnosed as borderline personality disorder, 17% as narcissistic personality disorder, 11% as affective disorders, 9% as conduct disorder, 5% as other personality disorders, and 20% were in the "other" diagnostic category, which included such disorders as anxiety disorder, opposition disorder, eating disorders, and substance abuse.

Shortly after admission, these 130 inpatients completed the LSI and the Beck Depression Inventory (BDI). They also completed a number of additional tests that will not be reported on here. The 78 high school students completed only the LSI. Because Hebrew norms are not yet available for the LSI, the subscales and total score were analyzed in terms of raw scores. Two analyses were conducted. The first involved one-way ANOVAS to determine whether significant differences existed on the LSI subscales and total score among the patients characterized as suicidal at admission, those who were nonsuicidal at admission, and the individuals in the normal comparison group. Suicidals and nonsuicidals were also compared on the BDI.

Results from the ANOVAS and appropriate Sheffe post hoc comparisons of the raw scores for the suicidal, nonsuicidal, and comparison groups showed that they differed significantly on repression, regression, and total score. To determine whether transformation to percentiles utilizing U.S. norms would affect these results, such transformations were made and ANOVAS were again conducted. Findings demonstrated that the two procedures produced almost identical results in terms of $p$ values. Table 8–4 shows these findings in percentile form. As may be seen, the suicidal patients scored significantly higher than the comparison group on repression ($p < .002$), regression ($p < .001$), and total score ($p < .002$). They were also higher on regression than the nonsuicidals ($p < .003$). Nonsuicidal patients had higher scores than the high school students only on repression ($p < .003$) and total score ($p < .08$).

The findings in terms of total score are what would be theoretically predicted. The suicidal patients scored the highest, the nonsuicidal patients scored lower, and the comparison group of normal adolescents had the lowest scores. This same pattern holds for the defenses of repression and regression. What this suggests is that the patients admitted for a suicide attempt were more disturbed, in greater conflict and, therefore, in greater need of overall defense than the nonsuicidals, who in turn experienced a stronger need to be defended than did the normal comparison group. Interestingly, this need for defense is expressed most strongly

**TABLE 8-4**

**One-Way Analyses of Variance Comparing Adolescent Suicidal (S),**
**Nonsuicidal (NS), and Comparison (C) Groups on the Life Style Index**
**(Percentiles)**

| Variable | Suicidal (N = 40) | | Nonsuicidal (N = 90) | | Comparison (N = 78) | | F | Results |
|---|---|---|---|---|---|---|---|---|
| | Mean | SD | Mean | SD | Mean | SD | | |
| Denial | 53.48 | 32.33 | 63.88 | 33.12 | 59.13 | 31.24 | .23 | NS |
| Repression | 64.28 | 30.11 | 63.97 | 29.51 | 44.94 | 29.35 | 10.17 | S > C < .002 <br> NS > C < .003 |
| Regression | 70.49 | 26.49 | 51.37 | 34.29 | 48.33 | 27.11 | 7.48 | S > C < .001 <br> S > NS < .003 |
| Compensation | 50.10 | 26.38 | 55.62 | 32.20 | 49.67 | 26.88 | .98 | NS |
| Projection | 66.76 | 27.72 | 56.21 | 34.02 | 57.77 | 29.28 | .19 | NS |
| Displacement | 60.02 | 31.18 | 55.06 | 32.34 | 51.76 | 27.02 | 1.00 | NS |
| Intellectualization | 66.10 | 29.19 | 65.33 | 33.40 | 58.27 | 27.62 | 1.40 | NS |
| Reaction Formation | 76.92 | 19.09 | 74.74 | 23.12 | 68.49 | 22.52 | 2.51 | NS |
| Total | 69.89 | 26.51 | 62.27 | 35.25 | 48.88 | 29.77 | 6.58 | S > C < .002 <br> NS > C < . 08 |

through the use of repression and regression, with their implied exclusion from consciousness of anxiety-provoking emotions and retreat under stress to earlier and more immature patterns of behavior.

One other notable feature shown in Table 8–4 is the suicidal patients' lower mean score on denial compared with that of the nonsuicidal patients. While not significant in the overall analysis of variance, this 10-point difference suggests that the suicidal group experienced the reality of their problems more directly, leading them to attempt suicide, whereas the nonsuicidal group could be said to be more insulated from their problems. This interpretation is congruent with the fact that the suicidal patients reported themselves to be significantly more depressed on the BDI ($\overline{X} = 46.61$, $SD = 16.24$) than did the nonsuicidals ($\overline{X} = 38.10$, $SD = 14.05$, $t = 3.16$, $p < .002$).

Figure 8–1 presents a profile in terms of percentile scores of the ego defenses of the suicidal patients. As may be noted, they are considerably above the norm (the 50th percentile) on reaction formation, regression, projection, and intellectualization. From a clinical point of view, and in terms of the way these suicidal adolescents described themselves on the items of the LSI, their high scores on reaction formation suggest that they believe they have very high moral standards, particularly as concerns sexual matters such as the use of dirty language, pornography, and promiscuity. This image is buttressed by their high scores on intellectualization, implying that they are not particularly emotional or affectionate, see themselves as more rational, logical, and objective than most people, and believe themselves to be hard workers.

The conflict inherent in these adolescents is put into relief as we note that they simultaneously scored high on projection and regression. This means that they tend to project their own unacceptable impulses onto others, as evidenced by their reporting that they "hate" hostile people and those who boss people around, and that they think people are basically selfish, insincere, and will take advantage of them if given the chance. If you add to this description their frequent use of regression as a defense mechanism (which implies that they are impulsive, tend to oversleep, cry easily, and become irritable, moody, and act childishly when upset or frustrated), you have a picture of a group of conflicted young people who describe themselves as high-minded and mature and simultaneously as angry and childish.

The second analysis consisted of one-way ANOVAS on the same variables for patients who were characterized at admission as "suicidal only" ($N = 20$), "destructive only" ($N = 24$), or "neither suicidal or

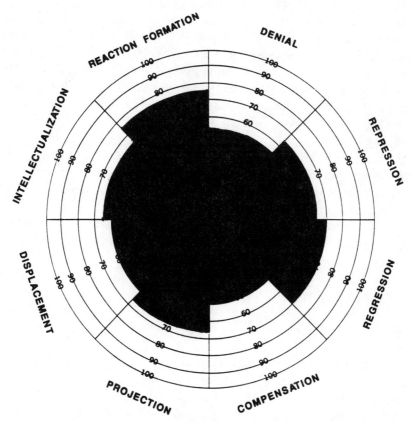

**Figure 8–1.** Percentile scores on the Life Style Index of 40 suicidal adolescents.

destructive" ($N = 50$). These analyses showed three significant differences among the groups. The patients characterized as destructive only had significantly higher scores on repression ($\overline{X} = 75.75$, $SD = 20.76$) than did those patients who were neither suicidal nor destructive ($\overline{X} = 57.04$, $SD = 29.76$, $p < .05$). This could be interpreted to mean that these destructive patients were not conscious of or did not feel such emotions as guilt or shame, thereby reducing any conflict over their behavior.

The suicidal-only patients were significantly higher on regression ($\overline{X} = 72.90$, $SD = 24.27$) than were patients who were neither suicidal nor destructive ($\overline{X} = 45.10$, $SD = 32.14$, $p < .01$). This is consistent with Apter et al.'s (1989) finding that suicidal inpatients scored significantly higher on regression than did a comparison group of nonsuicidal patients. The suicidal-only inpatients were also significantly higher on depression as measured by the BDI ($\overline{X} = 47.89$, $SD = 18.01$) than were those labeled destructive only ($\overline{X} = 34.43$, $SD = 12.16$, $p < .01$). These findings replicate the results of the comparisons among the suicidal, nonsuicidal, and comparison adolescents. Another finding that is replicated is the suicidals' lower utilization of denial than the destructive patients ($\overline{X} = 53.00$, $SD = 73.33$ vs. $\overline{X} = 73.33$, $SD = 31.24$, respectively, $p < .07$).

The results of this study indicate that the Israeli adolescent patients, as a group, used ego defenses to a greater extent than did a group of students who were not under psychiatric care. The finding that psychiatric patient groups tend to be higher on the use of defense mechanisms than comparable groups of nonpatients has been frequently noted. The profile depicting the use of defenses by the adolescent patients who were considered suicidal, but not destructive to others, is congruent with the image of suicidal individuals as highly conflicted with no clear notion of how to resolve their problems.

## CONCLUSION

The background, construction, and use of the Life Style Index has been described. It appears to be a reasonable and comprehensive test for measuring the conscious derivatives of a relatively well-agreed-on selection of defense mechanisms defined as unconscious mental processes. Among the salient characteristics of the LSI is that it has a self-report format and is thus easy to administer and to score. Because observer judgment is irrelevant, the self-report format also has the advantage of potentially enhancing the reliability of the scales.

That some of the scales' reliability coefficients are not as high as would be desirable is probably a function of at least two factors. First, as Vaillant and Drake put it, "Defenses are, after all, metaphors; they are a shorthand way of describing different cognitive styles and modes of rearranging inner and outer realities" (1985, p. 601). As such, they reflect integrated processes that are both difficult to identify and to define. There is, therefore, bound to be some slippage when investigators take the additional step of translating these abstract concepts into conscious derivatives.

Second, as previously pointed out, combining several of these somewhat diffuse concepts into a single scale, even when empirically and theoretically advisable, requires some sacrifice of internal consistency. This phenomenon has been noted by other investigators as well. Bond et al. (1989) and Perry and Cooper (1989), for example, note that studies have shown that it is likely that a scale with a limited number of clustered defenses or perhaps utilizing only a total score would prove more reliable than a schema in which identification of single defenses was required. Studies using the LSI have shown that total score is consistently the best discriminator among groups. However, the use of clusters or only a total score would mean a disregard for the structural model on which the LSI is based (Plutchik et al., 1979), with the subsequent loss of its heuristic value in terms of personality dynamics and diagnoses. The richness of the potential data inherent in the implicit similarity and polarity structure of defense mechanisms is one of the LSI's strongest points.

Laplanche and Pontalis (1973) posited that the type of illness a patient has in large measure determines which defense mechanisms will predominate. Vaillant and Drake (1985) and Bond and Vaillant (1986) investigated the relations among ego defenses and diagnoses with somewhat inconsistent results. More recently, Greenwald (1991) tested the relations between defense mechanisms and diagnoses postulated by Plutchik's structural model (Plutchik et al., 1979) and partially confirmed the hypothesized relations.

Further such investigations would help to provide a clearer picture of the extent to which defense mechanisms relate to an aspect of human functioning that is distinct from that encompassed in diagnoses or whether the use of particular defenses is an integral part of a given diagnostic status. In addition to investigating the relations between defense mechanisms and diagnoses, future research should also address the relationship between ego defenses and general level of adjustment in varying psychiatric populations.

One final point concerns the use of the LSI in translation. Only the Dutch and Norwegian versions have been directly compared with the U.S. version (Olff & Endresen, 1991). There was greater agreement between the results of the Dutch and Norwegian versions, obtained from subjects from two related cultures, but with different languages, than between these subjects and the U.S. samples. In contrast, the use of U.S. norms did not substantially alter the findings obtained with the Israeli adolescents (Apter, personal communication, 1992) using the Hebrew version of the LSI. These inconsistencies should encourage further comparisons to help clarify the extent to which environment and cultural context affect the use of the various defense mechanisms. In fact, such comparisons may be used as a way of testing the psychological robustness and soundness of the underlying concepts.

# REFERENCES

Ablon, S. L., Carlson, G. A., & Goodwin, F. K. (1974). Ego defense patterns in manic-depressive illness. *American Journal Psychiatry, 131,* 803–807.

American Psychiatric Association Committee on Nomenclature and Statistics. (1987). *Diagnostic and statistical manual of mental disorders* (3rd ed., rev.). Washington, DC: American Psychiatric Association.

Andrews, G., Pollock, C., & Stewart, G. (1989). The determination of defense style by questionnaire. *Archives of General Psychiatry, 46,* 455–460.

Apter, A., Plutchik, R., Sevy, S., Korn, M., Brown, S., & van Praag, H. (1989). Defense mechanisms in risk of suicide risk of violence. *American Journal of Psychiatry, 146,* 1027–1031.

Bellak, L., Hurvich, M., & Gediman, H. K. (1973). *Ego functions in schizophrenics, neurotics, and normals.* New York: Wiley.

Bendig, A. W. (1956). The development of a short form of the Manifest Anxiety Scale. *Journal of Consulting Psychology, 20,* 384–387.

Bond, M., Gardner, S. T., Christian, J., & Sigal, J. J. (1983). Empirical study of self-rated defense styles. *Archives of General Psychiatry, 40,* 333–338.

Bond, M., Perry, J. C., Gautier, M., Goldenberg, H., Oppenheimer, J., & Simand, J. (1989). Validating the self-report defense styles. *Journal of Personality Disorders, 3,* 101–112.

Bond, M. P., & Vaillant, J. S. (1986). An empirical study of the relationship between diagnosis and defense style. *Archives of General Psychiatry, 43,* 285–288.

Brenner, C. (1973). *An elementary textbook of psychoanalysis.* New York: International Universities Press.

Conte, H. R., & Plutchik, R. (1993). The measurement of ego defenses in clinical research. In U. Hentschel, G. Smith, W. Ehlers, & J. G. Draguns (Eds.), *The concept of defense mechanisms in contemporary psychology: Theoretical, research and clinical perspectives.* (pp. 275–289). New York: Springer-Verlag.

Conte, H. R., Plutchik, R., Buck, L., Picard, S., & Karasu, T. B. (1991). Interrelations among ego functions and personality traits: Their relation to psychotherapy outcome. *American Journal of Psychotherapy, 45,* 69–77.

Conte, H. R., Plutchik, R., Picard, S., Galanter, M., & Jacoby, J. (1991). Sex differences in personality traits and coping styles of hospitalized alcoholics. *Journal of Studies on Alcohol, 52,* 26–32.

Conte, H. R., Plutchik, R., Schwartz, B., & Wild, K. (1983). *Psychodynamic variables related to outcome in hospitalized schizophrenics.* Paper presented at the Convention of the American Psychological Association, Anaheim, CA.

Cooper, C., & Kline, P. (1986). An evaluation of the Defense Mechanism Test. *British Journal of Psychology, 77,* 19–31.

Endresen, I. M. (1991). A Norwegian translation of the Plutchik questionnaire for psychological defense. *Scandinavian Journal of Psychology, 32,* 105–113.

Endresen, I. M., Vaernes, R., Ursin, H., & Tonder, O. (1987). Psychological stress-factors and concentration of immunoglobulins and complement components in Norwegian nurses. *Work & Stress, 1,* 365–375.

Fitts, W. H. (1965). *The Tennessee Self-Concept Scale.* Nashville, TN: Counselor Recordings & Tests.

Freud, A. (1936). *The ego and the mechanisms of defense.* New York: International Universities Press.

Fromm, E. (1947). *Man for himself.* New York: Rinehart.

Gleser, G. C., & Ihilevich, D. (1969). An objective instrument for measuring defense mechanisms. *Journal of Consulting and Clinical Psychology, 33,* 51–60.

Greenwald, D. J. (1991). *Suicide and violence risk: Predictors of aggressive expression.* Unpublished doctoral dissertation, Fordham University, New York.

Hackett, T. P., & Cassem, N. H. (1974). Development of a quantitative rating scale to assess denial. *Journal of Psychosomatic Research, 18,* 93–100.

Horowitz, M. J. (Ed.). (1988). *Psychodynamics and cognition.* Chicago: University of Chicago Press.

Kline, P. (1987). The scientific status of the DMT. *British Journal of Medical Psychology, 60,* 53–59.

Kragh, U. (1969). *The Defense Mechanism Test.* Stockholm: Testforlaget.

Kragh, U. (1985). *DMT manual.* Stockholm: Persona.

Kreitler, H., & Kreitler, S. (1972). The cognitive determinants of defensive behavior. *British Journal of Social and Clinical Psychology, 11,* 359–373.

Laplanche, J., & Pontalis, J. B. (1973). *The language of psychoanalysis.* London: Hogarth Press.

Loevinger, J. (1976). *Ego development.* San Francisco: Jossey-Bass.

Loevinger, J., & Wessler, R. (1970). *Measuring ego development: Vol. 1. Construction and use of a sentence completion test.* San Francisco: Jossey-Bass.

Marshall, J. B. (1982). *Psychometric and validational studies of an objective test of Freudian defense mechanisms.* Unpublished doctoral dissertation, University of North Carolina at Chapel Hill.

Meissner, W. W., Mack, J. E., & Semrad, E. V. (1975). Theories of personality and psychopathology: Classical psychoanalysis. In A. M. Freedman & H. I. Kaplan (Eds.), *Comprehensive textbook of psychiatry II* (pp. 535–356). Baltimore: Williams & Wilkins.

Millon, T. (1987). *Manual for the MCMI-II* (2nd ed.). Minneapolis, MN: National Computer Systems.

Olff, M., & Endresen, I. (1991). The Dutch and the Norwegian translations of the Plutchik questionnaire for psychological defense. In M. Olff (Ed.), *Defense and coping: Self-reported health and psychobiological correlates* (pp. 57–69). Utrecht, Netherlands: ISOR.

Perry, J. C., & Cooper, S. H. (1989). An empirical study of defense mechanisms: I. Clinical interview and life vignette ratings. *Archives of General Psychiatry, 46,* 444–452.

Perry, J. C., & Vaillant, G. E. (1990). Personality disorders. In H. I. Kaplan & B. J. Sadock (Eds.), *Comprehensive textbook of psychiatry* (Vol. 2, pp. 1352–1395, 5th ed.). New York: Plenum.

Plutchik, L. (1991). *Ego defense style in mood-reactive compared to non-reactive depressed patients.* Unpublished manuscript, Albert Einstein College of Medicine, Bronx, NY.

Plutchik, R. (1962). *The emotions: Facts, theories, and a new model.* New York: Random House.

Plutchik, R. (1980). *Emotion: A psychoevolutionary synthesis.* New York: Harper & Row.

Plutchik, R., & Conte, H. R. (1989). Measuring emotions and their derivatives: Personality traits, ego defenses, and coping styles. In S. Wetzler & M. M. Katz (Eds.), *Contemporary approaches to psychological assessment* (pp. 239–269). New York: Brunner/Mazel.

Plutchik, R., Hyman, I., Conte, H. R., & Karasu, T. B. (1977). Medical symptoms and life stresses in psychiatric emergency room patients. *Journal of Abnormal Psychology, 86,* 447–449.

Plutchik, R., Kellerman, H., & Conte, H. R. (1979). The structural theory of ego defenses and emotions. In C. E. Izard (Ed.), *Emotions in personality and psychopathology* (pp. 229–257). New York: Plenum Press.

Plutchik, R., & van Praag, H. M. (1990). A self-report measure of violence risk: II. *Comprehensive Psychiatry, 31,* 1–4.

Plutchik, R., van Praag, H. M., & Conte, H. R. (1989). Correlates of suicide and violence risk: III. A two-stage model of countervailing forces. *Psychiatry Research, 28,* 215–225.

Plutchik, R., van Praag, H. M., Conte, H. R., & Picard, S. (1989). Correlates of suicide and violence risk: I. The suicide risk measure. *Comprehensive Psychiatry, 30,* 296–302.

Sackeim, H. A. (1983). Self-deception, depression, and self-esteem: The adaptive value of lying to oneself. In J. Masling (Ed.), *Empirical studies of psychoanalytic theory* (Vol. 1). Hillsdale, NJ: Analytic Press.

Sullivan, H. S. (1947). *The interpersonal theory of psychiatry.* New York: Norton.

Vaernes, R. J., Knardahl, S., Romsing, J., Aakvaag, A., Tonder, O., Walther, B., & Ursin, H. (1988). Relations between environmental problems, psychology and health among shift-workers in the Norwegian process industry. *Work & Stress, 2,* 7–15.

Vaernes, R. J., Myhre, G., Aas, H., Homnes, T., Hansen, I., & Tonder, O. (1991). Relationships between stress, psychological factors, health, and immune levels among military aviators. *Work & Stress, 5,* 5–16.

Vaillant, G. E. (1971). Theoretical hierarchy of adaptive ego mechanisms: A 30-year follow-up of 30 men selected for psychological health. *Archives of General Psychiatry, 24,* 107–118.

Vaillant, G. E. (1976). Natural history of male psychological health: The relation of choice of ego mechanisms of defense to adult adjustment. *Archives of General Psychiatry, 33,* 535–545.

Vaillant, G. E., Bond, M., & Vaillant, C. O. (1986). An empirically validated hierarchy of defense mechanisms. *Archives of General Psychiatry, 43,* 786–794.

Vaillant, G. E., & Drake, R. E. (1985). Maturity of ego defenses in relation to DSM-III, Axis II personality disorder. *Archives of General Psychiatry, 42,* 597–601.

Wong, N. (1989). Theories of personality and psychopathology. In H. I. Kaplan & B. J. Sadock (Eds.), *Comprehensive textbook of psychiatry* (Vol. 1, pp. 356–410, 5th ed.). Baltimore: Williams & Wilkins.

# 9

## The Development and Properties of the Defense Style Questionnaire

### MICHAEL P. BOND

The empirical study of defense mechanisms presents similar challenges to the researcher as does the study of most psychodynamically conceived processes. Definitions have been unclear, and different definitions from different theoretical perspectives make it difficult to know exactly to what investigators are referring when talking about defense mechanisms. In addition, intrapsychic and interpersonal processes are very difficult to measure so it is hard to develop valid instruments that render acceptable interrater reliability. Still, the concept of defense mechanism is accepted by the general public to a greater or lesser degree and is used by psychodynamic clinicians and theorists. Even cognitive psychologists explore seriously some of the basic defense mechanisms such as repression and dissociation (Singer, 1990).

The development of the Defense Style Questionnaire (DSQ) and the subsequent work with it represent efforts by myself and others to look at many facets of defense mechanisms. We have addressed these basic questions about defense mechanisms: Which phenomena can be called defenses? Are defenses to be considered adaptive or maladaptive? Are defenses unconscious processes or can they have conscious aspects? Can defense mechanisms be measured? Are specific defense mechanisms linked to specific illnesses or stages of development or levels of adaptiveness or maturity? Can defense mechanisms be grouped into defense styles that have theoretical and clinical relevance?

### DEFENSE MECHANISMS

To answer the first question, regarding which phenomena can be called defenses, Freud (1926/1973) listed regression, repression, reaction formation, isolation, undoing, projection, introjection, turning against the self, and reversal. A. Freud (1936) described sublimation, displacement, denial in fantasy, denial in word and act, identification with the aggressor, and altruism. Kernberg (1967) and Klein (1973) described splitting, omnipotence with devaluation, primitive idealization, projective identification, and psychotic denial.

Vaillant (1976) substituted some overt behaviors for intrapsychic processes in his study, claiming that "such substitution permits the examination of ego function in operational rather than in theoretical terms" (p. 54). In so doing, he added to the list of defenses fantasy, passive-aggression, hypochondriasis, acting out, suppression, humor, and anticipation.

An advisory committee to the work group creating the *Diagnostic and Statistical Manual of Mental Disorders,* Third Edition–revised (DSM-III-R), consisting of David Barlow, Michael Bond, Allen J. Frances, William A. Frosch, J. Christopher Perry, Andrew E. Skodol, Robert L. Spitzer, George Vaillant, Janet B. W. Williams and Jeffrey Young, prepared a list of defense mechanisms that appears in the glossary of technical terms of DSM-III-R (American Psychiatric Association, 1987). The list includes 18 defenses chosen by consensus. The committee proposed the following definition of defense mechanisms:

> Patterns of feelings, thoughts or behaviors that are relatively involuntary and arise in response to perceptions of psychic danger. They are designed to hide or to alleviate the conflicts or stressors that give rise to anxiety. Some defense mechanisms, such as projection, splitting, and acting out, are almost invariably maladaptive. Others, such as suppression and denial, may be either maladaptive or adaptive, depending on their severity, their inflexibility, and the context in which they occur. Defense mechanisms that are usually adaptive, such as sublimation and humor, are not included here.

This definition offers answers to some of the questions posed earlier, especially with regard to degree of awareness and relation to pathology or adaptiveness.

An important question remains: Can defense mechanisms be measured reliably and accurately? Investigators have tried several approaches for the study of defense mechanisms. Vaillant (1976) and Haan, Stroud, and Holstein (1973) used psychiatric interviews in combination with other measures, such as psychological tests, questionnaires, and autobiographical reports. Vaillant pointed out that the clinical judgment required in his study limited the objectivity and reliability of the judges' ratings. He went on to emphasize the need to make intrapsychic processes operational so that defenses could be studied experimentally.

Semrad, Grinspoon, and Feinberg (1973) created an ego profile scale that empirically measured different types of ego functioning. The items for the questionnaire were generated by two of the authors and then categorized into nine ego defense categories by 25 senior psychiatrists. An item was accepted as indicative of a particular ego defense if a sufficient number of raters independently agreed on its assignment to that category. The ego profile scale was filled out by patients' therapists on a weekly basis. The creation of this scale, as well as the scoring of the scale, depended solely on therapist's opinions and observations.

Perry and Cooper (1986) created the Defense Mechanism Rating Scale (DMRS) with a manual describing 22 defense mechanisms. Each defense was accompanied by a definition and a scale anchored by clinical examples of evidence for the defense's use. Two groups of three raters each scored the absence, probable presence, or definite presence of the defenses based on watching videotapes of dynamic, unstructured interviews of their subjects. This procedure yielded a median reliability of 0.57 for the consensus ratings of the individual defenses (Perry & Cooper, 1986).

The problem of interrater reliability is eliminated by using self-report scales, but validity becomes an even larger issue. Gleser and Ihilevitch (1969) devised the Defense Mechanism Inventory (DMI) to use the self-report approach, but the defenses that they identified have little overlap with those commonly referred to in clinical practice or those in the DSM-III-R list. We (Bond, Gardner, Christian, & Sigal, 1983) created the Defense Style Questionnaire (DSQ) to examine the range of defenses accepted by most psychodynamically oriented clinicians. Our list was a combination of Vaillant's defenses and those considered by Kernberg (1967) to be typical of patients with borderline personality organization.

We knew that a self-report questionnaire could only measure conscious derivatives of defense mechanisms and so thought that we could not measure individual defenses accurately. Instead, we aimed to measure clusters of defenses that we called *defense styles,* and we decided to use an empirical means, factor analysis, to decide which defenses belong to which group of defenses.

We hypothesized that defense styles might identify aspects of a person's stage of development and render other information about ego functioning independent of diagnosis. Vaillant (1975, 1976), who divided defenses into narcissistic, immature, neurotic, and mature groups, demonstrated that this theoretical hierarchy of defenses correlated with empirical definitions of mental health. Haan et al. (1973) and Haan (1969) divided ego processes into coping, defensive, and fragmentation, placing emphasis on different styles and not only on level of development.

Semrad et al. (1973) also proposed a hierarchy of ego functioning, specifically with regard to defense styles.

Shapiro (1965) used neurotic styles to refer to "a form or mode of functioning ... that is identifiable, in an individual, through a range of his specific acts" (page 1). He outlined four major neurotic styles: obsessive-compulsive, hysterical, paranoid, and impulsive, but he used no empirical data.

Linking defenses with specific illnesses can create confusion. Defense should refer to a style of dealing with conflict or stress, whereas diagnosis should refer to a constellation of symptoms and signs. Separating the examination of defenses from the issue of diagnosis would allow the use of the concept of defense more precisely during investigation of fluctuations in a person's style when dealing with a particular stress at a particular time and under particular circumstances. The use of that style would also reveal something about the level of that individual's psychosocial development.

A description follows of our preliminary attempt to contribute to the search for an objective, empirical method of studying the relations among defense mechanisms, diagnosis, level of maturity, and other ongoing psychological phenomena.

## Subjects

In our study, 209 volunteers participated, 98 patients and 111 nonpatients. The persons in the nonpatient sample, from their own point of view, were functioning adequately and at the time of testing were not undergoing psychiatric treatment. Their mean age was 31 years (range = 16–69 years). Of the subjects, 48 were male and 63 were female. The patient sample consisted of 98 persons drawn from the psychiatric wards ($N = 42$) or psychiatric outpatient departments ($N = 56$) of three university teaching or affiliated hospitals. The mean age of the 48 males and 50 females was 27 years (range = 25–64 years).

Using a simple, forced-choice evaluation sheet, the attending psychologist or psychiatrist made the following diagnoses: psychotic, 39; borderline, 26; neurotic, 22; personality disorder, 6; and other, 5.

## Methods

In the classical psychoanalytic sense, defense mechanisms are an unconscious process. A self-report questionnaire to measure defense styles, thus, may not detect a phenomenon of which a subject is unaware. Our approach to this objection was based on the following premises. There are times when defenses fail temporarily, and at those times subjects may become aware of the unacceptable impulses and their usual styles of defending against them. In addition, others often point out defense mechanisms to the person. A statement such as, "People tell me that I often take my anger out on someone other than the one at whom I'm really angry," might tap displacement even if the subject is unaware of defensive behavior at the time that it is happening. A statement such as, "When I have a close friend, I need to be with him all the time," can tap clinging behavior because the subject may have had this behavior pointed out to him or her, or the subject may have noted anxious or depressed feelings when unable to use this defensive behavior. The questionnaire was designed to elicit manifestations of a subject's characteristic style of dealing with conflict, either conscious or unconscious, based on the assumption that persons can accurately comment on their behavior from a distance. Only a clinical examination could identify unconscious processes as they are happening.

With this rationale, statements were designed to reflect behavior suggestive of the following 24 defense or coping mechanisms: acting out, pseudoaltruism, as-if behavior, clinging, humor, passive-aggressive behavior, regression, somatization, suppression, withdrawal, dissociation, denial, displacement, omnipotence-devaluation, inhibition, intellectualization, identification, primitive idealization, projection, reaction formation, repression, splitting, sublimation, and turning against self. These statements were subjected to an initial test of face validity by asking two psychologists and one psychiatrist (two of the three are psychoanalysts), independently, to match up each statement with its relevant defense or coping mechanism. Only the statements on which they all could agree formed our initial 97-statement questionnaire.

The following are some representative examples:

1. "If someone mugged me and stole my money, I'd rather he be helped than punished" (reaction formation).
2. "There's no such thing as finding a little good in everyone. If you're bad, you're all bad" (splitting).
3. "If my boss bugged me, I might make a mistake in my work or work more slowly so as to get back at him" (passive-aggressive behavior).
4. "I always feel that someone I know is like a guardian angel" (primitive idealization).

Subjects were asked to indicate their degree of agreement or disagreement with each statement on a 9-point scale, with 1 indicating strong disagreement and 9 indicating strong agreement. All scales were constructed so that a high score on any one defense measure indicated that subject was using that defense.

In a pilot project, we tested 30 patients on the first version of our questionnaire, which consisted of statements measuring self-appraisal of defense style. Internal consistency among statements designed to measure the same defense was assessed through item-to-total correlations. Based on these correlations and the earlier mentioned considerations of face validity, we retained 81 of the initial 97 statements measuring possible conscious derivatives of defense mechanisms and added 7 new statements.

Our hypotheses were that (a) factor analysis would demonstrate separate clusters of defense mechanisms—that is, defensive styles, and (b) defenses thought to be immature (e.g., acting out, projection, withdrawal, and passive-aggressive behavior) would be bipolar to defenses thought to be more mature.

The following measures of ego development were correlated with the data from the defense questionnaire to determine if there was a hierarchy of defense mechanisms:

1. *Ego Strength Questionnaire.* In an attempt to cross-validate Bellak, Hurvich, and Gediman's (1973) conclusions that ego functioning is multidimensional, Brown and Gardner (personal communication, 1981) constructed a questionnaire designed to measure a number of different ego functions. Since only one factor was found, Brown and Gardner argued that a subject's total score on the questionnaire, which is referred to as the "ego strength score," reflected the person's general level of adaptation.

2. *Sentence Completion Test of Loevinger.* The second measure of ego development was a sentence completion test that is well described elsewhere (Loevinger, 1976).

## Results

As in the pilot project, item-to-total correlations were carried out for each question, and then for the total score of the questions attributed to each defense mechanism in relation to the factor to which it belonged, to ensure that reliability had been retained and that the statements still correlated with the other statements in the relevant defense category. All correlations remained significant at a greater than .001 level.

Principal component (type PA1, quartimax rotation) (Nie, Hull, Jenkins, Steinbrenner, & Bent, 1975, pp. 484–485) factor analyses were carried out on the sets of statements on the 24 postulated defenses for the entire sample and for the patient and nonpatient samples taken separately. A four-factor solution provided an adequate representation of the data for the combined group and for the nonpatient and patient samples taken separately. (See Table 9–1 for factor loadings.) In the factor analysis carried out on the combined group, and in that on the nonpatient and patient samples taken separately, the same defenses clustered together. Factor 1 accounted for 50% of the variance; factor 2, 10%; factor 3, 9%; factor 4, 8%.

Defense Style 1 (Factor 1) consisted of apparent derivatives of defense mechanisms usually viewed as immature: withdrawal, regression, acting out, inhibition, passive-aggression, and projection. All of the preceding mechanisms produced factor loadings greater than .65 on the combined

**TABLE 9–1**
**Factor Loadings on Defenses (Combined Sample)\***

| Defense | Factor 1 | Factor 2 | Factor 3 | Factor 4 |
|---|---|---|---|---|
| Acting out | .76 | .11 | −.10 | −.23 |
| Regression | .67 | −.01 | −.09 | −.29 |
| Passive-aggressive behavior | .74 | .10 | −.02 | −.09 |
| Withdrawal | .75 | −.17 | .11 | .05 |
| Projection | .69 | .31 | .02 | −.41 |
| Inhibition | .69 | −.20 | .17 | −.01 |
| Omnipotence-devaluation | .17 | .70 | −.10 | .21 |
| Splitting | .38 | .60 | −.05 | −.20 |
| Primitive idealization | .36 | .54 | .36 | .15 |
| Pseudoaltruism | .33 | −.08 | .62 | .06 |
| Reaction formation | .36 | −.07 | .56 | .06 |
| Sublimation | −.09 | .12 | .17 | .64 |
| Humor | −.14 | .02 | −.27 | .63 |
| Suppression | −.10 | .02 | .00 | .62 |
| As if behavior | .62 | .05 | .07 | .32 |
| Clinging | .64 | .34 | .04 | .02 |
| Denial | .33 | .04 | .52 | −.05 |
| Displacement | .49 | .15 | −.19 | .05 |
| Dissociation | .63 | .22 | .15 | −.17 |
| Identification | .45 | .32 | .19 | .29 |
| Intellectualization | .49 | −.12 | −.11 | .33 |
| Repression | .53 | −.08 | .05 | −.17 |
| Somatization | .56 | .19 | .11 | .10 |
| Turning against self | .61 | −.26 | .02 | −.03 |
| % variance | 50% | 10% | 9% | 8% |

*Source:* Reprinted from "Empirical Study of Self-Rated Defense Styles," by M. Bond, S. T. Gardner, J. Christian, and J. J. Sigal, 1983, *Archives of General Psychiatry, 40*, 333–338, March 1983. Copyright 1983 by the American Medical Association. Reprinted by permission.

\*Type PA1, quartimax rotation.

analyses and greater than .55 on the separate analyses, except for regression, which only loaded at .40 for the nonpatients.

Defense Style 2 (Factor 2) consisted of apparent derivatives of omnipotence, splitting, and primitive idealization. All three defenses loaded greater than .50 on all three of the factor analyses.

Defense Style 3 (Factor 3) consisted of apparent derivatives of only two defense mechanisms: reaction formation and pseudoaltruism. There was some question as to whether to include denial within Defense Style 3, since it loaded fairly highly on both the factor analysis of the combined sample and that of the patient sample taken separately. However, denial was eliminated because it loaded negatively on this factor when the analysis was carried out on the nonpatient sample alone.

Defense Style 4 (Factor 4) consisted of apparent derivatives of suppression, sublimation, and humor, all of which loaded at a greater than .50 level on all three factor analyses, with the exception of sublimation, which loaded at the .47 level when factoring was done on the nonpatient sample alone.

The level of development of these four defense styles was assessed in a number of ways. Defense Style 1 has a significant negative correlation with Style 4 ($t = -.28$, $p < .001$). Table 9–2 shows the correlations of the four defense styles with the two measures of maturity: ego strength score and ego development score. These correlations indicate that Defense Styles 1 through 4 can be ranked in that order; that is, the ego strength score has a high negative correlation with Style 1, a lower negative correlation with Styles 2 and 3, and a significantly positive correlation with Style 4. The same pattern holds for the ego development score (the Loevinger test).

When the ego strength and ego development scores were factor analyzed (type PA1, quartimax rotation) (Nie et al., 1975) along with the

**TABLE 9–2**
**Correlations of Defense Styles with Loevinger's Ego Development and Brown and Gardner's Ego Strength Measure**

|  | Style 1 | Style 2 | Style 3 | Style 4 |
|---|---|---|---|---|
| Ego Strength | −.91** | −.37** | −.38** | .32** |
| Loevinger's development | −.42** | −.22 | −.29* | .19* |

*Source:* Reprinted from "Empirical Study of Self-Rated Defense Styles," by M. Bond, S. T. Gardner, J. Christian, and J. J. Sigal, 1983, *Archives of General Psychiatry, 40,* 333–338. Copyright 1983 by the American Medical Association. Reprinted by permission.
*$p < .01$.
**$p < .001$.

separate defenses that constitute the four defense styles, a four-factor solution resulted, with the ego strength and ego development scores loading negatively with Style 1 defenses and positively with Style 4 defenses.

The mean scores on Defense Styles 1 through 3 are higher for the patients than the nonpatients (132.7, $SD = 34$ vs. 91.7, $SD = 24.7$, $p < .001$, $t = 9.86$; 36.9, $SD = 14.8$ vs. 30.3, $SD = 9.9$, $p < .001$, $t = 3.73$; and 25.8, $SD = 9$ vs. 22.6, $SD = 6.1$, $p < .01$, $t = 2.96$); whereas the score on defense style 4 was higher for the nonpatients (28.2, $SD = 5.9$ vs. 24.4, $SD = 7.8$, $p < .001$, $t = -3.96$).

This difference between the nonpatient and the patient sample in the use of defense styles is again borne out by examining the defense styles used by individual subjects. If a subject's score was 0.5 $SD$ above the mean on a particular factor, we assumed that the subject used that corresponding defense style. Using a cutting point of 0.5 $SD$ provided the best discrimination. Of those with computable scores, 60% of the patients used Defense Style 1 in conjunction with other styles, and 16% used it exclusively. In contrast, 11% of the nonpatients used Style 1 in conjunction with other styles and only 3% used it exclusively. With regard to Defense Style 4, 48% of the patients used it in conjunction with other defense styles and only 9% used it exclusively. In contrast, 90% of the nonpatients used Defense Style 4 in conjunction with other defenses and 42% used it exclusively. What this implies is that patients use Style 1 more than nonpatients and the latter use Style 4 more than patients do.

The following clinical example illustrates how scores on our scales might be related to clinical information. The patient had a diagnosis of an acute schizophrenic episode and borderline personality at different times. At the time that she was tested, she was an outpatient. At her worst, she showed signs of regression, withdrawal, and primitive projection. She had delusions of persecution, influence, and grandiosity; however, by structuring her life and by encouraging her activity in the creative arts and music, she was helped to cope.

This patient had high scores on Defense Styles 1, 2, and 4. We believe that Style 1 reflected her regressive behavior, Style 2 reflected her omnipotence and primitive idealization, and Style 4 reflected her adaptive coping mechanisms. A subject's use of multiple styles might provide clues as to why he or she would receive different diagnoses at different times. According to the DSM-III, a diagnosis of schizophrenia rules out the diagnosis of borderline personality disorder, but if this patient was using Styles 2 and 4 most strongly and her regressive behavior was under control, then she would seem borderline to some clinicians.

## The Questionnaire

A questionnaire has some important advantages over the clinical interview for the assessment of defensive functioning. It saves time, does not require highly trained and highly paid professionals to administer it, eliminates problems of interrater reliability, provides a measure of the degree to which defenses are present on a standardizable continuum; and it provides an opportunity to gather normative data. As a result, it permits the development of cutting points that may discriminate between impaired and unimpaired functioning.

Our results demonstrate that the construction of such a questionnaire is feasible. We have produced an instrument that has desirable statistical properties. Even more important, the factors make clinical sense. We do not presume, however, that the present questionnaire is complete. It does not measure all the possible conscious derivatives of defense mechanisms. Nonetheless, it does provide a frame to which questions measuring other defenses or more items measuring the same defenses can be added. It must be stressed, however, that we are only measuring self-appraisals of defensive styles and not actually measuring defense mechanisms. A further study is needed to validate the relationship between what we are measuring and the traditional notion of defense.

A number of findings lend support to the validity of the questionnaire. First, the defenses clustered in the factor analysis along lines that make theoretical sense. Thus, "immature" defense maneuvers (e.g., regression, acting out) clustered together on Factor 1; splitting, primitive idealization, pseudoaltruism on Factors 2 and 3, were intermediate in maturity; and the defenses clustered in factor 4 (sublimation, suppression, and humor) are commonly associated with the idea of greater maturity. Second, the high negative correlation of the expected primitive defenses with the expected higher level defenses provides additional evidence for validity.

The criterion validity of the questionnaire was supported in two ways. First, the defense styles related to other indexes of ego development, as expected; that is, the relative correlations of Styles 1 through 4 with the scores on the Loevinger and ego strength tests indicate that they can be ranked, in that order, on a continuum of development or adaptation. Second, the fact that patients tend to use the less mature defenses and nonpatients the higher level defenses adds credence to the questionnaire. The patient sample had significantly higher mean scores than the nonpatient sample on Defense Styles 1 through 3. The nonpatient sample had a significantly higher mean score on Style 4 defenses. When factor scores were computed for individual subjects, the patients tended to use

Style 1 defenses much more and the Style 4 defenses much less than the nonpatients.

## Clusters of Self-Perceptions of Characteristic Defenses

It was clear from our data that subjects' perceptions of their own characteristic behaviors clustered into what we call defensive styles. It is interesting to speculate, for each style, about the common elements that might apply to all the inferred defenses associated with that style. For the six defenses that clustered on Factor 1—withdrawal, acting out, regression, inhibition, passive-aggression, and projection—immaturity may not be the best term since these defenses can sometimes be found in well-functioning persons. Perhaps the common feature of this factor is that all these behaviors indicate the subjects' inability to deal with their impulses by taking constructive action on their own behalf. The acting-out subject requires controls. The withdrawn or inhibited person needs to be actively drawn out. The passive-aggressive person acts to provoke anger in the person with whom he or she is involved. The regressed person requires someone to take over and do something for him. The projecting person puts the blame and responsibility on others instead of accepting his or her own impulses. Thus, this style might be labeled "maladaptive action patterns."

The essence of the inferred defenses that clustered on Factor 2—splitting, primitive idealization, and omnipotence with devaluation—is splitting of the image of self and other into good and bad, strong and weak. This differs from the Style 1 defenses in that it is image-oriented rather than action-oriented. Although Style 2 could interfere with object relations, it need not necessarily affect achievement and accomplishment. In situations of stress, these defenses could be invoked for constructive adaptation by persons who do not use them habitually; for example, one way of dealing with a severe physical illness may be to trust in the omnipotence of the physician. These defenses may also be used nonadaptively by persons with chronic difficulty in forming mature relationships. In the literature, this style is associated with narcissistic and borderline personality disorders (Kernberg, 1967). These clustered defenses, then, can be described as the "image-distorting" style.

The items designed to test the two inferred defenses constituting Style 3—reaction formation and pseudoaltruism—reflect a need to perceive one's self as being kind, helpful to others, and never angry. This is characteristic of martyr types and "do-gooders." It is our impression that these people are often involved in stable but not necessarily healthy relationships and that they are usually able to function adequately. They often come to the attention of psychiatrists when they suffer a loss and their characteristic defense pattern cannot contain their anger and anxiety. They then become depressed. Style 3 can be characterized as consisting of "self-sacrificing" defenses.

The inferred defenses for Style 4—humor, suppression, and sublimation—are strongly associated with good coping. Suppression allows an anxiety-producing conflict to be put out of awareness until the individual is ready to deal with the issue. Humor reflects a capacity to accept a conflictual situation while taking the edge off its painful aspects. Sublimation uses the anxiety-provoking impulse in the service of creative response. All three defenses are associated with a constructive type of mastery of the conflict. Style 4 can be labeled the "adaptive" defense style.

For the most part, the defense styles are different from the "neurotic styles" Shapiro (1965) outlined by means of theoretical construction from psychoanalytic descriptions rather than by using empirical data. He described the obsessive, paranoid, hysterical, and impulsive styles. Our maladaptive action patterns probably correspond to his impulsive style, but the other "neurotic styles" seem to be organized along factors different from our defense styles.

## Maturity and Defense Styles

The correlations of each of the defense styles with two measures of maturity—ego strength and Loevinger tests—indicate that in developmental terms there is a progression from the maladaptive action patterns, through the image-distorting defenses, and the self-sacrificing defenses to the adaptive defenses, along the line of increasingly constructive dealing with the vicissitudes of life.

The least mature people have behavior problems. Those in the image-distorting group have problems in realistically viewing themselves and others, which lends to relationship problems. The self-sacrificing persons have more stable relationships but cannot fulfill their creative potential. The adaptive defenses reflect less preoccupation with relationships and allow more creative expression of the individual's inner self. Thus, the defense styles reflect a shift from preoccupation with control of raw impulses, to preoccupation with all-important others, to creative expression of self.

Other studies also reflect this shift. With a clinical population, Semrad et al. (1973) suggested that as patients improve, their defenses become less primitive and more mature. One patient in their study moved from what they labeled as narcissistic patterns, to affective defensive patterns to neurotic defensive patterns as therapy progressed. Vaillant (1976), in his 20-year follow-up study of a normal male college-age population, found an increasing use of more mature defenses over time. Mature defenses not only enhanced the men's ability to work but also enhanced their ability to love. Thus, Vaillant's study of normal subjects, the study of patients by Semrad et al., and our study of both patients and nonpatients indicate that defenses can be arranged in a hierarchy of maturity that relates to a person's successful adaptation to the world.

## FURTHER ATTEMPTS AT VALIDATION

A second study involving 156 subjects was carried out to compare subjects' responses on the DSQ with their scores on the Defense Mechanism Rating Scale (DMRS; Perry & Cooper, 1986) in which judges rated defense mechanisms from a videotaped clinical assessment interview (Bond et al., 1989). These ratings are assumed to be as valid a measure of defense mechanisms as researchers can achieve empirically and, thus, were used as a standard with which to compare the self-report scores.

In the period from July 1985 to October 1986, 333 people who came for psychiatric assessments to the Department of Psychiatry of the Jewish General Hospital, Montreal, were asked to participate in our research project. Of these, 179 agreed to participate and signed informed consent forms. Complete data were collected on 156 subjects, of whom 66 were male and 90 female. Their ages ranged from 16 to 73, with a median of 39, a mode of 24, and a mean of 36 with a standard deviation of 14.7.

There were 130 patients from the adult outpatient department and 26 patients from an outpatient youth service for patients ages 16–20. There were 66 single patients, 69 married, 9 separated, and 23 divorced.

The four measures were the Defense Style Questionnaire, the Defense Mechanisms Rating Scale, the Life Events Scale, and the Health-Sickness Rating Scale.

Space limitations restrict us to only a summary of the relevant findings in this study. There were significant positive correlations between the use of the DSQ maladaptive defense style and the ratings of immature defenses (DMRS) by the clinical judges and a significantly negative correlation between DSQ maladaptive defense style and DMRS mature defenses. DSQ maladaptive defenses correlated negatively with age and scores on the Health Sickness Rating Scale (HSRS) (a measure of overall health functioning) and positively with a high degree of life stress (measured by the Life Events Scale).

The DSQ image-distorting defense style was significantly positively correlated with DMRS immature defenses, with divorced or single status, and with high life stress. It was negatively correlated with age and healthy functioning (HSRS). Further details of the methodology and results are presented in Bond et al., 1989.

In 39 cases, the Defense Style Questionnaire was repeated 6 months later. The correlations using Pearson's correlations for the four defense styles at the two times were highly significant, $p = 0.001$; for Style 1, $r = .73$; for Style 2, $r = .71$; for Style 3, $r = .68$; and for Style 4, $r = .69$. In other words, the style used by an individual did not change in relation to the group of subjects. However, there was a tendency for subjects to report less use of Styles 1 and 2 when tested 6 months later ($p < 0.005$ and $< 0.003$, respectively), and for them to report more use of Style 4 ($p < 0.01$). Thus, although the defense style profile of an individual remained stable, there was a trend toward more mature defense style reporting 6 months later. This might reflect spontaneous improvement, treatment effect, or regression toward the mean.

Two case examples are provided. (The criterion for the use of a style is a score of 0.5 *SD* above the mean for that style.)

*Case 1.* Mrs. N, a 54-year-old, married woman, presented to the outpatient department with a 7-month history of early morning wakening and a 3-month history of decreased appetite: weight loss of 18 lb; withdrawal; loss of interest, energy, and concentration; feelings of worthlessness; sadness; and suicidal thoughts. She worried about losing her job and not having enough money for her old age. She was diagnosed as having a major depression.

On her initial visit, the Defense Style Questionnaire showed her to be using Defense Styles 1, 2, and 3; and the DMRS showed her to be using hypochondriasis, passive-aggression, reaction formation, and devaluation. After treatment, 6 months later, she was doing well, her HSRS score improved by 10 points, and the questionnaire showed her to be using Style 4. Thus, with improvement, her defense style changed from immature to mature. Her treatment consisted of antidepressants and group and milieu therapy in a day hospital setting. She was actively encouraged to focus on others, not on herself. In this case, the change in defense style was dramatic and in the direction of the therapeutic focus, which encouraged suppression, sublimation, affiliation, and altruism. Defense style behaved like a state phenomenon, changing with improvement.

*Case 2.* This 23-year-old single female nurse's aide, who lived alone, used the maladaptive and image-distorting defense styles on initial testing and also on testing 6 months later. The HSRS score dropped by 25 points despite 10 sessions of psychotherapy. Her DMRS showed use of immature, neurotic, and image-distorting defenses on initial presentation.

She presented with suicidal ideas since she took an overdose of over-the-counter sleeping medications while drinking wine 6 months previously. A friend helped her get over this episode but suicidal thoughts recurred whenever she felt overwhelmed by stress. She was in recurrent financial crisis and had a relationship with a man whom she perceived as taking advantage of her. She felt unrecognized at her job in spite of her hard work.

She presented as an attractive, friendly, fashionably dressed young woman who smiled a lot, did not seem depressed, and denied suicidal intent. She was seen as having an adjustment disorder and referred for psychotherapy. After 10 sessions of psychotherapy, she was "somewhat confused about her life" and appeared depressed and regressed (looking and acting like a teenager). She was not attending school, had difficulty coping at work, and was living with a married man. At this point, she was suspected of having borderline personality disorder.

This is an example of how defense style did not change over a 6-month period. The maladaptive and image-distorting defense styles are consistent with the behavioral outcomes of acting out, regression, and problematic relationships, and might have been an important warning of problems ahead, despite her superficially healthy presentation, which led to a falsely hopeful diagnosis.

### Diagnosis and Defense Style

It is interesting to speculate about the relationship between defense style and diagnosis. In the two preceding studies, no diagnostic group was significantly correlated with any DSQ defense style or DMRS subscale. However, a later study (Bond, Paris, & Zweig-Frank, 1994) that focused on female patients diagnosed as personality disorders found significant differences. The sample was divided into 78 subjects who scored 8 or over on the Diagnostic Interview for Borderlines-Revised (DIB-R) (Zanarini, Frankenburg, Chauncey, & Gunderson, 1987) and 72 subjects (other personality disorders) who scored less than 7 on the DIB-R. The borderline group reported using the maladaptive and image-distorting defense styles significantly more often and the adaptive defense style significantly less often than the nonborderline but personality-disordered group. This finding is in line with Kernberg's (1967) view of borderlines using image-distorting defenses and being lower level personality disorders. The lack of use of adaptive defenses (suppression, sublimation, and humor) is consistent with an incapacity to master anxiety, painful emotion, or threatening impulse, which leaves borderline patients in a poorly modulated state of mind. The nonemergence of this particular finding in our previous two studies (Bond, 1990) can be explained by the smaller sample of borderlines and by the fact that we did not use as specific a diagnostic tool as the DIB-R, but instead chart diagnoses.

## DISCUSSION

This research elucidates both what is possible in the empirical measurement of defense mechanisms and what difficulties continue to exist. The Defense Style Questionnaire seems to be most accurate when discriminating between adaptive and maladaptive defense styles. The self-reported use of the maladaptive defense style was significantly positively correlated with the group of immature-level defenses rated by the Defense Mechanism Rating Scales and significantly negatively correlated with the DMRS mature-level defenses. Of 25 items identified as tapping maladaptive defenses, 23 items positively correlated with Perry and Cooper's group of immature level defenses (1986). When this is added to Vaillant, Bond, and Vaillant's (1986) results, there is compelling evidence that the Defense Style Questionnaire can identify immature defenses as a group validly and reliably.

Defense mechanisms from other groupings did show significant correlations on an individual basis: Neurotic denial, splitting, projective identification, and omnipotence/devaluation all showed significant correlations between their DMRS and DSQ ratings.

The maladaptive defense style also correlated significantly negatively with both age and healthy functioning on the HSRS, and positively with a high life events score. The use of any given defense style remained stable 6 months later. All these data are consistent with what we would theoretically expect, including the notion that a defense style would be stable over a 6-month period. That there is a trend toward greater maturity and toward a higher HSRS score 6 months after seeking help indicates that as patients are functioning better, they report using more adaptive defenses, but still maintain the same basic defensive profile. Thus, it would seem that the state-or-trait question cannot be given an all-or-none answer. Defense styles seem to be a trait phenomenon, but some change within a given profile seems likely over time. However, there is much variation among individuals, as shown by our case examples. The correlation of high life stress with low Health Sickness Rating Scale scores and with a maladaptive defense style is logically consistent. The three variables are probably all part of a vicious cycle of stress and poor functioning.

The two case examples illustrate the variety among the many dimensions of functioning of human beings. In the first case, there was a change in the use of defense style as the individual's level of functioning or state of crisis changed. The change may have been a result of therapy encouraging new ways of dealing with conflicts. In the second case, defense style seemed to be more of a trait. In this case, the DSQ elicited evidence of a tendency toward regression that was not apparent in the clinical interview, as is often the case with borderlines who appear neurotic at first blush. Thus, the DSQ can be a useful adjunct to clinical diagnosis but is not predictive on its own. It may indicate directions to take in therapy. If the use of more adaptive defenses can be fostered by therapy, the patient's clinical state could improve.

Generally, defense style cannot predict specific diagnoses, which indicates that each measures different dimensions. Certain defense styles are significantly correlated with borderline personality disorder, but still, there are patients who use these maladaptive and image-distorting defenses who are not borderline just as many disturbed patients may still use some adaptive defenses. Thus, although some specific defenses may be associated with some specific illnesses, the correlations are not high enough or exclusive enough to use defenses as an indicator of diagnosis in most cases.

The DSQ might have some value in predicting outcome of psychotherapy. Piper, de Carufel, and Szkrumelak (1985) studied 21 psychiatric outpatients who were treated with short-term psychoanalytically oriented individual psychotherapy. Pretherapy defense mechanisms were an excellent predictor of outcome, with the adaptive ones predicting the best outcome and maladaptive defenses predicting the worst.

Our questionnaire relies on patients' self-reports, which are limited by their motivation at the moment of responding, by their openness, and by their self-awareness. Also, the statements are merely indirect measures of defenses, tapping conscious derivatives of these unconscious intrapsychic processes. These limitations require us to be very cautious about disentangling trait versus state issues from our results. Although Vaillant (1976) was able to show the predictive power of defenses for large groups, we must be wary of predicting outcome with individuals.

Despite the caveats, the DSQ seems to have real usefulness in discriminating adaptive from maladaptive defense styles, which in turn allows predictions about level of development and measures of health and outcome in at least one form of therapy.

# REFERENCES

American Psychiatric Association. (1987). *Diagnostic and statistical manual of mental disorders* (3rd ed., rev.; DSM-III-R). Washington, DC: American Psychiatric Press.

Bellak, L., Hurvich, M., & Gediman, H. K. (1973). *Ego functions in schizophrenics, neurotics, and normals.* New York: Wiley.

Bond, M. (1990). Are "borderline defenses" specific for borderline personality disorders? *Journal of Personality Disorders, 4,* 251–256.

Bond, M., Gardner, S. T., Christian, J., & Sigal, J. J. (1983). Empirical study of self-rated defense styles. *Archives of General Psychiatry, 40,* 333–338.

Bond, M., Paris, J., & Zweig-Frank, H. (1994). Defense styles and borderline personality disorders. *Journal of Personality Disorders, 8*(1), 28–31.

Bond, M., Perry, J. C., Gautier, M., Goldenberg, H., Oppenheimer, J., & Simand, J. (1989). Validating the self-report of defense styles. *Journal of Personality Disorders, 3,* 101–112.

Freud, A. (1936). *The ego and the mechanisms of defense.* New York: International Universities Press.

Freud, S. (1973). Inhibitions, symptoms and anxiety. In J. Strachey (Ed. and Trans.), *The standard edition of the complete psychological works of Sigmund Freud* (Vol. 20). London: Hogarth Press. (Original work published 1926)

Gleser, G. C., & Ihilevich, D. (1969). An objective instrument for measuring defense mechanisms. *Journal of Consulting and Clinical Psychology, 33,* 51–60.

Haan, N. A. (1969). Tripartite model of ego functioning values and clinical research applications. *Journal of Nervous and Mental Disease, 148,* 14–30.

Haan, N. A., Stroud, J., & Holstein, J. (1973). Moral and ego stages in relationship to ego processes: A study of "hippies." *Journal of Personality, 41,* 596–612.

Kernberg, O. (1967). Borderline personality organization. *Journal of the American Psychoanalytic Association, 15,* 641–685.

Klein, M. (1973). *The psychoanalysis of children.* London: Hogarth Press.

Loevinger, J. (1976). *Ego development.* San Francisco: Jossey-Bass.

Nie, N. H., Hull, C. H., Jenkins, J. G., Steinbrenner, K., & Bent, D. H. (1975). *Statistical package for the social sciences* (2nd ed.). New York: McGraw-Hill.

Perry, J. C., & Cooper, S. H. (1986). A preliminary report on defenses and conflicts associated with borderline personality disorder. *Journal of the American Psychoanalytic Association, 34,* 863–893.

Piper, E. W., de Carufel, F. L., & Szkrumelak, N. (1985). Patient predictors of process and outcome in short-term individual psychotherapy. *Journal of Nervous and Mental Disease, 173,* 726–733.

Semrad, E. V., Grinspoon, L., & Feinberg, S. E. (1973). Development of an ego profile scale. *Archives of General Psychiatry, 28,* 70–77.

Shapiro, D. (1965). *Neurotic styles*. New York: Basic Books.

Singer, J. L. (1990). *Repression and dissociation*. Chicago: University of Chicago Press.

Vaillant, G. E. (1975). Natural history of male psychological health, III: Empirical dimensions of mental health. *Archives of General Psychiatry, 32,* 420–426.

Vaillant, G. E. (1976). Natural history of male psychological health, V: The relation of choice of ego mechanisms of defense to adult adjustment. *Archives of General Psychiatry, 33,* 535–545.

Vaillant, G. E., Bond, M. P., & Vaillant, C. O. (1986). An empirically validated hierarchy of defense mechanisms. *Archives of General Psychiatry, 43,* 786–794.

Zanarini, M. C., Frankenburg, F. R., Chauncey, D. L., & Gunderson, J. G. (1987). The diagnostic interview for personality disorders: Interrater and test-retest reliability. *Comprehensive Psychiatry, 28,* 467–480.

# 10

# The Defense Mechanisms Inventory
## Its Development and Clinical Applications

DAVID IHILEVICH AND
GOLDINE C. GLESER

Over the past three decades, empirical studies have demonstrated that the individual's sense of mastery or control over perceived threat is much more important for adaptation and health than is the actual nature of the threat (cf. Friedman, 1991; Lazarus & Folkman, 1984; Rabkin & Struening, 1976; Taylor & Brown, 1988). The robustness of these findings has propelled the dynamic concepts of coping and defense into the center stage of inquiry in such fields as stress research, psychosocial adaptation, and psychoimmunology. It thus appears that Freud's conclusion that the defense mechanisms of the mind constitute "the cornerstone on which the whole structure of psychoanalysis rests" (Freud, 1914/1957, p. 16) was prescient.

Although the definition of defense mechanisms has not changed substantially since Freud's conceptualization, the presumed functions of psychological defenses have expanded considerably. Freud described defense mechanisms as unconscious mental processes that are activated involuntarily when the individual experiences intrapsychic conflicts which produce excessive psychic pain or anxiety. Freud observed that under certain circumstances, these "techniques [defenses] which the ego makes use of in conflicts may lead to neurosis" (Freud, 1926/1959, p. 163). By adopting the concept of unconscious defense, Freud linked, in a network of seemingly naturalistic, logically consistent principles, the etiology of various disorders, the therapeutic methods, and intervention strategies needed to effect cures. He did not elucidate however, when the use of defenses is healthy and when pathological. It remained for Anna Freud to address that issue. She concluded, "Whether defense leads to symptom formation rather than to healthy social adaptation depends on quantitative factors even more than on qualitative ones" (A. Freud, 1965, p. 117).

In addition to the role of defenses in psychopathology, Anna Freud suggested that they also fulfill vital functions in normal personality development. She observed that although the defense of turning against self is clinically linked to depression, used in moderation, it contributes to the development of the child's superego. Whereas the excessive use of reaction formation is associated with development of neurosis, its moderate deployment stabilizes a child's values. Relying excessively on projection can lead to paranoia, yet its moderate use protects a child's vulnerable self-esteem against excessive criticism and lasting damage (A. Freud, in Hoffer, 1954, p. 196). In a similar vein, Van der Leeuw (1971) concluded that although defense mechanisms can lead to neurosis, they are simultaneously indispensable for normal psychic functioning. For example, he notes that whereas denial hinders perception, it also protects the ego from being overwhelmed. Identification and projection disturb reality testing, but they also facilitate insight into others and are a necessary condition for learning compassion (Van der Leeuw, 1971, p. 56).

Vaillant suggested that the function of defenses entails (a) keeping affects within bearable limits, (b) postponing or redirecting biological drives, (c) integrating changes in self-concept, and (d) managing unresolved conflicts with others (Vaillant, 1971, p. 107). Object relation theorists (e.g., Kohut, 1984; Modell, 1984) emphasize the function of defenses as protectors against the fear of separation and abandonment that they believe are more important sources of anxiety than intrapsychic conflicts. More recently, Nesse (1990), expanding on the findings of the biologists Trivers and Alexander, suggested that by concealing motives from the self, defenses make it easier to conceal motives from others, thus conferring to their users an evolutionary adaptive advantage.

Available empirical evidence generally supports the position that, to some extent, all defense mechanisms perform the following four functions: (a) falsifying the meaning or significance of perceived threats; (b) creating the illusion of mastery over perceived dangers, whether from internal or external sources; (c) eliminating or reducing to tolerable levels the experience of conscious anxiety, and (d) protecting or enhancing the individual's sense of well-being.

Following the empirical work of Miller and Swanson (1960), we conceptualized defense mechanisms as relatively stable, unconscious response dispositions for resolving conflicts between internalized values and opposing internal or external demands experienced by the individual. Defenses reconcile or resolve these conflicts by attacking, distorting, or becoming selectively unaware of certain aspects of the internal or external world. Several empirical studies in the 1960s raised serious doubt that the approaches to evaluating defenses available at that time (clinical interview, projective tests, existing objective measures) were adequate. It is in this context that we undertook the development of the Defense Mechanisms Inventory (DMI) in 1962.

To organize the currently available data on the DMI, we have divided this chapter into eight sections. The first will describe the classification system of defenses we have adopted for constructing the DMI. The second section will describe the construction of the DMI as an assessment instrument for measuring the defense styles in the classification system. The third section describes some psychometric properties of the inventory. The fourth section will present demographic correlates and normative data obtained for male and female general adults, college students, and psychiatric outpatients. The fifth section will analyze the reliability of individual defense scales and profiles. The sixth section will examine some of the data gathered relevant to the construct validity of the DMI scales as measures of defense mechanisms. The seventh section will illustrate possible clinical applications of the DMI. We shall conclude with a brief review of the implications of empirical findings gathered with the DMI for several theoretical issues pertaining to defenses.

## THE CLASSIFICATION SYSTEM OF THE DEFENSE MECHANISMS INVENTORY

Freud's clinical and theoretical papers described nine unconscious modes of operation that he designated as defense mechanisms. Anna Freud (1936/1946) conceptualized several additional mechanisms of defense. Because of the striking originality of these concepts, their explanatory power, and not least the stature of the authors, these have been frequently designated the "classical defenses." In the past three decades, there has been an explosion in the number of new defense mechanisms described in the clinical literature. Most of these "new defenses," however, are either a redefinition of familiar symptoms (e.g., "sexualization," "counterphobic behavior," "excessive eating"), a revised use of established diagnostic categories (e.g., "delinquency," "anorexia," "hypochondriasis"), or the equating of various forms of behavior or cognitive processes (e.g., "acting out," "anticipation," "fantasy") with constructs that denote unconscious mechanisms activated for defensive purposes.

This proliferation of defenses has made meaningful communication, empirical research, and development of measurement instruments all but impossible. As a result, several theoreticians have concluded that a classification system is needed based on a few simple "strategies," "forms," or "processes" from which most defenses are derived. In this debate, a few investigators have pointed out that even the differences among the classical defense mechanisms identified by Freud have barely been spelled out. For example, Suppes and Warren (1975) concluded that in "Anna Freud's work, it is difficult to find any systematic statement which clearly differentiates reversal from reaction-formation . . . [or] isolation from intellectualization" (p. 410). Suggestions were advanced to classify defenses on the basis of such criteria as their degree of "unconsciousness," "complexity," "source of anxiety," and "maturity." As of now, no particular classification system of defenses has emerged that is fully satisfactory. Ultimately, the comprehensiveness, heuristic value, and clinical usefulness of a classification system, need to be determined by empirical studies.

While gathering preliminary data from 352 male and female college students, we found that the defensive responses to three conflictual story vignettes could be parsimoniously classified into the following five defense categories: aggressive, projective, intellectualizing, intrapunitive, and repressive. These five defense styles had the advantage of being economical, sufficiently distinct from each other to allow their separate measurement, yet general enough to encompass most of the classical defense mechanisms previously identified (Gleser & Ihilevich, 1969). Our definition of each style and the classical defenses it encompasses is as follows:

*Turning Against Object (TAO).* This class of responses manages internal conflict or external threats to well-being by excessive and inappropriate attack on the real or presumed source of the perceived danger. Such attacks diminish anxiety by transforming the experience of feeling threatened into an experience of making the threat. When deployed as a defense mechanism, aggression creates an illusion of power and strength, which bolsters the person's sense of well-being. The classical defenses of identification with the aggressor and displacement can be subsumed under this category.

*Projection (PRO).* Included here are defensive responses to perceived threat and conflict that justify the expression of hostility or rejection by first attributing to others negative intent or characteristics on the basis of distorted evidence. Such negative attribution and rejection have the effect of diminishing the person's anxiety concerning his or her own undesirable characteristics by indirectly creating the illusion of superiority and mastery over these traits, thus enhancing self-esteem.

*Principalization (PRN).* Under the guise of espousing general principles, this class of defenses invokes platitudes, truisms, cliches, and sophistry to obfuscate the inner conflict or perceived external threat. This process has the effect of splitting off the awareness of perceived threats from their emotional significance. By creating the illusion of "understanding," a sense of mastery is established, emotional detachment from perceived threat is achieved, anxiety is diminished, and self-esteem is enhanced. The classical defenses of intellectualization, rationalization, and isolation of affect fall into this category.

*Turning Against Self (TAS).* In the face of perceived conflicts and threats, this class of defensive responses directs excessive disapproval, anger, or uncalled for hostility toward the self. Such forms of preemptive punishment and self-derogation create a "cushion" that softens the impact of negative or less than perfect outcomes. This strategy has the effect of protecting vulnerable self-esteem against further diminution. The process of anticipating the worst creates an illusion of existential control over undesirable outcomes, thus diminishing the impact of perceived threats and containing, if not eliminating, conscious anxiety. Self-handicapping, pessimistic, masochistic, and autosadistic responses are subsumed under this category.

*Reversal (REV).* This class of defensive responses diminishes inner conflict or perceived external threats by minimizing their importance or totally removing them from awareness. The process entails responding in a positive or neutral fashion to a frustrating event that might otherwise be expected to evoke a negative reaction. Obliterating unpleasant reality creates an illusion of mastery over it that diminishes conscious anxiety and enhances a sense of well-being. Defenses such as negation, denial, reaction formation, and repression are subsumed under this category.

The lines of evidence for the classification system of defenses we have adopted emerges from the work of other investigators as well as from research we have conducted. Due to space limitations, most of the supporting studies in this and subsequent sections will be omitted. However, these can be found in our two books, *Defense Mechanisms: Their Classification, Correlates and Measurement with the Defense Mechanisms Inventory* (Ihilevich & Gleser, 1986), henceforth referred to as the "DMI Manual," and *Defenses in Psychotherapy: The Clinical Application of the Defense Mechanisms Inventory* (Ihilevich & Gleser, 1991), henceforth referred to as the "Clinical Manual."

The clinical and social psychology literature contains many studies of psychological reactions to real-life threatening situations where the defensive reactions deployed bear a close similarity to three, four, or all five defense styles measured by the DMI. These studies describe nondefensive reactions as well (e.g., hope, prayer, stoicism), which we consider to be coping responses. The studies in question encompass analyses of (a) the defense mechanisms deployed by desperate concentration camp victims in the face of extreme threat to their survival (Bettelheim, 1943); (b) the typical defenses of psychiatric casualties during war (Grinker & Spiegel, 1945); (c) parents' reactions to their children's impending death from leukemia (Friedman, Chodoff, Mason, & Hamburg, 1963); (d) reactions of women awaiting the results of breast tumor biopsies (Katz, Weiner, Gallagher, & Hellman, 1970); (e) the defenses deployed by the elderly in response to unavoidable relocations (Aldrich & Mendkoff, 1963); (f) graduate students' use of defense mechanisms in the face of qualifying doctoral examinations (Mechanic, 1962); and (g) the psychological reactions of the Japanese people to their defeat in World War II (Kitahara, 1981). All these studies describe responses that can be encompassed by and that bear a close similarity to the five defense styles measured by the DMI.

## CONSTRUCTION OF
## THE DEFENSE MECHANISMS INVENTORY

### Story Vignettes

After examining the written responses of college students to three conflictual story vignettes, we decided that an expanded inventory was needed to represent a wider variety of situations where people might experience conflicts. In particular, a larger number of stories was necessary to achieve reliability of measurement of a person's typical defense style. For this purpose we constructed 12 story vignettes involving 6 conflict areas (2 per area). We hoped that this would enable us to study whether there is a systematic association between specific conflicts and defenses or whether individuals differed in defense style as a function of the type of conflict. The conflict areas tapped were as follows:

1. Conflict with *authority figures,* where self-assertion might provoke severe retribution.
2. Conflicts around expressing *needs for independence,* where to express such needs risks more severe deprivation.
3. Conflicts around expressing *competitive needs,* where ambition is threatened by fear of failure and humiliation.

4. Conflicts around *masculinity* (two stories) and
5. *Femininity* (two stories), where the individual's assertion of gender identity is threatened with sexual rejection.
6. *Situational* conflicts, where the person's needs for security, predictability, and control are pitted against random, threatening, uncontrollable events.

To ascertain whether the 12 stories matched the intended conflict areas, five clinical psychologists were given the names of the six conflict areas and were asked to classify the stories, assigning two to each conflict area. Four accomplished the task in perfect agreement and in accord with the authors' intent. The fifth psychologist did not note that he was to assign only two stories to each area and combined the stories involving "authority" and "independence" into one category. All the others were correctly classified.

## Scales and Defensive Responses

Examining the written reactions of college students to three conflictual story vignettes, we noted that about half of their responses could be classified into the five defense categories previously described. The balance of their responses consisted of either reasonable accommodations with or constructive solutions to the conflicts described in the stories. Since we did not want to tap coping or problem-solving responses in our instrument, we decided to forgo the free-response format and develop sets of structured responses corresponding to the five defense styles we had identified. These sets followed four questions that were asked about each story regarding (a) anticipated overt behavioral reactions to the conflictual event described in the story, (b) fantasies about what the respondent might wish to do impulsively, (c) anticipated emotional reactions, and (d) what thoughts the respondent might have in the situations described.

For example, in a story designed to portray a conflict around expressing needs for *independence,* an orphaned college student is living with his/her aunt and uncle. It is raining heavily, and the aunt and uncle insist that the student cancel a date with his/her "steady." The following statements are response alternatives to the question, "What thought might occur to you?"

1. "Why don't they shut up and leave me alone?" (TAO)
2. "They never have really cared for me." (PRO)
3. "You can't take without giving something in return." (PRN)
4. "It's all my own fault for planning such a late date." (TAS)

5. "They are so good to me, I should follow their advice without question." (REV)

## Profile Analysis

We have recently developed a system for classifying the set of five scores obtained on the DMI into profiles. This system, which attempts to be all-inclusive, takes into account both the elevation and spread of scores among the defenses. The most useful profiles to date are those with one or two salient defenses. One-point profiles are those in which one defense is predominant, rising at least 1.5 standard deviations above the norm for general adults and .5 *SD*'s above the next highest score. Two-point profiles have two defenses, each one *SD* or more above the norm and within about .6 *SD*'s of each other. Approximately 50% of the 476 males and female outpatients in the sample we reported on in the Clinical Manual had profiles falling into these two major categories.

## PSYCHOMETRIC CHARACTERISTICS

To ascertain the psychometric characteristics of the scales and responses we developed, we conducted studies of their (a) face validity, (b) alternative instructional formats, (c) intercorrelations, (d) level of adjustment and frequency distribution of scores, and (e) social desirability. Some of these studies will be briefly summarized in this chapter. More detailed analyses are presented in the DMI Manual.

## Face Validity

Three face validity studies were conducted to determine the degree to which the defensive responses we had developed corresponded to the defense styles we intended. In one, we asked 10 practicing psychotherapists from a community mental health center (7 social workers and 3 psychologists) to match each of the 240 DMI responses with one name from a list of 15 classical defenses. No definitions of the DMI styles or of the classical defenses were given. The judges were also permitted to mark the name of a defense not mentioned in the list or to note that, in their opinion, the response did not represent a defense mechanism. This methodology was designed to give us an estimate of the extent to which our defensive responses correspond to responses from which clinicians infer the operation of classical defenses and to discover to what extent these responses collapse into the five styles we intended. Results revealed that there was reasonably good matching of the classical defenses on the list with PRN, TAS, and REV styles (60%, 80%, and 70%, respectively).

However, there was less satisfactory matching between classical defenses and PRO and TAO defense styles (45% and 43%, respectively). The TAO and PRO responses are adequately differentiated from other defensive responses, since relatively few were assigned to other categories. However, about 30% of the TAO responses and 20% of the PRO responses were not considered defensive. A study by Blacha and Fancher (1977) essentially replicated our results.

These findings suggest that practicing therapists frequently do not consider aggressive and accusatory responses as modes of defense. Furthermore, they use varying definitions of projection based on differing theoretical explanations of paranoia. Subsequent item analysis and construct validity studies have justified our use of TAO and PRO as categories of defense and the assignment of responses to these categories.

## Alternative Instructional Formats

An early decision that we had to make was the type of format that would be used with the DMI—free choice or forced choice. After some preliminary experiments, we decided to use the forced choice or ipsative format for our measuring instrument. Our primary reason was that we believed that the free choice format introduced unwanted variance in the scores by virtue of response biases. Persons tending to be hypercritical or suspicious and those fearful of revealing self-inadequacies might reject most items. Such response tendencies confound interpretation of the defense scores obtained using the free choice format but are eliminated by the forced choice, together with any overall measure of defensiveness.

## Intercorrelations among Defense Styles

The intercorrelation matrices among DMI scales have been found to be remarkably similar for men and women college students, general adults, and psychiatric outpatients, using the forced choice scoring format. TAO and PRO are positively correlated as are PRN and REV, whereas the two pairs are negatively correlated with each other. TAS tends to be uncorrelated with the other scales.

These correlations are in the expected direction and are not so large as to make independent associations between the correlated defense styles and other variables impossible to achieve. Thus, for example, even though the TAO and PRO scales are positively correlated in several samples (.42 to .64), only TAO, as expected, correlated significantly with an established measure of *aggression* and *displacement*. Conversely, only PRO was found to be significantly associated with *suspicion* and *paranoia* (see Tables 10–3, 10–4, and 10–5). In a similar vein, despite the positive correlations between REV and PRN (.36 to .57), only PRN is significantly associated with effective *coping skills* and *obsessive-compulsive* neurosis, whereas REV is significantly associated with *denial* and a *hysterical* personality organization.

## DEMOGRAPHIC CORRELATES AND NORMS

To ascertain whether incidental factors such as intelligence, education, gender, age, socioeconomic status, and birth order are associated with defense mechanisms, several researchers have gathered information on the correlation of DMI scales with these variables. The findings reveal that the DMI scales are mainly associated (although weakly) with gender, age, and education and/or intelligence. As noted also in studies of mean differences, these correlations reveal that, as a group, men use more aggressive defenses (TAO & PRO) whereas women prefer to use intrapunitive defenses (TAS) when confronted with threats to their well-being. The data also show a mild decrease in TAO defenses and an increase in REV with age and somewhat higher scores on TAO and PRN and lower scores on TAS and REV with higher education and/or verbal intelligence. Taken together, these findings imply that scores on the DMI should be compared with those from an appropriate normative group with respect to gender, age, and education for proper interpretation.

Table 10–1 provides norms for men and women general adults, college students, and psychiatric outpatients. In both the general adult and college samples and also in the psychiatric outpatient samples, males are significantly higher than females on TAO and significantly lower on TAS. Males are also consistently higher than females on PRO and significantly so in the student sample. The male psychiatric patients tend to have higher scores on TAS and lower scores on TAO and PRO than do either of the nonpatient samples. The typical pattern for normative men is PRN followed by REV. The least preferred are TAS, followed by PRO and TAO. For women, the most preferred are PRN, TAS, and REV, and the least preferred are TAO and PRO. The typical defense preferences for college men, however, are PRN followed by TAO and PRO, while the least preferred are TAS and REV. For college women, PRN is the preferred defense, followed by TAS, whereas the least preferred are TAO and PRO.

The means for psychiatric outpatients differ very little from general population norms. However, their standard deviations tend to be larger for several defenses. This would indicate that the scores are more extreme among psychiatric patients than among the general population, particularly on the TAS and REV scales.

**TABLE 10–1**
**Means and Standard Deviations of DMI Scores for Male and Female General Adults, College Students, and Psychiatric Outpatients**

| Population | | Age | Ed. | TAO | PRO | PRN | TAS | REV |
|---|---|---|---|---|---|---|---|---|
| | | | | Defenses | | | | |
| *General Adults* | | | | | | | | |
| Males (*N* = 558) | $\overline{X}$ | 41.8 | > 12 | 37.6 | 38.5 | 46.7 | 35.5 | 41.6 |
| | *SD* | 14.2 | NA | 9.8 | 6.4 | 6.5 | 6.4 | 8.2 |
| Females (*N* = 438) | $\overline{X}$ | 29.9 | > 12 | 33.9 | 35.9 | 46.1 | 42.6 | 41.4 |
| | *SD* | 11.7 | NA | 9.0 | 7.0 | 6.3 | 6.5 | 8.8 |
| *College Students* | | | | | | | | |
| Males (*N* = 958) | $\overline{X}$ | > 18 | > 13 | 41.6[a] | 40.0 | 44.9 | 36.4 | 37.1[b] |
| | *SD* | NA | NA | 9.2 | 5.8 | 6.3 | 6.8 | 7.4 |
| Females (*N* = 987) | $\overline{X}$ | > 18 | > 13 | 36.7[a] | 36.8 | 46.6 | 42.0 | 38.0[b] |
| | *SD* | NA | NA | 8.8 | 6.0 | 6.2 | 7.2 | 8.0 |
| *Psychiatric Outpatients* | | | | | | | | |
| Males (*N* = 124) | $\overline{X}$ | 32.6 | 12.3 | 36.8 | 36.2 | 45.6 | 39.6[a] | 41.9 |
| | *SD* | 8.3 | 2.3 | 10.7 | 6.1 | 6.2 | 7.4[a] | 9.4 |
| Females (*N* = 110) | $\overline{X}$ | 31.6 | 12.1 | 33.8 | 35.4 | 45.5 | 44.2[a] | 41.1 |
| | *SD* | 7.8 | 1.9 | 10.4 | 7.2 | 7.3 | 7.9[a] | 10.7[a] |

[a]Significantly higher (*p* < .05) than general norms for adults.
[b]Significantly lower (*p* < .05) than general norms for adults.
NA = Not Available.

# GENERALIZABILITY OF SCORES AND PROFILES

## Internal Consistency Estimates

Alpha coefficients were obtained in six large studies of male and female subjects. These were averaged and are shown in Table 10–2 together with the range of estimates found for each defensive scale. The sources from which these statistics were obtained and a more detailed discussion of the internal consistency of the scales are presented in the DMI Manual.

## Stability of Scales

The average internal consistency for the DMI scales based on six studies varies from .61 to .80. Stability of scales, over occasions for periods of from 2 weeks to 12 months, has been reported in five American studies and one Dutch study. Coefficients from the American studies were averaged and are presented in Table 10–2 together with the range of values obtained for each defense scale. The average stability coefficient ranged from a low of .62 for Projection to a high of .81 for Turning against Others. The Clinical Manual presents a more detailed description of the results of these and other reliability studies. In particular, an analysis

**TABLE 10–2**
**Reliability**

| Defense | Range | Average |
|---------|-------|---------|
| *Internal Consistency Estimates from Six Studies* | | |
| TAO | .76–.86 | .80 |
| PRO | .47–.73 | .61 |
| PRN | .65–.74 | .69 |
| TAS | .59–.78 | .70 |
| REV | .71–.83 | .78 |
| *Stability Estimates from Five Studies* | | |
| TAO | .77–.87 | .81 |
| PRO | .48–.73 | .62 |
| PRN | .65–.79 | .73 |
| TAS | .63–.82 | .70 |
| REV | .70–.84 | .79 |

extracting variance components for conflict area, stories, and occasions revealed considerable situation specificity and led to our recommendation that the vignettes be considered as randomly parallel situations and that all 10 should be used to obtain adequate generalization to a subject's typical pattern of defense preference (see DMI Manual, pp. 42–43).

### Stability of Profiles over Occasions

Stability of profiles over a 12-month period was investigated for a sample of 94 normative women who completed the DMI on three occasions, 6 months apart.

The study indicated that 75% of the one-point or two-point profiles would yield stable interpretations over time, making them useful for clinical practice (see Clinical Manual, pp. 13–17). Similar information has seldom if ever been available on other psychological measures.

## CONSTRUCT VALIDATION

To establish the validity for the five defense styles measured with the DMI, we examined their convergence with other measures of defense as well as with certain theoretically relevant variables such as field dependence-independence, locus of control, self-esteem, anxiety, and diagnosis. Additionally, we explored whether the scales correlated as expected with other constructs in the behavioral, cognitive, affective, and personality domains.

Tables 10–3, 10–4, and 10–5 show a small sample of the correlates that have been found in many studies reported in dissertations and

## TABLE 10-3
### The Association of Defense Styles to Selected Measures of Behavior, Cognition, and Affect

| Construct (Study) | Sample | Gender | (N) | Defenses TAO | PRO | PRN | TAS | REV |
|---|---|---|---|---|---|---|---|---|
| *Behavior Level* | | | | | | | | |
| Rebellious/ISI (Shea, 1981) | General Adults | Males | (55) | .21 | .25 | NA | .16 | .09 |
| | | Females | (95) | .33** | .16 | NA | .07 | -.26** |
| Hostile/ISI (Shea, 1981) | General Adults | Males | (55) | .51** | .36** | NA | -.02 | -.48** |
| | | Females | (95) | .47** | .27** | NA | -.24* | -.27** |
| Harmonious/WRMS (Clum & Clum, 1973) | College Students | Males | (23) | -.49* | -.21 | .38* | -.26 | .48* |
| | | Females | (23) | ns | ns | ns | ns | ns |
| Introverted/MMPI (Gleser & Ihilevich, 1969) | Psychiatric Outpatients | Males | (67) | .16 | .06 | -.24* | .32** | -.35** |
| | | Females | (93) | .05 | .04 | -.22 | .32** | .04 |
| Tolerant/ISI (Shea, 1981) | General Adults | Males | (55) | -.55** | -.38** | NA | .07 | .41* |
| | | Females | (95) | -.50** | -.37** | NA | .11 | .43* |
| *Cognition Level* | | | | | | | | |
| Catastrophizing/RBI (Morelli & Andrews, 1982) | College Students | Males | (23) | .45** | .26* | -.37** | .03 | -.41** |
| | | Females | (37) | | | | | |
| Suspicious/ESS (Bornstein et al., 1989) | College Students | Males | (30) | .11 | .47** | .11 | -.26 | -.14 |
| | | Females | (34) | .07 | .38* | .21 | .02 | .04 |
| Novelty Seeking/OMI (Hornyak, 1978) | College Students | Males | (30) | .13 | .00 | .30** | -.16 | .05 |
| | | Females | (31) | | | | | |
| Doubting/Haan (Gleser & Ihilevich, 1969) | Psychiatric Outpatients | Males | (67) | .09 | .04 | -.17 | .26* | -.25* |
| | | Females | (93) | .01 | .05 | -.26* | .30** | -.10 |
| Field-Dependence/EFT (Erikson et al., 1976) | Alcoholic Inpatients | Males | (160) | -.22* | -.25* | .05 | .16* | .32** |

**TABLE 10-3** (*Continued*)

| Construct (Study) | Sample | Gender | (N) | Defenses | | | | |
|---|---|---|---|---|---|---|---|---|
| | | | | TAO | PRO | PRN | TAS | REV |
| *Affect Level* | | | | | | | | |
| *Aggression/MMPI* (Gleser & Ihilevich, 1969) | Psychiatric Outpatients | Males | (67) | .25* | .09 | −.08* | −.02 | −.28* |
| | | Females | (93) | .32** | .21 | −.39** | −.21 | −.32** |
| *Anxiety/STAI* (Ritigstein, 1974) | College Students | Males | (123) | .12 | .28* | −.17 | .28* | −.38** |
| | | Females | (238) | .11 | .31** | −.36** | .37** | −.48** |
| *Experienced* | | | | | | | | |
| *Control/COIF* (Rohsenow et al., 1978) | Alcoholic Inpatients | Males | (92) | −.20* | −.29** | .40** | .11 | .17 |
| *Depression/SCL-90* (Kaley & Hovey, 1983) | Planned Parenthood | Females | (90) | −.11 | .08 | −.19 | 26** | −.24* |
| *Elation/WRMS* (Clum & Clum, 1973) | College Students | Males | (23) | −.57** | −.21* | 43* | −.28* | 55** |
| | | Females | (32) | ns | ns | ns | ns | ns |

*p < .05 two-tailed test; **p < .01; ns = not significant; NA = not available.

*Note:* Significant correlations for convergent validity are boxed for emphasis.

*Legend:* Aggression/MMPI = Sum scores of *F*, *PD*, and *Ma* scales from the MMPI combined according to Huesmann et al., (1978) formula; COIF = Control Over Internal Forces; EFT = Embedded Figure Test; ESS = Experimental Study of Suspicion (Bornstein et al., 1989); FCI = Family Coping Index; HAAN = Haan's scale (derived from MMPI items); ISI = Interpersonal Style Inventory; OMI = Orientation and Motivation Inventory; RBI = Rational Behavior Inventory; STAI = State-Trait Anxiety Inventory; SCL-90 = Derogotis Symptom Checklist; WRMS = Wiseman & Ricks Mood Scale.

**TABLE 10-4**
**Correlations between DMI Scales, Selected Personality Dimensions, and Other Defense Measures**

| Construct (Study) | Sample | Gender | (N) | Defenses | | | | |
|---|---|---|---|---|---|---|---|---|
| | | | | TAO | PRO | PRN | TAS | REV |
| *Extraversion/HOQ* (Tauschke et al., 1991) | Medical & Psychiatric Patients | Males | (40) & | .30* | .20 | -.02 | -.37* | -.13 |
| | | Females | (64) | | | | | |
| *Displacement/J&N* (Shea, 1981) | General Adults | Males | (55) | .33* | .25 | -.44** | -.02 | -.07 |
| | | Females | (95) | .24* | .15 | -.31** | .24* | -.23* |
| *Expediency/ISI* (Shea, 1981) | General Adults | Males | (55) | .36** | .28* | NA | -.07 | -.16 |
| | | Females | (95) | .44** | .36** | -.46** | -.16 | -.36** |
| *Cynicism/ISI* (Shea, 1981) | General Adults | Males | (55) | .33* | .30* | NA | .01 | -.31* |
| | | Females | (95) | .24* | .22* | NA | -.13 | -.22* |
| *Self-Ideal Discrepancy/IAV* (Narov, 1983) | College Students | Males | (51) | .43* | .33** | -.44** | .14 | -.49** |
| | | Females | (63) | .16 | .19 | -.07 | .00 | -.29* |
| *Coping Ability/FCI* (Yu, 1981) | Parents of Handicapped Children | Mothers & Fathers | (54) & (25) | .03 | .05 | .24* | .01 | -.23* |
| *Self-Esteem/RSE* (Kaley & Hovey, 1983) | Planned Parenthood | Females | (90) | -.08 | -.09 | .34** | -.38** | .20 |
| *Ego Strength/MMPI* (Rohsenow et al., 1978) | Alcoholic Inpatients | Males | (219) | .04 | -.06 | .21* | -.15 | .02 |
| *Attention Avoiding/ISI* (Shea, 1981) | General Adults | Males | (55) | -.06 | .06 | NA | .36** | .14 |
| | | Females | (93) | -.12 | .02 | NA | .22** | .05 |
| *Internalizing Symptoms/YSR* (Noam & Recklitis, 1990) | Adolescent Inpatients | Males | (85) | -.06 | .18 | -.12 | .27* | -.14 |
| | | Females | (111) | .09 | .01 | -.21* | .38** | -.22* |

**TABLE 10—4** (*Continued*)

| Construct (Study) | Sample | Gender | (N) | Defenses | | | | |
|---|---|---|---|---|---|---|---|---|
| | | | | TAO | PRO | PRN | TAS | REV |
| *Trusting/ISI* (Shea, 1981) | General Adults | Males | (55) | −.25* | −.34* | NA | −.09 | .41** |
| | | Females | (31) | −.18 | −.19 | NA | .03 | .19 |
| *Altruism/OMI* (Hornyak, 1978) | College Students | Males | (45) & | −.25 | −.12 | .13 | −.04 | .31* |
| | | Females | (31) | | | | | |
| *Denial/COPE* (Vickers & Hervig, 1981) | Marine Recruits | Males | (79) | −.19 | −.10 | .12 | −.15 | .24* |
| *Controlled/16PF* (Gleser & Ihilevich, 1979) | Psychiatric Outpatients | Males | (56) | −.29* | −.18 | .05 | .01 | .39* |
| | | Females | (62) | −.35* | −.49* | .33* | −.07 | .45* |

\**p* .05 two-tailed test; \*\**p* < .01; ns = not significant; NA = Not Available.

*Note:* Significant correlations for convergent validity are boxed for emphasis.

*Legend:* COPE = Coping Operations Preference Enquiry; FCI = Family Coping Index; HOQ = Hysterioid/Obsessoid Questionnaire (reported in Tauschke et al., 1991); IAV = Index of Adjustment & Values; ISI = Interpersonal Style Inventory; J&N = Joffe and Naditch Defense Scales (derived from CPI items); MMPI = Minnesota Multiphasic Personality Inventory; OMI = Orientation and Motivation Inventory; RSE = Rosenberg Self-Esteem Scale; 16 PF = Sixteen Personality Factor Questionnaire; YSR = Youth Self Report Inventory.

## TABLE 10–5
### The Relationship of Defense Styles to Selected Diagnostic Categories

| Diagnosis (Study) | Sample | Gender | (N) | Defenses | | | | |
|---|---|---|---|---|---|---|---|---|
| | | | | TAO | PRO | PRN | TAS | REV |
| *Delinquency* (Noam & Recklitis, 1990) | Adolescent Psychiatric Inpatients | Males | (85) | .31** | .12 | −.14 | −.18 | −.24* |
| | | Females | (111) | .37** | .18 | −.30** | −.13 | −.25** |
| *Narcissism* (Biscardi, 1984) | College Students | Males | (97) | .36** | .27** | −.34** | −.21* | −.22* |
| | | Females | (89) | .16 | .19 | .07 | −.17 | −.13 |
| *Paranoia* (Schueler, 1981) | Psychiatric Inpatients | Males | (40) | NS | SH* | NS | NS | SL* |
| | | Females | (40) | NS | SH* | NS | NS | SL* |
| *Obsessive-Compulsive* (Seif & Atkins, 1979) | Psychiatric Outpatients | Males | (03) & | | | | | |
| | | Females | (15) | NS | SL* | SH** | NS | SL* |
| (Cooper & Kline, 1982) | College Students | Males | (112) | NS | NS | SH** | NS | NS |
| *Depression* (Gleser & Ihilevich, 1969) | Psychiatric Outpatients | Males | (67) | −.03 | −.10 | −.17 | .42** | −.15 |
| | | Females | (93) | −.04 | .02 | −.13 | .24* | −06 |
| *Hysteria* (Seif & Atkins, 1979) | Psychiatric Outpatients | Males | (03) & | | | | | |
| | | Females | (15) | NS | SH* | SL** | NS | SH* |
| (Cooper & Kline, 1982) | College Students | Males | (112) | NS | NS | NS | NS | SH* |

$*p < .05$ two-tailed test; $**p < .01$.

*Note:* Significant correlations for convergent validity are boxed for emphasis.

*Legend:* SH = Significantly High mean differences relative to comparison group. SL = Significantly Low mean difference; NS = No Significant mean difference.

journal articles in the past 30 years. A more complete listing can be found in the DMI and Clinical Manuals together with a discussion of their theoretical relevance.

Additionally, as reported in the Clinical Manual, MMPI scores on 120 male and 145 female outpatients and 16 PF scores on 85 males and 93 females were used to formulate descriptions of clients whose scores fit the criteria for one- or two-point DMI profiles. These descriptions can be found in the Clinical Manual.

Finally, we have developed dynamic formulations and preliminary treatment intervention guidelines for 5 one-point profiles and for 4 two-point profiles based on the clinical experience of one of us (D.I.). Since no empirical studies relying on these formulations have been conducted, no validity is claimed for them. At the present time, they are best regarded as conceptual frameworks aimed at explaining clinical observations and inferring their therapeutic implications.

## CLINICAL APPLICATIONS

In spite of the great emphasis placed by Freud and other psychoanalysts on the importance of defense mechanisms in the assessment and treatment of psychopathology, by the mid-1950s it was acknowledged that "we do not know enough about their modification as a result of psychoanalytic treatment" (Lowenstein, 1954, p. 192). More recently, a reviewer of the clinical literature concluded that there have been "few attempts to assess therapeutic improvement in psychoanalysis [or other treatment approaches] in terms of alterations in defense patterns" (Brenner, 1975, pp. 2–3).

To alter excessively used defenses, we have proposed two strategies:

1. Help patients identify and confront the covert sources of their anxiety.
2. Help patients acquire effective coping skills, so that defenses do not need to be deployed in the face of mild or moderate perceived threats.

In general, we recommend that interpretations be used sparingly to modify defenses since such interpretations often come perilously close to "blaming the victim." In two studies (cited in the Clinical Manual), teaching effective coping skills through group instruction and practice produced changes in defenses used even though the interventions did not include interpretation, reconstruction of the past, or resolution of unconscious conflicts. However, since these were nonpatient samples, the generalizability of this approach to psychiatric patients is as yet uncertain.

Even though there is broad consensus among dynamically oriented therapists that it is insufficient to plan treatment interventions on the basis of knowledge or patients' symptoms and diagnosis alone, a prominent reviewer has recently concluded: "Our treatments are at best symptomatic" at this time (Freedman, 1992).

Therapists cannot agree on what actually helps in treatment: Is it insight and interpretation or the experience of the therapeutic relationship, cognitive assimilation of psychic trauma or its reframing, being understood or intellectual understanding, conflict resolution or compensation for deficits? We propose that once a therapeutic relationship is established and an alliance to work on the patient's difficulties is formed, treatment should focus on identifying, and modifying if necessary, the patient's *methods* of dealing with internal conflicts and externally perceived threats. These methods include *problem-solving efforts, coping skills,* and the unconscious *defense mechanisms* deployed by patients to avoid confronting the sources of their anxiety. Knowledge of a patient's defensive configuration can help guide treatment interventions and make his or her behavior and motivations more intelligible and less subject to countertransference phenomena. For example, we found that patients who present themselves with depressed symptoms or mood, might be high on intrapunitive defenses (TAS), intrapunitive and repressive defenses (TAS/REV), intrapunitive and projective or aggressive defenses (TAS/PRO/TAO) or high on aggressive defenses only (TAO). To be efficient, we believe that treatment interventions for depressive patients need to be guided by their underlying defensive organizations (see Clinical Manual).

In the following three examples, we will show how knowledge that a patient is high on *anxiety*, unduly *aggressive*, or low on *self-esteem* can by itself lead to misguided interventions. Each of these "problems" may need to be managed differently in therapy, depending on which defense mechanisms underlay these difficulties.

## Anxiety and Defenses

A perusal of Table 10–3 reveals that anxiety is positively correlated with blaming others (PRO), as well as with self-blame (TAS). The reduction of anxiety associated with these different defense styles, however, requires different forms of intervention. With high TAS patients, interventions need to focus on helping these patients cope with chronic feelings of dissatisfaction, hopelessness, and need for perfection. To improve, these patients have to develop the capacity for putting things in perspective, finding the "silver lining," making positive comparisons, taking setbacks in their stride, and accepting imperfections as natural. To diminish the anxiety that accompanies high PRO defenses, interventions should aim to help these patients cope with distrust and with fear of intimacy, victimization, and loss of autonomy. Guidelines for interventions to affect these conditions are described in the Clinical Manual.

## Defenses and Aggressive Behavior

It is clinically important to keep in mind the essential difference in the function of aggression for patients high on PRO versus those high on TAO defenses. Whereas high PRO patients feel persecuted and erect a hostile front as a defense against anticipated attack, high TAO patients respond to actual threats with exaggerated aggressive defenses designed to diminish their fear, enhance their sense of power, and bolster their sense of superiority. By provoking rejection and retaliation, PROs confirm their basic conviction that they are victimized by those who treat them unfairly. Through excessive aggression, TAOs shield their feelings of inferiority by transforming the experience of being threatened into an empowering experience of making the threats. The expression of anger by high PROs is usually accompanied by self-righteousness and mounting indignation; the expression of anger by high TAOs is usually accompanied by catharsis and a reduction in emotional tension. Whereas the hostile ruminations of high PRO patients need to be deflected in therapy, the ventilation of aggressive thoughts and feelings by high TAO patients is usually beneficial.

## Defenses and Self-Esteem

Several studies have found that low self-esteem, as measured by Rosenberg's (1965) Self-Esteem Scale, is associated with high scores on intrapunitive defenses (TAS). On closer examination however, this finding appears to be purely an artifact of the scale chosen to measure self-esteem. When a different measure is used to assess self-esteem, such as the Self-Ideal Discrepancy Scale (Bills, Vance, & McLean, 1951), low self-esteem is significantly correlated with high scores on the aggressive (TAO and PRO), not intrapunitive (TAS) defenses. These findings lend support to the dynamic formulation that whereas intrapunitive defenses cushion and protect self-esteem through lowered expectations and systematic self-derogation, aggressive defenses provide a protective shield to self-esteem through boasting, domineering behavior, and self-aggrandizement.

## THEORETICAL ISSUES

Data gathered with the DMI sheds light on several controversial issues concerning defense mechanisms. This section discusses two such issues: (a) the emergence of defense mechanisms, and (b) the relationship of defenses to physical symptoms.

### Chronological Emergence of Defenses

In her classic monograph, Anna Freud (1936/1946) tried in vain to link the evolution of defense mechanisms to developmental phases. After reviewing a variety of positions on that issue, she concluded: "The chronology of psychic processes is still one of the most obscure fields of analytic theory . . . it will probably be best to abandon the attempt to so classify them . . ." (p. 53).

In recent years, a number of investigators conducted empirical studies with children of various age groups to explore the prevalence and presumably the sequence of emergence of defense mechanisms. Several researchers have concluded that "less complex" defenses are deployed earlier in life whereas "more complex" defenses emerge later. There is no consensus, however, on which defenses are less and which are more complex. For example, Freud believed, "All repressions take place in early childhood; they are primitive defensive measures adopted by the immature, feeble ego" (Freud, 1937/1959, p. 328). Other theoreticians have suggested that the capacity to use repression emerges only in later years, after the child establishes a strong enough ego and a clear demarcation of self from nonself.

Cramer (1983) adopted the DMI classification system to analyze the defensive reactions of elementary schoolchildren to several conflictual situations depicted in videotaped vignettes. The children in the study were drawn from the second, fourth, and fifth grades. Over half of their responses were defensive (59%), while most of the others were characterized as "coping behaviors." Out of the 301 responses categorized as defensive, 41.9% were classified as falling under the TAO defense style; 46.8% were subsumed under the REV style; 8.1% were classified as TAS responses; and 3.1% as PRO responses. Only *one* reaction was categorized as a rationalization (PRN). Several other studies that used the DMI have found that intellectualizing defenses (PRN) become prominent only in adolescent populations. Taken together, these findings suggest that denial and attack are the earliest modes of defense to emerge in childhood. Apparently, the preferred way for a young child to deal with conflict or perceived threat is either to obliterate it internally by using denial or to obliterate it externally by attacking the source of threat. These two defense styles employ "concrete" thought processes, characteristic of Piaget's *preoperational* stage of cognitive development.

The next two most frequently used defenses in Cramer's study, PRO and TAS, require the more complex mental operations characteristic of Piaget's *egocentric* level of development. The capacity to deploy these defenses reflects the child's experience of being at the hub of the universe. At this stage, the child presumably relates all that happens to herself or himself ("They are against *me*" (PRO); "It's *my* fault" (TAS). Only during adolescence does the third protective layer, intellectualizing defenses (PRN), become available as a mode of reaction to internal conflict and external threats. Intellectualizing defenses require for their operation the ability to simultaneously entertain alternative hypotheses, find common elements in different situations, and formulate self-serving interpretations to modify the meaning of perceived threat. This method of conflict resolution corresponds to Piaget's *formal* (abstract) thought operations, which were found empirically to make their appearance only in early adolescence.

### Relationship of Defenses to Physical Symptoms

The psychodynamic literature has long regarded different psychosomatic symptoms as representing unique repressed conflicts that reemerge in disguised form ("return of the repressed"). In this vein, theoreticians have suggested that certain personality dynamics and defenses characterize the "arthritic personality," the "hypertensive personality," the "migraine personality," the "duodenal ulcer personality," and so on (Alexander, 1950; Dunbar, 1948; Graham, 1962). As recently as 1992, theoreticians were still suggesting "It is through resistances and symptoms that we infer defenses" (Vaillant, 1992, p. 50). Empirical research, however, has failed to confirm specific relationships between various physical symptoms, conflicts, and defenses. Data gathered with the DMI on medical patients with *cardiovascular disease, hypertension, ulcers, migraine* and *tension headaches, psoriasis, rheumatoid arthritis, backaches,* and *chronic pain* shows that some of these groups score higher on repressive (REV) and/or intrapunitive (TAS) defenses and lower on aggressive and/or projective defenses (TAO and PRO). However, the amount of variance explained is too small for individual prediction. Research findings with the DMI indicate that defenses correspond, as expected, with personality variables and particular psychiatric diagnoses (see Table 10–5). However, the "specificity hypotheses," that certain physical symptoms imply the use of certain defenses, receives no support from our data.

## CONCLUSION

In closing, we need to emphasize that only a fraction of the needed research on defense mechanisms has yet been done. Although we have found various connections and regularities, we know next to nothing about how defenses are acquired, their multifarious positive effect on adaptation, or how to go about modifying their deleterious effects when their use becomes thwarted or excessive. We expect that future research, using the DMI along with other measures of defense, will be able to provide answers to these questions.

## REFERENCES

Aldrich, C. K., & Mendkoff, E. (1963). Relocation of the aged and disabled: A mortality study. *Journal of American Geriatrics Society, 11,* 185–194.

Alexander, F. (1950). *Psychosomatic medicine.* New York: Norton.

Bettelheim, B. (1943). Individual and mass behavior in extreme situations. *Journal of Abnormal and Social Psychology, 38,* 417–445.

Bills, R. E., Vance, E. L., & McLean, O. S. (1951). An index of adjustment and values. *Journal of Consulting Psychology, 15,* 257–261.

Biscardi, D. (1984). *The relationship between a measure of narcissistic traits and defensive style, Machiavellianism, and empathy.* Unpublished doctoral dissertation, Southern Illinois University at Carbondale. (University Microfilm No. DA8414000)

Blacha, M. D., & Fancher, R. E. (1977). A content validity study of the Defense Mechanisms Inventory. *Journal of Personality Assessment, 41,* 401–404.

Bornstein, R. F., Scanlon, M. A., & Beardslee, L. A. (1989). The psychodynamics of paranoia: Anality, projection and suspiciousness. *Journal of Social Behavior and Personality, 4,* 275–284.

Brenner, C. (1975). Alterations in defenses during psychoanalysis. In H. F. Waldhorn & B. D. Fine (Eds.), *Monographs of the Kris Study Group of the New York Psychoanalytic Institute* (Vol. 6, pp. 1–22). New York: International Universities Press.

Clum, G. A., & Clum, J. (1973). Choice of defense mechanisms and their relationship to mood level. *Psychological Reports, 32,* 507–510.

Cooper, C., & Kline, P. (1982). A validation of the Defense Mechanisms Inventory. *British Journal of Medical Psychology, 55,* 209–214.

Cramer, P. (1983). Children's use of defense mechanisms in reaction to displeasure caused by others. *Journal of Personality, 51,* 63–73.

Dunbar, F. (1948). *Mind and body: Psychosomatic medicine.* New York: Random House.

Erickson, R. C., Smyth, L., Donovan, D. M., & O'Leary, M. R. (1976). Psychopathology and defensive style of alcoholics as a function of congruence-incongruence between psychological differentiation and locus of control. *Psychological Reports, 39,* 51–54.

Freedman, D. (1992). The search: Body, mind, and human purpose. *American Journal of Psychiatry, 149,* 858–866.

Freud, A. (1946). *The ego and the mechanisms of defense.* New York: International Universities Press. (Original work published 1936)

Freud, A. (1965). *Normality and pathology in childhood.* New York: International Universities Press.

Freud, S. (1957). On the history of the psychoanalytic movement. In J. Strachey (Ed. and Trans.), *The standard edition of the complete psychological works of Sigmund Freud* (Vol. 14, pp. 3–66). London: Hogarth Press. (Original work published 1914)

Freud, S. (1959). Inhibitions, symptoms and anxiety. In J. Strachey (Ed. and Trans.), *The standard edition of the complete psychological works of Sigmund Freud* (Vol. 20, pp. 77–174). London: Hogarth Press. (Original work published 1926)

Freud, S. (1959). Analysis terminable and interminable. In J. Strachey (Ed. and Trans.), *The collected papers of Sigmund Freud* (Vol. 5, pp. 316–357). New York: Basic Books. (Original work published 1937)

Friedman, H. S. (1991). *The self-healing personality: Why some people achieve health and others succumb to illness.* New York: Holt.

Friedman, S. B., Chodoff, P., Mason, M. J., & Hamburg, D. A. (1963). Behavioral observations on parents anticipating the death of a child. *Pediatrics, 32,* 10–25.

Gleser, G. C., & Ihilevich, D. (1969). An objective instrument for measuring defense mechanisms. *Journal of Consulting and Clinical Psychology, 33,* 51–60.

Gleser, G. C., & Ihilevich, D. (1979). Personality factors and ego defenses. *Academic Psychology Bulletin, 1,* 171–179.

Graham, D. T. (1962). Some research on psychophysiologic specificity and its relation to psychosomatic disease. In R. Roessler & N. S. Greenfield (Eds.), *Physiological correlates of psychological disorder* (pp. 221–238). Madison: University of Wisconsin Press.

Grinker, R. R., & Spiegel, J. P. (1945). *Men under stress.* Philadelphia: Blakiston.

Hoffer, W. (1954). Defensive process and defensive organization: Their place in psychoanalytic technique. *International Journal of Psychoanalysis, 35,* 194–198.

Hornyak, L. M. (1978). *Relationships of cognitive orientation, defense style and OMI personality variables on the dimension of field dependence-independence.* Catholic University of America, Washington, DC. (Unpublished Study)

Huesmann, L. R., Lefkowitz, M. M., & Eron, L. (1978). Sum of MMPI Scales F, 4 and 9 as a measure of aggression. *Journal of Consulting and Clinical Psychology, 46,* 1071–1078.

Ihilevich, D., & Gleser, G. C. (1986). *Defense mechanisms: Their classification, correlates and measurement with the Defense Mechanisms Inventory.* Odessa, FL: Psychological Assessment Resources.

Ihilevich, D., & Gleser, G. C. (1991). *Defenses in psychotherapy: The clinical application of the Defense Mechanisms Inventory.* Odessa, FL: Psychological Assessment Resources.

Kaley, M., & Hovey, J. (1983). *A prevention program for adult women at risk for maladjustment.* (Unpublished study submitted to Michigan's Department of Mental Health)

Katz, J. L., Weiner, H., Gallagher, T. G., & Hellman, L. (1970). Stress, distress, and ego defenses. *Archives of General Psychiatry, 23,* 131–142.

Kitahara, M. (1981). The Japanese and defense mechanisms. *The Journal of Psychoanalytic Anthropology, 4,* 465–479.

Kohut, H. (1984). *How does analysis cure?* Chicago: University of Chicago Press.

Lazarus, R. S., & Folkman, S. (1984). *Stress, appraisal and coping.* New York: Springer.

Loewenstein, R. M. (1967). Defensive organization and autonomous ego functions. *Journal of the American Psychoanalytic Association, 15,* 795–809.

Mechanic, D. (1962). *Students under stress.* New York: Free Press.

Miller, D. R., & Swanson, G. E. (1960). *Inner conflict and defense.* New York: Holt.

Modell, A. (1984). *Psychoanalysis in a new context.* New York: International Universities Press.

Morelli, G., & Andrews, L. (1982). Cognitive irrationality and defensiveness. *Psychological Reports, 51,* 387–393.

Narov, D. (1983). *The relationship of gender, self-esteem and cognitive style to ego defense mechanisms.* Unpublished doctoral dissertation, Loyola University of Chicago. (University Microfilm No. DA8327270)

Nesse, R. M. (1990). The evolutionary functions of repression and the ego defenses. *Journal of the American Academy of Psychoanalysis, 18,* 260–285.

Noam, G. G., & Recklitis, C. J. (1990). The relationship between defenses and symptoms in adolescent psychopathology. *Journal of Personality Assessment, 54,* 311–327.

Rabkin, J. G., & Struening, E. L. (1976). Life events, stress and illness. *Science, 194,* 1013–1020.

Ritigstein, J. M. (1974). *The relationship of defense mechanisms to trait anxiety and state anxiety in female college students.* Unpublished doctoral dissertation, New York University. (University Microfilm No. 758560)

Rohsenow, D. J., Erickson, R. C., & O'Leary, M. R. (1978). The Defense Mechanisms Inventory and alcoholics. *The International Journal of the Addictions, 13,* 403–414.

Rosenberg, M. (1965). *Society and the adolescent self-image.* Princeton: Princeton University Press.

Schueler, D. E. (1981). *Defensive preference, premorbid adjustment and the schizophrenic symptoms.* Unpublished doctoral dissertation, St. John's University, Jamaica, NY (University Microfilm No. 8119621)

Seif, M. N., & Atkins, A. L. (1979). Some defensive and cognitive aspects of phobias. *Journal of Abnormal Psychology, 88,* 42–51.

Shea, M. T. (1981). *On the relationship between interpersonal styles and defense mechanisms.* Unpublished doctoral dissertation, Catholic University of America, Washington, DC (University Microfilm No. 8126909)

Suppes, P., & Warren, H. (1975). On the generation and classification of defense mechanisms. *International Journal of Psychoanalysis, 56,* 405–414.

Tauschke, E., Helmes, E., & Merskey, H. (1991). Evidence that defense mechanisms are more related to personality than to symptoms. *British Journal of Medical Psychology, 64,* 137–146.

Taylor, S. E., & Brown, J. D. (1988). Illusion and well-being: A social psychological perspective on mental health. *Psychological Bulletin, 103,* 192–210.

Vaillant, G. E. (1971). Theoretical hierarchy of adaptive ego mechanisms: A 30-year follow-up of 30 men selected for psychological health. *Archives of General Psychiatry, 24,* 107–118.

Vaillant, G. E. (1992). *Ego mechanisms of defense: A guide for clinicians and researchers.* Washington, DC: American Psychiatric Press.

Van der Leeuw, P. J. (1971). On the development of the concept of defense. *International Journal of Psychoanalysis, 52,* 51–58.

Vickers, R. R., & Hervig, L. K. (1981). Comparison of three psychological defense mechanism questionnaires. *Journal of Personality Assessment, 45,* 630–638.

Yu, Muriel Mei-Ton. (1981). *Personal defensive disposition and coping ability among parents of the deaf-blind multihandicapped children.* Unpublished doctoral dissertation, University of Oklahoma, Norman, OK (University Microfilm No. 8122791)

# 11

---

# The Defense Mechanism Profile
## A Sentence Completion Test

NANCY L. JOHNSON AND
STEVEN N. GOLD

Defense mechanisms are hypothetical constructs that have long been considered useful in clinical work. Historically, several instruments developed or adapted to measure defense mechanisms or defensive functioning have received short-term attention or sparse use: the Blacky Defense Preference Inventory (Blum, 1956), the Repression-Sensitization Scale (Byrne, 1961; Byrne, Barry, & Nelson, 1963), Haan's structured interview (1963), the Defense Mechanism Test (Kragh, 1960), Rosenzweig's Picture Frustration Study (1976), and the Ego Profile Scale (Semrad, Grinspoon, & Feinberg, 1973). In addition to their having psychometric problems, these efforts have been criticized in that the tests either measured defensiveness instead of specific or clustered defenses, assessed a very limited number of defenses, were found to measure something other than defenses (e.g., anxiety), utilized concepts or definitions outside the mainstream of traditional defense theory, or involved an impractical approach to assessment (e.g., extensive interview or tachistoscopic method). However, the works of both Vaillant (1971, 1976; Vaillant, Bond, & Vaillant, 1986) and Gleser and Ihilevich (1969) have had a significant impact on the study and assessment of defenses.

The Defense Mechanism Inventory (DMI), an objective instrument authored by Gleser and Ihilevich (1969), is the instrument most actively used in defense mechanism research today and the only defense mechanism assessment tool listed in *The Tenth Mental Measurements Yearbook* (Conoley & Kramer, 1989). A serious difficulty with the DMI is raised by Cooper and Kline (1982), who note that the ipsative method of scoring renders the DMI scales statistically uninterpretable when correlated with any other criterion measure. Thus, while the DMI achieves a measure of objectivity, its usefulness as a research instrument is limited by its statistical properties.

Analyzing longitudinal data, extending to a 30-year follow-up (1971), Vaillant conceptualized a four-level hierarchy of defenses, offered clear definitions for specific defenses, and studied the development of defenses as the individual matures (1976). The two most serious methodological problems in Vaillant's work involve the method of data collection through individual interviews, making interrater agreement difficult to achieve and maintain, and the use of male subjects only.

Recently, Bond, Gardner, Christian, and Sigal (1983) developed a Defense Style Questionnaire, later used to explore the validity of Vaillant's defense hierarchy (Vaillant et al., 1986). The Defense Style Questionnaire requires the subject to indicate his/her degree of concurrence (on a nine-point scale) with statements that describe behavior. Though each statement represents a defense, 24 defenses are evaluated by only 81 statements, with some defenses represented by a total of two statements. No reliability data are provided. Given the format of the questionnaire, the subject can only respond to those behavioral descriptions presented, thus severely limiting, or missing, information most needed: the individual's preferred, typical, idiosyncratic defensive response.

The Defense Mechanism Profile was developed with the aim of providing an instrument that would (a) avoid the interrater reliability problems of the time-consuming interview method of obtaining data; (b) eliminate the response constricting fixed-choice method, in favor of an open-ended format; and (c) provide objective criteria for scoring an open-ended response test. The following report describes the development and preliminary research on an instrument that may prove to be a useful addition to the current means of assessing and studying defense mechanisms.

## THE DEFENSE MECHANISM PROFILE: DESCRIPTION AND DEVELOPMENT

### Test Items

The Defense Mechanism Profile (DMP) is a self-administered, projective sentence completion instrument. The open-ended aspect of the sentence completion format permits the responder a complete range of expression without forcing a response that may be neither representative nor accurate.

To provide a stimulus sufficiently anxiety provoking to elicit a defensive response, each of the 40 DMP sentence stems was designed to (a) state or imply a situation generally considered to be at least mildly psychologically uncomfortable, or (b) express a distressing emotion or feeling. Both the situation and accompanying affect are given; the subject is instructed to respond with what he/she would do, behaviorally, in the situation. (Examples: When I am really worried, I _____. When I'm around someone who doesn't like me, I _____.)

It is assumed, given the "projective hypothesis," and given repeated opportunity to respond, that the pattern of an individual's typical manner of acting will emerge. It is also reasoned that, as is typical of clinical work, the defense mechanisms represented at the unconscious level may be inferred from self-reported, conscious behavior.

Each response is assigned to 1 of 14 categories. Subjects often give more than one scorable response per stem. The response frequency is summed for each individual defense, which, when placed in a normative context, reflects the individual's preference for and avoidance of specific defenses. No overall, total score is generated since the DMP assesses defensive styles, rather than degree of general defensiveness.

## Scoring Criteria

Working with pilot data, subjects' responses were matched with an extensive compilation of defense mechanism definitions drawn from the literature. It became apparent that the test format permitted responses indicative of some defenses but not others. For example, no responses reflecting splitting or projection were observed, most likely because of the relatively unstructured, noncomplex situations depicted in the sentence stems. Although not all major defenses were represented, the matching process eventually culminated in 14 scoring categories. Table 11–1 provides a complete listing of the 4 tension reducers (precursors of defenses) and 9 defenses measured by the DMP, accompanied by brief definitions, plus a category representing an unscorable response.

Whether attending to characteristics of adaptiveness or structural complexity, defense mechanisms are routinely conceptualized and categorized along a developmental hierarchy (Fenichel, 1945; Freud, 1936/1966; Gero, 1951; Gill, 1963; Rapaport, 1951/1967; Sperling, 1958).

Similarly, DMP scoring categories are grouped hierarchically as follows:

1. *Tension reducers.* Incorporation-physical, Incorporation-indirect, Expulsion-physical, Expulsion-verbal.
2. *Early Defenses.* Denial, Withdrawal.
3. *Middle-Range Defenses.* Undoing, Displacement, Turning against Self, Reaction Formation, Compensation.
4. *Advanced Defenses.* Substitution, Rationalization/Intellectualization.

**TABLE 11–1**
**DMP Scoring Category Definitions**

| Category | Code | Definition |
|---|---|---|
| Incorporation-physical | IP | The assimilation of something from the external environment. Something is brought into, or brought to, the self-system. The goal is essentially to reduce discomfort through nurturance. |
| Incorporation-indirect | II | The assimilation of something abstracted from other people. II is qualitatively different from IP, in that no concrete, physical assimilation, or acquisition occurs. The individual must draw comfort, or extract relief, from the words, presence, attitudes, or actions of others. |
| Expulsion-physical | EP | Simple, uncomplicated behaviors that do not require a mental detour for organization or delay of expression. Responses scored EP usually fall into three major groupings: direct expression of emotion or tension, physical expulsion or destruction of an object, or implied physical attack on an external object. |
| Expulsion-verbal | EV | Expressions that permit verbal release or verbal ventilation of an affect or verbal attack on an object (person). These behaviors are largely impulsive and do not reflect well-planned, thought-out discussions or logical arguments. |
| Denial | Den | An unconscious mechanism that attempts to keep some acceptable aspect of reality out of awareness or attempts to reject the existence of aversive reality. Because all defenses involve some degree of denial and repression, the scoring of Den is reserved for those responses that deny the existence of an event or object (usually via withdrawal of attention) or deny the meaning of a fact, event, or situation. |
| Withdrawal | WD | Retreat, avoidance, or attempts to hide or conceal oneself or aspects of oneself. Resigning or giving up in difficult situations is also interpreted as withdrawal. |
| Undoing | Undo | Confession, expiation, rituals, and magical solutions. Undo is scored when responses indicate efforts to extricate the responder from uncomfortable thoughts, actions, events, or consequences through ritualistic, placative, or magical means and efforts to undo the behaviors and suspected motives, actions, and thoughts of others through ritualistic, placative, or magical means. |
| Displacement | Dis | The transference, deflection, or redirection of affect from one object to another (or others). The form of displacement (physical or verbal) is not a relevant issue; redirection is the critical variable. It is important to note that most often Dis involves an additional displacement in time. That is, there is some direct or implied indication that the action is delayed and not immediate. |

**TABLE 11-1** *(Continued)*

| Category | Code | Definition |
|---|---|---|
| Turning against Self/Reaction Formation | TAS RF | Responses that indicate negative emotions or judgments are directed toward the self rather than toward others. Strong or blatant expression by a behavior, feeling, or attitude that contradicts other (opposite) behaviors, feelings, or attitudes. |
| Compensation | Comp | Statements reflecting that a perceived strength or valued attribute is being substituted for a self-perceived weakness, failing, or fault. |
| Substitution | Sub | An attempt to rechannel positive affect when the original object of the affect is unavailable, unobtainable, or inappropriate, or to rechannel negative affect when the individual has imposed sufficient organization on the situation to discharge the affect in a substitute, socially appropriate, releasing, or gratifying manner. |
| Rationalization/ Intellectualization | RI | All attempts to explain or justify behavior, attitudes, thoughts, or emotions, often in abstract or intellectual terms. It is imperative to note that RI responses, by their very nature, require a delay for thinking, analyzing, or planning. |
| Unscorable Response | ? | These responses generally fall into one of three instances: (1) the item was left blank; (2) the responder answered with an emotion or feeling rather than a behavioral description; (3) the response was too vague to understand what was done or what transpired. |

To maximize objective aspects of scoring, a scoring manual was developed that outlines the procedures for administering and scoring the DMP, defines each defense utilized in the test (conceptual definition), gives specific criteria and behavioral examples for each scoring category (application), and notes common scoring difficulties.

As an example, the conceptual definition of Withdrawal (Table 11-1) is translated into the following application: The DMP interprets all responses that indicate *retreat, avoidance, or attempts to hide or conceal oneself,* or aspects of oneself, as evidence of withdrawal. *Resigning or giving up* is also interpreted as withdrawal.

The specific criteria for scoring Withdrawal are those responses that indicate (a) physical or emotional withdrawal, retreat, or avoidance of an event or object; (b) efforts to conceal or hide oneself or aspects of oneself; (c) resignation or giving up. Each specific criterion is clarified by a sampling of actual and frequently occurring DMP responses. A partial listing of responses reflecting efforts to hide or conceal includes these statements: Keep quiet, retreat to my room, stop talking, keep it to myself, stay in the background.

To test content (sampling) validity of the behavioral examples, four experts (one psychiatrist and three clinical psychologists, two of whom were psychologist-psychoanalysts) read both the conceptual and applied definitions from the DMP Manual and selected from a list of 20 responses those that matched the defense being defined (Johnson, 1986). The target responses were embedded in a list of responses randomly selected from all examples, across all defenses, in the manual. A different list was generated for each defense. From the resulting 260 possible agreements/disagreements, three experts concurred with the manual in 94% of the choices, and one expert had a 95% agreement rate. Given the level of inference and abstraction involved in the task, the results were considered to support strongly the DMP translation of defense definitions into specific behavioral examples.

### Training Procedures and Interrater Reliability

Scorers are considered satisfactorily trained when they can achieve and maintain an 80% agreement level with the scoring manual, the external criterion for accuracy. When scoring actual DMP data, differences between pairs of trained raters are resolved through discussion to consensus (Loevinger, Wessler, & Redmore, 1970) in a group comprising all raters involved in the research project. Numerous scoring manual clarifications and revisions resulted from the early consensus meetings.

Fassman (1984) examined two methods of training scorers, an in-class group ($N = 12$) and a home-study group ($N = 13$). Results indicated no significant differences between the training methods in total mean scoring errors ($t = -1.39$). While both training methods appeared to be equally effective in Fassman's study, neither method produced a level of accuracy (63% agreement) sufficient for research purposes within the 5-week training period. Subsequent work indicates that adequate scoring performance can be achieved with 6 weeks of training, with practice and feedback on a total of 12 to 14 protocols (Johnson, 1984).

In calculating the agreement level achieved between pairs of scorers (prior to the consensus group meeting), a scoring was considered in error if *any part of the scoring* of an item was in disagreement. Because the majority of items elicit more than one scorable response per stem, this method is the most conservative and rigorous manner in which to assess interrater agreement. The consistency of the percentages (range: .790 to .916) across 12 studies indicates that the DMP Scoring Manual provides sufficient structure and clarity to permit scorers to achieve and maintain a satisfactory level of interrater agreement on the open-ended responses obtained on the DMP.

## DMP STUDIES

### Test-Retest Reliability

In general, establishing reliability in the assessment of personality traits has proven a difficult psychometric task, even with objective measures (Bem & Allen, 1974; Mischel, 1969; Paunonen & Jackson, 1985; Zuckerman et al., 1988).

Consistency of DMP responses across time has been explored in four studies using the test-retest paradigm. Study 1 utilized a 3-week interval between testings of 14 male and 21 female graduate students (Johnson, 1982a). Using a nonstudent group of 15 male and 14 female adults, Study 2 was also conducted over a 3-week interval (Larkin, 1983). As defense mechanisms are thought to be a very durable aspect of personality, stability over a 3-month interval was investigated using a (different) class of graduate psychology students (Study 3, Johnson, 1982b). Subjects in Study 3 consisted of 7 males and 17 females. In Study 4, White (1989) investigated stability of adolescent responses over a 3-week interval (24 male and 23 female 8th-grade students; 9 male and 26 female 11th-grade students).

Correlation coefficients and significance levels for the overall test and for each individual DMP scale from all four studies are reported in Table 11–2. Comparison of the DMP correlations from the two adult 3-week interval studies (Studies 1 and 2) reveals highly consistent results. Only the Den and Dis scales differ. As expected, stability of the defense scales (Den through RI) in Study 3, a 3-month interval, was highly comparable to the 3-week studies.

Tension reducer scales (IP through EV), thought to represent more impulsive, situational responses, were expected to be less stable over a 3-month interval. However, in Study 3, only two of the tension reducers scales, IP and II, failed to reach significance, whereas EP and EV appeared as stable over a 3-month period as in the shorter term studies.

Among adolescents (Study 4), test-retest reliability was established for all four tension reducers over a 3-week interval and for six of the nine defense scales.

Reliability has not been satisfactorily demonstrated on four scales—Undo, Dis, RF, and Comp—three of which (Undo, Dis, and Comp) have

**TABLE 11–2**
**Correlation Coefficients in Test-Retest Reliability Studies**

| Time Interval | Study 1 (N = 35) 3 Week | | Study 2 (N = 29) 3 Week | | Study 3 (N = 24) 3 Month | | Study 4 (N = 86) 3 Week | |
|---|---|---|---|---|---|---|---|---|
| Scale | r | p | r | p | r | p | r | p |
| IP | .691 | .001 | .689 | .001 | .164 | NS | .41 | .001 |
| II | .720 | .001 | .756 | .001 | .372 | .10 | .59 | .001 |
| EP | .604 | .001 | .663 | .001 | .538 | .01 | .66 | .001 |
| EV | .512 | .01 | .428 | .05 | .793 | .001 | .58 | .001 |
| DEN | .717 | .001 | .085 | NS | .853 | .001 | .67 | .001 |
| WD | .565 | .001 | .709 | .001 | .692 | .001 | .51 | .001 |
| UNDO | .319 | NS | .099 | NS | .299 | NS | .18 | NS |
| DIS | .836 | .001 | .008 | NS | .426 | .05 | .46 | .001 |
| TAS | .623 | .001 | .677 | .001 | .655 | .001 | .75 | .001 |
| RF | .247 | NS | .291 | NS | .396 | .10 | a | a |
| COMP | .586 | .001 | .409 | .05 | .096 | NS | .29 | NS |
| SUB | .478 | .01 | .753 | .001 | .389 | .10 | .71 | .001 |
| RI | .736 | .001 | .730 | .001 | .739 | .001 | .63 | .001 |
| Overall (mean *r*) | .523 | .01 | .484 | .01 | .493 | .05 | .53 | .001 |

[a]These figures are unavailable; they were erroneously omitted from the original report of Study 4.

a very low frequency of response rate both within groups and within subjects. The mean response rate in these three scales is generally less than one per protocol.

## Normative Data and Demographic Trends

To put normal defensive functioning into proper perspective, normative empirical data are sorely needed, and scores on assessment instruments must be placed within the meaningful context of means and standard deviations.

### Mean Profile

DMP data from the first 250 nonpsychiatric, adults tested (101 males, 149 females) were compiled to form a "normal" profile. Subjects in the normative sample ranged in age from 18 to 81, with a mean age of 35.5. Education level (available on only 186 subjects) was skewed toward the higher range, with the mean for both males and females falling at college level.

Means, standard deviations, and probability values of univariate *F*-tests for gender differences for each scale are listed in Table 11–3.

**TABLE 11–3**
**Average DMP Scores for the DMP Normative Sample**

| Mean Age<br>DMP Scale | Combined<br>(N = 250)<br>35.5<br>Mean | SD | Male<br>(N = 101)<br>35.9<br>Mean | SD | Female<br>(N = 149)<br>35.3<br>Mean | SD | p value<br>(male/female<br>differences) |
|---|---|---|---|---|---|---|---|
| IP | 2.52 | 2.26 | 2.36 | 2.29 | 2.64 | 2.25 | .338 |
| II | 3.14 | 3.07 | 2.57 | 2.88 | 3.52 | 3.14 | .015 |
| EP | 4.90 | 3.37 | 3.89 | 2.92 | 5.58 | 3.49 | .000 |
| EV | 3.47 | 3.07 | 2.69 | 3.20 | 3.99 | 2.87 | .001 |
| DEN | 2.86 | 2.51 | 3.15 | 2.72 | 2.66 | 2.35 | .131 |
| WD | 8.94 | 4.25 | 8.70 | 4.55 | 9.11 | 4.03 | .468 |
| UNDO | 1.26 | 1.48 | 1.10 | 1.42 | 1.38 | 1.52 | .144 |
| DIS | 0.42 | 0.78 | 0.39 | 0.80 | 0.44 | 0.77 | .624 |
| TAS | 0.57 | 1.04 | 0.46 | 0.79 | 0.65 | 1.17 | .139 |
| RF | 3.09 | 2.07 | 2.99 | 1.99 | 3.16 | 2.12 | .530 |
| COMP | 0.57 | 0.88 | 0.56 | 0.85 | 0.57 | 0.90 | .911 |
| SUB | 3.81 | 2.96 | 3.77 | 3.28 | 3.83 | 2.72 | .849 |
| RI | 9.44 | 5.84 | 10.39 | 6.93 | 8.81 | 4.90 | .032 |
| ? | 3.32 | 3.46 | 3.57 | 3.85 | 3.15 | 3.18 | .351 |

*df*(1,248)

## Gender and Age

Only two studies to date have compared age and gender patterns of response with the DMP. In analyzing the responses of 80 men and 80 women between the ages of 20 and 59, Lindeman (1990) found several scales—three tension reducers and two defenses—that differentiated men from women: II, EP, EV, Undo, and TAS. In every instance, women scored significantly higher than men; none of the tension reducers or defenses were more frequently utilized by men than women. With 40 subjects in each age group (20 male and 20 female), Lindeman found no significant differences across age groups (20 to 29; 30 to 39; 40 to 49; 50 to 59) on any DMP scales.

In her study of adolescent patterns of response to the DMP, White (1989) found a significantly higher use of II among females than males. Adolescent males employed Sub significantly more than did females. She found a significantly higher use of RI and TAS among 16- to 17-year-olds than among 13- to 14-year-olds.

## Educational Status

O'Donnell (1992) administered the DMP to two groups of 16- to 17-year-old males, 31 "regular education students" (RES) and 27 "alternative education students" (AES). He hypothesized that the RES group would employ more developmentally mature defenses, as measured by the DMP, than the AES group, on the assumption that the RES were more well-adjusted than the AES. Consistent with O'Donnell's hypothesis, RES were found to be significantly higher than AES in use of advanced defenses (Sub and RI) and middle-range defenses (Comp and Undo). AES generated significantly more Unscorable (?) responses.

## Influence of Social Desirability

Reynolds (1985) examined the manner in which 38 subjects, 28 females and 10 males, responded to instructions to distort DMP responses in a specified direction, specifically to "fake good" or to "fake bad." After completing the DMP under standard instructions, the "fake good" group was instructed to complete the test again answering "with actions which you consider to be ideal, socially acceptable actions . . ." (p. 24), while the "fake bad" group was instructed to answer with actions "which you consider to be undesirable and socially unacceptable . . ." (p. 24).

A multivariate analysis of variance yielded no significant differences between the two groups on the initial testing under standard instructions; however, significant between-group differences occurred under the manipulated conditions. Univariate analyses demonstrated significant differences under "fake good" or "fake bad" instructions on 9 of the 13 scales.

Further analyses (2-factor MANOVA for repeated measures and univariate ANOVA for repeated measures) revealed that all significant differences in response patterns were accounted for by the "fake bad" group. In summary, the "fake bad" profile was characterized by a deviation from the "norm" consisting of a marked increase in developmentally early defenses (IP and EP), and a significant decrease in advanced defenses (RF, Comp, Sub, and RI). No "fake good" pattern was established.

These findings are consistent with those on the Washington University Sentence Completion Test (WU-SCT), a measure of hierarchical stages of ego development (Loevinger, Wessler, & Redmore, 1970; Redmore, 1976); when instructed to do so, subjects were able to "fake bad" on the WU-SCT, lowering their apparent stage of ego development, but were unsuccessful in "faking good." Redmore (1976) argued that the latter finding was accounted for by subjects' inability to simulate responses representative of an ego level higher than the one they have achieved (just as a child would be unable to simulate a level of cognitive development higher than that he/she has attained). The similar finding by Reynolds (1985) regarding the DMP, therefore, may be taken as providing indirect evidence for the validity of the developmental-hierarchical ordering of defenses.

## Convergent Validity

### Consistency of DMP Self-Report Data and Observer Ratings

The question of the degree to which DMP self-report data accurately reflect overt behavior was the impetus for research conducted by Saluk (1990). Saluk administered the DMP to 20 married couples. In addition, he constructed and administered to all 40 subjects a modified, multiple-choice version of the DMP, the DMP II.

The DMP II consisted of the 40 sentence stems of the original DMP, each followed by five responses. Four of the five responses to each stem were randomly chosen from the DMP scoring manual to represent four different defense mechanisms; one of the five was the actual response of the subject's spouse, with any identifying or idiosyncratic information deleted. In completing the DMP II, each subject was instructed to select the response out of the five provided for each stem that "reflects what *your spouse* would most likely do in the situation described" (p. 87).

Item-by-item agreement between the DMP and DMP II was 51.8% and was significant at the .001 level. Rank order correlations of husbands' DMP self-reports and their wives' DMP II observational reports ($r = .90$) and wives' DMP self-reports and their husbands' DMP II observational reports ($r = .94$) were significant at the .01 level. Saluk (1990) concluded that these results seem to support strongly the belief that DMP responses accurately reflect actual behavior.

### Consistency of DMP Scores and Daily Behavioral Diary

Adapting suggestions offered by Epstein (1979, 1980), Mastriana (1988) administered the DMP to 23 first-year psychology graduate students who kept a behavioral diary in which they recorded stressful events occurring in their lives, along with their emotional and behavioral reactions to those events, for 30 consecutive days. Behavioral reactions from the diary were scored following the same criteria used to rate DMP responses.

A comparison of the same 13 defenses, rank ordered from most to least preferred (highest to lowest frequency), demonstrated a positive and significant correlation between the DMP and the diary (Spearman's rho = .868). Importantly, results indicate that the most and least preferred defenses reflected by the DMP correlate strongly with recorded behavioral reactions made in response to a wide variety of unstructured, naturally occurring, unpleasant events. Although both the diary and the DMP are self-report measures, the results demonstrate that the brief administration of the DMP yields the same profile as that gathered from a markedly increased number of events over an extensive period of time.

**Discriminant Validity**

*Severe Psychological Disorders*

To explore differences in defense patterns between normal and inpatient populations, Quick (1987) compared the DMP profiles of three groups: (a) 17 male and 11 female schizophrenic patients, (b) 9 male and 12 female affective-disordered patients, and (c) 15 male and 15 female nonpatients ("normals" randomly selected from archival data). A one-way MANOVA revealed significant differences between these three groups. Univariate analyses indicated significant differences between the schizophrenic and normal groups on 6 of the 14 DMP scales, between the affective disordered and normal groups on 2 scales, and between the affective disordered and schizophrenic groups on one scale.

It is commonly held that normally adjusted persons have greater flexibility and variety in defensive styles than those suffering severe pathology (e.g., Fenichel, 1945). Quick's (1987) data revealed that with the exception of the Unscorable category, schizophrenics scored *below* normals on all DMP scales on which they significantly differed, specifically IP, EV, RF, Comp, and RI. The schizophrenic group also gave more Unscorable responses than the affective group, the only DMP variable on which these two groups differed significantly. Finally, the affective group scored significantly higher than either the normal or schizophrenic groups on WD and significantly lower than either on RI.

In addition, post hoc comparisons indicated significant group differences in the number (variety) of responses given for each stem. Whereas the normal and affective-disordered subjects were able to respond to situations with more than one response option, the schizophrenic subjects were less able to generate more than one behavioral reaction, if that.

In another study of 22 males and 13 female schizophrenic inpatients, O'Connell (1990) administered the DMP within 24 hours of admission and again within 12 hours before discharge. No significant differences were found in individual DMP scales between admission and discharge (mean length of hospital stay was only 12.3 days). However, consistent with Quick's (1987) findings, O'Connell (1990) reported a significant increase between admission and discharge in the mean number of categories of defense generated in response to each stem. In addition, when the individual DMP scales were clustered into the hierarchical categories of early, middle, and advanced, the advanced defenses proved to be significantly higher at discharge than on admission.

*Substance Abuse*

Two studies have examined patterns of response to the DMP among substance abusers with similar, although not identical, results. Bodie (1989) administered the DMP to three all-male groups, each comprising 30 subjects: (a) an alcoholic group, consisting of inpatients admitted to a chemical dependency treatment program with a primary diagnosis of alcohol dependency; (b) a drug-dependent group, also inpatients in the same treatment program with a primary diagnosis of drug dependency; and (c) a control group consisting of medical outpatients. Serpico's (1990) subjects, divided into alcoholic, substance abusing, and control groups, were recruited from an outpatient treatment setting. Her drug-dependent subjects were primarily heroin addicted, and her control group consisted of employees at a large computer company.

The results of both studies (Bodie, 1989; Serpico, 1990) indicated the presence of significant differences in DMP scores between alcoholics and controls and between drug-dependent subjects and controls, but not between the alcohol and drug-dependent groups. The major findings of both studies were consistent in revealing (a) significantly greater use of advanced defenses among controls than among either the alcohol or drug-dependent groups, (b) significantly greater use of the tension reducer IP among drug-dependent subjects than among controls, and (c) significantly greater use of Sub among alcoholics than among controls.

## CONCLUSION

Early work with the DMP is encouraging, though the instrument and supporting research are currently limited in several important aspects. The DMP does not measure use of all major defenses. The normative sample distribution is skewed in education, age, race, and geographic location. Further examination of normative performance by gender and age groupings is needed as well. Ethnic and racial influences need investigation. Although initial studies suggest robust stability in an adolescent population, 4 of the 14 scales are, thus far, inadequate in test-retest stability for an adult population.

The DMP was created to develop an instrument that would allow much needed empirical exploration of widely accepted, but untested, defense theory. It is hoped that sufficient preliminary work has been presented to generate interest, thought, and further investigation into the usefulness and validity of the Defense Mechanism Profile.

## REFERENCES

Bem, D., & Allen, A. (1974). On predicting some of the people some of the time: The search for cross-situational consistencies in behavior. *Psychological Review, 81,* 506–520.

Blum, G. S. (1956). Defense preferences in four countries. *Journal of Projective Techniques, 20,* 33–41.

Bodie, L. (1989). *Defense mechanisms of alcoholics and drug addicts: A comparison study.* Unpublished doctoral research project, Nova University, Fort Lauderdale, FL.

Bond, M., Gardner, S., Christian, J., & Sigal, J. (1983). Empirical study of self-rated defense styles. *Archives of General Psychiatry, 40,* 333–338.

Byrne, D. (1961). The repression-sensitization scale: Rationale, reliability and validity. *Journal of Personality, 29,* 334–349.

Byrne, D., Barry, J., & Nelson, D. (1963). The relation of the revised repression-sensitization scale of measures of self-description. *Journal of Psychological Reports, 13,* 323–334.

Conoley, J. C., & Kramer, J. J. (Eds.). (1989). *The tenth mental measurements yearbook.* Lincoln: University of Nebraska Press.

Cooper, C., & Kline, P. (1982). A validation of the Defense Mechanism Inventory. *British Journal of Medical Psychology, 55,* 209–214.

Epstein, S. (1979). The stability of behavior: I. On predicting most of the people much of the time. *Journal of Personality and Social Psychology, 37,* 1097–1126.

Epstein, S. (1980). The stability of behavior: II. Implications for psychological research. *American Psychologist, 35,* 790–806.

Fassman, F. (1984). *A comparison of training methods for use of the Defense Mechanism Profile.* Unpublished doctoral dissertation, Nova University, Ft. Lauderdale, FL.

Fenichel, O. (1945). *Psychoanalytic theory of neurosis.* New York: Norton.

Freud, A. (1936/1966). *The ego and the mechanisms of defense.* New York: International Universities Press.

Gero, G. (1951). The concept of defense. *Psychoanalytic Quarterly, 20,* 565–578.

Gill, M. (1963). Topography and systems in psychoanalytic theory. *Psychological Issues, 3* (2, Whole No. 10).

Gleser, G., & Ihilevich, D. (1969). An object instrument for measuring defense mechanisms. *Journal of Consulting and Clinical Psychology, 33,* 51–60.

Haan, N. (1963). A proposed model of ego functioning: Coping and defense mechanisms in relationship to IQ change. *Psychological Monographs, 77* (8, Whole No. 571).

Johnson, N. (1982a). *Test-retest reliability of the Defense Mechanism Profile.* Unpublished research project, Nova University, Fort Lauderdale, FL.

Johnson, N. (1982b). *Three month interval test-retest reliability of the Defense Mechanism Profile.* Unpublished research project, Nova University, Fort Lauderdale, FL.

Johnson, N. (1984). *Defense Mechanism Inventory scorer training follow-up.* Unpublished research project, Nova University, Fort Lauderdale, FL.

Johnson, N. (1986). *A content validation study of the Defense Mechanism Profile.* Unpublished research project, Nova University, Fort Lauderdale, FL.

Kragh, U. (1960). The Defense Mechanism Test: A new method for diagnosis and personnel selection. *Journal of Applied Psychology, 44,* 303–309.

Larkin, V. (1983). *Reliability study of the Defense Mechanism Profile.* Unpublished doctoral dissertation, Nova University, Fort Lauderdale, FL.

Lindeman, J. B. (1990). *The effect of age and gender group differences on defense mechanism utilized.* Unpublished doctoral research project, Nova University, Fort Lauderdale, FL.

Loevinger, J., Wessler, R., & Redmore, C. (1970). *Measuring ego development: I. Construction and use of a sentence completion test.* San Francisco: Jossey-Bass.

Mastriana, L. (1988). *A validity study of the Defense Mechanism Profile by means of a natural process method: Daily diary.* Unpublished doctoral research project, Nova University, Fort Lauderdale, FL.

Mischel, W. (1969). Continuity and change in personality. *American Psychologist, 24,* 1012–1018.

O'Connell, P. (1990). *A criterion related validity study of the Defense Mechanism Profile with hospitalized schizophrenics.* Unpublished doctoral research project, Nova University, Fort Lauderdale, FL.

O'Donnell, J. E. (1992). *An evaluation of differences in Defense Mechanism Profiles of alternative program and general education adolescents.* Unpublished doctoral research project, Nova University, Fort Lauderdale, FL.

Paunonen, S., & Jackson, D. (1985). Idiographic measurement strategies for personality and prediction: Some unredeemed promissory notes. *Psychological Review, 92,* 486–511.

Quick, J. (1987). *A criterion related discriminant validation study of the Defense Mechanism Profile.* Unpublished doctoral research project, Nova University, Fort Lauderdale, FL.

Rapaport, D. (1951/1967). The autonomy of the ego. In M. M. Gill (Ed.), *The collected papers of David Rapaport.* New York: Basic Books.

Redmore, C. (1976). Susceptibility to faking of a sentence completion test of ego development. *Journal of Personality Assessment, 40*(6), 607–615.

Reynolds, D. (1985). *A validity study: Social desirability and the Defense Mechanism Profile.* Unpublished doctoral dissertation, Nova University, Fort Lauderdale, FL.

Rosenzweig, S. (1976). Aggressive behavior and the Rosenzweig picture-frustration (P-F) study. *Journal of Clinical Psychology, 32,* 885–891.

Saluk, J. (1990). *An empirical comparison of subject (self)-spouse (observer) agreement on reports of behavior manifested under stress: A validity study of the Defense Mechanism Profile.* Unpublished doctoral research project, Nova University, Fort Lauderdale, FL.

Semrad, E. V., Grinspoon, L., & Feinberg, S. E. (1973). Development of an ego profile scale. *Archives of General Psychiatry, 28,* 70–77.

Serpico, F. (1990). *A comparison of locus of control and defense mechanisms of outpatient alcoholics and opiate addicts.* Unpublished doctoral research project, Nova University, Fort Lauderdale, FL.

Sperling, S. J. (1958). On denial and the essential nature of defense. *International Journal of Psychoanalysis, 39,* 25–58.

Vaillant, G. E. (1971). Theoretical hierarchy of adaptive ego mechanisms. *Archives of General Psychiatry, 24,* 107–118.

Vaillant, G. E. (1976). Natural history of male psychological health: The relation of choice of ego mechanisms of defense to adult adjustment. *Archives of General Psychiatry, 38,* 535–545.

Vaillant, G., Bond, M., & Vaillant, C. (1986). An empirically validated hierarchy of defense mechanisms. *Archives of General Psychiatry, 43,* 786–794.

White, D. (1989). *A reliability study and profile study of the Defense Mechanism Profile with adolescents.* Unpublished doctoral research project, Nova University, Fort Lauderdale, FL.

Zuckerman, M., Koestner, R., DeBoy, T., Garcia, T., Maresca, B., & Sartoris, J. (1988). To predict some of the people some of the time: A reexamination of the moderator variable approach in personality theory. *Journal of Personality and Social Psychology, 54,* 1006–1019.

# 12

## The Rorschach
### *Defense or Adaptation?*

BARRY RITZLER

Because the Rorschach test was adopted early by the psychoanalytic community as a technique particularly well suited for the assessment of psychodynamic concepts (Schafer, 1954), it is not surprising that it frequently has been used to assess defense mechanisms. This chapter, in summarizing the major contributions to the Rorschach defense literature, will address the following question: Does the Rorschach adequately operationalize defense mechanisms, thereby providing a method for the validation of the theoretical concepts, or has the work on Rorschach assessment of defenses merely identified differences in level of adaptation that more parsimoniously account for differences in test results? In other words, has the Rorschach given us reason to believe that defense mechanisms actually exist as distinct psychological structures as psychodynamic theories have hypothesized?

The discussion begins with a brief summary of early and partial contributions followed by a critique of the more extensive work of Schafer (1954) who first proposed a comprehensive methodology for assessing defenses on the Rorschach. Next, Holt's method for measuring defenses on the Rorschach based on the concepts of primary and secondary process thinking (Holt, 1977) is reviewed. The chapter ends with critiques of the contemporary work of Lerner and his associates (Lerner, 1991; Lerner, Albert, & Walsh, 1987; Lerner & Lerner, 1980; Lerner, Sugarman, & Gaughran, 1981) and Cooper and his colleagues (Cooper & Arnow, 1986; Cooper, Perry, & Arnow, 1988; Cooper, Perry, & O'Connell, 1991; Perry & Cooper, 1985; Perry & Cooper, 1989). In each case, research evidence and the logical consistency and methodological soundness of the different systems will be considered in evaluating the Rorschach's contribution to the measurement of defense mechanisms.

## EARLY AND PARTIAL CONTRIBUTIONS

As scoring-based Rorschach assessment developed in the 1940s and early 1950s, some limited attention was given to identifying derivatives of defense operations on the test. Beck (1952) and, later, Molish and Beck (1958) offered some suggestions for defining specific scoring criteria with particular emphasis on projection and obsessive-compulsive defenses. Rapaport (1946), Schachtel (1945), and Schafer (1948) also made some interesting suggestions for interpreting defenses. No validation studies, however, were conducted on these early ideas.

In a rare empirical study, Baxter, Becker, and Hooks (1963) developed a fairly extensive set of Rorschach criteria based primarily on response content and test behavior for the assessment of denial, projection, isolation, undoing, and displacement. Subjects were parents of neurotics and good and poor premorbid schizophrenics. Differences in Rorschach-measured defensive styles were found between the parents of good and poor premorbid schizophrenics, but no systematic Rorschach pattern of defenses discriminated the parents of neurotics. No external criteria for defenses were used in the study. The Rorschach criteria, though promising in this initial study, have not been investigated in further published research. Also, the unusual samples of parents rather than the patients themselves may not have provided the best assessment of the validity of the Rorschach scores.

Although this chapter focuses on scoring systems that cover comprehensive sets of ego defense mechanisms, some contributions regarding individual defenses are worth mentioning. Gardner, Holtzman, Klein, Linton, and Spence (1959) used formal scores and content analysis to find correlations between cognitive styles of leveling and sharpening and the defenses of repression and isolation.

Repression has received relatively extensive treatment with the Rorschach Index of Repressive Style (RIRS; Levine & Spivak, 1964). The RIRS correlated positively with the capacity to tolerate sensory isolation, and such cognitive-perceptual phenomena as field independence and leveling-sharpening (Levine & Spivak, 1964). Also, certain clinical diagnostic categories theoretically associated with repression such as obsessive-compulsive, hysteria, and borderline have been discriminated by the RIRS (Levine & Spivak, 1964). The RIRS also attains good reliability results in the 90%–95% range of interrater agreement. Lerner (1991) points out some ambiguity in the RIRS criteria and criticizes some of the methodology of Levine and Spivak, but evaluates the scale highly enough to incorporate most of it in his criteria for repression on the Lerner Defense Scales. Aronow and Reznikoff (1976) leveled some rather harsh criticism toward the RIRS for relying too heavily on verbal expressive style, which may be influenced by many factors other than repression.

Bahnson and Bahnson (1966) also had some success in finding relationships between a 16-item Rorschach index of repression and behavioral repression in cases of malignant neoplasm; however, poor controls and a narrow range of generalization limit the validity of this study.

Bellak, Hurvich, and Gediman (1973) found correlations between levels of pathology (schizophrenia, neurosis, and normal) and global Rorschach criteria of defensive failure and pathology based on theoretical concepts associated with repression, isolation, and projection; these defenses, however, were not operationally defined in the study, but were inferred from the clinical diagnoses of the subjects—a method that is used all too frequently in Rorschach studies of defense mechanisms.

Other than the studies already mentioned and the four major projects covered in the remainder of the chapter, no other investigations of the Rorschach as a measure of defense mechanisms have appeared in the literature.

## SCHAFER'S SYSTEM

The first theoretically based, comprehensive attempt at developing a Rorschach assessment method for defenses was presented by Schafer (1954). In his thorough, erudite style, he combined theory and assessment technique to fashion an impressive set of criteria for each defense from all aspects of the Rorschach protocol and test situation. Compared with other methods for assessing defense mechanisms on the Rorschach, Schafer's system remains, by far, the most complex. He covers *repression, projection,* and a set of defensive operations he terms "obsessive-compulsive"; namely, *regression, isolation, intellectualization, reaction formation,* and *undoing.* In all, his system covers nearly 250 pages of text and is too lengthy to summarize completely in this chapter. Consequently, *projection* has been chosen for the purpose of general illustration and critique of the system.

In an introductory discussion of the psychoanalytic theory of projection, Schafer defines it as ". . . a process by which an objectionable internal tendency is unrealistically attributed to another person or to other objects in the environment instead of being recognized as part of one's self" (p. 279). Schafer presents a concise summary of the psychoanalytic theory of projection and then proceeds to base his criteria for Rorschach assessment of the defense on the specific elements of the theory he has discussed.

As is the case for all defenses assessed by his system, Schafer groups his criteria for projection under three general headings: Test Scores, Test Attitudes and Behaviors, and Thematic Analysis of Content. For test scores, he uses the Rapaport system (Rapaport, 1946): Beginning with location, Schafer proposes that an inflated number of Whole responses (W) is indicative of lofty ambition ($W > 10$), grandiosity ($W > 15$), and megalomania ($W > 20$) of individuals with projection as a primary defense (paranoid patients). Often, this expansiveness is accompanied by rather shallow, poorly organized pretentiousness captured by the poor form Whole response ($W-$). In contrast, when projection is characterized by suspiciousness rather than grandiosity, the defense usually is manifested in a high percentage of unusual detail responses (greater than 20%) or by an increased number of space responses indicative of the oppositional distrust of paranoid individuals.

In regard to determinants, Schafer proposes a high pure $F\%$ as indicative of an excessive need for control, an emphasis on good form as a way of preserving self-justification and social invulnerability (although as simple projection edges into paranoia, less accurate interpretation of reality may become more apparent), and an underemphasis on color (especially $Cf$ and $C$) suggesting overcontrol of affect and impulse. Schafer argues that human movement ($M$) may persist in a paranoid record because of the strong ideational component in projection. Special emphasis is given to small detail and poor form $M$ responses because they combine a predisposition toward ideation with narrow focus and/or autistically distorted perceptions of others.

Schafer goes on to propose that some standard Rorschach content categories may be sensitive to the cautious constriction ($A\%$) and/or suspicious overattention to detail ($Ad$ and $Hd$) indicative of many paranoid individuals. Magical thinking and ideas of reference may result in an increase in overabstract forms such as "triangles" in the Card I white spaces, the letter "H" in the middle of Card III, and a "question mark" around the lower edge of Card I.

Concluding his discussion of determinants and the defense of projection, Schafer cites confabulatory elaboration of responses as indicative of the paranoid's ". . . efforts to ferret out hidden or obscure meanings and to avoid being taken by surprise, as well as to reorganize reality along lines that are not intolerable. . . ." (p. 286). He also finds paranoid implications in peculiar notions concerning resemblances and common meanings among the cards or parts of the cards, and wary remarks concerning hidden or obscure meanings in the blots. . . . Responses may take on a fluid, elusive quality [and] in the inquiry, the patient may reject a previous response and may even deny that he gave it. (p. 286)

Indeed, such tendencies have been identified by others (e.g., Johnston & Holtzman, 1979; Powers & Hamlin, 1955; Watkins & Stauffacher, 1952) as associated with schizophrenic thought disorder.

Turning to test attitudes and behavior, Schafer argues that the relative lack of structure in the Rorschach test situation is a threat to the paranoid subject and often will elicit heightened suspiciousness that

may take many specific forms: (a) intense interest in what the test records; (b) anxiety over verbatim recording, particularly verbatim recording of asides, interjections, sighs and the like; (c) evasive, querulous, elusive, defensive responses to inquiry; (d) continued demands for more explicitness in the test instructions; (e) emphasis on similarities and differences between the cards and on the lack of perfect symmetry between opposite sides of single cards; (f) legalistic documenting or critical evaluation of each detail in each response; (g) preoccupation with what the test is "really" after (e.g., sex, gore, morbid matters). (p. 287)

Schafer goes on to suggest that in certain paranoid individuals, meglomania may override suspiciousness resulting in

a benign, patronizing pose, or an inscrutable pose that combines a frozen smile with steely eyes, or a supremely self-assured pose that is saturated with a holier-than-thou loftiness, disdain and even disgust. (p. 287)

At times, both suspicious and grandiose attitudes may appear in the same test performance.

Schafer discusses thematic analysis of content *after* he covers evidence from scoring and observation of test attitudes. Although he obviously regards content analysis as vital, he does not propose it until he has established a framework of a more operationalized and less inferential assessment.

For content analysis of projection, Schafer refers to three general categories of paranoid function, each of which he associates with corresponding content groupings. These categories are (a) the paranoid fear of external threat; (b) need for and modes of self-protection; and (c) impulse problems. Schafer proposes that external threat is the most specific indicator of paranoia and may be signified by contents such as ". . . eyes, pointing fingers, blood stains, fingerprints or footprints, detectives or policemen, leering faces. . . ." (p. 288). Also, a sense of danger resulting from projection of hostility may result in such contents as ". . . fierce, threatening, sinister, evil, approaching or hovering figures, . . . along with traps, webs, pits, poison, electrical or radio waves, concealing darkness, and hidden or partly concealed or obscured figures" (p. 288).

Schafer divides the paranoid's preoccupation with self-protection into three areas:

1. An emphasis on concealment and flight signified by such contents as ". . . shields, armor, masks, the shells of turtles or crabs, and crouching or fleeing figures . . ." (p. 288).

2. An expansive, meglomaniacal mode ". . . expressed through such images of status, omnipotence or omniscience as coats of arms, emblems, idols, gods, prophets, crowns, thrones, sceptres, kings and queens, monuments, and persons famous for their achievement, wisdom, goodness, power, or supernatural attributes . . ." (p. 288).

3. An emphasis on defense failure and victimization resulting in such contents as ". . . mangled butterfly wings, a bombed building, and a person being tortured on a rack . . ." (p. 288).

Schafer finishes his prescription for the Rorschach assessment of projection as a defense by suggesting that paranoid protocols will contain more regressive content indicative of the breakthrough of primitive impulses. He is less specific in identifying the types of content that represent such regression, but his ideas are similar to those of Holt, which are summarized in the following section. Schafer refers generally to ". . . formal primitivization of thought and perception but also in a coming to the fore of various pregenital (oral, anal, phallic-aggressive, homosexual, etc.) impulse representations" (p. 289). He concludes his remarks with an interesting caution:

Those impulses which are crucial in the development of the paranoid disorder may be represented in the test imagery, but they may not be singled out for special emphasis and clearly indicated to be pathogenic. They may merely take their place along with other archaic expressions of impulse. There is no clear evidence as yet that one or another type of pregenital content prevails in the records of paranoid patients, and certainly not content that neatly fits the theory that paranoid pathology is primarily a defense against homosexuality. (p. 289)

Now that Schafer's assessment method for projection has been summarized, the reader is encouraged to compare his work with the Rorschach defense assessment procedures that follow in this chapter. It will be obvious that Schafer's is the most comprehensive system in terms of using the total Rorschach protocol for interpretation. Unfortunately, little research validation for Schafer's system has appeared in the literature. Only Haan (1964) has reported on the empirical validity of a comprehensive set of Rorschach variables for discriminating between different defense mechanisms. Curiously, although she cites Schafer as a primary source in her introduction, Haan uses the Klopfer system (Klopfer, Ainsworth, Klopfer, & Holt, 1954) in her analysis rather than the Rapaport system used by Schafer. Nevertheless, she found some suggestive but inconclusive results with a nonpatient sample of 88 adults. Using the rather liberal significance level of $p > .10$, she found significant relationships between 10 defense mechanisms and such Klopfer variables as $M$, $M:FM$, and $W:M$, but not (as hypothesized) $A$, $F$ extended, and $F:Fk + Fc$. Haan found better correlations between defenses and such Rorschach test attitudes and behaviors as (a) sensitive reaction to the examiner's structuring of instructions; (b) elaboration of good $F$ responses; (c) ambivalent approach to percept formation; (d) affective enjoyment of the situation; (e) intellectual, cognitive enjoyment of the situation; (f) restructuring of blot areas; and (g) attention focused on task.

Although her results were roughly consistent with many of Schafer's hypotheses, Haan's use of the Klopfer method, her failure to sample pathological subjects, the liberal significance level, and disregard for content analysis prevent the study from being a conclusive test of the Schafer propositions.

Recently, Viglione, Brager, and Haller (1991) used the Exner Comprehensive System to test Schafer's general proposition that a thorough application of Rorschach variables would result in a significant discrimination between defense mechanisms. The authors took responses from Schafer's original illustrations of defensive styles and found that the Comprehensive System distinguished the repressive style from other defensive operations. This study, while suggesting that the Comprehensive System would be appropriate for testing Schafer's hypotheses, did not assess a representative sample of Rorschach protocols from individuals identified as having specific defensive styles. Such a comprehensive study remains to be done.

## HOLT'S CONTRIBUTIONS

Following Schafer's work on the psychoanalytic interpretation of defenses, Holt (1977) used the Rorschach to measure derivatives of primary and secondary thought processes as defined by Freud (1900/1938). In using the Rorschach to operationalize secondary process thinking, Holt recognized issues of control and defense that distinguished secondary process from primary process and seemed to have manifestation on the Rorschach. Consequently, he devoted an entire section of his scoring manual to control and defense. Although, unlike Schafer, he did not focus on specific defenses, he concentrated on particular defensive operations that are consistent with the operations characteristic of most of the defenses of psychoanalysis. These operations are *remoteness, context, postponing,* and *overtness.* Holt also included a miscellaneous category for operations less frequently apparent than those previously mentioned.

Briefly, *remoteness* refers to response content that is distant in time, place, person, or reality level from the subject's current experience; *context* makes the response less primitive by giving it cultural, aesthetic, intellectual, and/or humorous qualities; *postponing* simply refers to delay and blocking of a response; and *overtness* is the distinction between potential and active aggression in the response content—the more overt the aggression, the less the defensive control.

In addition to the specific defense operation scores, corresponding ratings of effectiveness in the Holt system yielded three *overall* scores. The first, the *defense demand rating,* used a six-point scale to estimate the amount of primary process in a response. The second overall score in Holt's system is *defense effectiveness,* which also involved a six-point rating of the degree to which a defense operation in a response was successful in modifying primary process material into a secondary process idea. Finally, the third overall defense and control score was *adaptive regression,* which attempted to assess the adaptive potential of the subject by multiplying the defense demand rating by the defense effectiveness rating, summing the products, and dividing by the number of defense operation responses.

Obviously, Holt's system does not have the potential to directly validate the existence of specific defense mechanisms. Nevertheless, if the

**TABLE 12–1**
**Reliability Estimates of the**
**Holt Defense Operation Scoring System**

| Study | Reliability Estimates | | |
| | Defense Effectiveness | Defense Demand | Adaptive Regression |
| --- | --- | --- | --- |
| McMahon (1964) | .56 | — | — |
| Allison (1967) | .81 | .99 | .67 |
| Benfari & Calogeras (1968) | .90 | .95 | — |
| Rabkin (1967) | .90 | .86 | — |
| Russ (1980) | .80 | .76 | .90 |

*Note:* Studies summarized in this table are reviewed in Lerner (1991) pp. 164–165.

defense operations he proposes are supported by research hypothesis testing, the basic theoretical concept of distinct defense mechanisms would be supported by association. Unfortunately, reliability is a serious problem for the specific defense operation scores. Holt has made numerous revisions of his scoring manual (the last known revision is number 15) in an effort to improve the reliability of the defense operations scores; however, regardless of the revision used, reliability estimates (usually interrater agreement) consistently fail to exceed the 50% level of agreement for any specific defense operation.

The reliability of the overall scores is more encouraging. Table 12–1 summarizes the reliability estimates from several research studies of the Holt system. The overall scores are consistent in attaining reliability estimates that appreciably exceed the .50 level—most are in the .80–1.00 range.

Given these contrasting reliability findings for specific defense operations and overall effectiveness, it is not surprising to learn that reported research supports the validity of the overall scores but does not show significant results for the highly unstable defense operation scores. Table 12–2 summarizes the essential significant results of studies of the Holt system. The last study was published in 1982—a fact representative of the declining interest in the Holt system, probably because most psychodynamically oriented investigators are interested in assessing specific defenses as opposed to obtaining overall estimates of effectiveness.

There are three logical possibilities to explain why Holt's system does not yield reliable estimates of defense operations:

1. The theoretical concept of defense operations is not valid—a nonexistent phenomenon cannot be measured reliably.
2. Defense operations exist, but the Rorschach does not measure them.

3. Defense operations exist, the Rorschach measures them, but the Holt system is not correct or precise enough in its definitions to provide a stable measure.

The point is that studies of the Holt control and defense measures give no logical support for the existence of defense mechanisms (or, at least,

**TABLE 12–2**
**Summary of Results of Validation Studies**
**of Holt Defense Operation Scoring System**

| Study | Subjects | Results Summary* |
|---|---|---|
| Pine & Holt (1960) | College students ($n = 27$) | Quality of imagination related to AR and DE. |
| Goldberger (1961) | College students ($n = 14$) | Controlled primary process thinking during perceptual isolation related to DE. |
| Pine (1962) | Unemployed actors ($n = 56$) | Failed to replicate Pine & Holt (1960). |
| Maupin (1965) | Male college students ($n = 29$) | Positive response to mediation correlated with DE. |
| Wright & Abbey (1965) | ($n = 21$) | Ability to tolerate perceptual deprivation related to DD/DE. |
| Zimet & Fine (1965) | Schizophrenics; reactive ($n = 23$) process ($n = 36$) | Reactives > process on DD, AR, and DE. |
| Saretsky (1966) | Male schizophrenics ($n = 40$) | Improvement in DE scores for chlorpromazine and placebo groups. |
| Allison (1967) | Male divinity students ($n = 20$) | Intensity of religious conversion experience related to DD and AR but not DE. |
| Feirstein (1967) | Male graduate students ($n = 20$) | Tolerance for unrealistic experience related to AR, DE, and DD. |
| Benfari & Calogeras (1968) | College students ($n = 40$) | Punitive and conflicted conscience negatively correlated with AR, DE, and DD. |
| Blatt, Allison, & Feirstein (1969) | Male college students ($n = 50$) | Ability to handle cognitive complexity related to DE and AR but not DD. |
| Greenberg, Ramsay, Rakoff, & Weiss (1969) | 17-year-old patient with myxedema psychosis | Improvement following thyroxin treatment related to increases in DE. |
| Murray & Russ (1981) | College students ($n = 42$) | Cognitive complexity related to AR for males, but not females. |
| Dudek & Chamberland-Bouhadana (1982) | Mature artists ($n = 20$) Young artists ($n = 20$) | Mature artists showed more DE, DD, and AR. |

*DD = Defense Demand; AR = Adaptive Regression; DE = Defense Effectiveness.

*Note:* Studies summarized in this table are reviewed in Lerner (1991), pp. 165–170.

their hypothetically underlying operations). Although the overall defense scores seem to have some validity, the significant findings in all cases can be explained by the concept of adaptive potential—individuals who have healthier, more adaptive personalities receive higher defense effectiveness scores on their Rorschachs. The concept of specific defense mechanisms is not necessary since the overall scores are the only scores that yield significant results. Still, the concept of defense mechanisms is not *disproved*, because of the previously listed logical possibilities 2 and 3.

## LERNER DEFENSE SCALES

The first Rorschach method that promoted validation research on specific defense mechanisms was the Lerner Defense Scales (Lerner & Lerner, 1980). Essentially, the scales are designed to measure defenses that operate at a lower, more pathological level of personality functioning. The specific defenses measured are *splitting, devaluation, idealization, projective identification,* and *denial.* For devaluation, idealization, and denial, the scale requires a rating on a developmental continuum from low to high (maturity). Only responses with some form of human content are scored. Scored elements of the response are the specific type of figure, the action (if any), and numerous descriptive embellishments. In addition, the form level of the scored responses is included in the rating of projective identification and denial.

The basic definitions of the scoring categories will be summarized and critiqued. (For a more complete scoring manual, consult Lerner, 1991.) For the most part, the definitions are clear, straightforward, and accompanied by helpful examples. A number of the scoring definitions lack exclusion criteria and examples that would help refine the scoring decision. Nevertheless, reliability estimates have been very good. Lerner and Lerner (1980) reported the following interrater agreements: splitting, 100%; devaluation, 91%; idealization, 87%; projective identification, 100%; and denial, 83%. Later, Lerner et al. (1981) obtained reliability coefficients ranging from .94 to .99 for the specific defense categories. Other investigators not of the Lerner team found acceptable alpha coefficient levels of 1.00 to .80 (Van-Der Keshet, 1988) and interrater agreements of 100% to 88% (Gacono, 1988).

Definitions for scoring the Lerner system are guided by psychodynamic theories of defenses. For instance, *splitting* ". . . involves a division of internal and external into (1) parts, as distinct from wholes, and (2) good and bad part-objects" (Lerner, 1991; p. 182). Briefly, the scoring criteria are (a) a sequence of human responses in which the affective descriptions are opposite (Lerner's example: "'. . . an ugly criminal . . . .' followed by 'couples . . . cheek to cheek,'" p. 182); (b) a human response in which part of the figure is opposite to another part ("'A giant. His lower part here conveys danger, but his top half looks benign,'" p. 182); (c) a response involving two human figures described in opposite ways ("'Two figures, a man and a woman. He is mean and shouting at her. Being rather angelic, she's standing there and taking it,'" p. 182); and (d) a tarnished idealized figure or an enhanced devalued figure ("'A headless angel,'" p. 182). These definitions are very straightforward in that they seem to be direct manifestations of "splitting" with little inference necessary to make the connection. In other words, these definitions have high *face validity*.

*Devaluation* is the ". . . tendency to depreciate, tarnish, and lessen the importance of one's inner and outer objects" (p. 182), and it is scored on a five-point scale based on the degree of humanness of the figure(s), the severity of depreciation, and temporal distancing. The levels of the scale are as follows:

1. Real human qualities, slight depreciation, and no distancing (example: "'a girl in a funny costume,'" p. 183—if distancing occurs, the response must be rated at a lower level.
2. Real human, with blatant depreciation ("'a woman defecating,'" p. 183).
3. Quasi-human, slight depreciation ("'sad looking clowns,'" p. 183).
4. Quasi-human, blatant depreciation ("'. . . evil witches,'" p. 183).
5. Nonhumans with human characteristics, depreciation not necessary ("'mannequins . . . ,'" p. 183).

Here, the depreciation has clear face validity, but some inference is necessary to equate quasi- or nonhuman with devaluation; distancing takes even more inference, most of which would probably not occur to those who are not psychoanalytic.

*Idealization* ". . . involves a denial of unwanted characteristics of an object and then enhancing of the object by projecting one's own libido or omnipotence onto it" (p. 184). The scoring involves the same five-point scale and the same three dimensions as devaluation except for the evaluative dimension being one of positive evaluation or aggrandizement. The same comments are pertinent regarding level of inference.

*Projective identification* ". . . refers to a process in which parts of the self are split off and projected onto an external object or part-object" (p. 185). It differs from projection proper in that what is projected onto the object is not experienced as ego alien. There are two distinctly different criteria for scoring this defense:

1. An overly embellished, confabulatory human response of form level *w*— or — on the Mayman (1970) form level scoring system. (Example: "'A huge man coming to get me. I can see his huge teeth. He's staring straight at me. His hands are up as if he will strike me,'" p. 185) and

2. human responses in which the location is small, rarely used, and arbitrarily formed by using inner shading detail to delimit the figure. ("'an ugly face' . . . in reference to the inner portion of Card IV . . . ," p. 185). Here, face validity is almost entirely lost and the inference involved in getting from the response content to the specific defense mechanisms is daunting.

## COOPER ET AL. AND
## THE RORSCHACH DEFENSE SCALE

The latest formal attempt to measure defense mechanisms with the Rorschach is that of Cooper and his colleagues (Cooper & Arnow, 1986; Cooper, Perry, & Arnow, 1988; Cooper, Perry, & O'Connell, 1991; Perry & Cooper, 1989), who have developed the Rorschach Defense Scale (RDS). The RDS is similar in format to the Lerner Defense Scale (LDS) with substantial overlap in the scoring criteria. The RDS, however, is a much longer scale primarily because it is designed to measure 15 (compared with 5) defenses: *isolation, intellectualization, reaction formation, reationalization, repression, devaluation, primitive idealization, projective identification, splitting, omnipotence, projection, massive denial, hypomanic denial, Pollyannish denial,* and *higher level denial.* Also, the RDS relies even more heavily on content analysis and is based on somewhat different theoretical concepts—object relations, Kohut's narcissism concept (Kohut & Wolf, 1978), and developmental arrest and structural deficiency as defined by Stolorow and Lachmann (1980)—compared with the theoretical basis of the Lerner Defense Scales, which are derived from Kernberg's theory of borderline pathology (Kernberg, 1975). The broader theoretical base of the RDS is primarily responsible for the wider range of defenses it covers and for the designation of *all* responses as potentially scorable compared with limiting the scale to responses with human qualities.

As a more comprehensive scale for measuring defenses, the RDS is applicable to a much wider range of psychopathology and yields many more scorable responses, thereby increasing its discriminatory potential. Unfortunately, the scale has reliability problems. Only the defense subscale of *omnipotence* yields an intraclass correlation coefficient for interrater reliability that exceeds .80. All other reliability estimates for the individual subscales range between .45 and .76 with 8 of the 15 subscales failing to exceed .65. The authors group the subscales into larger categories of Neurotic, Borderline, and Psychotic defenses with somewhat more encouraging reliability results (Neurotic category = .71; Borderline category = .81; and Psychotic category = .72). These groupings, however, lose the integrity of the specific defenses so that the scale becomes more like the general defense effectiveness measures of Holt.

In spite of the discouraging reliability figures, Cooper and his colleagues have demonstrated that the RDS has some discriminatory power. Positive correlations were obtained between the subscales of devaluation, projection, splitting, hypomanic denial (all Borderline subscales except hypomanic denial) and the total score from the Borderline Personality Disorder Scale (BPD) (Perry & Cooper, 1985), an interview-based continuous measure of borderline pathology as defined by object relations theory. Significant negative correlations were obtained between the BPD and the RDS subscales of intellectualization and isolation (Neurotic defenses). The only specific defense score from the BPD that correlated significantly with its counterpart on the RDS was splitting.

In a study of the RDS as a predictor of levels of depression, anxiety, and psychosocial role functioning of patients with personality and affective disorders, Cooper et al. (1991) found that the RDS was a less powerful predictor than a basic clinical interview (Perry & Cooper, 1989). Only devaluation and projection were associated with poor outcome of affective disturbance and impaired social functioning, whereas intellectualization, isolation, reaction formation, and Pollyannish denial were associated with good outcome.

The modest results for the RDS are not surprising in light of the questionable reliability of the subscales. In a study comparing the Lerner Defense Scales and the RDS Borderline subscales of splitting, devaluation, idealization, projective identification, and omnipotence with samples of neurotic, borderline, and psychotic subjects, Lerner et al. (1987) found the same suggestive, but hardly confirming results for both scales. Generally, the RDS was more effective in discriminating between healthier subjects (e.g., between outpatient neurotics and outpatient borderlines), whereas the LDS did better with more severely disturbed patients (e.g., discriminating between inpatient borderlines and inpatient psychotics). The specific defense subscales of both the RDS and LDS differentiated between some, but not all pairings of the patient groups—again, showing some promise in spite of the questionable reliability of the RDS (Lerner et al. achieved greater than 80% interrater agreement with the LDS, but only 64% with the RDS).

In the Lerner et al. study, correlations between the RDS and LDS revealed significant results for splitting ($r = .49$) and devaluation ($r = .64$); the results for projective identification ($r = .30$) and idealization ($r = .13$) indicate that the corresponding subscales from the two systems are not measuring the same personality processes. Indeed, close inspection of the criteria for projective identification and idealization on the LDS and RDS reveals several differences that are not apparent when the criteria for splitting and devaluation are compared across scales. The extension of the RDS to all Rorschach responses and the reliability problem mentioned earlier may also contribute to the low correlations. Finally, the LDS subscales were all significantly intercorrelated, while the RDS subscales were much less closely associated with each other. This not only suggests that the LDS has a more unitary theoretical basis (Kernberg's theory versus the multitheory basis of the RDS), but gives reason to believe that the RDS subscales are more likely to be measuring separate processes—a more admirable psychometric property for a scoring system for defense mechanisms.

In summary, although evidence exists that indicates the two systems are measuring *something* relevant to defense mechanisms, the results for both reliability and validity are not robust enough to confidently make the claim at this time that the scales are actually measuring the hypothesized defensive processes. A noteworthy criticism by Carr (1987) further addresses this issue.

## CARR'S CRITICISM

Arthur Carr, a long-time associate of Kernberg (e.g., see Carr, Goldstein, Hunt, & Kernberg, 1979), presents a critique of the Lerner et al. (1987) comparison study that injects further uncertainty into the question of the validity of the defense scales (Carr, 1987).

Carr criticizes Lerner et al. for combining DSM-III borderline and schizotypal patients into their "borderline" category; this strategy, he argues, is not consistent with Kernberg's theory, which places schizotypals more in the schizophrenic than the borderline spectrum. Furthermore, Carr notes that Lerner et al. used three different diagnostic systems for identifying their experimental groups: schizophrenia was diagnosed by the Research Diagnostic Criteria (Spitzer, Endicott, & Robbins, 1975);

borderline diagnosis was by the DSM-III (American Psychiatric Association, 1980); the neurotic criteria were unspecified, but certainly were not from the Research Diagnostic Criteria or DSM-III. Such mixed criteria further scramble the meaning of the marginal results obtained by Lerner et al.

Perhaps Carr's most telling criticism is summarized by the following quote:

> Although those systems [LDS and RDS] may show differences between various diagnostic groups (better arrived at, it is hoped, than those offered in the Lerner study), the convincing validation will have to come from evidence that shows that a Rorschach measure for a specific defense is correlated adequately with some clinical or behavioral evidence of that particular defense, rather than that a plethora of defenses differentiates large diagnostic groups that, on the basis of somebody's theory, presumably use these defenses. (p. 353)

The following—and final—section addresses this criticism.

## CONCLUSION

Reliability and validity are essential to personality assessment. Lack of evidence for these key principles, however, has not kept clinicians from using the Rorschach to assess defenses—the practice is performed often in many clinical settings. The efforts of Schafer, Holt, Lerner, and Cooper and his colleagues, however, provide us with substantial springboards for the search for valid derivatives of defense mechanisms in the Rorschach. To date, none of these systems has given us much reason to believe that what passes for defenses on the Rorschach is what Freud, or the ego psychologists, or the object relations theorists, or even Kernberg (or Schafer, for that matter) meant by defenses.

It has been nearly four decades since Schafer presented his elaborate system for assessing defenses on the Rorschach, and yet very few studies have been published showing validation of the system. It is difficult to believe that only a small handful of investigators have attempted to validate Schafer's system. Could it be that many who have tried have obtained negative results and either abandoned their investigations or had their manuscripts rejected? Schafer's system respects the time-honored approach of using all facets of the Rorschach procedure for interpretation (scores, behavioral observations, and content analysis) and, consequently, would seem to have the most promise for detecting defensive operations if they occur. Until a definitive validity study has been conducted following Carr's suggestions, it may be unwise to abandon Schafer's system in favor of simpler procedures that perhaps rely excessively on content analysis.

Holt's system also comes with little evidence for the validity of specific defense mechanisms on the Rorschach. His measures of *defense effectiveness,* however, yielded promising results, thereby raising the critical question: Is Holt really measuring *defense* effectiveness or could his system instead be measuring general coping capacity or overall level of adjustment? In other words, is the concept of defenses necessary to explain Holt's positive results?

It may seem like heresy to suggest that there are no such phenomena as ego defenses, but the Rorschach data have not unequivocally verified their existence. Lerner and Cooper and their colleagues have shown that their simplified modifications of Schafer's system have some diagnostic and behavioral discriminatory power, but they have yet to demonstrate that their Rorschach measures have convergence with independent assessments of defense mechanisms. Carr's call for comparisons between Rorschach measures and clinical or behavioral assessments of defenses is a crucial next step for the scoring systems developed by Lerner and Cooper. Until such a comparison is made, the status of the Rorschach as a technique for assessing defense mechanisms must be rated "uncertain."

## REFERENCES

Allison, J. (1967). Adaptive regression and intense religious experiences. *Journal of Nervous and Mental Disease, 145,* 452–463.

American Psychiatric Association. (1980). *Diagnostic and statistical manual of mental disorders* (3rd ed.). Washington, DC: Author.

Arnow, E., & Reznikoff, A. (1976). *Rorschach content interpretation.* New York: Grune & Stratton.

Bahnson, J., & Bahnson, T. (1966). The role of the ego-defenses: Denial and repression in the etiology of malignant and neoplasm. *Annals of New York Academy of Sciences, 125,* 826–844.

Baxter, J., Becker, J., & Hooks, W. (1963). Defensive style in the families of schizophrenics and controls. *Journal of Abnormal and Social Psychology, 66,* 512–518.

Beck, S. (1952). *Rorschach's test: III. Advances in interpretation.* New York: Grune & Stratton.

Bellak, L., Hurvich, M., & Gediman, H. (1973). *Ego functions in schizophrenics, neurotics and normals.* New York: Wiley.

Benfari, R., & Calogeras, R. (1968). Levels of cognition and conscience typologies. *Journal of Projective Techniques and Personality Assessment, 32,* 466–474.

Blatt, S., Allison, J., & Feirstein, A. (1969). The capacity to cope with cognitive complexity. *Journal of Personality, 37,* 269–288.

Carr, A. (1987). Borderline defenses and Rorschach responses: A critique of Lerner, Albert, and Walsh. *Journal of Personality Assessment, 51,* 349–354.

Carr, A., Goldstein, E., Hunt, H., & Kernberg, O. (1979). Psychological tests and borderline patients. *Journal of Personality Assessment, 43,* 582–590.

Cooper, S., & Arnow, D. (1986). An object relations view of the borderline defenses: A Rorschach analysis. In M. Kissen (Ed.), *Assessing object relations* (pp. 143–171). New York: International Universities Press.

Cooper, S., Perry, J., & Arnow, D. (1988). An empirical approach to the study of defense mechanisms: I. Reliability and preliminary validity of the Rorschach defense scales. *Journal of Personality Assessment, 52,* 187–203.

Cooper, S., Perry, J., & O'Connell, M. (1991). The Rorschach defense scales: II. Longitudinal perspectives. *Journal of Personality Assessment, 56,* 191–201.

Dudek, S., & Chamberland-Bouhadana, G. (1982). Primary process in creative persons. *Journal of Personality Assessment, 46,* 239–247.

Feirstein, A. (1967). Personality correlates for unrealistic experiences. *Journal of Consulting Psychology, 31,* 387–395.

Freud, S. (1938). The interpretation of dreams. In *The basic writings of Sigmund Freud* (179–549). New York: Modern Library. (Original work published 1900)

Gacono, C. (1988). A Rorschach analysis of object relations and defensive structure and their relationship to narcissism and psychopathy in a group of antisocial offenders. Unpublished doctoral dissertation, United States International University.

Gardner, R., Holtzman, P., Klein, G., Linton, H., & Spence, D. (1959). Cognitive control: A study of individual consistencies in cognitive behavior. *Psychological Issues, Monograph 4.*

Goldberger, L. (1961). Reactions to perceptual isolation and Rorschach manifestations of the primary process. *Journal of Projective Techniques, 25,* 287–302.

Greenberg, N., Ramsay, M., Rakoff, V., & Weiss, A. (1969). Primary process thinking in myxedema psychosis: A case study. *Canadian Journal of Behavioral Science, 1,* 60–67.

Haan, N. (1964). An investigation of the relationship of Rorschach scores, patterns and behavior to coping and defense mechanisms. *Journal of Projective Techniques, 28,* 429–441.

Holt, R. (1977). A method for assessing primary process manifestations and their control in Rorschach responses. In M. Rickers-Ovsiankina (Ed.), *Rorschach psychology* (pp. 375–420). New York: Krieger.

Johnston, M., & Holtzman, P. (1979). *Assessing schizophrenic thinking: A clinical and research instrument for measuring thought disorder.* San Francisco: Jossey-Bass.

Kernberg, O. (1975). *Borderline conditions and pathological narcissisms.* New York: Aronson.

Klopfer, B., Ainsworth, M., Klopfer, W., & Holt, R. (1954). *Developments in the Rorschach technique: Vol. 1. Technique and theory.* Yonkers-on-Hudson, NY: World Book.

Kohut, H., & Wolf, E. (1978). The disorders of the self and their treatment: An outline. *International Journal of Psychoanalysis, 59,* 413–425.

Lerner, P. (1991). *Psychoanalytic interpretation of the Rorschach.* Hillsdale, NJ: Analytic Press.

Lerner, P., Albert, C., & Walsh, M. (1987). The Rorschach assessment of borderline defenses: A concurrent validity study. *Journal of Personality Assessment, 51,* 334–348.

Lerner, P., & Lerner, H. (1980). Rorschach assessment of primitive defenses in borderline personality structure. In J. Kwawer, H. Lerner, P. Lerner, & A. Sugarman (Eds.), *Borderline phenomena and the Rorschach test* (pp. 257–274). New York: International Universities Press.

Lerner, P., Sugarman, A., & Gaughran, J. (1981). Borderline and schizophrenic patients: A comparative study of defensive structure. *Journal of Nervous and Mental Disease, 169,* 705–711.

Levine, M., & Spivak, G. (1964). *The Rorschach index of repressive style.* Springfield, IL: Charles C. Thomas.

Maupin, E. (1965). Individual differences in response to a Zen meditation exercise. *Journal of Consulting Psychology, 29,* 139–145.

Mayman, M. (1970). Reality contact, defense effectiveness, and psychopathology in Rorschach form level scores. In B. Klopfer, M. Meyer, & F. Brawer, *Developments in Rorschach technique* (Vol. III, pp. 11–44). New York: Harcourt, Brace Jovanovich.

McMahon, J. (1964). *The relationship between "overinclusive" and primary process thought in a normal and a schizophrenic population.* Unpublished doctoral dissertation, New York University.

Molish, B., & Beck, S. (1958). Psychoanalytic concepts and principles discernible in projective tests: 3. Mechanisms of defense in schizophrenic reaction types as evaluated by the Rorschach tests. *American Journal of Orthopsychiatry, 28,* 47–60.

Murray, J., & Russ, S. (1981). Adaptive regression and types of cognitive flexibility. *Journal of Personality Assessment, 45,* 59–65.

Perry, J., & Cooper, S. (1985). Psychodynamics, symptoms and outcomes in borderline and antisocial personality disorders and bipolar type II affective disorder. In T. McGlashan (Ed.), *The borderline: Current empirical research* (pp. 63–78). Washington, DC: American Psychiatric Press.

Perry, J., & Cooper, S. (1989). An empirical study of defense mechanisms: I. Clinical interview and life vignette ratings. *Archives of General Psychiatry, 46,* 444–452.

Pine, F. (1962). Creativity and primary process: Sample variations. *Journal of Nervous and Mental Disease, 134,* 506–511.

Pine, F., & Holt, R. (1960). Creativity and primary process: A study of adaptive regression. *Journal of Abnormal and Social Psychology, 61,* 370–379.

Powers, W., & Hamlin, R. (1955). Relationship between diagnostic category and deviant verbalizations on the Rorschach. *Journal of Consulting Psychology, 19,* 120–124.

Rabkin, J. (1967). Psychoanalytic assessment of change in organization of thought after psychotherapy. Unpublished doctoral dissertation, New York University.

Rapaport, D. (1946). *Diagnostic psychological testing: Vol. II.* Chicago: Year Book.

Russ, S. (1980). Primary process integration on the Rorschach and achievement in children. *Journal of Personality Assessment, 44,* 338–344.

Saretsky, T. (1966). Effects of chlorpromazine on primary process thought manifestations. *Journal of Abnormal Psychology, 71,* 247–252.

Schachtel, E. (1945). Subjective definitions of the Rorschach test situation and their effect on test performance. *Psychiatry, 8,* 419–448.

Schafer, R. (1948). *The clinical application of psychological tests.* New York: International Universities Press.

Schafer, R. (1954). *Psychoanalytic interpretation in Rorschach testing.* New York: Grune & Stratton.

Spitzer, R., Endicott, J., & Robbins, E. (1975). Research diagnostic criteria: Rationale and reliability. *Archives of General Psychiatry, 35,* 773–782.

Stolorow, R., & Lachmann, F. (1980). *The psychoanalysis of developmental arrest.* New York: International Universities Press.

Van-Der Keshet, Y. (1988). Anorexic patients and ballet students: A Rorschach analysis. Unpublished doctoral dissertation, University of Toronto.

Viglione, D., Brager, R., & Haller, N. (1991). Psychoanalytic interpretation of the Rorschach: Do we have better hieroglyphics? *Journal of Personality Assessment, 57,* 1–9.

Watkins, J., & Stauffacher, J. (1952). An index of pathological thinking in the Rorschach. *Journal of Projective Techniques, 16,* 276–286.

Wright, N., & Abbey, D. (1965). Perceptual deprivation tolerance and adequacy of defense. *Perceptual Motor Skills, 20,* 35–38.

Zimet, C., & Fine, H. (1965). Primary and secondary process thinking in two types of schizophrenia. *Journal of Projective Techniques and Personality Assessment, 29,* 93–99.

# 13

## A Review of the Defense
## Mechanism Rating Scales

### J. CHRISTOPHER PERRY AND
### MARIANNE E. KARDOS

The scientific study of psychodynamics is a difficult challenge for re-searchers. Because the assessment of dynamic phenomena requires infer-ence, the measures must be capable of guiding the observer in arriving at each inference and/or justifying that an inference is warranted. The usual alternative is between a measure that is easily learned and reliably ap-plied, but not truly dynamic, versus a measure that attempts to assess dy-namic phenomena at too deep a level, but fails to do so reliably. However, defense mechanisms lend themselves to study more readily than other as-pects of dynamics, such as intrapsychic conflict or transference. This is because patterns of affect, behavior, and cognition indicating an underly-ing defense are less complex or require less inference than other dynamic phenomena. According to Vaillant, defense mechanisms are ". . . largely unconscious regulatory mechanisms that allow individuals to reduce cog-nitive dissonance and to minimize sudden changes in internal and exter-nal environments by altering how these events are perceived" (Vaillant, 1985, p. 171). Observing defensive phenomena provides a window into other intrapsychic processes and helps determine links between them and external behavior and adaptation. This chapter will review research on de-fense mechanisms that has used the same measurement instrument, the Defense Mechanisms Rating Scales (DMRS), developed by the first au-thor (JCP). The review of defenses encompasses their relationship to men-tal disorders (Axis I and II diagnoses), psychiatric symptoms, and global adaptation.

### HISTORY OF THE DEFENSE MECHANISMS
### RATING SCALES

The first author (JCP) developed an interest in defense mechanisms while studying with Dr. George Vaillant, a pioneer in the empirical study of defenses and adaptation (see Vaillant, 1971, 1976, 1977). Dr. Vaillant's rating of defenses was based on a list of definitions that were applied to selected life vignettes resulting in a rank ordering of a given subject's most important defenses. The first author (JCP) set out to devise a rating system that would be applicable to a wider variety of data, especially dynamic interviews and would incorporate prototypical examples to aid raters.

Work on the Defense Mechanism Rating Scales (DMRS) was begun in 1980 resulting in a suitable instrument by the third version. Initially, 22 defense mechanisms were chosen representing two of three levels proposed by Vaillant (1971) (immature and neurotic) and the borderline level of organization proposed by Kernberg (1975). They were tested on a sample of young adults with personality and affective disorders. The mature defense level was subsequently added in the fourth edition of the DMRS to yield a total of 30 defenses. Each defense was given a definition, a description of its intrapsychic function (how it protects the subject, and what it trades off), a list of near neighbor defenses and how to differentiate them and, finally, a rating scale itself. The scale has three points anchored by examples to make the qualitative observation of whether the subject does not use, probably uses, or definitely uses the defense. In the fifth edition, directions have been added to make quantitative ratings of defenses from tapes and transcripts by identifying each defense as it is used. In addition, the preparation of the fifth edition employed an editorial process in which several defense researchers (Drs. Michael Bond, Steven Cooper, George Vaillant) suggested emendations to yield a consensus instrument reduced to 27 defenses. Finally, some terms were updated by substituting terms with functional implications for older terms with diagnostic implications: Borderline and narcissistic defenses were renamed major and minor image-distorting defenses, respectively.

The DMRS is organized around the concept of a hierarchy of the adaptiveness of defenses. Defenses are presented in a particular order, based on early empirical study with the DMRS. The most maladaptive defenses are rated first, given that they often contain the most dramatic and obvious behavioral referents. Although the ordering and grouping of defenses warrants further empirical refinement, the DMRS divides the defenses among the following seven defense levels (presented in Table 13–1), within each of which the defenses share some functional properties:

1. The *action defenses* temporarily bypass conflicts by releasing feelings and impulses directly through impulsive action, often toward

**TABLE 13–1**
**Hierarchical Listing of Defense Mechanism Rating Scales**
**(Fifth Edition, 1990)**

Mature Defenses
  Affiliation
  Altruism
  Anticipation
  Humor
  Self-Assertion
  Self-Observation
  Sublimation
  Suppression
Obsessional Defenses
  Isolation
  Intellectualization
  Undoing
Other Neurotic Defenses
  Repression
  Dissociation
  Reaction Formation
  Displacement
Minor Image-Distorting Defenses (Narcissistic)
  Omnipotence
  Idealization
  Devaluation
Disavowal Defenses
  Denial
  Projection
  Rationalization
  Fantasy (not a disavowel defense but scored at same level)
Major Image-Distorting Defenses (Borderline)
  Splitting (Object Images)
  Splitting (Self Images)
  Projective Identification
Action Defenses
  Acting Out
  Passive-Aggression
  Hypochondriasis

others. They include acting out, passive-aggression, and hypochondriasis (help-rejecting complaining).

2. The *major image-distorting defenses* (formerly called borderline) distort self and object images to conform totally with a particular meaning or emotional state. They include splitting of self and others' images, and projective identification. The distinction between borderline and narcissistic defenses was supported by previous factor analysis (Perry & Cooper, 1986a).

3. The *disavowal defenses* disavow subjective experiences, affects, or impulses to preserve self-image. They include denial (minor or neurotic denial), projection, and rationalization.

   *Autistic fantasy* also is associated with the same overall level of adaptiveness as the disavowal defenses, although it does not share the disavowal function.

4. The *minor image-distorting defenses* (narcissistic) distort aspects of self or others' images to regulate self-esteem and mood. The distortions are not as complete and widespread as in the major image-distorting defenses. They include omnipotence, primitive idealization, and devaluation. In earlier work (Perry & Cooper, 1986a), this group also included mood-incongruent denial (manic or depressive denial).

5. *Other neurotic defenses* keep conflict and stressors out of conscious awareness and include two groups. The so-called hysterical defenses of repression and dissociation, which keep emotional conflict and stress out of conscious awareness with or without allowing its symptomatic expression. The other neurotic defenses of reaction formation and displacement allow the expression of emotional conflicts through changing by altering the original impulse or affect, or the target.

6. The *obsessional defenses* neutralize or minimize affects without distorting associated external reality. They include isolation, intellectualization, and undoing.

7. The *mature defenses* maximize gratification and allow the conscious awareness of feelings, ideas, and their consequences, while promoting an optimal balance between conflicting motives. They include five defenses originally proposed by Vaillant (1971), anticipation, altruism, humor, sublimation, and suppression. Three additional defenses were added, suggested by the DSM-III-R subcommittee on defenses, including affiliation, self-assertion, and self-observation.

## THE DEFENSE MECHANISMS RATING SCALES, FIFTH EDITION

The DMRS manual contains descriptions of 27 individual defense mechanisms, with definitions, explanations of how each defense functions, and ways to differentiate it from similar presentation defenses (e.g., splitting vs. projective identification vs. devaluation). Defenses are qualitatively rated as (0) absent, (1) probable, or (2) definite. Each scale is anchored by prototypical examples of the specific defense, thus adding ostensive examples to the definition. However, because an exhaustive list of examples is not possible, and even a large list would prove cumbersome, the ratings will always involve some degree of inference.

## Qualitative versus Quantitative Scoring

The DMRS can yield either qualitative or quantitative ratings. The qualitative method, representing the original scoring system of the DMRS, was designed for rating videotapes of one hour, initial, dynamic assessment interviews for whether a subject used each defense or not. A defense rating of definite versus probable would depend on the amount of supporting evidence in the interview, based on the clarity or frequency of the examples. Only current use of a defense is considered, given that individuals may have used a defense during an earlier time period but no longer use it. Thus, along with the observations of defenses in use during the interview itself, scoring directions allow use of historical data from only the most recent 2-year period.

The qualitative method does not assess the frequency of use of a defense, and thus is not designed to measure changes in defensive functioning. That is achieved by the quantitative method. This method counts the number of instances in which a defense is identified in an interview, irrespective of whether the particular example is deemed a "probable" or "definite" use of the defense. Because a defense may be overlooked on first pass, it is imperative that the rater have a written transcript of the interview, therapy session, or life anecdote being scored. In the best of circumstances, both a videotape or audiotape and a transcript of the interview would be available. While watching the interview, the rater marks down each particular defense used and the location in the text where the defense begins and ends. A less accurate but acceptable method is for the rater to make a verbatim transcript upon listening to the taped interview, and then rate it. In either case, after completing the ratings, the investigator counts the number of instances each defense occurred and divides it by the total number of defenses rated in the session, thus obtaining the proportion or percentage of all defenses rated attributable to each defense. The advantage of the quantitative method is that it permits quantitative comparisons of defensive functioning within individuals over time, thus allowing the assessment of change, as well as comparison between groups of individuals.

## Overall Defensive Functioning

After scoring each interview by either the qualitative or quantitative method, the subject's overall maturity score may be calculated. Each defense is assigned to one of seven hierarchically arranged groups, according to the level of maturity or adaptiveness. Level 1, the action defenses, is least adaptive, while Level 7, the mature defenses, is the most adaptive. Each defense is then multiplied by a weight that is the number of the level (1 to 7). Then the weights of the individual defense mechanisms are summed, and the total is divided by the total number of defenses rated, thereby yielding a weighted average score, called the Overall Defensive Functioning (ODF) score, ranging from 1 to 7. This was formerly named the Overall Defense Maturity Score. The term *maturity* however, is not meant to imply a certain developmental order of acquiring defenses. The process that leads individuals to "specialize" in using certain defenses is an open question for empirical investigation. While the term maturity has been used because of historical convenience, it seems more appropriate to replace it with the term *functioning* to avoid confusion with the developmental term.

## Reliability

There are reliability estimates for dynamic interviews, life vignettes, and psychotherapy sessions. Perry and Cooper (1989) studied the reliability of the qualitative method using two groups each with three master's-level students. Each rater independently and blindly rated 46 videotaped 50-minute initial dynamic interviews. Subsequently each group met, discussed the individual ratings, and established consensus ratings. For the individual ratings, the median intraclass $R$ $(I_R)$ was .36 (range .11 to .59); whereas for the group consensus ratings, the reliability was generally higher: median $I_R$ = .57 (range .35 to .79). Higher reliabilities were obtained when conceptually and empirically related defenses were summed into groups or levels of defenses (e.g., passive-aggression, hypochondriasis, acting out = action defenses). These defense summary scores yielded median intraclass $R$'s of .53 and .74 for the individual and consensus ratings, respectively. In general, irrespective of whether defenses were considered individually or in groups, consensus ratings proved to be more reliable than individual ratings.

In a pilot psychotherapy study, experienced raters scored one or two consecutive therapy sessions from eight patients using the quantitative method (Perry, Kardos, & Pagano, 1993). Raters listened to the audiotapes and scored accompanying typed transcripts. Each session was rated independently by two raters, who then met and reached a consensus.

Only consensus ratings were used for further data analysis. Interrater reliabilities were obtained for the individual scores, but not for the consensus scores. The interrater reliability for the individual defense scores (based on 11 therapy sessions) resulted in a median intraclass $R$ of .70 (range .43 to .83). However, if only the last 7 sessions rated were taken into account, the reliability figures were all $> .70$, reflecting most probably increased cross-calibration and experience. The intraclass $R$ for the Overall Defensive Functioning scores was .89. Taken together, these figures suggest that higher reliabilities are obtainable with the quantitative than with the qualitative method.

In a second reliability study, transcripts alone, from six therapy sessions, were rated independently by two raters. Four trained, experienced raters scored one or two sessions, while a fifth rater scored each session. The interrater reliability yielded a median intraclass $R$ of .75 (range .58 to .92) (Perry et al., 1993). Given that four of the five raters in this study first participated in the previous reliability study, it suggests that increased rating experience and learning from the consensus process may improve reliability. Of course, this does not necessarily imply increased validity, unless investigators ensure that there is no rater drift away from the DMRS manual.

## THE HIERARCHY OF DEFENSES

Vaillant (1971) first proposed that there are four groups of defenses, in order of increasing adaptiveness: psychotic, immature, neurotic, and mature. He did not include the "borderline" level defenses described by Kernberg (1975). He tested the idea of this hierarchy using two longitudinal samples, one of college males (Vaillant, 1976), the other of inner-city boys (Vaillant, Bond, & Vaillant, 1986), with both samples followed into mid-adulthood. In both studies, there were positive correlations between mature defenses and adult adjustment in such areas as work, marriage, and physical health, and negative correlations between immature defenses and adjustment.

Perry and Cooper (1989) also found significant correlations between defense mechanisms measured by the DMRS and global functioning. Table 13–2 summarizes these findings on the association between the groups or levels of defenses at intake and other measures of adjustment: the Global Assessment Scale (GAS) (Endicott, Spitzer, & Fleiss, 1976) at intake and follow-up, and impairment over follow-up in two factors of psychosocial role functioning. The correlations were in the predicted direction, and furthermore the findings at intake were maintained over 1 to

**TABLE 13–2**
**Summary Defense Scales**

**(Spearman correlations between individual defenses and GAS and psychosocial role functioning over one year of follow-up; $n = 53$)**

|  | GAS | | Mean Score over One Year | |
|---|---|---|---|---|
|  | | | Factor I Occupation, | Factor II Spouse/Lover, Friends, |
|  | Intake $n = 76$ | Follow-Up $n = 53$ | Relatives, Satisfaction | Socializing, Recreation |
| Action | −.38*** | −.49*** | .41** | .29* |
| Borderline | −.30* | −.34** | .40** | .22 |
| Disavowal | −.19+ | −.12 | .27* | .06 |
| Narcissistic | −.14 | −.22 | .23+ | .13 |
| Obsessional | .21+ | .20 | −.24+ | −.25+ |
| Overall Defense Maturity Scale | .38*** | .37** | −.39** | −.28* |

*Note:* From "An Empirical Study of Defense Mechanisms" by J. C. Perry and S. H. Cooper, 1989, *Archives of General Psychiatry, 46,* 444–452. Copyright 1989 by the American Medical Association. Reprinted by permission.

Psychosocial Role Impairment: + direction = greater impairment.

$^+p < .10$; $^*p < .05$; $^{**}p < .01$; $^{***}p < .001$.

2 years of follow-up. Generally, both action and major image-distorting (borderline) level defenses were associated with lower GAS and higher impairment in both psychosocial role factors. Both disavowal and minor image-distorting (narcissistic) level defenses also correlated negatively with GAS and with impairment in Factor I role functioning (with occupation, relatives, and satisfaction). The obsessional defenses correlated positively with GAS and with lower levels of role impairment, demonstrating that in a sample in which many individuals have personality disorders, obsessional defenses may have some positive adaptive value. Mature defenses were not rated in this report.

Several other studies support the hypothesis that defenses may be hierarchically arranged in order of their adaptive value (Battista, 1982; Bond, Gardner, Christian, & Sigal, 1983; Jacobson et al., 1986; Vaillant & Drake, 1985). Although the preceding studies employed different methods for rating defenses, involved variations in the definitions of individual defenses, used different measures of adaptation and mental health, and employed different types of samples and different follow-up times, they show consistent results. Elsewhere, Perry (1993) compared the studies' findings and calculated the median correlation between each group of defenses and adult adaptation, regardless of how it was assessed.

The median correlations between global measures of mental health and large groups of defenses were as follows: psychotic (median $-.57$), immature (median $-.28$) and image-distorting defenses ($-.12$), neurotic (.04), and mature (.33), respectively. Interestingly, within the neurotic level defenses, the obsessional defenses, which keep ideas intact while minimizing affect, appear to have somewhat more adaptive value (median .14) than the other neurotic defenses (median $-.05$).

Despite using different assessment methods, Perry and Cooper (1989) and Vaillant (1976) assess 10 defenses in common. When each defense is arranged in order of its correlation with GAS (Perry & Cooper, 1989) or adult adjustment (Vaillant, 1976), the order of the defenses is quite similar between the two studies (Spearman $r = .79$). This further suggests that both studies measured the same phenomena, a conclusion that strengthens the construct validity of the hierarchical adaptive value of defenses.

## CONCURRENT VALIDITY OF THE DMRS

One study compared defense ratings from the DMRS with the Defense Style Questionnaire (DSQ), a self-report measure of defenses developed by Michael Bond (Bond et al., 1983). The DSQ questionnaire was administered to 156 subjects, each of whom had an independent assessment of their defense mechanisms by raters scoring initial videotaped interviews using the DMRS (Bond, Perry, Gautiec, Goldenberg, Oppenheimer, & Simand, 1989). The results showed positive correlations between Styles 1 (maladaptive), 2 (image distorting), and 3 (self-sacrificing), of the DSQ and the immature level (action) defenses of the DMRS, as well as with low scores on the Health Sickness Rating Scale. At the same time, the maladaptive style of the DSQ was negatively correlated with the mature-level defenses of the DMRS.

## DEFENSES AND PROSPECTIVELY MEASURED SYMPTOMS

After assessing defenses at intake, Perry and Cooper (1989) prospectively assessed symptoms on multiple occasions over 1 to 2 years of follow-up. Subjective mood symptoms by the POMS (McNair, Lorr, & Droppleman, 1971) were positively correlated with action and major image-distorting (borderline) defenses, and negatively correlated with obsessional defenses. Objectively rated symptoms of anxiety and depression using the Hamilton Scales (Hamilton, 1959, 1960) followed a similar pattern with one addition. Whereas the disavowal defenses did not correlate with subjectively rated mood symptoms, they did correlate with mood symptoms when rated by interview, confirming that disavowal defenses protect the individual from awareness of affective experiences that are nonetheless still observable to others.

The action defenses had the highest correlations with alcohol, drug abuse, and antisocial symptoms. The disavowal defenses correlated with alcohol abuse and antisocial symptoms, whereas minor image-distorting (narcissistic) defenses correlated with antisocial symptoms. By contrast, obsessional defenses correlated negatively with all affective and impulse symptoms. Although these findings generally follow the hierarchy of defenses, they also suggest some differential relationships between defenses and specific impulses. The association between minor image-distorting (narcissistic) defenses and antisocial behaviors (and antisocial personality disorder, as noted later in this chapter), suggest that narcissistic and antisocial symptoms share some common psychopathology. Second, the association between action and disavowal defenses, on the one hand, and alcohol abuse and antisocial behaviors, on the other, is expected, given that antisocial behaviors and alcohol abuse often occur together. Similarly, it is a common clinical finding that alcohol abusers have a tendency to deny or rationalize the occurrence or extent of their drinking. Finally, it is noteworthy that major image-distorting defenses correlated with subjective distress and objectively rated mood symptoms, but not with objectively rated antisocial and substance abuse symptoms. This suggests that major image-distorting defenses serve some different functions than the other near neighbor defenses (action and disavowal) in the hierarchy of adaptation.

## DEFENSE MECHANISMS AND
## DESCRIPTIVE DIAGNOSIS

### Defenses and Axis I Diagnosis

Perry and Cooper (1986a) found that chronic depression with a duration of 2 years or longer, as assessed by the Diagnostic Interview Schedule, was associated with the action defenses of passive-aggression and hypochondriasis, and with the minor image-distorting defense of devaluation. Using subsequent follow-along data on the same sample, Perry (1990b) found that the action defenses were associated with the duration of dysthymia. The preceding findings were replicated on a separate sample of individuals with DSM-III-R dysthymia (Bloch, Shear, Markowitz, Leon, & Perry, 1993). They found that the same three defenses plus acting out and projection were more common in adults with dysthymia than with panic disorder. The convergence of these independent studies suggests that chronic depression is associated with conflicted affects and motives surrounding issues of hostility and dependency and with defenses that misdirect these by turning anger toward the self, reproaching oneself and perceiving reproach by others, much as postulated by Freud, Abraham, and other early psychoanalysts.

Using the same sample described previously (Perry & Cooper, 1986b, 1989), Perry (1988) investigated the relationship between defense mechanisms and recurrent depression. Subjects were reinterviewed at 6-month intervals over a median length of 2 years' follow-up. Systematic interviews were conducted about intercurrent life events and how subjects coped with them. These were subsequently rated for defenses, blind to diagnostic information. Greater reliance on action and major image-distorting (borderline) defenses was associated with higher rates of recurrence for acute major depressive disorder and more generally for exacerbations of depressive symptoms. In addition, life events that were rated higher on subjective stressfulness or on objectively rated long-term contextual threat were followed by higher rates of recurrence or exacerbation in depression. This suggests that stressful events may trigger the recurrence or exacerbation of depression, whereas the psychological vulnerability to recurrence is reflected in maladaptive defenses that lower the individual's resistance to stress.

In the same study, use of major image-distorting defenses in response to life events was associated with having psychotic and psychoticlike symptoms over follow-up (Perry, 1988). This suggests that defenses such as splitting, which keep contradictory self and object images rigidly apart, may leave the individual vulnerable to the intrusion of hostile impulses and memories in the externalized guise of hallucinations, ideas of reference, and illusions.

Perry (1990) also looked at a possible relationship between defense mechanisms and duration of time spent ill with episodes of affective and anxiety disorders. The action defenses correlated positively with the proportion of time spent in dysthymia, as noted earlier. Major image-distorting (borderline) defenses correlated with time spent in panic disorder episodes, whereas both major image-distorting and action defenses correlated positively with the duration of agoraphobia. On the other hand, the action defenses correlated negatively with the duration of manic episodes, and obsessional defenses correlated with the duration of hypomanic episodes. Obsessional defenses also correlated negatively with time spent in major depression and panic disorder.

These latter findings are consistent with the construct of obsessional defenses, since these function to minimize the intensity of unpleasant affective experience.

### Defenses and Axis II Diagnosis

Perry and Cooper (1986a) examined the differential relationship between defenses and either borderline (BPD) or antisocial (ASP) personality disorder. First, they examined the eight borderline-level defenses that Kernberg postulated represented a single level of personality organization (1975). Alternatively, Perry and Cooper hypothesized that these defenses represented two separate dimensions. A factor analysis did separate into two factors or dimensions. The first, so-called borderline factor, included splitting of self-images, splitting of others' images, projective identification, and bland denial. The second, so-called narcissistic factor, included omnipotence, primitive idealization, devaluation, and mood-incongruent denial (manic or depressive denial). These dimensions were later renamed major and minor image-distorting defenses, respectively, to emphasize their functional aim rather than their diagnostic association (Perry, 1993). Bland denial and mood-incongruent denial were subsequently dropped because they occurred with very low frequency.

Perry and Cooper (1986a) found that borderline psychopathology (as measured by the Borderline Personality Disorder Scale) was significantly correlated with the major image-distorting defenses and action defenses (acting out, passive aggression, and hypochondriasis). Antisocial personality symptoms correlated with the minor image-distorting defenses and disavowal defenses (denial, projection, rationalization). The findings were consistent with literature on borderline patients. They also suggested that antisocial psychopathology overlaps with narcissistic psychopathology, in the same vein as findings by Vaillant and Drake (1985). Yet, contrary to expectation, and to Drake's and Vaillant's findings as well, Perry and Cooper did not find a significant association between antisocial personality and action defenses. However, because the defense ratings were based on a single dynamic interview, it is possible that someone who also uses disavowal defenses may disavow some evidence of his or her acting out and other action defenses.

Despite the associations, Perry and Cooper (1986a) and others (Vaillant, 1985; Skodol & Perry, 1993) have not found that Axis II disorders could be discriminated solely on the basis of defenses, which is consistent with the conclusion that defenses and Axis II are separate constructs.

## FUTURE DIRECTIONS FOR RESEARCH

### Relationship between Defenses and Physical Health or Illness

The relationship between coping and the development and course of illness and its treatment is a major area for exploration. Recently, Perry and colleagues have started to examine the defenses of patients who have undergone bone marrow transplantation for leukemia, to determine whether defense mechanisms have a role to play in an individual's survival from such drastic treatment of life-threatening illness. Study of this population has the unique property of examining the importance of psychological defenses during a period in which immunological defenses are nonexistent. This study was inspired by a study done in Germany, by Schwilk, Kachele, and colleagues (1989), who examined the defenses found in those who survived bone marrow transplantation. Although the study is not completed, it is hypothesized that the overall hierarchy of defenses will hold true regarding what is and what is not adaptive in such extreme life-threatening circumstances. Whether or not certain defenses have a differential relationship to survival or adaptation during the recovery period also remains to be seen.

### Defenses and Psychotherapy Research

In an ongoing study of a small sample of patients, the authors and colleagues have followed the course of defense mechanisms over 1 to 2 years of psychotherapy. Defenses were measured in five consecutive sessions at the beginning of therapy, at 1, and at 2 years into the therapy, respectively. Defenses were rated from audiotapes of therapy sessions accompanied by transcripts. Some of the questions posed by this pilot study were whether defense mechanisms show short-term stability and whether they change over 1 to 2 years. Whereas the answer for the latter question is yet not available, it appears that in the very short term, from one therapy session to the next, one week apart, defense mechanisms are highly stable. Specifically the Overall Defensive Functioning Score demonstrated a Pearson $r$ of .90 between two contiguous sessions (Perry et al., 1993).

Defenses have a fortunate characteristic from a research point of view. Because they are a basic building block of psychodynamic psychopathology, they function as markers of the patient's functioning in psychotherapy, which is useful for process research. However, when summed up over a session or series of sessions, they also serve as an outcome measure representing how the person is doing over that same time period. In the same psychotherapy pilot study previously noted, the authors have begun to examine the relationship between defense mechanisms, motives (wishes and fears), conflicts, therapeutic alliance, and outcome assessed by other measures of psychopathology. The study will also examine the relationship between the patient's defenses and the therapist's interventions and subsequent outcome.

This pilot data will help us develop hypotheses about some old questions. Is there a differential relationship between the patient's defenses used at one point in a session and is it more effective for the therapist to address the defense or the underlying motive? To what extent does defensive function change in a successful therapy? As the use of less adaptive defenses decreases, are they supplanted by specific defenses that are more adaptive? Is there a differential relationship between the prominent constellations of defenses (such as the major or minor image-distorting defenses) and the mix of therapeutic techniques that predict successful outcomes? To what extent is the maturity of defenses at the start of therapy related to the patient's ability to form and maintain a therapeutic alliance? Although questions such as these will require a generation of research, the advent of methods such as the DMRS makes it possible to address these clinically important issues. Whereas recent papers describe how clinicians should deal with patients' specific defenses (Perry & Cooper, 1987; Vaillant, 1992), research on defenses in psychotherapy also should provide an empirical foundation for what is now left to clinical acumen.

### Should an Axis for Defenses Be Included in DSM-IV?

Early critiques of both DSM-III (Karasu & Skodol, 1980) and DSM-III-R (Cooper & Michels, 1988) noted that the diagnostic systems did not include the assessment of dynamics that would be helpful in guiding treatment planning. In the preparation for DSM-IV, Allen Frances, MD, Chairman of the DSM-IV Task Force, appointed an ad hoc committee on defense mechanisms* to advise the DSM-IV Multiaxial Issues Work Group on this issue. The ad hoc committee proposed an optional sixth axis for DSM-IV consisting of up to seven of the most prominent or frequent individual defense mechanisms and up to three of the most prominent defense levels that a patient uses. The rationale for the Defense Axis is presented fully elsewhere (Skodol & Perry, 1993).

---

*Members: Michael Bond, MD, Steven Cooper, PhD, Bram Fridhandler, PhD, Mardi Horowitz, MD (Co-Chair), J. Christopher Perry, MPH, MD (Co-Chair), and George Vaillant, MD.

The ad hoc committee then conducted a field trial of the proposed axis in three sites, Massachusetts, New York, and Norway, to test the feasibility and reliability of the axis. The DMRS served as the basic training tool for the field trial, with slight modifications of some defense definitions by the committee. The data suggests that clinicians can learn to use the axis with some training. Although reliability is lower than in a research study, the overall kappa values are fair to moderately good, which is very acceptable for a clinical field trial. The proposed Defense Axis has been accepted as an optional axis for DSM-IV, listed in the Appendix. This should provide an incentive for further attention to the usefulness of defense mechanisms for the planning and conduct of treatment.

## CONCLUSION

It is exciting that the idea of defense mechanisms, which Freud originated 100 years ago, is robust enough for the scientific study of defenses still to show acceleration. As in all empirical science, scientific tools are necessary to bring ideas to measurement and testing. The DMRS is one such tool. It has the advantage that it may be applied to any type of clinical data and yields quantitative scores. The rating process still requires judgment as well as observation, but the DMRS manual helps guide or justify the observer's inferences to protect against wild speculation. This review of the research suggests that the DMRS is playing a useful scientific role in addressing clinically meaningful questions. With increasing scientific attention, and inclusion in the diagnostic system, we can look forward to increasing our understanding of the effects of defenses and to improving our ability to facilitate more adaptive defensive functioning in our patients.

## REFERENCES

Battista, J. R. (1982). Empirical test of Vaillant's hierarchy of ego functions. *American Journal of Psychiatry, 139,* 356–357.

Bloch, A. L., Shear, M. K., Markowitz, J. C., Leon, A. C., & Perry, J. C. (1993). An empirical study of defense mechanisms in dysthymia. *American Journal of Psychiatry, 150,* 1194–1198.

Bond, M., Gardner, S. T., Christian, J., & Sigal, J. J. (1983). Empirical study of self-rated defense styles. *Archives of General Psychiatry, 40,* 333–338.

Bond, M., Perry, J. C., Gautier, M., Goldenberg, M., Oppenheimer, J., & Simand, J. (1989). Validating the self-report of defense styles. *Journal of Personality Disorders, 3*(2), 101–112.

Cooper, A. M., & Michels, R. (1988). Diagnostic and statistical manual of mental disorders (3rd ed., rev.) [book review]. *American Journal of Psychiatry, 145,* 1300–1301.

Endicott, J., Spitzer, R. L., & Fleiss, J. L. (1976). The Global Assessment Scale. *Archives of General Psychiatry, 33,* 766–771.

Hamilton, M. (1959). The rating of clinical anxiety. *British Journal of Medical Psychology, 32,* 30–55.

Hamilton, M. (1960). A rating scale for depression. *Journal of Neurological and Neurosurgical Psychiatry, 23,* 56–62.

Jacobson, A. M., Beardslee, W., Hauser, S. T., Noam, G. G., Powers, S. I., Houlihan, J., & Rider, E. (1986). Evaluating ego defense mechanisms using clinical interviews: An empirical study of adolescent diabetic and psychiatric patients. *Journal of Adolescence, 9,* 303–319.

Karasu, B. T., & Skodol, A. E. (1980). VI[th] Axis for DSM-III: Psychodynamic evaluation. *American Journal of Psychiatry, 137,* 607–610.

Kernberg, O. F. (1975). *Borderline conditions and pathological narcissism.* New York: Aronson.

McNair, D. M., Lorr, M., & Droppleman, L. F. (1971). *Profile of mood states.* San Diego, Educational and Industrial Testing Service.

Perry, J. C. (1988). A prospective study of life stress, defenses, psychotic symptoms, and depression in borderline and antisocial personality disorders and bipolar type II affective disorder. *Journal of Personality Disorders, 2*(1), 49–59.

Perry, J. C. (1990). Psychological defense mechanisms and the study of affective and anxiety disorders. In J. D. Maser & C. R. Cloninger (Eds.), *Comorbidity of mood and anxiety disorders* (pp. 545–562). Washington, DC: American Psychiatric Press.

Perry, J. C. (1993). The study of defense mechanisms and their effects. In N. Miller, L. Luborsky, J. Barber, & J. Docherty (Eds.), *Psychodynamic treatment research: A handbook for clinical practice.* New York: Basic Books.

Perry, J. C., & Cooper, S. H. (1986a). Preliminary report on conflicts and defenses associated with borderline personality disorder. *Journal of the American Psychoanalytic Association, 34,* 863–893.

Perry, J. C., & Cooper, S. H. (1986b). What do cross-sectional measures of defense mechanisms predict? In G. E. Vaillant (Ed.), *Empirical studies of the ego mechanisms of defense* (pp. 31–46). Washington, DC: American Psychiatric Press.

Perry, J. C., & Cooper, S. H. (1987). Empirical studies of psychological defense mechanisms. In R. Michels & J. O. Cavenar (Eds.), *Psychiatry, 1*(30). New York: J. B. Lippincott, and Basic Books, 1–19.

Perry, J. C., & Cooper, S. H. (1989). An empirical study of defense mechanisms. *Archives of General Psychiatry, 46,* 444–452.

Perry, J. C., Kardos, M. E., & Pagano, C. J. (1993). The study of defenses in psychotherapy using the Defense Mechanism Rating Scales (DMRS). In

U. Hentschel & W. Ehlers (Eds.), *The concept of defense mechanisms in contemporary psychology: Theoretical, research, and clinical perspectives.* New York: Springer.

Schwilk, C., & Kachele, H. (1989, September). *Defense mechanisms during severe illness.* Paper delivered at the third European Conference on Psychotherapy Research, Bern.

Skodol, A., & Perry, J. C. (1993). Should an axis for defense mechanisms be included in DSM-IV? *Comprehensive Psychiatry, 34,* 108–119.

Vaillant, G. E. (1971). Theoretical hierarchy of adaptive ego mechanisms. *Archives of General Psychiatry, 24,* 107–118.

Vaillant, G. (1976). Natural history of male psychological health: The relation of choice of ego mechanisms of defense to adult adjustment. *Archives of General Psychiatry, 33,* 535–545.

Vaillant, G. E. (1977). *Adaptation to life.* Boston: Little Brown.

Vaillant, G. E. (1985). An empirically derived hierarchy of adaptive mechanisms and its usefulness as a potential diagnostic axis. *Acta Psychiatrica Scandinavica,* Supplementum 319, *71,* 171–180.

Vaillant, G. E. (1992). The beginning of wisdom is never calling a patient a borderline; or, The clinical management of immature defenses in the treatment of individuals with personality disorders. *Journal of Psychotherapy Practice and Research, 1*(2), 117–134.

Vaillant, G. E., & Drake, R. E. (1985). Maturity of ego defenses in relation to DSM-III Axis II personality disorder. *Archives of General Psychiatry, 42,* 597–601.

Vaillant, G. E., Bond, M., & Vaillant, C. O. (1986). An empirically validated hierarchy of defense mechanisms. *Archives of General Psychiatry, 43,* 786–794.

# 14

# The Inventory of Defense-Related Behaviors—An Approach to Measuring Defense Mechanisms in Psychotherapy
## A Preliminary Report

STEPHEN F. BAUER AND
LAWRENCE H. ROCKLAND

In this chapter, we present a new scale for measuring defense mechanisms as they reveal themselves in patient behaviors in the clinical interview. The scale consists of 60 behaviors that are associated with 20 defenses; there are three scale behaviors related to each defense mechanism. We hoped that by asking raters to evaluate the presence or absence of clinical behaviors, rather than of inferred defense mechanisms, we could obtain better interrater reliability and minimize halo effects.

We have omitted most of the high-level mature defenses because we feel that they are either derivatives of more classical defenses or are better conceptualized as ego functions than as defenses (e.g., anticipation, humor).

We have called the scale the Inventory of Defense-Related Behaviors (IDRB). Here we describe the development of the IDRB, its properties, and some preliminary findings.

The authors wish to thank Francine S. Mandel, PhD, for statistical consultation. Dr. Mandel is Research Statistician, Department of Research, North Shore University Hospital and Assistant Professor of Biostatistics, School of Public Health, Cornell University Medical College.

This work was done in conjunction with the Psychotherapy of Borderline Patients Research Group: Drs. John Clarkin, Harold Koenigsberg (co-directors), Ann Appelbaum, Lisa Gornick, Otto Kernberg, Paulina Kernberg, Michael Selzer, Thomas Smith, and Frank Yeomans. The authors appreciate their criticism and assistance.

## BACKGROUND THEORY

Defense is inextricably bound up with conflict, and because conflict is quintessentially "dynamic," the problem of defense has occupied many psychoanalytic and psychodynamic authors. Wallerstein (1983) has clarified some of the central issues; Vaillant (1986) has presented a concise but searching conceptual history; and Cooper (1989), writing of the most recent 20 years, has discussed "diverse trends . . . (that) . . . have emerged in psychoanalytic understandings of the defense mechanism concept, involving elaborations of both the intrapsychic and object-relational contexts" (p. 865). The following paragraphs summarize their collective observations.

Although Freud wrote about defense as early as 1894, he tended to use the term interchangeably with repression, gradually replacing the former with the latter. It was only when he posited his new "structural" theory in 1923 that he differentiated the ego mechanisms of defense from other ego functions (S. Freud, 1923/1961). This sweeping change in theory, with the formulation of a tripartite mental apparatus, ushered in new possibilities for thinking about what gradually had been generically characterized as repression. Thus in 1926, in "Inhibitions, Symptoms and Anxiety," Freud began to describe individual ego mechanisms of defense such as repression, isolation, regression, reaction formation, and undoing. In that work, Freud revived the concept of defense, which, he said, "can cover all these processes that have the same purpose—namely, the protection of the ego against instinctual demands—and subsuming repression under it as a special case" (1926/1959, p. 164). In this scheme, defense mechanisms are processes (or functions) of the ego. They are irreducible, not-observable entities—constructs—whose activity and presence can only be inferred from behaviors. In analysis, for example, defense mechanisms are inferred from defensive behaviors, particularly during states of resistance.

Anna Freud (1936) summarized the earlier contributions of her father (1894/1962, 1915/1957, 1922/1955, 1926/1959) and the nine methods of defense he had described: repression, isolation, regression, reaction formation, undoing, introjection, projection, turning against the self, and reversal. To these she added a tenth, sublimation. Explicit in Anna Freud's creative synthesis, bringing together Freud's 1923 structural theory and his 1926 revision of the theory of anxiety, is the idea that the ego's defensive functions are carried out by defense mechanisms. These mechanisms are ego functions that are used for defense, and defense only. This idea is one with which Brenner (1981) would later take exception, when he stated that all mental products could be used defensively, while none is used for defense only.

At the same time that Anna Freud was conducting studies of ego psychology, Melanie Klein began to espouse the view (1930) that from the very earliest stages of life impulses had accompanying fantasies. In Klein's view, defense too could be conceived in terms of fantasy. The external object was represented by an internal object, constructed by the infant from instinctually and defensively based fantasies and projections. In this scheme, one fantasy defends against another. The nature of fantasy (Isaacs, 1948), its relation to the process of "fantasying" (Sandler & Joffe, 1969), and the relationship of fantasy to intrapsychic structure has become a subject of intense scrutiny (Sandler & Nagera, 1963). Klein's thinking culminated in her description in 1946 of ego defenses such as splitting, idealization, projective identification, devaluation, and omnipotence becoming operative during the first 3 months of life. When these defenses persisted in later life, they tended to be associated with severe psychopathology.

Anna Freud had also referred to a "chronology" of defenses in her 1936 monograph (from primitive to advanced), but indicated that a developmental chronology of defense mechanisms still remained obscure. The incompatibility of Klein's ideas about structure and fantasy with Freudian ego psychology made it difficult for Anna Freud to incorporate Kleinian observations into her own work. Nevertheless, Anna Freud suggested in 1965, "Defenses have their own chronology . . . they are more apt to have pathological results if they come into use before the appropriate age or are kept up too long after it. Examples are denial and projection, which are 'normal' in early childhood and lead to pathology in later years; or repression and reaction formation, which cripple the child's personality if used too early" (p. 177).

Later, Kernberg (1966, 1967) integrated Klein's primitive defenses into an object relations/ego psychological model. His scheme, based on clinical observations in the modified psychoanalytic treatment of borderline patients, although not framed in Klein's developmental and theoretical scheme, nonetheless emphasized the importance of "primitive" (developmentally early) defenses in borderline conditions.

Despite a general acceptance among many psychoanalytic clinicians of a developmental hierarchy that characterizes some defenses as primitive, (related to the earliest years of life and to more severe psychopathology) and others as higher-level, (associated with a later stage of development when object constancy has been achieved and with less severe pathology) the whole subject remains controversial (Willick, 1983).

As momentum has propelled the "widening scope" of analysis (Stone, 1954) and psychiatrists and psychoanalysts have become increasingly concerned with the treatment of severely ill patients, there has been a burgeoning parallel interest in the clinical study of defense (Brenner, 1981; Cooper, 1989; Wallerstein, 1983; Willick, 1983). Furthermore, the relationship of defense to coping and the related notions of compromise formation and adaptation have been steadily reported in the psychoanalytic and psychiatric literature (Brenner, 1981; Schafer, 1968; Vaillant, 1977; Valenstein, 1961).

Some implications of the foregoing deserve to be emphasized:

1. Defense *mechanisms* are constructs or theoretical abstractions, whereas defensive *behaviors* are observable phenomena (Wallerstein, 1983).

2. *Fantasying* is a mental process, a construct, in contrast to *fantasies,* which are experiential and a product of fantasying; one fantasy can be viewed as "defending" against another fantasy as a result of fantasying (Sandler & Joffe, 1969).

3. Defense mechanisms, or clusters of mechanisms, may be associated with specific psychopathological entities, but precise relationships, especially to newer nosologies (e.g., DSM-III-R), remain to be specified (A. Freud, 1936; Willick, 1983).

4. Defense mechanisms may be hierarchically differentiated (Vaillant, 1986), that is, arranged in relationship to severity of psychopathology (or degree of health), but as with item 3, this has not been firmly established.

## EMPIRICAL STUDIES

It was inevitable that the importance of the subject and its clinical relevance would lead to empirical studies of defense. Current efforts have been reviewed in a monograph edited by Vaillant (1986) that presents the work of a number of authors. Four major lines of approach to empirical study have been taken.

The first is exemplified by Gleser and Ihilevich (1969), who developed a paper-and-pencil test—the Defense Mechanism Inventory (DMI). It consists of 10 brief stories followed by questions in which subjects indicate their response to the situations through selecting among responses (representing five defenses) the most and least representative of their reaction. The scale has shown acceptable reliability and construct validity, and has become widely used for research purposes. An important advantage lies in the use of standardized conflicts with which to compare subjects (or patients). A variant of this is the use of psychological tests to develop a defense profile. For example, a series of special measures of defense mechanisms, based on the MMPI item pool, have been developed by Haan (1965).

A second approach is that of Bond, Gardner, Christian, and Sigal (1983), who developed a defense style questionnaire to be completed by the patient. Because the inventory is a self-report, the problem of inter-rater reliability was eliminated. Items were designed to capture conscious manifestations of 24 unconscious defenses or coping mechanisms with the hypothesis that defense styles or mechanisms thought to be immature would factor out at the opposite pole from those thought to be more mature. Subsequent analysis from 209 subjects revealed that there was a clustering of the items into 4 separate factors (defense styles). Although promising, the defense styles correlated neither with specific defenses nor with clinical diagnosis. Work by the Bond group continues and has been extended by Andrews and colleagues (Andrews, Pollock, & Stewart, 1989; Pollock & Andrews, 1989), who are attempting to bring the Bond self-report into closer apposition to defense mechanisms by using the inventory to study defense mechanisms in a variety of clinical conditions.

The third major approach is exemplified by the work of Vaillant (1971, 1977, 1986) and colleagues (McCullough, Vaillant, & Vaillant, 1986). Vaillant developed a series of definitions of defenses, hierarchically arranged, and has trained independent raters to achieve reliability, using 150 examples of defenses embedded in 10 interview reports. He then had the raters read and code complete case histories (each about 300 pages long). These extensive biographical data, supplemented by questionnaires completed by the subjects, were the clinical data studied. Using this method, raters tended to agree about predominant defense style.

A fourth approach is exemplified by Hauser (1986) and Perry (1986; Perry & Cooper, 1986). These investigators developed a series of definitions of defenses, used these definitions in the development of a rating scale, trained raters, and then had them rate psychodynamic interview material (videotape, audiotape, or typed transcripts). In these studies, the rating scale was applied to direct clinical data.

As Vaillant observes (1986, p. 75) about rating defenses from clinical material, "The difficulty with clinical methods is that reliability is often suspect because of observer bias." It may be difficult for a rater to evade halo effects once he or she notes that a given defense is present because the rater may be inclined to see "related" defenses present as well. The advantage of the method is that it approximates the measurement of defense in the actual clinical situation.

# THE INVENTORY OF DEFENSE-RELATED
# BEHAVIORS (IDRB)

As previously noted, the appeal of directly rating clinical material is offset by the rating problems it creates, primarily the halo effect that identifying a given defense has on subsequent observations. That is, because of theoretical bias, an observer may be predisposed either toward "seeing" certain "clusters" of defenses or, because of belief, to not see other defenses at all. Nevertheless, we have concluded that the value of studying direct clinical material and the actual process of psychotherapy is justified. In addition, we hope that the rating of behaviors, not defenses, will minimize the problem of halo effect. The basis of our method is simple: to ask raters to identify behaviors as being either present or absent. These behaviors are instigated by the defensive activity of the ego and are therefore considered to be manifestations of the presence of related defense mechanisms.

## Scale Construction

### Defense List

After surveying the defenses described by Hauser and colleagues, Kaplan and Sadock, Perry, and DSM-III-R (Vaillant, 1986 [appendix]), and after reviewing the psychoanalytic literature, we selected 19 defense mechanisms. The list included the classic mechanisms of Anna Freud, others that we found repeated in all lists, and, finally, a number of those identified by Kernberg and others as characterizing primitive defenses. Thus our initial list consisted of (alphabetically):

Denial, Devaluation, Displacement, Identification with the Aggressor, Intellectualization, Isolation (of Affect), Primitive Idealization, Projection, Projective Identification, Rationalization, Reaction Formation, Repression, Splitting, Suppression, Transforming Psychological Conflict into Physical Symptomatology (Somatization), Transforming Psychological Conflict or Dysphoric Affects into Behavior (Acting Out), Turning Against the Self, Undoing, Withdrawal into Fantasy

### Interview Behaviors

For each defense, a definition was constructed. Vignettes were then developed from clinical practice to demonstrate the activity of defense in actual clinical situations. Finally, we devised brief statements for each defense, based on the vignettes, exemplifying behaviors or attitudes to be expected in a psychotherapy or evaluative session when a given defense is activated. When completed, the 19 defenses were associated with 79 interview behaviors.

### Clinician Agreement Study and Construct Validity

Randomized lists of the 79 interview behaviors and the 19 defenses were given to seven experienced clinicians.* The clinicians were instructed to select the defense most associated with each behavior; if they selected more than one defense, they were asked to circle the most relevant one. We required that five of the seven clinicians agree that a given behavioral item was associated with a defense for us to retain the item; in addition, there should not be a concentration of linkages to another defense. The result was that 57 items survived this requirement. Furthermore, careful scrutiny of ambiguous items permitted re-writing to increase clarity. Some examples follow:

*Item 1.* The patient may characterize him/herself as totally stupid and worthless in comparison to others, on the basis of a minor or nonexistent failing.

Five clinicians rated this item as Devaluation, four as Turning against the Self, and one as Splitting. (Raters associated more than one defense with the behavior.) The item, on review, was seen as both ambiguous and inconsistent with the theory on which it was based and was rewritten.

*Revised Item 1.* A single failure or failing is generalized so that the other person is derogated and depreciated, without positive features. (Devaluation)

*Item 2.* The patient describes him/herself and others in categorical black and white terms, rather than in shades of gray. There is rarely an expression of a mixed feeling toward the self or others.

All seven clinicians rated this item as Splitting. The item was retained unchanged. (Splitting)

*Item 3.* A person in the patient's life is described as a powerful ally against equally powerful and dangerous others without there being a realistic appraisal by the patient of him/herself, the associate, or the "dangerous other."

The seven clinicians made a total of 12 ratings on this item. Three clinicians rated this item as Primitive Idealization, five as Splitting, two

---

* Drs. A. Appelbaum, S. Bauer, A. Carr, O. Kernberg, L. Rockland, M. Selzer, and F. Yeomans served as raters.

as Projective Identification, one as Projection, and one as Identification with the Aggressor. This item, originally conceived by the investigators as exemplifying Primitive Idealization, was dropped.

*Item 4.* Associations have the quality of a lecture in philosophy; they are lacking in "aliveness."

All seven clinicians rated this item as Intellectualization. Two also rated it as Isolation of Affect. The item was retained, unchanged. (Intellectualization)

The IDRB thus became a 57-item inventory of patient behaviors associated with the 19 selected defenses; each defense was linked with three behaviors. The behavioral items were related to individual defenses by experienced clinicians with a high level of agreement, thereby providing a measure of construct validity (Isaac & Michael, 1971). That is, experienced psychodynamically oriented clinicians, independently related clinical interview behaviors to specific defenses.

## Scale Application

The initial use of the scale by the authors was promising, in that our behavioral ratings were very similar on 15-minute segments of the five videotaped sessions we rated. Each of the 57 interview behaviors was scored as either absent (0), possibly present (1), or present (2). The scores for interview behaviors were combined into scores for defenses. A defense was considered to be present when the behavioral scores for the defense totaled two or more of a possible total of six.

For example, in a 15-minute segment in Tape 3, the authors were concordant for the presence or absence of 16 of the 19 defenses. That is, both agreed that 7 defenses were present and 9 defenses were absent. They disagreed about 3 defenses (see Table 14–1).

In addition to a high level of agreement between the authors on this tape segment, the clusters of defenses* present in the ratings made clinical sense based on our joint discussion of the session after ratings were made. Clinically, the diagnosis of this patient was borderline personality disorder with narcissistic and masochistic features.

As a result of these initial observations, we conducted a preliminary interrater reliability study, using ourselves as independent raters.

---

*Cluster 1: Denial, Projective Identification, Projection, Devaluation, Splitting.
Cluster 2: Identification with the Aggressor, Rationalization.

**TABLE 14-1**
**Ratings of a Videotaped Psychotherapy Session**

| Defense | Rater 1 | Rater 2 |
|---|---|---|
| Splitting | 2 | 3 |
| Devaluation | 2 | 4 |
| Projective Identification | 6 | 2 |
| Projection | 4 | 4 |
| Denial | 4 | 6 |
| Repression | 2 | 1 |
| Rationalization | 4 | 3 |
| Identification with the Aggressor | 4 | 3 |
| Primitive Idealization | 0 | 0 |
| Isolation | 0 | 0 |
| Intellectualization | 0 | 0 |
| Reaction Formation | 0 | 0 |
| Somatization | 0 | 0 |
| Suppression | 0 | 0 |
| Turning against the Self | 0 | 0 |
| Undoing | 0 | 0 |
| Withdrawal into Fantasy | 0 | 0 |
| Displacement | 2 | 0 |
| Acting Out | 0 | 2 |

*Note:* Maximum score for each defense = 6 (present on all 3 items).

## Method and Results

Ten 45-minute videotaped sessions were used in their entirety for the study. Each session was rated as follows: Each 15-minute segment was rated independently using the scoring scheme previously noted. In addition, a fourth overall rating was made for the entire 45-minute session. Thus each session had four scores, representing segments 1, 2, 3, and 4 (the overall score). The maximum score for each defense in each session was 24 ("present" on all three items in all four ratings).

Cohen's Kappa (1960) was used to estimate the degree of agreement between raters about the presence or absence of the 19 defenses in the 10 videotaped sessions. For purposes of calculation, a score of 0 through 4 for each defense in a session was defined as "defense absent"; 5 through 24, "defense present." As can be seen from Table 14-2, the percentage of agreement varied between 40% and 100%, with a mean percentage of agreement of 80%.

The Kappa coefficient for interrater agreement ranged from mild to strong levels (between 0.35 and 1.00) for 5 of the 19 defenses (suppression, repression, isolation, projective identification, and rationalization). In 6 defenses, Kappa could not be calculated due to a "0" cell, causing an incalculable result. In 4 of those (reaction formation, displacement,

**TABLE 14–2**
**Interrater Agreement**

| Defense | Kappa | % Agreement |
|---|---|---|
| Suppression | 1.00 | 100 |
| Repression | 0.62 | 90 |
| Isolation | 0.52 | 80 |
| Projective Identification | 0.40 | 70 |
| Rationalization | 0.35 | 70 |
| Projection | 0.21 | 70 |
| Turning against Self | 0.21 | 70 |
| Denial | 0.20 | 60 |
| Devaluation | 0.20 | 60 |
| Splitting | 0.09 | 40 |
| Identification with the Aggressor | −0.18 | 60 |
| Acting Out | −0.25 | 60 |
| Intellectualization | −0.32 | 50 |
| Primitive Idealization | * | 90 |
| Reaction Formation | * | 100 |
| Somatization | * | 80 |
| Displacement | * | 100 |
| Undoing | * | 90 |
| Fantasy | * | 80 |

*Kappa cannot be calculated.

primitive idealization, and undoing), the percentage of agreement between raters was good (between 90% and 100%); for two (somatization, fantasy) percentage of agreement was satisfactory (80%). In 4 defenses (projection, turning against the self, denial, and devaluation), agreement showed a trend that was promising (Kappas between 0.20 and 0.21).

For 4 defenses (splitting, identification with the aggressor, acting out, and intellectualization), agreement was clearly unsatisfactory (Kappas between 0.09 and −0.32).

We also determined in what order each rater ranked the 10 videotaped sessions for each defense. A Spearman rank-order correlation (Siegel, 1956) was performed to determine the extent of agreement between the raters in the way they ranked the sessions for each defense (from the highest score for the defense to the lowest). The Spearman correlation coefficients and their related probabilities are displayed in Table 14–3.

As can be seen, 2 defenses (projective identification, primitive idealization) were ranked with strong levels of correlation by the two judges ($r_s$ values >0.70); 3 (splitting, denial, repression) with good levels ($r_s$ values between 0.50 and 0.69); and 3 (devaluation, isolation, identification with the aggressor) with weak levels ($r_s$ values between 0.30 and 0.49). That is, scores generated through IDRB ratings by each rater ordered the

**TABLE 14–3**
**Rank Order Correlations**

| Defense | Spearman $r_s$ | p *value* |
|---------|----------------|-----------|
| Projective Identification | 0.79 | 0.01 |
| Primitive Idealization | 0.71 | 0.02 |
| Splitting | 0.66 | 0.04 |
| Denial | 0.62 | 0.06 |
| Repression | 0.57 | 0.09 |
| Devaluation | 0.45 | 0.19 |
| Isolation | 0.38 | 0.28 |
| Identification with the Aggressor | 0.31 | 0.38 |
| Somatization | 0.25 | 0.48 |
| Suppression | 0.25 | 0.49 |
| Acting Out | 0.13 | 0.71 |
| Projection | 0.11 | 0.77 |
| Rationalization | 0.11 | 0.77 |
| Displacement | 0.09 | 0.80 |
| Turning against the Self | −0.01 | 0.99 |
| Intellectualization | −0.01 | 0.97 |
| Undoing | −0.17 | 0.65 |
| Fantasy | −0.17 | 0.64 |
| Reaction Formation | −0.32 | 0.37 |

cases for these defenses similarly. For all other defenses, there was no correlation. The associated *p* values (Table 14–3) probably do not do justice to the correlations because of the small sample size.

Tinsley and Weiss (1975) have usefully distinguished between interrater agreement and interrater reliability. Whereas agreement represents the "extent to which different judges tend to make exactly the same judgments about the rated subject" (p. 359), interrater reliability, in practice, means that "the relationship of one rated individual to other rated individuals is the same although the absolute numbers used to express this relationship may differ from judge to judge" (p. 359). That is, it is possible for agreement between judges to be low, but reliability high.

For example, the two raters had very poor agreement in their scores for the defense of splitting (Kappa = 0.09). However, the same scores ranked the 10 videotaped sessions in almost the identical order ($p = 0.0384$), from the highest to the lowest scores on splitting. This may be one instance where interrater reliability is high despite low interrater agreement.

Nevertheless, both high interrater agreement and reliability are important to achieve. The small sample size, which leads to underpowered results, may have contributed to our weak agreement in some of the defenses. All told, these preliminary results on interrater agreement and

reliability are encouraging. Review of the scale items with colleagues*
collaborating with us led us to rewrite some of the items to achieve
greater clarity, thereby hopefully improving agreement and reliability.
We have also decided to add three behaviors relating to a 20th defense,
omnipotence. Not only is this defense one of the major primitive defenses
described in the literature, but we found in doing ratings that some observed behaviors fit best with that defense.[†]

It is difficult to interpret the data in Table 14–3, because the case material derives from a narrow spectrum of psychopathology—patients
with borderline personality disorder. Expanded replication studies using
patient material from a wider range of psychopathology will widen the
range of defensive behaviors observed.

## DISCUSSION

We have presented a scale that is behaviorally based, and therefore may
prove to be a more reliable research tool for the study of defense mechanisms than those that rely more heavily on rater inference. Our scale asks
raters to decide whether a given behavior is present or absent, rather than
whether a defense mechanism is present or absent; this should present an
easier task. That the behaviors are reliably related to the defense mechanisms of which they are manifestations is confirmed by the clinician
agreement study that was carried out.

The scale can be used to study shifts in defensive functioning during
the course of a single session (a microscopic analysis) as well as during
the course of an entire psychotherapy (a macroscopic analysis). Although
character, and the constellation of defenses that support it, tends to remain relatively constant over time, variations from moment to moment
under the influence of conflict are of importance and interest.

"Structural" (in the sense of intrapsychic structure) diagnosis may
have a relationship to descriptive diagnosis (e.g., DSM-III-R). For example, elucidating characteristic defensive patterns (or clusters of defense
mechanisms) could be an important structural factor in differentiating
subgroups of borderline patients.

The scale can be employed in personality disorders and clinical conditions other than borderline personality disorder to determine whether
specific diagnostic entities are characterized by specific defensive constellations.

---

*Drs. L. Amsel, A. Donatelli, S. Kulchycky, A. Rotter, A. Stern, and S. Theoharakis have served
as raters and have assisted in scale revision.
†The latest version of the IDRB is a 60-item, 20-defense scale. Copies are available from the authors.

As studies are done, it will be possible to compare the findings obtained with the IDRB with those of Gleser and Ihilevich (the DMI) and Bond (the Defense Style Questionnaire) and obtain additional measures of concurrent validity.

## CONCLUSION

A new approach to rating defense mechanisms is presented that builds on the work of previous investigators. Initial experiences with the scale (the IDRB) have been promising and its use should contribute to the developing body of empirical knowledge about the nature, function, and consistency of defense mechanisms, their relationship to psychopathology, and possible implications for treatment.

## REFERENCES

Andrews, G., Pollock, C. & Stewart, G. (1989). The determination of defense style by questionnaire. *Archives of General Psychiatry, 46,* 455–460.

Bond, M., Gardner, S. T., Christian, J., & Sigal, J. J. (1983). Empirical study of self-rated defense styles. *Archives of General Psychiatry, 40,* 333–338.

Brenner, C. (1981). Defense and defense mechanisms. *Psychoanalytic Quarterly, 50,* 557–569.

Cohen, J. (1960). A coefficient of agreement for nominal scales. *Educational and Psychological Measurement, 20,* 37–46.

Cooper, S. H. (1989). The theory of defense mechanisms: A comparative view. *Journal of the American Psychoanalytic Association, 37,* 865–891.

Freud, A. (1936). *The ego and the mechanisms of defense.* New York: International Universities Press.

Freud, A. (1965). *Normality and pathology in childhood.* New York: International Universities Press.

Freud, S. (1955). Certain neurotic mechanisms in jealousy, paranoia, and homosexuality. In J. Strachey (Ed. and Trans.), *The standard edition of the complete psychological works of Sigmund Freud* (Vol. 18, pp. 223–232). London: Hogarth Press. (Original work published 1922)

Freud, S. (1957). Instincts and their vicissitudes. In J. Strachey (Ed. and Trans.), *The standard edition of the complete psychological works of Sigmund Freud* (Vol. 14, pp. 117–140). London: Hogarth Press. (Original work published 1915)

Freud, S. (1959). Inhibitions, symptoms and anxiety. In J. Strachey (Ed. and Trans.), *The standard edition of the complete psychological works of Sigmund Freud* (Vol. 20, pp. 87–172). London: Hogarth Press. (Original work published 1926)

Freud, S. (1961). The ego and the id. In J. Strachey (Ed. and Trans.), *The standard edition of the complete psychological works of Sigmund Freud*

(Vol. 19, pp. 12–66). London: Hogarth Press. (Original work published 1923)

Freud, S. (1962). The neuropsychoses of defence. In J. Strachey (Ed. and Trans.), *The standard edition of the complete psychological works of Sigmund Freud* (Vol. 3, pp. 45–61). London: Hogarth Press. (Original work published 1894)

Gleser, G. C., & Ihilevich, D. (1969). An objective instrument for measuring defense mechanisms. *Journal of Counseling and Clinical Psychology, 33,* 51–60.

Haan, N. (1965). Coping and defense mechanisms related to personality inventories. *Journal of Consulting Psychology, 29,* 373–378.

Hauser, S. T. (1986). Conceptual and empirical dilemmas in the assessment of defenses. In G. E. Vaillant (Ed.), *Empirical studies of ego mechanisms of defense* (pp. 89–100). Washington, DC: American Psychiatric Press.

Isaac, S., & Michael, W. B. (1971). *Handbook in research and evaluation.* San Diego: Robert R. Knapp.

Isaacs, S. (1948). The nature and function of phantasy. *International Journal of Psychoanalysis, 29,* 73–97.

Kernberg, O. (1966). Structural derivatives of object relationships. *International Journal of Psychoanalysis, 47,* 236–253.

Kernberg, O. (1967). Borderline personality organization. *Journal of the American Psychoanalytic Association, 15,* 641–685.

Klein, M. (1930). The importance of symbol-formation in the development of the ego. *International Journal of Psychoanalysis, 11,* 27–34.

Klein, M. (1946). Some notes on schizoid mechanisms. *International Journal of Psychoanalysis, 27,* 99–110.

McCullough, L., Vaillant, C. O., & Vaillant, G. E. (1986). Toward reliability in identifying ego defenses through verbal behavior. In G. E. Vaillant (Ed.), *Empirical studies of ego mechanisms of defense* (pp. 62–72). Washington, DC: American Psychiatric Press.

Perry, J. C. (1986). Perry's clinical defense mechanism rating scales, and glossary of defenses. In G. E. Vaillant (Ed.), *Empirical studies of ego mechanisms of defense* (pp. 121–136). Washington, DC: American Psychiatric Press.

Perry, J. C., & Cooper, S. H. (1986). A preliminary report on defenses and conflicts associated with borderline personality disorder. *Journal of the American Psychoanalytic Association, 34,* 863–893.

Pollock, C., & Andrews, G. (1989). Defense styles associated with specific anxiety disorders. *American Journal of Psychiatry, 146,* 1500–1502.

Sandler, J., & Joffe, W. G. (1969). Towards a basic psychoanalytic model. *International Journal of Psychoanalysis, 50,* 79–90.

Sandler, J., & Nagera, H. (1963). Aspects of the metapsychology of fantasy. *Psychoanalytic Study of the Child, 18,* 159–194.

Schafer, R. (1968). The mechanisms of defense. *International Journal of Psychoanalysis, 49,* 49–62.

Siegel, S. (1956). *Nonparametric statistics for the behavioral sciences.* New York: McGraw-Hill.

Stone, L. (1954). The widening scope of indications for psychoanalysis. *Journal of the American Psychoanalytic Association, 2,* 567–594.

Tinsley, H. E. A., & Weiss, D. J. (1975). Interrater reliability and agreement of subjective judgments. *Journal of Counseling Psychology, 22,* 358–376.

Vaillant, G. E. (1971). Theoretical hierarchy of adaptive ego mechanisms. *Archives of General Psychiatry, 24,* 107–118.

Vaillant, G. E. (1977). *Adaptation to life.* Boston: Little, Brown.

Vaillant, G. E. (Ed.). (1986). *Empirical studies of ego mechanisms of defense.* Washington, DC: American Psychiatric Press.

Valenstein, A. F. (1961). In G. L. Bibring et al., A study of the psychological processes in pregnancy and of the earliest mother-child relationship. *Psychoanalytic Study of the Child, 16,* 9–72.

Wallerstein, R. S. (1983). Defenses, defense mechanisms, and the structure of the mind. *Journal of the American Psychoanalytic Association, 31* (supplement), 201–225.

Willick, M. S. (1983). On the concept of primitive defenses. *Journal of the American Psychoanalytic Association, 31* (supplement), 175–200.

# Epilogue

The panorama of views presented in this volume about the mechanisms of defense suggests a number of conclusions and insights. Unlike some other psychoanalytic ideas, the concept of defenses is widely accepted, and it continues to be of interest to an increasing number of theoreticians and clinicians. In recent years, academic psychologists and psychometricians have also attempted to contribute to an understanding and measurement of these concepts.

Given these trends, how can the current landscape be best described? A question that recurs in the writings of most commentators is, How adaptive are ego defenses? The early (classical) psychoanalytic view was that defenses were rigid and unconscious forms of self-deception used by the young developing ego in an attempt to deal with severe conflicts and existential threats. The reason for the rigid quality of the defenses is simply that the ego is not well developed when some of these major conflicts occur. The classical view assumes that many individuals who have experienced developmental traumas and fixations may continue to use the unconscious self-deceptive defenses even in adult life, and that such use is one of the indicators of neuroses.

Over the years, influenced by the writing of Hartmann and others, the view has evolved among psychoanalysts that not all defenses are maladaptive, rigid, or unconscious and that some are, in fact, forms of successful adaptation to a complex world. This view tends to interpret some defenses as more primitive and thus less adaptive, whereas others are used by the more highly developed ego and are thus more "mature." An alternative way to represent the same idea is to describe primitive defenses as "narcissistic," whereas more mature defenses are described as "neurotic." Implicit in these ideas are two concepts:

1. There is a developmental sequence to the appearance of defenses, reflecting in some sense the development of the ego itself.
2. Some defenses are less adaptive, whereas others are more adaptive.

There is thus an implicit dimension of adaptiveness in the types of ego defense that have been recognized. The chapters of the present volume

315

suggest that these two ideas—the development of defenses and the adaptiveness of defenses—tend to be accepted by most of the authors, although some authors make a distinction between relatively maladaptive, unconscious ego defenses and conscious, relatively effective coping mechanisms.

The thinking and agreement are less clear concerning the sequential development of defenses. There is only speculation on which defenses develop first and which last, and whether there is any universality to the proposed sequence. Evidence on this point is obviously difficult to obtain; and the issue may, therefore, remain debatable for some time.

Part of the theoretical ferment concerns how best to conceptualize defenses within a broader framework. One of the new approaches attempts to relate defenses to emotions; this is proposed independently by both Plutchik and Dahl. From Plutchik's viewpoint, defenses appear during development of the individual as methods for influencing or controlling specific emotions related to life crises. Based on the assumption that there are eight basic emotions, Plutchik hypothesizes eight basic ego defenses, related to one another in terms of similarity and polarity. Support for the idea of the relationship between defenses and emotions comes from research that has shown that both can be described in terms of a circular (or circumplex) similarity structure. One of the values of this approach is that it has led to the development of specific scales for the measurement of the basic ego defenses.

Dahl's approach to emotions and defenses assumes that defenses function to restrict an individual's awareness of unacceptable emotional experiences. They also function to inhibit acts related to emotional impulses and thus become expressed by variations in the intensity of emotional experiences. Another important point made by Dahl is that the patterns of behavior associated with defenses against the expression of emotions may result in the persisting styles of interpersonal interaction that we call personality traits. Of significance in both Plutchik's and Dahl's attempts to relate emotions to defenses is the idea of the interconnectedness of affects, personality traits, personality disorders, and ego defenses.

An alternative theoretical framework for conceptualizing defenses is based on the idea of defenses as "control processes." Horowitz and Stinson point out that control processes are part of the machinery of the mind for all individuals and include such processes as focusing of attention, establishing thresholds for action, planning acts, and having thresholds for affective arousal. All these processes are assumed to control the levels and types of emotions an individual expresses, and thus to keep them within acceptable limits defined by implicit homeostatic needs.

Of major importance in these authors' viewpoint is that defenses are intimately related to control processes (e.g., thresholds for interruption or decision), and to person schemas. Thus, for example, the use of the displacement defense influences the nature of the role relationship between the individual and other people, and it may result in antisocial or passive-aggressive personality styles. Here again, personality, emotions, and defenses appear to be intimately related.

Benjamin presents yet another approach to placing defenses within a larger theoretical framework by relating them to her circumplex model of personality. Benjamin assumes that there are two types of defenses: normal ones that enhance feelings of love and affirmation, and abnormal ones that are associated with acts of blame and attack. Although she admits that defenses typically distort perceptions, she also believes that defenses are sometimes necessary to preserve attachments to others. Benjamin also takes the view that defenses may or may not be unconscious. As a result, defenses are potentially subject to persuasion, discussion, and other forms of therapeutic interventions.

A fifth approach that attempts to embed defenses within a broader theoretical framework is offered by Slavin and Greif. They attempt to relate repression, conceptualized as the prototypical defense, to certain theories of evolutionary biology. From this point of view, children must adapt to the fundamental fact that their self-interests are not identical to the self-interests of their parents. The most effective way for a young child to deal with the resulting conflict is by utilizing the ego defense of repression, which diverts subjective experience from unacceptable but important needs. Repression is thus conceived as a form of deception that has at least two functions: It avoids painful confrontations, and it may deceive parents into providing greater investment in the individual who is repressing aggressive or conflictual impulses.

In addition to a discussion of the various ways that theoreticians have conceptualized the nature and function of defense mechanisms, this volume has presented a variety of approaches to their assessment. Still, running through all of them are some common themes. The first concerns a determination of the number of defenses to be measured. In the present chapters, this varies from 28 to 5, but the optimum number for comprehensive coverage of the domain of defense mechanisms remains unclear. What can be said, however, is that the greater the number of defenses measured, the more likely are they to be clustered or grouped into categories.

The 24 defenses assessed by Bond, for example, are grouped into four clusters called defense styles. Similarly, Perry's Defense Mechanisms

Rating Scale groups 28 defenses into seven categories plus an Overall Defense Maturity Score. Ihilevich and Gleser chose not to identify individual defenses at all, preferring, rather, to classify the classical defense mechanisms into five defense styles. After sampling the domain, Plutchik and his colleagues opted to measure 8 defenses separately and included a total score to measure overall defendedness.

In some cases there was an a priori reason for clustering or developing categories. Nevertheless, in all cases this process, or the use of a total score, has resulted in greater reliability in terms of internal consistency, test-retest stability, or interrater agreement. In all likelihood, this is because there is a good deal of similarity, or overlap, among the defenses that obscures their distinctiveness as individual entities.

A second theme touched on by investigators using these different methodologies is the extent to which they are useful not only for research but for clinical applications as well. In terms of diagnostic value, the results have been decidedly mixed. Plutchik et al.'s Life Style Index has shown modest but significant correlations between several defense mechanisms and personality styles/clinical syndromes as determined from self-report data. Bond, utilizing patients who had been diagnosed clinically or with a specific diagnostic instrument, found some evidence that the Defense Style Questionnaire had predictive value for diagnosis of some psychiatric disorders. In general, however, it appears that the assessment instruments that have been described are not adequate indicators of diagnosis.

In contrast, all the instruments have been shown to be valuable not only for research but also for actual or potential clinical applications. These applications are in terms of treatment planning, predictions about outcome, and the measurement of changes during the course of a psychotherapy session as well as over the course of an entire therapy. For example, inasmuch as knowledge of the way in which an individual utilizes the various defense mechanisms provides information over and beyond data provided by Axis I and Axis II diagnoses, it can be helpful in fine-tuning treatment interventions to an individual's level of functioning and specific areas of maladaptation.

Knowledge of defensive functioning, both in terms of overall defensive functioning and in terms of the level of the most prominent defenses employed, may allow both researchers and clinicians to make predictions about the possible outcome of psychotherapy. Similarly, measurement of the extent to which a given defense changes over one or more sessions or of shifts in the type or level of the defenses employed may serve as the basis for examining both psychotherapy process and outcome.

A number of conclusions may be drawn from the theoretical and measurement issues we have discussed. In terms of theory, it appears that
regardless of conceptualization, there is general agreement among psychodynamically oriented theoreticians that defense mechanisms are a
necessary and basic aspect of an individual's mental functioning. Second,
there has been a trend toward viewing defense mechanisms not as isolated phenomena but, rather, as related to such broader domains as emotions, personality, and evolutionary biology.

Conclusions may also be drawn from the chapters dealing with issues
of measurement. The first is that there is no "best" way either for obtaining or for measuring data relating to an individual's use of defense
mechanisms. It has been shown that clinicians' ratings as well as paper-
and-pencil tests involving self-ratings of behavioral derivatives of defenses, ratings of vignettes, and projective tasks all produce data that
are, in varying degrees, reliable and valid. The second conclusion is that,
like the theoreticians, the psychometricians have shown defense mechanisms to be part of a broader nomothetical network that includes such
concepts as self-esteem, ego strength, stress, aggression, anxiety, and
depression.

# Author Index

321

# Subject Index